DRUMMER HODGE

DRUMMER HODGE

The Poetry of the
Anglo-Boer War
(1899-1902)

M. van WYK SMITH

1978

Clarendon Press Oxford

Oxford University Press, Walton Street, Oxford OX2 6DP

OXFORD LONDON GLASGOW NEW YORK
TORONTO MELBOURNE WELLINGTON CAPE TOWN
IBADAN NAIROBI DAR ES SALAAM LUSAKA ADDIS ABABA
KUALA LUMPUR SINGAPORE JAKARTA HONG KONG TOKYO
DELHI BOMBAY CALCUTTA MADRAS KARACHI

British Library Cataloguing in Publication Data
Van Wyk Smith, M
 Drummer Hodge.
 1. South African War, 1899–1902, in literature
 I. Title
 809.1′93   PN1083.S/
 ISBN 0-19-812082-6

*Printed in Great Britain by
Butler & Tanner Ltd
Frome and London*

They throw in Drummer Hodge, to rest
Uncoffined—just as found:
His landmark is a kopje-crest
That breaks the veldt around;
And foreign constellations west
Each night above his mound.
Thomas Hardy, 'Drummer Hodge'.

Acknowledgements

THE author and publishers wish to express their gratitude to the following copyright holders, publishers, and institutions for permission to quote or use illustrations from the works and manuscript collections listed below:

George Allen and Unwin Ltd., London: George Ives, *Eros' Throne* (1900).

Angus and Robertson (Publishers) Ltd., Sydney, and the Copyright Proprietors: A. B. Paterson, *Rio Grande's Last Race* (1902); George Essex Evans, *Collected Verse*, ed. F. McKinnon (1928); and Henry Lawson, *Collected Verse*, ed. Colin Roderick (1967).

Edward Arnold Ltd., London: James Rennell Rodd, 1st Baron Rennell, *The Violet Crown* (1913).

Associated Book Publishers Ltd. incorporating Methuen and Co. Ltd., London: Lawrence Binyon, *The Death of Adam* (1904); Alice Buckton, *The Burden of Engela* (1904); and Edgar Wallace, *Writ in Barracks* (1900).

Messrs. Pierre Barbier and France Vernillat, Paris: Pierre Barbier and France Vernillat, eds. *L'Histoire de France par les chansons*, vol. 7 (1956).

Ernest Benn Ltd., London: Robert Service, *Songs of a Sourdough* (Fisher Unwin, 1907); and Sir Wilfred Lawson and F. Carruthers Gould, *Cartoons in Rhyme and Line* (Fisher Unwin, 1905).

William Blackwood and Sons Ltd., Edinburgh, and the Estate of the late Dr. Alfred Noyes: Alfred Noyes, *The Enchanted Island* (1909), and *The Wine-Press* (1913).

Burns and Oates Ltd., London: G. K. Chesterton, *Poems* (1915).

Cassell and Co. Ltd., London: H. A. Chilvers, *Out of the Crucible* (1929).

Constable and Co. Ltd., London: St. John Lucas, *Poems* (1904); Sir George Arthur, *The Story of the Household Cavalry* (1909); Gen. C. R. de Wet, *Three Years War* (1902).

Department of National Education, Cape Archives Depot, Cape Town, and Transvaal Archives Depot, Pretoria: Photograph of Lotter's Commando; verses from the P. R. de Villiers Papers; and Hester van Zyl's poem on the Mafeking Camp.

Gerald Duckworth and Co. Ltd., London: Hilaire Belloc, *Verses* (1910).

Faber and Faber Ltd., London, and Farrar, Straus and Giroux Inc.,

New York: Robert Lowell, 'The Sleeper in the Valley', from *Imitations* (1962).

Horace W. E. Green, Johannesburg: Poems in manuscript by Mark Walter West.

Hollandsch Afrikaansche Uitgeversmaatschappij, Cape Town: C. Louis Leipoldt, *Oom Gert Vertel en Ander Gedigte*, 2nd ed. (1917).

George G. Harrap and Co. Ltd., London: Sir William Watson, *For England* (1904).

Albert Langen Georg Müller Verlag GMBH, Munich: Ludwig Thoma, *Der Burenkrieg* (1900).

Lawrence and Wishart Ltd., London: A. L. Lloyd, *Folk Song in England* (1967).

Longman Group Ltd., Harlow: Alfred Cochrane, *Collected Verses* (1903).

Macmillan London and Basingstoke, Macmillan Co. Canada, and the Trustees of the Hardy Estate: Thomas Hardy, *Collected Poems* (1930).

National Army Museum, Chelsea: Harold Hardy, 'The C.I.V.; or, The British Volunteer'; and 'The Cock and the Buller'.

Peter Newbolt, Cley near Holt: Sir Henry Newbolt, *The Sailing of the Long Ships* (1902), and *Poems New and Old* (1912).

Dr. M. Nijland-Verwey, Santpoort-Zuid, Holland: Albert Verwey, *Dagen en Daden* (1901).

Oxford University Press, Cape Town: C. J. D. Harvey and A. P. Grové, eds. *Afrikaans Poems with English Translations* (1962).

Polak & Van Gennep Uitgeversmaatschappij BV, Amsterdam: P. C. Boutens, 'Twee Sonnetten voor S. J. P. Kruger' (1901).

Routledge and Kegan Paul Ltd., London: 'Centurion', *Ante-Room Ballads* (1905).

The Society of Authors as the literary representative of the Estate of A. E. Housman; Jonathan Cape Ltd., London; and Holt, Rinehart and Winston, New York: A. E. Housman, *Collected Poems* (1939).

The Society of Authors as the literary representative of the Estate of Richard Le Gallienne: Richard Le Gallienne, *New Poems* (1910).

Strange Library of Africana, Johannesburg: 'The Black Watch at Magersfontein'.

Tafelberg Publishers Ltd., Cape Town: J. D. du Toit ('Totius'), *Rachel* (1913) and *By die Monument*, 5th ed. (1917); Jan F. E. Celliers, *Die Vlakte en Ander Gedigte*, 4th ed. (1917); and Johannes Meintjes, *Stormberg: A Lost Opportunity* (1969).

The Thomson Organization Ltd. and the *Illustrated London News*: Spenser Wilkinson, *The Illustrated London News Record of the Transvaal War* (1900).

University of Cape Town Libraries, Cape Town: Letters of Olive Schreiner in the Murray-Parker Collection.

J. L. van Schaik (Pty.) Ltd., Pretoria: Jan F. E. Celliers, *Die Lewen-stuin* (1925); and Eugène N. Marais, *Versamelde Gedigte* (1933).
W. Versluys Uitgeversmaatschappij B. V., Amsterdam: Willem Kloos, *Verzen III* (1913).
War Museum, Bloemfontein: Verse from *De Strever, De Krijgsgevan-gene* and *De Prikkeldraad*, and from the MS collections of G. J. van Riet, C. D. Oberholzer, and J. C. van Zyl.
A. P. Watt and Son, the Executors of the Estate of the late Mrs. E. Bambridge; Macmillan London and Basingstoke; and Doubleday and Co. Inc., New York: Rudyard Kipling, *Stalky and Co.* (1899); *Departmental Ditties* (1890); and *The Five Nations* (1903).
Witwatersrand University Press and *English Studies in Africa*, Johannesburg, for permission to reproduce here, with a few changes, 'Kipling and Kiplingson: Some Poetry of the Anglo-Boer War' which had appeared in that journal.

Every effort has been made to trace the holders of copyright in works from which substantial quotations appear in the following pages; where copyright has been inadvertently infringed, the author wishes to tender his apologies.

Preface

> But you've come
> To the wrong man; there must be many others
> Who'd tell the story straight, in the right order
> And with a moral too, and better grasp
> Of all the politics than I could have.
> C. Louis Leipoldt, 'Oom Gert Vertel', trans. C. J. D. Harvey.

THIS is not a history of the Boer War; nor is it an exclusively literary study of the poetry of that war. If the work that follows has to be defined generically at all, it may be called an exercise in cultural history. It attempts to assess the impact of a particular war on the literary culture, especially the poetry, of both the participants and the observers, whether in South Africa, in Britain and the rest of the English-speaking world, or in Europe. An assumption made throughout this study is that war poetry is not only verse written by men who are or have been under fire. Just as war poetry is not to be confused with political, polemical, or patriotic verse, although it can contain elements of all of these, so it is also the work of observers at home as much as that of soldiers at the front.

It follows that I have not allowed myself the academic luxury of selecting, on the basis of literary merit only, a handful of outstanding war poems for rigorous analysis and discussion. 'Doggerel can express the heart', wrote one of these late-Victorian soldierly versifiers, and I have roamed widely in the attempt to assemble the material which, I believe, records the full range of the impact that the Boer War made not only on Briton and Boer, but on the world at large.

A major thesis of this study is that the Boer War marked the clear emergence of the kind of war poetry which we have come to associate almost exclusively with World War I. Poems in the style and spirit of 'The Charge of the Light Brigade' were written in profusion, but the work which serves as this study's masthead, Hardy's 'Drummer Hodge', clearly has—like many of its contemporaries—more in common with Owen's verse than with

Tennyson's. The reasons for the appearance of such poetry are discussed in Chapter I; the rest of the book provides the evidence of it.

I have quoted liberally, believing both that the verse should largely speak for itself and that much of what I am writing about is all but unknown. Except for the work of the few well-known poets who responded to the war—Kipling, Hardy, Housman—still readily available in standard editions, important poems have usually been given in full. All quotations from non-English verse are immediately followed by prose translations.

The historical background and development of the Boer War are fairly well-known, but since I say little about these in the rest of the study, I offer here a brief resumé. After the Cape of Good Hope became a permanent British colony in 1806 increasing tension between the authorities and the original Dutch settlers (generally known as 'Boers' well into the present century, though 'Afrikaners' is now the common term) led to the latter's moving off into the interior regions of South Africa, especially from 1836 onwards. Much slaughter between Boer and Black followed, but the Boers established two republics between the Orange and Limpopo rivers; the Orange Free State and the South African Republic or Transvaal. Over two or three generations the Boers developed into redoubtable hunters, riders, and riflemen, became shrewd practitioners of the diplomacy of Bible and gun, and were all but forgotten by the rest of the world.

But the discovery of diamonds and gold in these territories in the last third of the century brought them suddenly to the world's attention. Fortune seekers flocked from all over the earth, creating two alien, cosmopolitan communities, Kimberley and Johannesburg, amidst the farms of suspicious and resentful Boers. Tensions were inevitable, and they came to a head over the Transvaal Government's refusal to grant the franchise to these new settlers, known as 'Uitlanders' ('Outlanders'), most of whom claimed British nationality. The franchise issue very soon merged into the larger issue of who would control the mines, their labour, and their profits: Britain or the Transvaal?

Complex diplomatic manœuvres failed to achieve a solution. The first Boer War of 1880–1—chiefly remembered for the British defeat at Majuba Hill—and the Jameson Raid of 1896, an attempt by the Prime Minister of the Cape, Cecil John Rhodes, to jockey the imperial authorities into annexing the Transvaal, destroyed whatever good faith remained between the opposing parties. Sir Alfred Milner, British High Commissioner for South Africa from 1897 and a confirmed neo-imperialist, believed that the Transvaal president, S. J. P. Kruger, could be squeezed into submission by 'a show of force', and his persuasions found a fertile field in the jingoism of the post-Jubilee years.

War broke out on 11 October 1899, the Boers striking first. They quickly lay siege to Kimberley, Ladysmith, and Mafeking, with the result that the first few months of the campaign saw the action mainly confined to attempts to relieve Kimberley in the Cape and Ladysmith in Natal. Lord Methuen failed, with great loss of life, in the first task, and Sir Redvers Buller even more disastrously in the second, the climax coming with a series of British defeats—Stormberg, Magersfontein, Colenso—during the so-called 'Black Week', 10–16 December 1899.

Britain despatched massive reinforcements under Lords Roberts and Kitchener, contingents were raised in Canada, Australia, and New Zealand, and what had started as only another Victorian colonial fray had become the twentieth century's first major war. Anglophobia was rife on the Continent, and the Boers became the heroes of an anti-British world. In Britain itself a strong pro-Boer movement led to trenchant questioning of the aims and methods of both war and imperialism, a process directly responsible for the appearance of a significant body of anti-war verse.

In South Africa, however, an imperial army numbering eventually almost half-a-million men inevitably meant doom for the Boers, who never mustered more than 50,000 men all told. The surrender of General Cronjé and 4,000 men at Paardeberg on 27 February 1900 broke the back of the conventional war, and with the fall of Pretoria, the Transvaal capital, in June, Roberts declared that the war was over and went home. With him departed most of the correspondents, colonials, and volunteers who had added glamour to the campaign. Now, however, ensued two years of guerrilla warfare under the outstanding leadership of Generals Botha, De Wet, and Smuts. Kruger, in exile in Europe, elicited even more popular continental support for the Boers, thus encouraging them to continue with their impossible war. Kitchener, left behind to clean up, had a new campaign on his hands, which he only managed to end by bringing the whole Boer nation to its knees with his 'burnt earth' policy of total war.

One point remains to be made. The Boer War was a White man's war in a predominantly Black country. Few Whites at the time, whether British or Boer, thought the fact at all remarkable. True, J. A. Hobson claimed, in *The War in South Africa* (1900), that the war was essentially a battle between rival exploiters for the control of cheap labour, and a cartoon in the German *Woche*, 21 October 1899, showed two Blacks watching a battle and remarking: 'Thank God, this time they're not shooting at us!' but both sides seemed to be in tacit and mutual agreement that the Blacks did not form an issue in their quarrel. That the following study is almost completely silent on the experiences and attitudes of South African Blacks during the Boer War must therefore be seen not as an omission, but as a function of most White thinking at the time, however reprehensible it may now seem to us.

This study was conceived and written as a book, not as a dissertation. I have, hence, avoided the inch-by-inch footnoting of purely academic writing by including, as far as possible, all references in the body of the text, or by consolidating closely related references into single footnotes. Full bibliographical details appear in footnotes and in the selected bibliography at the end, but references in the text are usually limited to author, title, and date. The reader curious to know more about the methods and research tools used in the compilation of this study is referred to my 'Poetry of the Anglo-Boer War: Anatomy of a Research Project', *English in Africa*, 1 (Sept. 1974).

My debts to institutions and individuals are vast, and I can hope to discharge only some of them in thanking the following institutions and individuals:

The Human Sciences Research Council for awarding me an *ad hoc* grant in 1970 and a senior bursary and travel grant in 1971–2 to pursue, in South Africa and Europe, the search for Boer War poems. (The opinions expressed and conclusions reached in the following study are not to be regarded as those of the HSRC or any of its officers.)

The Council of Rhodes University for granting me a year's sabbatical and study leave during 1971–2, and for a series of research grants from 1968 to 1973.

The Keepers of Printed Books, Librarians, Curators, or Directors—and their staffs—of the following institutions who welcomed me to their domains, often made special arrangements to facilitate my work, or answered numerous queries, both in person and by letter:

the British Library, the BL Newspaper Library, the Library of the Royal Commonwealth Society, the National Army Museum, and the National Register of Archives, all in London;

the Bodleian Library, Rhodes House, and Taylor Institution in Oxford;

the Bibliothèque Nationale, Paris;

the Bayerische Staatsbibliothek, Munich;

the Koninklijke Bibliotheek, The Hague;

the Nederlandsch Zuid-Afrikaansche Vereeniging, Amsterdam;

several regimental museums in Britain;

the Cape Archives, the South African Library, and the Library of Parliament in Cape Town;

the Transvaal Archives and the State Library in Pretoria;

the War Museum and Orange Free State Archives in Bloemfontein;

the Libraries of the Universities of Rhodes, Cape Town, Stellenbosch, and Witwatersrand;

and the Public Libraries of Johannesburg, Grahamstown, Durban, Port Elizabeth, and Pietermaritzburg.

The editors of about seventy South African newspapers and periodicals who, during 1970, published an appeal for Boer War poetry and reminiscences in private hands.

The more than 180 correspondents, mainly South African, who responded to that appeal and loaned or presented material, much of which is used, with grateful acknowledgement, in the following pages.

Mr. Johannes Meintjes, who presented me with a substantial typescript collection of Boer War poems he had assembled over many years.

The late Professor Rob Antonissen, Professor C. A. Bodelsen, Professor C. E. Carrington, Professor J.-L. Cattanéo, Major C. Congreve, Dr. Arthur Davey, Professor A. R. W. de Villiers,

Professor H. Erbe, Mr. John A. Hogan, Dr. Rubin Musiker, Dr. Richard Rive, Mr. Jon Stallworthy, Dr. Donald J. Weinstock, and Mr. Lewis S. Winstock, who in various ways directed my thoughts or my searches.

Dr. Beverley Brooks, Dr. W. Jonckheere, Mr. I. Pinchuck, and members of the Rhodes University Department of Translation, who provided me with draft translations of the French, Dutch, and German verse used in Chapters I, VII, and VIII.

Rex and Barbara Reynolds, who prepared immaculate prints for the illustrations, often from poor originals.

Miss Lorna Dixon, who typed the whole work, Miss Dorothy Driver, who proof-read the typescript, and Mrs. Priscilla Hall, who read the proofs.

My final two debts are the greatest, but also the happiest to acknowledge. Professor Guy Butler has, both as friend and supervisor, not only encouraged my enthusiasm for Boer War poetry over many years, but has throughout lavished a generous fund of comments, insights, and goodwill on this study. I shall remain deeply thankful to him.

My wife and children have cheerfully put up with the Boer War for longer than they may care to or can remember. Their willingness to do so is largely responsible for the completion of this work, and to Rosemary, Matthew, Anna, Charlotte, and Lucy I dedicate these fruits of their patience and love.

M. van W. S.

Rhodes University
Grahamstown

Contents

List of Illustrations

I

Prelude to Pity: War Poetry of the Nineteenth Century

> And ever since historian writ,
> And ever since a bard could sing,
> Doth each exalt with all his wit
> The noble art of murdering.
> Thackeray, 'The Chronicle of the Drum'.

IN a letter to the *Spectator* at the close of the Boer War in 1902 an army chaplain, the Revd. H. J. Rose, drew attention to the therapeutic effects of quoting Newbolt's 'Vitaï Lampada' to soldiers at the front: 'Over and over again, the sick man wasted by wounds and disease; the strong man, doomed to inaction on the lines of communication; the man at the very front, almost within range of the enemy's fire—has been nerved and cheered "to play the game", against all odds.'[1] The following week Violet Brooke-Hunt, recently returned from a spell of nursing in South Africa, gave further evidence of the great popularity among soldiers of Newbolt, Henley, Doyle's 'Corporal Dick', Harte's 'Song of the Drum', and Lionel Johnson's 'Comrades'. She quoted a private from a Lancashire regiment who had said, apropos of Browning's 'One who never turned his back, but marched breast forward', 'Words like that stick in a fellow's head, and come to his mind more than once or twice, I can tell you.' In the course of the next few weeks a considerable correspondence developed on the subject, with some reminders that the phenomenon was not new. One writer pointed out that men lying prostrate before Torres Vedras had listened with enthusiasm to their Captain's reading of Scott's latest verses on the Peninsular War.

Soldiers and their verse, and the poetry of war have been studied seriously and extensively as far as the two great wars of the twentieth century are concerned, but the *Spectator* correspondence

---

[1] *Spectator*, 89 (1902), 566.

suggests that the literature of previous wars might well warrant a closer look than the customary glance of dismissal that opens most studies of modern war poetry.[2] The assumption too often has been that for all pre-1914 war verse Tennyson's 'Charge of the Light Brigade' might serve as a perfect epitome, and that Owen's poetry of 'The pity of war, the pity war distilled', was a rare new plant that sprang from the mudbanks of the Somme. War poetry 'began and ended with the First World War', claims a reviewer in the *Times Literary Supplement* (29 September 1972)— 'There were poems written about earlier wars but they were battle-pieces, not war poems in the 1914–18 sense.'

This proposition rests on several questionable assumptions; for instance, that the only great war poetry is that which grows from and dwells on personal experience of the horror of war; that only verse written by soldiers can count as war poetry; and that the Great War produced a particular lyrical sensibility of martial disillusionment that had never existed before. But the story of war poetry is more complex than that. In the following discussion I shall attempt to show that in English, French, and German a wide range of war (and anti-war) poetry existed long before the Great War, and that a wider definition of war verse, somewhat along the lines of that suggested by Julian Symons during World War II, might well be more fruitful in the examina-of such poetry:

A good poem may be written about war from any possible attitude, that of Rudyard Kipling or that of Wilfred Owen. War poetry is not a specialized department of poetry; it is ... quite simply the poetry, comic or tragic, cynical or heroic, joyful, embittered or disillusioned, of people affected by the reality of war.[3]

My purpose, furthermore, will be to show that the 'development' of war poetry to the heights of World War I depended not only, or even primarily, on the increasing fatality and horror of methods of warfare, but also on wide-ranging Victorian changes in attitude towards the army, the soldier, the volunteer, and war itself. These changes were connected, in turn, with the rise of

[2] See, for instance, J. E. Johnston, *English Poetry of the First World War* (Princeton: Oxford University Press, 1964); B. Bergonzi, *Heroes' Twilight: A Study of the Literature of the Great War* (London: Constable, 1965); and Jon Silkin, *Out of Battle: The Poetry of the Great War* (Oxford: Clarendon Press, 1972).

[3] *An Anthology of War Poetry*, ed. Julian Symons (Harmondsworth: Penguin, 1942), p. viii.

democracy and universal education, and made themselves felt in the radical, socialist, and humanitarian opposition to war which by 1899 was well organized, articulate, and influential.

All wars must seem equally cruel to the people involved in them. Contemporary sketches of the field of Waterloo (1815) and photographs of trenches full of bodies after the Battle of Spionkop (1900) reveal an image of war not very different from scenes on the Somme in 1916. Candide's experiences in the battle between the Bulgars and the Abars may stand for the impact of any war on a bewildered participant. What distinguishes the men who fought at Waterloo from those on Spionkop and the Somme is not how they fared but what they could say about their experiences. While literacy was almost non-existent in the ranks and rare even among non-commissioned officers in the Peninsular War,[4] the men who went to South Africa in 1899 were the products of several decades of universal literacy and franchise. They were the beneficiaries of almost a century of democratic campaigns in the fields of politics, education, social organization, humanitarianism, and, more specifically, army reform. But their great-grandfathers who died at Waterloo were either of the elitist few who accepted almost unquestioningly the military and social code that gave them their superior position, or they belonged to the multitude who had no voice, either political or literary. As one of the many popular and rather self-conscious eulogies of the 1890s on the rise of the 'common' soldier put it:

Literature contains no adequate picture of a great battle as seen through the eyes of the private in the ranks. The men who make history, un-fortunately, cannot write it. . . . The average soldier belongs to the inarticulate class. It is not that, like the 'needy knife-grinder' of Canning's squib, he has 'no story to tell'; he cannot tell it.[5]

Within a few years of the writing of these words the Boer War was to prove them wrong. If Hardy's 'Drummer Hodge' who

never knew—
Fresh from his Wessex home—
The meaning of the broad Karoo,
The Bush, the dusty loam,

[4] See H. de Watteville, *The British Soldier: His Daily Life from Tudor to Modern Times* (London: Dent, 1954), p. 100.
[5] W. H. Fitchett, *Fights for the Flag* (London: Smith, Elder, 1898), p. 296.

>   And why uprose to nightly view
>   Strange stars amid the gloam,

serves as one image of the Boer War soldier—uncouth, uneducated, fighting for an unknown cause—E. W. Hornung's 'In
Memoriam' presents a picture, just as valid, of educated men on
both sides of the fray:

>   These twenty years ago and more,
>   'Mid purple heather and brown crag,
>   Our whole school numbered scarce a score,
>   And three have fallen for the Flag.
>
>   You two have finished on one side,
>   You who were friend and foe at play;
>   Together you have done and died;
>   But that was where you learnt the way.
>
>   And the third face! I see it now,
>   So delicate and pale and brave.
>   The clear grey eye, the unruffled brow,
>   Were ripening for a hero's grave.[6]

These two poems, written by non-combatant poets 6,000 miles
from the front, might suggest no more than that the soldier had
received a compassionate voice at home before he found his own
at the front in 1914; the 'undistinguished dead' was a subject for
memorial verse throughout the Boer War, as in Austin Dobson's
'Rank and File':

>   O Undistinguished Dead!
>   Whom the bent covers, or the rock-strewn steep
>   Shows to the stars, for you I mourn—I weep,
>   O Undistinguished Dead!
>
>   None knows your name.
>   Blacken'd and blurr'd in the wild battle's brunt,
>   Hotly you fell—with all your wounds in front:
>   This is your fame.[7]

We shall see, however, that the Boer War soldier had a great deal
to say about his own experiences, both in prose and in verse.

By 1899 the literacy of the common soldier and his willingness
to write about and publish his experiences had become one of the

[6] *Spectator*, 84 (1900), 172.
[7] *Complete Poetical Works* (London: Oxford University Press, 1923).

most striking features of military life. The first few months of the
Boer War confirmed it: 'Never before has Britain sent forth to the
battlefield so large a force of men sufficiently educated to write
home. The war, therefore, has been described from day to day,
not like all other wars, by professional journalists or by literary
officers, but by the rank and file.'[8] A reviewer in the *Bookman*
remarked: 'Few of the rough campaigners of the Low Countries
and the Peninsular could, or did write home. . . . But think of our
army of a quarter million, each one almost to a man a war correspondent.'[9] It is this evolution of the soldier from 'rough
campaigner' to articulate 'war correspondent' that needs more
careful attention in the history of war poetry.

One way of tracing out the pattern of war poetry through the
ages is to see it as a constant oscillation between two equally
ancient views of war as either heroic and ennobling or tragic and
brutalizing, with the latter conception of war gradually gaining
dominance from the mid-nineteenth century onwards. Bernard
Bergonzi (*Heroes' Twilight*) sees these two notions of war enshrined in Hotspur and Falstaff, but Falstaff, as largely a foil for
and even parody of Hotspur (he is only too eager to affect martial
glory when an easy opportunity presents itself) is perhaps a less
helpful and humane counterpart for Hotspur's idealistic belligerence than the thoughtful, unspectacular family man, Williams,
in *Henry V*: 'I am afeard there are few die well that die in battle;
for how can they charitably dispose of anything when blood is
their argument?' (IV. i. 144–7). The voice of Williams is a rare
one in English literature much before the nineteenth century. He
is described from the outside, as in Massinger's lines:

> To dare boldly
> In a fair cause, and for their country's safety:
> To run upon the cannon's mouth, undaunted;
> To obey their leaders, and shun mutinies;
> To bear with patience the winter's cold
> And summer's scorching heat, and not to faint
> When plenty of provisions fails, with hunger,
> Are the essential parts make up a soldier[10]

---

[8] Anon., *Pen Pictures of the War by Men at the Front* (London: Simpkin Marshall,
1900), preface.

[9] *Bookman*, 22 (1902), 131–3.

[10] Quoted as epigraph in Reginald Hargreaves, *This Happy Breed: Sidelights on
Soldiers and Soldiering* (London: Skeffington, 1951).

and he is sometimes the subject of sympathy, but when we hear him it is usually a poet adopting his voice in some satiric *persona*, like Peter Woodhouse in 1605:

> I see a Soldiers service is forgot,
> In time of peace the worlde regards us not.[11]

That Williams was rarely heard in literature is, however, not strange when one considers that he was heard even less frequently in politics and society during the same period. Correlli Barnett, in *Britain and her Army* (1970), has traced the complex and intimate connection between traditional British distrust of a standing army and the equally traditional ambivalence in English attitudes towards officers and the ranks. Since all British armies since the Civil War have been expeditionary forces, operating largely out of sight of people at home, Englishmen could, until late in the nineteenth century, cultivate the illusion of being an 'unmilitaristic' nation, look on officers as gentlemen, and despise the rank and file as vagabondage who, in common with convicts and other undesirables, could be sent abroad. During the early eighteenth century 'soldiering reached the low place in British society it was to occupy until the Great War in 1914, an occupation despised by the middle and working classes as a disgrace hardly less than prison' (Barnett, p. 139).

At the end of the eighteenth century, however, developments began which were to change public attitudes to war and soldiering, not only in England but throughout Europe. The Napoleonic wars introduced something like 'total war' into Europe; that is, war between nations rather than rulers, involving large numbers of civilians not only as volunteers and victims, but also as sharers in the ideals—however imperfectly conceived—of nationalism, patriotism, and liberty that inspired the struggle: 'A greater contest than that in which we are engaged the world has never seen, for we are not fighting the battle of England alone, but we are fighting to decide this question, whether there shall be any more freedom upon the earth,' the Revd. Sydney Smith told the Marylebone Volunteers in 1803.[12] At the same time the humanitarian principles that underlay the less sanguinary aspects of the French Revolution and which were to lead to the great radical

[11] *Democritus his Dream* (London, 1605).
[12] *Patriots in Arms: Addresses and Sermons . . . in Praise of the Volunteer Movement*, ed. Thomas Preston (London: Whittaker, 1881), p. 14.

movements of the nineteenth century for the improvement of the common man's (and soldier's) lot, began to fire poets with compassion for the soldier as outcast, and with an ideological rejection of war. Thus Wordsworth, while prescribing a humane but still heroic ethic of conduct for his 'Happy Warrior', could also be aware of the profound and speechless dignity conferred on the soldier through misery, as in his moving description of the destitute soldier in *The Prelude*, Book 4.

Illiterate as the Napoleonic armies may have been, the recollections of Rifleman Harris, Private Wheeler, and Sergeant Donaldson showed that henceforth the common soldier would not remain quite silent,[13] just as Goya's 'Third of May 1808' landmarked a new ideological horror of war in the artist. In England, too, a movement had started that would eventually bring soldiering much closer to the lives of respectable Englishmen. The large number of Volunteer Associations formed on the threat of a French invasion fostered a new concept of soldiering and of public involvement in matters military: 'No sooner did the insulting menace of invasion come forth from the enemy, but an union in arms took place which has put the nation in a posture of defence heretofore unknown.... Persons of rank and property mingle with manufacturers and mechanics, and they form a body of men trained to the use of arms who, without forsaking the occupations of peace, are ready to repress internal tumult and to guard our shores against the approach of the foe,' marvelled the rector of Stoke-Newington (Preston, *Patriots in Arms*, p. 38), and he is echoed by several other divines in this collection.

In Preston's pages, too, we often hear the alarums of another conflict that was to grow mightily as the nineteenth century proceeded, namely the clash between national necessity and Christian conscience. But, like all the other preachers in the volume, the Revd. John Evans, addressing a Finsbury congregation on 'The Duty of Every Briton at this Perilous Moment', had no qualms about his choice: 'That war is a serious calamity will not be denied. The moralist and divine have lifted up their voice against it in all ages, and have justly exposed it to the abhorrence

[13] *The Recollections of Rifleman Harris*, ed. C. Hibbert (London: Leo Cooper, 1971); *The Letters of Private Wheeler 1809–1828*, ed. B. H. Liddell Hart (London: Michael Joseph, 1951); and Joseph Donaldson, *Recollections of the Eventful Life of a Soldier* (Glasgow, 1825).

of the world. . . . Offensive war is to be condemned without
hesitation. But no law, human or divine, condemns resistance
against an invading enemy.' The ambivalence that lies behind
Evans's thinking manifests itself in much Romantic war verse,
too. Bernard Bergonzi and Jon Silkin have shown how ideological
and humanitarian objections to war in the verse of Wordsworth,
Coleridge, Byron, and others are often vitiated by their willingness to argue that certain kinds of war (e.g. defensive or nationalistic ones) are sometimes justifiable:

> I would fain say 'fie on't',
> If I had not perceived that revolution
> Alone can save the earth from hell's pollution.
>
> (*Don Juan*, VIII. 51)

As the nineteenth century advanced the arguments for and
against war, nascent in the Napoleonic period, developed,
diverged, and, as education grew to be universal and the popular
press ubiquitous, became established on a wide base of public
awareness and articulation. The professedly nationalistic and
libertarian nature of most European wars during the century,
culminating in the Franco-Prussian War of 1870–1, condoned the
use of force in the attainment of elevated ideological objectives.
These wars turned military preparedness into a major item of
national policy and expenditure, enhanced the image of the soldier
as protector of the state, and firmly drew civilians into the ambit
of conflict.

Yet the very increase in the currency of militaristic ideologies
stimulated reaction; the humanitarian ideals of the Revolution
modulated into the philanthropic, radical, and socialist concerns
of the later nineteenth century, all essentially pacifist. Much of this
opposition to war was cast in explicitly Christian terms, as in the
words of Henry C. Wright in 1846: 'Especially do I regard a
church and clergy who patronize war as pre-eminent in guilt, for
they give to deeds at which humanity shudders, whatever
respectability and attraction the sanctions of Christianity can
impart to them.'[14] But Dickens's famous exposure in *The Uncommercial Traveller* (1861) of the treatment of men returned from
the Indian Mutiny indicates the more generally philanthropic
form that such condemnation took as the century wore on.

---

[14] *Defensive War Proved to be a Denial of Christianity* (Dublin, 1864), preface.

By the end of the century a whole battery of socialist or humanitarian newspapers and periodicals existed which attacked war as the product and tool of capitalism, the established church, and the state. When the Boer War broke out, the editors of *Brotherhood*, *Coming Day*, *Commonwealth*, *Daylight*, the *Labour Leader*, and *Reynold's Newspaper* all came out with statements similar to that of their colleague in *Justice*:

Armies, mercenary armies, have always been maintained by the dominant classes for the purpose of repression at home and aggression abroad. . . . We must aim at democratising militarism by the abolition of the barrack system, and by abolishing the *army* altogether, while fitting every citizen for the duties of the soldier. (6 January 1900.)

The Boers, he claimed (18 November 1899), 'are fighting the battle of the workers against the capitalists, and as fully deserve the sympathy and support of British workers as any body of workmen on strike have ever done'.

Darwinism, by the end of the century appearing in garbs that Darwin would hardly have recognized, was invoked by pro- and anti-war factions alike—by the former to substantiate Nietzschean vindications of the use of force to establish the ascendancy of superior (which in practice meant 'imperial') races;[15] and by the latter to argue that war had become an anachronism. 'We disguise the transaction with uniforms and music; but the thing we do remains. We sacrifice human victims; we kill our brothers. . . . Our national and imperial creed in action . . . is an ignoble creed; a low stage of thought; a state of ignorance and darkness.' Thus wrote J. Bruce Wallace in his monthly *Brotherhood*, November 1899, supporting his argument with anti-Kipling poems:

> Your bugle-note is that which calls
> Rameses to the fight,
> Sculptured on Karnac's crumbling walls
> At twenty times his height.
> Again you blow his ancient horn,
> That pigmy tribes may fear,
> You're harking back to times out-worn,
> A-bugling in the rear.[16]

---

[15] See Karl Pearson, quoted in Gertrude Himmelfarb, 'Varieties of Social Darwinism', in G. Himmelfarb, *Victorian Minds* (London: Weidenfeld & Nicolson, 1968).
[16] Ernest H. Crosby, 'The Bugler in the Rear', *Brotherhood*, Jan. 1900.

These papers repeatedly stressed the individual suffering that national military glory brought in its wake:

> They'll never have done with fightin' on land an' over sea;
> Government—government, what does it care—what does it care for me?
> Bugles must blow an' flags must wave, an' the muffled drums must beat,
> An' what to a lass is a lover when they lay him dead at her feet?[17]

If we turn from the ideologies of war to the poetry of war in the nineteenth century we shall find that it flowed mainly in the two diverging channels charted so far. War poetry flourished while popular pacifism grew, both phenomena encouraged by the fact that in Victorian England war became a distant glory and foreign barbarity. If poets like Scott, Campbell, and Mrs. Hemans could make a corner in rousing, facile, patriotic battle-pieces such as 'Ye Mariners of England' and 'The Field of Waterloo', others, like Southey, Hood, Wolfe, and Peacock, were casting a colder eye on the glories of war. The beguiling irony of 'The Battle of Blenheim', or the haunting exposition of furtive glory in Wolfe's 'The Burial of Sir John Moore'—

> Not a drum was heard, not a funeral note,
>   As his corse to the ramparts we hurried;
> Not a soldier discharged his farewell shot
>   O'er the grave where our hero we buried.
>
> We buried him darkly at dead of night,
>   The sods with our bayonets turning;
> By the struggling moonbeams' misty light,
>   And the lantern dimly burning—

suggest moods which, if not entirely new, were from now on more frequently expressed, appearing sometimes in the mouth of a fictional common soldier, like Charles Lever's 'Irish Dragoon':

> Bad luck to this marching,
> Pipeclaying and starching;
> How neat we must be to be shot by the French!
> I'm sick of parading,
> Through wet and cold wading,
> Or standing all night to be shot in a trench.

[17] Frank L. Stanton, 'And Women Must Weep', *Coming Day*, Feb. 1902.

The demythologizing of war continued in Peacock's 'To Battle'—

> Drink and sing, and eat and laugh,
> And so go forth to battle:
> For the top of a skull and the end of a staff
> Do make a ghostly rattle—

and in the hideous puns of Thomas Hood's many verses on the gruesome delights of soldiering:

> Alas! a splinter of a shell
> Right in my stomach sticks;
> French mortars don't agree so well
> With stomachs as French bricks.

> This very night a merry dance
> At Brussels was to be;—
> Instead of opening a ball,
> A ball has open'd me.
>
> ('A Waterloo Ballad')

The Crimean War brought the two opposing concepts of war into sharper focus. While it was still possible for large sections of the British public to see the war as a glorious, God-ordained and invigorating challenge to a too-prosperous England,[18] and 'The Charge of the Light Brigade' as an apt expression of the sentiments appropriate to war, it had also become impossible for such views to thrive on ignorance of what was actually happening at the front. Whereas the circulation of *The Times* during the Napoleonic wars had been 5,000, it now sold 40,000 copies and was only one of several newspapers with correspondents at the front who had the use of the telegraph to speed their reports (Barnett, *Britain and her Army*, p. 285). The philanthropic spirit of the age urged Florence Nightingale to the hospitals of Scutari and her revelations sparked off a blaze of hysterical public compassion for the soldier, though much of this concern was directed at the poor treatment of soldiers, not at war itself. Indeed, among the many verses on the war propounding the ethics of Hotspur one heard now an alarmingly strident, pugnacious note of savagery indicative of the extent to which ancient and elitist codes of war

[18] See Olive Anderson, 'The Reaction of Church and Dissent to the Crimean War', *J. of Eccl. Hist.*, 16 (1965), 209–20.

were being lost in new doctrines of total war and material force
that anticipated the crazed jingoism of the end of the century:

> No more words:
> Try it with your swords!
> Try it with the arms of your bravest and your best,
> You are proud of your manhood, now put it to the test;
> Not another word:
> Try it by the sword.
>
> . . . . . .
>
> Serve out the deadliest weapons that you know,
> Let them pitilessly hail in the faces of the foe.[19]

Compared with this proto-jingo blood-lust, 'The Charge of the
Light Brigade' is still a masterpiece. The lineal descendant of 'The
Battle of Maldon', Drayton's 'Agincourt', Aytoun's 'Flodden',
Scott's 'Waterloo', and Macaulay's 'Battle of Naseby', it was
probably the last great battle-piece that could be written in
English. Like its famous predecessors in the heroic vein, it turns
the immediate horror of war into a distant, larger-than-life
pageant. Though dealing in ferocious action, it freezes the on-
slaught, the panic, the butchery into an eternally still and heroic
gesture:

> Flash'd all their sabres bare,
> Flash'd as they turn'd in air
> Sabring the gunners there,
> Charging an army.

True to its kind, it distills out the emotions of fear, funk, and
doubt ('Their's not to reason why') in favour of the more stoic,
and socially conforming, virtues of honour, duty, manhood,
loyalty, and camaraderie. Horror and slaughter are redeemed by
the necessity for heroic affirmation and patriotic rationalization.

Tennyson's achievement is the more amazing when one
considers that the foolishness of the charge was well known at the
time, thanks to war correspondents like W. H. Russell of *The
Times*, and is, indeed, acknowledged in the poem: 'Some one had
blunder'd'. That the charge was conducted almost as a cavalry
display for the benefit of the host of prestigious onlookers on
both sides of the valley—'Never did the painter's eye rest on a
more beautiful scene that I beheld from the ridge' (*The Times*,

[19] Franklin and Henry Lushington, 'Laissez Aller!', *Points of War* (1854).

14 March 1854)—no doubt encouraged a heroic view of the affair. But basically the poem's success is due to Tennyson's exploitation of a still-dominant heroic tradition, and his superb handling of the infectious rhythms and memorable clichés of the genre.

The glamour of 'The Charge of the Light Brigade' has obscured poetry of a very different kind which the Crimean War produced. Public hysteria after the revelations of Florence Nightingale and greater knowledge of conditions at the front moved some poets to frame a vision of war as futile horror and individual disaster. Thackeray, anticipating Siegfried Sassoon, etched the ironic contrast between cant at home and slaughter at the front; his socialites,

> in smooth dinner-table phrase,
> Twixt soup and fish, discuss the fight;
> Give to each chief his blame or praise;
> Say who was wrong and who was right.
>
> . . . .
>
> Meanwhile o'er Alma's bloody plain
> The scathe of battle has rolled by—
> The wounded writhe and groan—the slain
> Lie naked staring to the sky.[20]

Alexander Smith, designing lace in Glasgow and apparently never near the Crimea, saw the war in these terms:

> 'Thou canst not wish to live,' the surgeon said.
> He clutched him, as a soul thrust forth from bliss
> Clings to the ledge of Heaven! 'Would'st thou keep this
> Poor branchless trunk?' 'But she would lean my head
> Upon her breast; oh, let me live!' 'Be wise.'
> 'I could be very happy; both these eyes
> Are left me; I should see her; she would kiss
> My forehead; only let me live.'—He dies
> Even in the passionate prayer.[21]

At the front, a letter tells us, 'our men used to sit in some old redoubt or abandoned trench, and there the song and toast went round, and once or twice I heard some original or extemporaneous verses, *apropos* to the time and place, to our Government at home, to our Generals at headquarters, to the Czar in his palace, and to

---

[20] 'The Due of the Dead', *Punch*, 28 Oct. 1854.
[21] 'The Army Surgeon' *Sonnets on the War* (London: David Bogue, 1855).

Johnny Russ in front, which were not only witty and satirical, but highly indicative of poetic genius'.[22] Unfortunately the writer furnished no examples of the products of this trench muse, but they were probably no different from the sardonic verses that came out of the French lines:

> Le Français qu'au feu l'on admire
> Est vraiment gai dans le malheur.
> Éclats de bombe, éclats de rire
> Ont pour lui la même valeur.
> Dans la tente est notre demeure,
> Sebastopol est à deux pas,
> Le canon tonne, le vent pleure,
> Et pourquoi n'en ririons-nous pas ?[23]

(The Frenchman is to be admired under fire: he is truly cheerful in disaster. Bursts of shrapnel and bursts of laughter are all the same for him. We have made our home in tents, Sebastopol is a stone's throw away; the cannon roars, the wind weeps—and why not treat it all as a joke?)

After the war Britain took stock of her military establishment and her findings further changed the public and literary image of the soldier from 1859 onwards. The war marked a turning-point in the traditionally amateur conception of the English army; British methods and weapons were shown to be utterly out of date, and the army was found to have no public image and no depth of civilian reserves (Barnett, *Britain and her Army*, p. 286). It was only after the Franco-Prussian War that Cardwell hit on the essential reforms, but in the meantime national anxiety led to the resuscitation of the Volunteer Movement, a step of considerable significance in the development of war poetry. Tennyson's 'Riflemen Form!' introduced into English literature the view of the volunteer soldier as a respectable figure protecting the nation:

> Let your Reforms for a moment go,
> Look to your butts, and take good aims.
> Better a rotten borough or so,
> Than a rotten fleet or a city in flames!

[22] Quoted in *A Pedlar's Pack of Ballads and Songs*, ed. W. H. Logan (Edinburgh, 1869), preface.

[23] Sergeant-Major Émile Carré, 'Et pourquoi n'en ririons-nous pas?', in *Histoire de France par les chansons*, ed. P. Barbier and F. Vernillat, vol. vii (Paris, 1956).

Nugent Taillefer's collection of *Rondeaus of the British Volunteer* (1871) is one of several works which record the vogue for vociferous patriotic jingle that the Volunteer Movement brought in, just as Sir Francis Doyle's 'Private of the Buffs' (1859) manifests a new, if still patronizing, respect for the uncouth soldier's conception of his duty. The patriotic fervour of late-Victorian activist verse had been born:

> Last night, among his fellow roughs,
>   He jested, quaffed, and swore;
> A drunken private of the Buffs,
>   Who never looked before.
> To-day beneath the foeman's frown,
>   He stands in Elgin's place,
> Ambassador from Britain's crown,
>   And type of all her race.

Private Moyse of the East Kent regiment celebrated here also has the further honour of being one of the first of a long line of soldiers to be eulogized as upholders of Victorian empire, a sphere of activity that was to improve the soldier's image markedly as the century wore on.[24] The foundation of the Staff College at Camberley, 1857, was a forward step in changing the image of the officer, too, from that of a privileged, thoughtless prig to that of a professional man doing a job. Although Alfred Austin could towards the end of the century still speak of soldier and officer in terms of 'lowly valour led by lofty will', it is in verse like the following that one recognizes the controversial officer of the late-nineteenth century:

> Through bitter nights and burning days
>   He watched the veldt stretch bare and grim;
> At home beside the cheerful blaze
>   We wrote our views of him.
>
> We mourned his curious lack of brain;
>   We judged him stupid, judged him slow;
> How much of what he knew was vain—
>   How much he did not know!

[24] Doyle's note on the indomitable Moyse appears in many anthologies, e.g. in *Ballads of the Brave*, ed. Frederick Langbridge, 4th ed. (London: Methuen, 1911), p. 444.

B

> Where Duty called, he pressed in haste;
>   That, too, was wrong, that haste undue;
> Why practise with such wanton waste
>   The only art he knew?
>
> Too well he loved each foolish game;
>   'Is War a game?' we sternly cried.
> And while we talked of England's name
>   For England's sake he died.

H. C. Macdowall's poem, which appeared in the *Spectator*, 15 December 1900, shows the effects of several controversies about army reform that raged between the Crimean and Boer wars, but before we turn to them we have to glance briefly at two other conflicts.

The American Civil War confirmed the all-engrossing and essentially civilian nature of all future large-scale wars. It involved large numbers of volunteers of whom many were educated men who, because American, were largely uninhibited by traditional European codes of military conduct and social distinctions between officers and subordinates. The result was a war which, waged between forces holding highly emotive but articulate points of view, became both gruesome and profoundly distressing. Edmund Wilson and Lee Steinmetz have sifted through the vast amount of verse that the war produced and have found that most of it now makes barren reading, mainly because even the better poets found it impossible to distance themselves sufficiently from the passionately partisan issues of the conflict.[25] Even Walt Whitman, serving as a hospital aide, aware of the suffering caused by the war, and capable of poems such as 'The Wound-dresser' and the prose of *Specimen Days*, could not resist the exhilarating challenge of combat:

> I'll pour the verse with streams of blood, full of volition, full of
>   joy,
> Then loosen, launch forth, to go and compete,
> With the banner and pennant a-flapping.[26]

But a few poems of the war, notably some by Herman Melville, show that in the American Civil War there existed for the first

[25] Edmund Wilson, *Patriotic Gore: Studies in the L terature of the American Civil War* (New York: Oxford University Press, 1966); *The Poetry of the American Civil War*, ed. Lee Steinmetz (East Lansing: Michigan State University Press, 1960).
[26] 'Song of the Banner at Daybreak', *Drum-Taps* (New York, 1865).

time all the conditions as well as the literary sensibility to produce poetry of the kind we normally associate with World War I. Quoting Froissart, thus recognizing that the *facts* of war have always been the same ('I dare not write of the horrible and inconceivable atrocities committed'), Melville puts forward a profoundly personal, compassionate vision of the dehumanizing effect of war and expresses it in a mode that modulates from the narrative or epic into the lyrical in poems like 'In the Prison Pen' and 'The College Colonel':

> A still rigidity and pale—
> An Indian aloofness lones his brow;
> He has lived a thousand years
> Compressed in battle's pains and prayers,
> Marches and watches slow.[27]

Another war that left a deep scar on a people sufficiently literate and motivated to articulate their responses in verse was the Franco-Prussian War, though it is necessary to remember that in France and Prussia, partly because of the continental situation of both countries, and partly because of conscription, the army and the soldier had always been much closer to the centre of national life than in Britain. In both countries this meant a tradition of war poetry, patriotic ballad, and soldier song much stronger than anything in England. If this tradition was at times more vociferous, it was often also more thoughtful than its British counterpart, and one therefore finds in both French and German articulate poems on the tragic futility and personal grief of war before the appearance of such works in English. The 'Soldatenliederbuch' and the patriotic chanson were integral parts of German and French popular culture in the nineteenth century, but so, too, were popular anti-war ballads, like the 'Deserteurlieder' which became widely current on the introduction of conscription in Germany,[28] or the revolutionary songs which expressed the perennial terror of life in the political maelstrom of post-Napoleonic France.

The radical-socialist commitments of German and French poets of the early nineteenth century frequently focused on the lot of the soldier. In Germany particularly, perhaps because of the close

[27] *Battle-Pieces and Aspects of the War* (New York: Harper & Bros., 1866).
[28] Karl Janicke, *Das deutsche Kriegslied: eine literarhistorische Studie* (Berlin, 1871), Vorwort.

relationship between 'Kunstdichtung' and 'Volkspoesie' in the
tradition of war verse and song, poets like Adelbert von Chamisso
and Georg Herwegh could cast their war poetry in the simple
elegiac mode of popular ballads of social protest, or could spike it
with the 'Galgenhumor' of the equally common 'Spotgedicht':

> Herr Wilhelm braucht ein grosses Heer,
> braucht Pulver und Patronen;
> an Jesum Christum glaubt er sehr,
> doch mehr noch an Kanonen.[29]

(Herr Wilhelm has need of a large army, he needs gun powder
and cartridges; he has great faith in Jesus Christ, but an even
greater faith in cannons.)

Even the German struggle for liberation and unification met with
some sardonic comment:

> Und ich lag, und abwärts wälzte
> unheilschwanger sich die Schlacht,
> über mich und über Leichen
> sank die kalte, finstre Nacht.
>
> . . . .
>
> Schrei ich wütend noch nach Freiheit,
> nach dem bluterkauften Glück,
> peitscht der Wächter mit der Peitsche
> mich in schnöde Ruh zurück.[30]

(And I lay, and away from me rolled the battle, pregnant with
disaster; over me and over the corpses sank the cold, dark night.
. . . Should I still, in fury, cry out for Freedom, for the reward of
happiness bought with so much blood, [Death] the guardian
lashes me with his whip back into my grim repose.)

As the century wore on and Prussian militarism became more and
more a pan-Germanic cult, the voices of opposition became
perhaps fewer, but lost none of their sharpness:

> Kruppschen Stahl, Kruppschen Stahl,
> und Soldaten ohne Zahl,
> und Stratechen ohnegleichen,
> die auf hunderttausend Leichen
> uns erbaut ein Ruhmesmal![31]

[29] Georg Herwegh, 'Herr Wilhelm' (1863), in *Deutschland, Deutschland: politische Gedichte vom Vormärz bis zur Gegenwart*, ed. Helmut Lamprecht (Bremen, 1969).
[30] Adelbert von Chamisso, 'Der Invalid im Irrenhaus', ibid.
[31] Herwegh, 'Immer Stärker', ibid.

(Krupp's steel, Krupp's steel, and soldiers without number, and strategists without peer, who, out of a hundred thousand corpses, have built us an epoch of fame!)

When the Franco-Prussian War broke out, a wave of patriotic verse swept over both France and Germany, engulfing both armies as well; Karl Janicke (*Das deutsche Kriegslied*) claims that not a regiment or a rank was without its poet, even the army fieldpost being elevated to the poetic pantheon. Ironically, though, it is from a French poet that we get our sharpest glimpse of the literacy of the invading Prussian army—Théodore de Banville, coming across a dead enemy soldier, comments:

> Il dormait, le jeune barbare,
> Avec un doux regard ami;
> Un volume Grec de Pindare
> Sortait de sa poche à demi.
>
> C'était un poète peut-être,
> Divin Orphée, un de tes fils,
> Qui pour un caprice du maître
> Est mort là, brisé comme un lys.[32]

(He slept, the young barbarian, with a gentle, friendly air. A volume of Pindar, in Greek, stuck out of his pocket. Perhaps he was a poet, one of your sons, divine Orpheus, who, for a whim of his master, lay there dead, broken like a lily.)

Among all these jubilating German soldier poets only a few were willing to say what war was really like, and through all the self-congratulatory euphoria on the humiliation of France, Moritz Hartmann's 'Genug des Mords, der Greul genug' and Edouard Mörike's 'Im Jahre 1871' must have rung like a cracked bell:

> Bei euren Taten, euren Siegen
> wortlos, beschämt hat mein Gesang geschwiegen:
> und manche, die mich darum schalten,
> hätten auch besser den Mund gehalten.[33]

(By our deeds, our victories, made speechless, my song fell silent in shame; and many who rebuked me for that had done better if they, too, had done the same.)

---

[32] 'Un Prussien Mort', *Idylles prussiennes* (Paris: Lemerre, 1872).
[33] Lamprecht, p. 208.

These sentiments, however, are mild compared with the effects defeat produced in France. Naturally, most of the French verse was hysterically patriotic, revanchist, or accusatory, attacking Teutonic barbarity and domestic ineptitude alike. Bismarck vied with Napoleon III for the position of chief public ogre in the chansons of the hour, but at the same time poems on the horror, devastation, humiliation, and pity of war came to a noticeable number. From the grim street and cabaret songs which lamented the bloodshed of the Paris Commune, of which many are recorded in Barbier and Vernillat's *Histoire de France par les chansons*, vol. viii (1961), to the more substantial poetry of the many writers who were either caught up in the campaign or witnessed its effects at close quarters, one may garner a striking body of verse on the shock and revulsion that the impersonal brute force of the first modern 'Blitzkrieg' produced. For Sully Prudhomme, Émile Bergerat, and Tristan Corbière the shock was registered in terms of the war's effect on the French countryside. Corbière could not believe that the corn would grow again where the blood of France had been spilt:

> Ne mangez pas ce pain, mères et jeunes filles!
> L'ergot de mort est dans le blé.[34]

Do not eat this bread, mothers and maidens! Death's sharp spur is in the wheat.)

Prudhomme, on the other hand, regarding flowers in a Paris park during the Commune, marvelled at nature's benign indifference to the scenes of carnage:

> Malgré les morts qu'elles recouvrent,
> Malgré cet effroyable engrais,
> Voici leurs calices qui s'ouvrent,
> Comme l'an dernier, purs et frais[35]

(In spite of the bodies beneath them, in spite of that fearful sustenance—look, how their petals unfold, as they did last year, fresh and innocent)

---

[34] 'La Pastorale de Conlie', *Les Amours jaunes* (1873), ed. Yves-Gerard le Dantec (Paris: Gallimard, 1953).
[35] 'Fleurs de sang', *Poésies* (Paris: Lemerre, 1872).

but Bergerat's village schoolmaster could find no such consolation on viewing the destruction of his little world:

> Des cadavres blêmis pourrissaient dans la boue;
> Des chevaux éventrés craquaient sous des caissons,
> Et des chemins affreux s'ouvraient dans les moissons
> Au sein des épis mûrs qu'avait fauchés la roue! . . .
> Le village n'était qu'un brasier.[36]

(Pallid corpses rotted in the mud; disembowelled horses split open under the wagons, and ghastly paths were opened up, cut through the crops in the very midst of ripe wheat that the wheel had mown down! . . . The village was no more than a burnt-out mass.)

If poets like Bergerat dwell perhaps too morbidly for our taste on scenes of devastation and corpses in mud, we may still concede that such verse, in its willingness to depict the nightmare of war compassionately and unheroically, marks a major step towards the poetry of Sassoon, Owen, and Rosenberg. Indeed, with the seventeen-year-old Rimbaud's 'Le Dormeur du val', written in October 1870, war poetry was pitched right into the world of 'Futility' and 'Anthem for Doomed Youth'. I quote it in Robert Lowell's translation.

> The swollen river sang through the green hole,
> and madly hooked white tatters on the grass.
> Light escaladed the hot hills. The whole
> valley bubbled with sunbeams like a beer-glass.
>
> The conscript was open-mouthed; his bare head
> and neck swam in the bluish water cress.
> He slept. The mid-day soothed his heaviness,
> sunlight was raining into his green bed,
>
> and baked the bruises from his body, rolled
> as a sick child might hug itself to sleep . . .
> Oh nature, rock him warmly, he is cold.
>
> The flowers no longer make his hot eyes weep.
> The river sucks his hair. His blue eye rolls.
> He sleeps. In his right side are two red holes.[37]

---

[36] 'Le Maitre d'école', *Poèmes de la guerre* (Paris, 1871).
[37] 'The Sleeper in the Valley', reprinted with the permission of Farrar, Straus & Giroux, Inc., and Faber & Faber Ltd. from *Imitations* by Robert Lowell, Copyright © 1958, 1959, 1960, 1961 by Robert Lowell.

The ambivalent treatment of death as both a negation of vitality and a peaceful release, offset against the incredulous, unwilling recognition that the sleeper is indeed dead, and the pointed exclusion of any reference to war except for the mention of 'conscript' and 'two red holes', here suggest the core of peacefulness that lies, ironically, at the heart of many of the great war poems of 1914–18. As in Owen's 'Asleep', we recognize here the conviction that ultimately war is naught and peace is all:

> He sleeps. He sleeps less tremulous, less cold
> Than we who must awake, and waking, say Alas!

In Europe the Franco-Prussian War inaugurated the 'Era of Violence' in international politics. Sheer force, based on material and technological superiority, was brilliantly vindicated as the most effective form of diplomacy. All over Europe governments took a searching look at their armies and launched out on the rapid mechanization of warfare and an arms race that would eventually lead to World War I. For the first time in English history the army became a permanent, obtrusive part of annual expenditure and national life.[38] The rapid growth of imperialist ideologies all over Europe, backed by Darwinian and Nietzschean slogans of 'survival of the fittest' and 'Wille zur Macht', rapidly established in England an image of and reliance on military superiority that lagged little, if at all, behind the traditional excesses of Prussian militarism and French 'gloire'.

The soldier became something of a national hero—if not always welcome, at least regarded with a grudging admiration or recognition of his necessity. 'The day has departed when civilians spoke with contempt of the private in the army and fawned upon the officer of the same. Even the rustic simpleton who, in a dazed and drunken mood, accepted the "shilling" ... has so often dignified by his after prowess, developed in the storms of war, the humble village of his birth, that British valour has come to be respected and feared wherever the British feet have trod';[39] or, in Kipling's more famous and more cynical words:

[38] Carlton J. H. Hayes, *A Generation of Materialism 1871–1900* (New York: Harper Torchbooks, 1963), *passim*; and G. M. Young, *Victorian England: Portrait of an Age*, 2nd ed. (London: Oxford Paperbacks, 1960), pp. 105 and 180.
[39] E. S. Macleod, *For the Flag: Lyrics and Incidents of the South African War* (Charlottetown, 1901), preface.

For it's Tommy this, an' Tommy that, an'
'Chuck him out, the brute!'
But it's 'Saviour of 'is country' when the guns
begin to shoot.[40]

Army reforms, like those of Cardwell, reorganized the army on a territorial basis, thus identifying regiments with local communities and pride, introduced short service and health and education qualifications, abolished the purchase of commissions, and began to make the army more popular and more democratic (Barnett, *Britain and her Army*, pp. 298 ff.). A new professionalism transformed European armies out of all recognition over the next thirty years. The introduction of mechanical transport, the telegraph, photographic reconnaissance, repeating rifles that could shoot a near-straight trajectory, machine-guns, and smokeless powder made armies more lethal and more respectable as they required more skill. The macabre situation developed, and grew to a nightmare in World War I, that soldiers became more efficient at killing each other as they became more educated and civilized.

The new militarist epoch also manifested itself in many other places. Doctrines of force came to permeate English culture to a striking extent, often in highly sublimated forms. Public schools, for instance, became more militarist in outlook as well as in method. At Wellington, established in 1858 for the sons of officers, boys wore uniforms, and rifle corps began to appear at several schools.[41] Brute force often paraded under the titles of 'muscular Christianity' and 'rugged individuality', as Kipling found:

There we met with famous men
Set in office o'er us;
And they beat on us with rods—
Faithfully with many rods—
Daily beat on us with rods,
For the love they bore us,[42]

or was sublimated in an ethos that eventually confused war with sport and life with a game, as enshrined in Newbolt's 'Vitaï Lampada':

---

[40] 'Tommy', *Barrack-Room Ballads* (London: Methuen, 1892).
[41] Marion Lochhead, *Young Victorians* (London: John Murray, 1959), p. 73.
[42] ' "Let us now praise famous men",' *Stalky & Co.* (1899).

> The river of death has brimmed his banks,
> And England's far, and Honour a name,
> But the voice of a schoolboy rallies the ranks:
> 'Play up! play up! and play the game!'

Popular culture, ferried on universal education from about the time of the Franco-Prussian War, became increasingly sensationalistic and force-oriented. The rapidly developing press and printing industry kept pace with and even outstripped these demands, thus foisting on its avid but still undiscriminating public books, newspapers, and magazines that dwelt on imperial and military adventure, eulogistic histories of nineteenth-century campaigns, the hero-worship of military commanders, fictitious wars and war-scares, elaborate speculations on the relevant strength of British and continental armies, and, above all, British racial superiority.[43] One result of all this was that the 1890s produced more popular anthologies of war poetry than any previous decade had done, Henley's *Lyra Heroica* (1892) leading the way in both kind and sentiment:

To set forth, as only art can, the beauty of the joy of living, the beauty and the blessedness of death, the glory of battle and adventure, the nobility of devotion—to a cause, an ideal, a passion even—the dignity of resistance, the sacred quality of patriotism, that is my ambition here.

Another, much more disastrous result was that the British, and European, public became accustomed to the idea of 'total war' and to the 'modern glorification of blood-lust' as Harold Spender called it in 1900,[44] ascribed by a contemporary reviewer of patriotic poetry directly to the superficial stimuli of popular education:

The vulgarity and ignorance that disfigure so many of these patriotic effusions must, we fear, be attributed to the elementary education of the last thirty years, which has given to crowds of people a certain capacity for self-expression without ideas to express, and an interest in reading without the taste to discriminate good from bad.[45]

[43] For instance, periodicals like *Regiment*, *Black and White*, and *Navy and Army Illustrated*; Fitchett's *Fights for the Flag*; Henty's juvenile novels; Charles S. Jerram's *Armies of the World* (1899); and the vast literature of Diamond Jubilee imperialism. See also I. F. Clarke, *Voices Prophesying War 1763–1984* (London: Oxford University Press, 1966).

[44] 'War and Poetry', *Pilot*, 16 June 1900.

[45] 'English Patriotic Poetry', *Quarterly Rev.*, 192 (Oct. 1900), 520–41.

'The mind of the multitude is beginning to resemble the contents of a number of *Tit-Bits*,' wrote O. Eltzbacher in the *Nineteenth Century*, aiming his strictures at the vast sub-culture of sixpenny novels, yellow press, and music hall.[46]

However, music hall belligerence at the end of the century was merely the most common form of a mood of savagery that stretched well up the social scale and found vociferous expression in much of the 'serious' verse of the period. Sentiments such as the following differ from more sophisticated expressions of the same thing—in, for instance, Alfred Austin—only in their greater Cockney honesty:

> When Tommy joins the 'unt,
> With the stabbin' of the baynit,
> The baynit, the bloody baynit,
> Gawd 'elp the man in front!
>
> . . . .
>
> And 'e'll get 'ome with the baynit,
> The flashing, gashing baynit,
> The ruddy, bloody baynit,
> Or 'e'll know the reason why![47]

Taken into the drawing-room and hedged about with ideologies of racial imperialism, these notions grew into

> We are the Choice of the Will: God, when He gave the word
> That called us into line, set at our hand a sword;
> Set us a sword to wield none else could lift and draw,
> And bade us forth to the sound of the trumpet of the Law[48]

or, elevated to the pages of *The Times*, they became Swinburne's 'Strike, England, and strike home' (11 October 1899) and the Archbishop of Armagh's ecstatic sadism (31 October 1899):

> Thus as the heavens' many-coloured flames
>   At sunset are but dust in rich disguise,
> The ascending earthquake dust of battle frames
>   God's picture in the skies.

If war became a popular theme towards the end of the century, so did peace, and if we return to the year 1871 and trace the growth

---

[46] 'The Disadvantages of Education', *Nineteenth Century*, 53 (1903), 314–29.
[47] *Literary World*, 6 July 1900.
[48] W. E. Henley, 'The Choice of the Will', *For England's Sake: Verses and Songs in Time of War* (London: David Nutt, 1900).

of pacifism from there onwards, we shall see that it developed in organization and articulation in proportion to the growth of doctrines of force, vitalism, and popular belligerence. If the establishment of universal education and the spread of literacy gave wider currency to militarist ideologies and literature, these developments also helped to disseminate the popular radical socialism of, for instance, *Reynold's Newspaper* and the *Labour Leader*, which were firmly opposed to war. Much-read social surveys, such as General Booth's *In Darkest England and the Way Out* (1890), and the popular works which they inspired, like Jack London's *The People of the Abyss* (1903), would turn to the case of the soldier as an example of injustice and expose the life of discharged soldiers in East End flop-houses. Shaw debunked military heroics in his plays and articles, for instance in *Arms and the Man* (1894) and 'Civilization and the Soldier': 'War is an orgy of crime based on the determination of the soldier to stick at nothing to bring it to an end and get out of [the] daily danger of being shot.'[49]

Just as the rise of a popular literate but unliterary culture encouraged the growth of music hall jingoism and exalted the *mores* of the street to middle-class ideologies of force, so the traditional outspokenness and irreverence of street ballads and soldier's 'grouse' rhymes became respectable fare for middle-class audiences. Unwritten folk ballads against soldiering must have existed for centuries. In *Folk Song in England* (1967) A. L. Lloyd has put on record some of the anti-pressing and deserter songs of the eighteenth and nineteenth centuries which express a strong animus against war, pieces such as 'Arthur McBride':

> Oh no, mister sergeant, we aren't for sale.
> We'll make no such bargain, and your bribe won't avail.
> We're not tired of our country, and don't care to sail,
> Though your offer is pleasant and charming.
>
> If we were such fools as to take your advance,
> It's right bloody slender would be our poor chance,
> For the Queen wouldn't scruple to send us to France
> And get us all shot in the morning.

[49] *Humane Rev.*, 1 (1900), 298–315.

An earlier collection, John Ashton's *Modern Street Ballads* (1888) shows that a close connection sometimes existed between social protest and anti-militarism in these songs:

> We're low—we're low—we're very very low,
>   And yet when the trumpets ring,
> The thrust of a poor man's arm will go
>   Thro' the heart of the proudest King.
> We're low—we're low—our place we know,
>   We're only the rank and file,
> We're not too low to kill the foe,
>   But too low to touch the spoil.
>   (Ernest Jones, 'The Song of the Lower Classes')

The influence of the sentiments and diction of songs like these on the poetry of Kipling is obvious, and it was indeed Kipling who, exploiting the idiom of music hall, street ballad, and barrack room, popularized the image of 'Tommy Atkins' as profane, rugged, ignorant, loyal, pugnacious, sentimental—in short, thoroughly human—that was to last right into World War II, a *persona* essential for the comprehension of all war poetry written from the 1890s onwards, since most of it either developed or reacted to this notion of the soldier as lovable rogue. 'Kipling', wrote B. H. Holland in the *Edinburgh Review* in 1902, 'has invented a style and discovered a subject matter. . . . He has translated into verse with extraordinary fidelity and skill the view taken of life by the unlettered Englishman of the roving disposition . . . who may be found taking the chances of life with the same ironical stoicism in every land and on every sea. . . . One hears his echoes everywhere.'[50] One did indeed. His verse could be easily imitated and parodied—the ballad-mongers of the hour, complained A. Waugh in the *Anglo-Saxon Review*, December 1900, had all caught 'the *argot* and the slang, the dropped aspirate and the sprinkled oath'—but this feature of Kipling's verse actually gave further currency to the image of the soldier it expressed, and provided, on the outbreak of the Anglo-Boer War, a common poetic patois for the men at the front, through which they could communicate a novel and unvarnished view of soldiering.

The popularity of Kipling's verse served, furthermore, to bring to the surface some of the genuine soldier verse on which his

[50] 'War and Poetry', *Edinburgh Rev.*, 196 (1902), 29–54.

idiom and portrayal of war and soldiering depended. In the last quarter of the nineteenth century there existed all over the empire a breed of pioneer poets and bush balladists who, it must be admitted, often merely fed the popular demand for 'colonial' literature and activist doggerel, but who sometimes managed to infuse into their verse the rugged excitement, humour, and pathos of building railroads in Africa, herding cattle in the Australian outback, waging punitive campaigns in India, or prospecting in Canada—'Diggers' Doggerel', as two of these mining-camp poets, C. and A. P. Wilson-Moore, called their work.[51] However, 'doggerel can express the heart', as Private Henry Surtees hopefully prefaced his rambling poem on 'The March to Khartoum and Fall of Omdurman' (1899), and his did:

> This journey was most trying,
>   The sun was very hot,
> And some weak constitutions
>   Were soon upon a cot,
> These men were very sorry
>   For having come so far,
> And being sent to Cairo
>   Without the longed-for 'bar'.

The Ashanti and Zulu Wars (1873 and 1879), the Chitral Relief expedition (1895), the Sudan campaign (1896–8), are only the better-known of the many late-Victorian conflicts that were celebrated in 'grouse' verse and popular ballads such as Surtees's. Much of it reveals a current of Victorian moralistic, denotative verse, untouched by the Romantic movement, which still ran strong in parlour, pub, and barrack room and inspired Kipling's most famous ballads. The Boer War gave birth to a vast amount of verse in this category, as the group of war correspondents found who, with Kipling, guest-edited the Bloemfontein *Friend* during the occupation of that city: 'The Tommies all did verse—or worse—and the example was epidemically contagious. Perhaps in another month we should all have turned versifiers, and produced copies of the *Friend* wholly in rhyme.'[52]

Kipling's portrayal of the soldier in more sympathetic and at least partly realistic terms was not an isolated one. Two other figures who produced significantly different war poems just before

[51] *Diggers' Doggerel: Poems of the Veldt and Mine* (Cape Town: Argus, 1890).
[52] Julian Ralph, *War's Brighter Side* (London: C. Arthur Pearson, 1901), p. 372.

the Boer War were A. E. Housman and, in America, Stephen Crane. *A Shropshire Lad* (1896) popularized a wistful, even sentimental image of the soldier as agent and victim of an inevitably tragic confrontation between man and circumstance:

> East and west on fields forgotten
>   Bleach the bones of comrades slain,
> Lovely lads and dead and rotten;
>   None that go return again.
>
> Far the calling bugles hollo,
>   High the screaming fife replies,
> Gay the files of scarlet follow:
>   Woman bore me, I will rise.
> (XXXV: 'On the Idle Hill of Summer')

If the seductive fatalism here were still too facile and the sentiments still too close to the sublimated brutality of the era, the death of a brother in the Boer War would bring Housman, as we shall see, to a sharper articulation of the poignancy already present in *A Shropshire Lad*.

In *War is Kind* (1899), published on the eve of the Boer War, Stephen Crane added aspic to *The Red Badge of Courage* (1895) and formulated the bitterest and most sardonic of all nineteenth-century lyrics attacking war. Some of these aphoristic verses hardly rise above snarling sarcasm:

> 'Have you ever made a just man?'
> 'Oh, I have made three', answered God,
> 'But two of them are dead,
> And the third—
> Listen! Listen!
> And you will hear the thud of his defeat.'

The title poem, however, shows a concept of war as hideous, mindless, and insulting to man that could perhaps, as Carl Sandburg claimed,[53] only be appreciated after 1914, but was certainly by 1899 no longer strange:

> Great is the battle-god, great, and his kingdom
> A field where a thousand corpses lie.
>
> . . . .
>
> Do not weep, babe, for war is kind.
> Because your father tumbled in the yellow trenches,

[53] Quoted in D. G. Hoffman, *The Poetry of Stephen Crane* (New York: Columbia University Press, 1957), p. 34.

> Raged at his breast, gulped and died,
> Do not weep.
> War is kind.

Compatriots of Crane, like Richard Burton, voicing their disenchantment with America's expansionist war against Spain in 1898, expressed views of war complementary to his:

> Beneath gray gloom they tramp along: their tread
>   Lacks rhythm; faded, soiled, and torn their dress;
> They wot of storm and peril, wounds that bled,
>   And pains beyond imagination's guess.
> The lookers-on, struck mute by tenderness,
> Hardly huzza: it is as if the dead
>   Walked with the quick. Beneath a brooding sky
>   The bronzed and battered veterans limp by.[54]

Crane's own *The Red Badge of Courage* had had some considerable part in the diffusion of anti-war attitudes at the end of the century, but it was not alone. The current literary modes of naturalism and realism, as exhibited in Zola's work on the Franco-Prussian War, *La Débâcle* (1892), Bertha von Suttner's *Die Waffen nieder* (1889), and Oswald Fritz Bilse's *Aus einer kleinen Garnison* (1903), all translated into English as soon as they appeared, fostered pacifist attitudes by the very realism with which they depicted military life, quite apart from their explicit crusading against war. The war reportage of the new journalism had a similar effect, in spite of frequent pandering to sensationalism. G. W. Steevens, who accompanied Kitchener to the Sudan and was to die a couple of years later in the Siege of Ladysmith, was one of many who created a vicarious immediacy for readers with reports such as the following:

Horses plunged, blundered, recovered, fell; Dervishes on the ground lay for the ham-stringing cut; officers pistolled them in passing over, as one drops a stone into a bucket; troopers thrust till lances broke, then cut; everybody went on straight, through everything.

And through everything clean out the other side they came—those that kept up or got up in time. The others were on the ground—in pieces by now, for the cruel swords shore through shoulder and thigh, and carved the dead into fillets.[55]

[54] 'The Return of the Veterans', *Lyrics of Brotherhood* (1899), in *Collected Poems* (Indianapolis: Bobbs-Merrill, 1931).
[55] *With Kitchener to Khartum* (London: Thomas Nelson, n.d.), p. 324.

The Boer War produced a plethora of similar efforts by war correspondents—*The Times* alone had twenty in South Africa[56]— and their influence on the poetry of war was considerable. Something of the new war reportage is clearly present in F. Whitmore's 'In the Trenches', which appeared just before the Boer War in the *Atlantic Monthly*, 83 (1899), inspired possibly by the Spanish-American War:

We lay among the rifle-pits, above our low heads streaming
Bullets, like sleet, with now and then, near by, the vicious screaming
Of shells that made us hold our breath, till each had burst and blasted
Its ghastly circle, hid in smoke—here, there—and while it lasted,
That murderous fume and fusillade, our hearts were in our throats;
For hell let loose about us raged, and in those muddy moats
The rain that fell was shot and shell, the plash it made was red,
And all about the long redoubt was garrisoned with dead.

During the 1890s pacifist and feminist movements gathered considerable momentum, women particularly playing a large part, under the inspiration of Emily Hobhouse in England and Olive Schreiner in South Africa, in mobilizing opposition to the Anglo-Boer War. The publications of these movements, for instance the *Humanitarian*, *Humane Review*, *Herald of Peace*, *Ethical World*, *Concord*, and, during the South African conflict, W. T. Stead's *War Against War*, were full of anti-war verses of usually a rather obvious kind, but on occasion rising to lines like the following:

Hot cannon heard upon the hills
And rifles in the glen;
Oh, all the world will listen, now:
For men are murdering men!

or:

For brave and simple are the gathering hosts,
Who move like dumb beasts to the shambles led,
Who hear the word and take their ordered posts,
Nor know the cause for which their blood is shed.[57]

In his *Quintessence of Ibsenism* Shaw, with characteristic rational impishness, showed how closely intertwined feminist and anti-militarist arguments often were: 'The domestic career is no more

[56] See L. S. Amery, *My Political Life*, vol. i: *England before the Storm 1896–1914* (London: Hutchinson, 1953), p. 115.
[57] Will Carleton, 'Song of the Wires', *Herald of Peace and International Arbitration*, 27 (1900), 87; B. Paul Neuman, 'The Voice of England', *Concord*, 15 (1900), 35.

natural to all women than the military career is natural to all men.'[58] His anti-militarist satire found frequent echoes in the verse of pacifist magazine poets:

> The Anglo-Saxon Christians, with Gatling gun and sword,
> In serried ranks are pushing on the gospel of the Lord,

sang William Lloyd Garrison near the end of the Anglo-Boer War (*Herald of Peace*, March 1902, p. 207), and earlier, when a large consignment of 'Khaki bibles' had been shipped to the troops in South Africa, an anonymous epigram in the *Academy*, 18 November 1899, suggested:

> Help us forget, till war is done
> That Little Englander, Thy Son.
>
> .   .   .   .
>
> Direct our Tommies when they con
> Thy Book of Books in khaki bound,
> (Which also cheers the Boers on);
> Lest any foe be left alive,
> Keep them from Matthew chapter five.

Indeed, the khaki bibles and tins of chocolates dispatched to the troops at about the same time threw the continental press, and even some British papers, into paroxysms of ridicule and caricature which eventually led to the demand and granting of a full diplomatic apology from the French government. But that is another story. What is relevant here is that the bibles and chocolates revealed a public and official willingness to concern itself, be it inadequately, with the soldier's welfare. Violet Brooke-Hunt's account of packets of tracts and shirts with biblical texts stitched on to their collars and cuffs which arrived in clothes parcels intended for hospitals at the front, illustrates the same benevolent ignorance.[59] By the time the chocolates and bibles arrived in South Africa, British troops had at Magersfontein, Stormberg, and Spionkop, to mention only a few fateful names, learnt something of the terrible accuracy of Ivan Bloch's prophetic *The Future of War* (1898), which appeared in England in W. T. Stead's popular version, *Is War now Impossible?*, just before the Boer War. Bloch exposed the massive fatality and stalemate that technological advances in warfare since 1870 had made inevitable

---

[58] Quoted in J. M. Kennedy, *English Literature 1880–1905* (London: Stephen Swift, 1912), p. 170.
[59] *A Woman's Memories of the War* (London: James Nisbet, 1901), p. 126.

in all future large-scale wars, and although he was not to be proved right before 1914, his six-volume study was welcomed by pacifists all over Europe as the final evidence for the urgency and validity of their cause. The Hague Peace Conference, concluded three months before the outbreak of the Boer War, was the outcome of this new impetus and the culmination of the nineteenth-century peace movement.

Barbara Tuchman has shown how suspicious the delegates, confused the aims, and negligible the results of the Conference were, but this gathering of the international pacifist clan served at least to focus public attention on the considerable fear of and opposition to war which existed by the end of the century.[60] It also provided the organizational framework for the feminist, radical, socialist, and humanitarian groups all over Europe that mounted a massive international protest against the Anglo-Boer War, thus preparing a growth-culture for the largest body of anti-war poetry that any war to date had produced. At the same time the Conference was the visible expression of a *fin-de-siècle* apprehension and pessimism about the continuation of Victorian security that inspired alike Hardy's 'Darkling Thrush', Arnold Böcklin's nightmare vision of impending doom in his painting, 'The War' (1896), Kipling's 'Recessional', Stephen Phillips's 'Midnight—The 31st of December, 1900'—

> I will make of your warfare a terrible thing,
>   A thing impossible, vain;
> For a man shall set his hand to a handle and wither
>   Invisible armies and fleets,
> And a lonely man with a breath shall exterminate armies,
>   With a whisper annihilate fleets;
> And the captain shall sit in his chamber and level a city,
>   The far-off capital city—

and Laurence Binyon's 'Europe, MDCCCCI—to Napoleon':

> A hundred years have flown, and still
> For peace they pine; peace tarries yet.
> These groaning armies Europe fill,
> And war's red planet hath not set.[61]

[60] *The Proud Tower: A Portrait of the World before the War 1890–1914* (London: Hamish Hamilton, 1966), ch. 5.
[61] Stephen Phillips, *New Poems* (London: John Lane, 1908); Laurence Binyon, *The Death of Adam and Other Verses* (London: Methuen, 1904).

On the eve of the South African War the two opposing forces of pacifism and militarism stood more clearly and firmly defined in public consciousness than they had probably ever done before. Every minor war brought forth a spate of catchpenny novels, like H. M. Brailsford's *The Broom of the War-God* (1898), on the Graeco-Turkish War of 1897. At the same time much evidence existed of a well-organized pacifist movement, as in William Jones's *Quaker Campaigns in Peace and War* (1899). On the one hand Julien Benda could believe: 'We were sincerely persuaded in 1898 that the era of wars was over. For fifteen years from 1890 to 1905 men of my generation really believed in world peace' (Tuchman, *Proud Tower*, p. 234). On the other hand Lord Fisher, referring to the Fashoda crisis of 1898, could lament: 'One ought not to wish for war I suppose, but it was a pity that it could not have come off just now, when I think we should have made rather a good job of it.'[62] The Boer War revealed that a spirit of blood-militarism existed all over Europe, but at the same time George Sturt found, after talking to the men of his village, that it was 'questionable if ever before men concerned themselves so much about the abstract morality of a war. . . . The old excuses for war are dying, if not dead. Lust of treasure, or of territory, will not be tolerated by the nations now taking into their hands the control of their affairs.'[63] By now it was clear, too, that war poems would no longer be mere 'battle-pieces' but would increasingly be concerned with the ethics of war and personal reactions to it. John Macleay, editing one of the many retrospective anthologies of war poems that the Boer War provoked, *War Songs and Songs and Ballads of Martial Life* (1900), was able to isolate two clear strains of war poetry that had emerged by 1900: 'On the one hand, we have wild animal spirits, a love of fighting, a passion for adventure, impatience of restraint . . . on the other, unobtrusive patriotism, a fear of expansion, a sincere horror of war.' Sir George Douglas, reviewing Hardy's *Poems of the Past and the Present* (1902), recognized that here the truly rich vein of war poetry was at last fully exposed. The book, he said, presented 'a sheaf of War Poems, which differ from the serviceable Kipling-isms and Begbie-isms of the hour most notably in this, that they

[62] Quoted in Dudley Barker, *Prominent Edwardians* (London, 1969), p. 34.
[63] *Journals, 1890–1927*, ed. E. D. Mackerness (Cambridge: Cambridge University Press, 1967), vol. i, entry for 10 June 1900.

dwell not on the glory, but on the piteousness of the struggle. Like other Gods, in Mr. Hardy's view, the God of Battles has had his day.'[64]

Hardy's reaction to the war no longer seems surprising. The Boer War brought together all the conditions essential for an articulate response to war: a literate, educated army consisting largely of volunteers, waging an expansionist war in full view of a large troop of war correspondents against two small republics whose life-style was popularly supposed to be pastoral and pacifist and who enjoyed the vociferous support of almost the whole civilized world as well as the whole socialist, radical, and pacifist movement in Britain. A flood of verse was inevitable and it was unlikely that it would all be in praise of the Union Jack and the bayonet.

[64] 'A New Note of Poetic Melancholy', *Bookman*, 21 (1902), 131–2.

II

Empire: Calling or Curse?

'Imperium et Libertas',
That's the motto for you, brothers;
Libertas for ourselves, boys,
And Imperium over others.

Punch, quoted in *Coming Day*, June 1900.

As early as 1883 Sir John Seeley in his seminal work on Victorian empire, *The Expansion of England*, identified two conflicting attitudes to imperial activity:

There are two schools of opinion among us with respect to our Empire, of which schools the one may be called the bombastic and the other the pessimistic. The one is lost in wonder and ecstasy at its immense divisions, and at the energy and heroism which presumably have gone to the making of it; this school therefore advocates the maintenance of it as a point of honour or sentiment. The other is the opposite extreme, regards it as founded in aggression and rapacity, as useless and burdensome, a kind of excrescence upon England, as depriving us of the advantages of our insularity and exposing us to wars and quarrels in every part of the globe; this school therefore advocates a policy which may lead at the earliest possible opportunity to the abandonment of it.[1]

Seeley's summation of British ambivalence about empire was to remain accurate for the rest of the century, and for many years after. As the fever of empire rose, so did serious doubts about its methods and aims. Hence the Boer War became a battle-field not only of opposing armies, but also of conflicting ideas on empire. If the war was the greatest of jingo outrages, it also served as a rallying point for a vociferous anti-imperialist movement, and ultimately formed the most effective antidote to the imperial fever that burned in Britain during the last decade of the nineteenth century.

The majority of the men involved in late-Victorian imperial

[1] 2nd ed. (London: Macmillan, 1900), pp. 340–1.

ventures would, of course, not have accepted our metaphor of disease. John Buchan, reflecting many years later on his feelings at the time of the war, wrote what is still one of the most idealistic accounts of imperialism:

Those were the days when a vision of what the empire might be made dawned upon certain minds with almost the force of a revelation. . . . It was an inspiration to youth to realize the magnitude of its material heritage, and to think how it might be turned to spiritual issues. . . . I dreamed of a world-wide brotherhood with the background of a common race and creed, consecrated to the service of peace.[2]

There was much dreaming. 'What's your dream?' blurted out Cecil Rhodes to Kipling on their first meeting (1896), and the phrase became something of an incubus in Kipling's imperialist verse after this date.[3] In contrast to Buchan, however, C. A. Parnell, like his famous compatriot and namesake, saw in imperialism only a blight:

The red wind sweeps from North to South,
　From West to the burning East,
And where it blows no good thing grows;
　But man, and woman, and beast
All wither and pine, and bodies and souls are blighted and slain,
　And the things that thrive are dull despair,
　Disease and vice, and sorrow and care,
And want and hate, and grief and pain.[4]

Between the poles of Buchan and Parnell a protean range of imperial creed or greed, violence or vision, can be found. One of the most fascinating exercises of recent historiography has been to lay bare the deep roots of late-Victorian imperialism and to trace them to mid-century ideologies of civilization and progress, public school cults of rugged idealism and British superiority, sublimated evangelicalism, and para-evolutionary doctrines of 'manifest destiny' and the need for racial conflict.[5] The ideas of

[2] *Memory Hold-the-Door* (London: Hodder & Stoughton, 1940), pp. 119–20.
[3] *Something of Myself* (London: Macmillan, 1937), p. 149.
[4] 'The British Empire', *Old Tales and New* (Dublin: Sealy, Bryers & Walker, 1905).
[5] Among the many works dealing with the Victorian origins of imperialism, I have found the following most illuminating: Elie Halévy, *Imperialism and the Rise of Labour*, 2nd ed. (London: Benn, 1951); C. E. Carrington, *The British Overseas* (Cambridge: Cambridge University Press, 1950); R. Robinson and John Gallagher, *Africa and the Victorians* (London: Macmillan, 1961); Richard Faber, *The Vision and the Need: Late Victorian Imperialist Aims* (London: Faber, 1966); L. H. Gann and

imperialism have turned out to be as manifold and contradictory as the growth of the empire itself was haphazard and speculative. Fortunately, the student of the poetry of the period will find that the imperialist verse of the 1890s covers a fairly narrow range of the imperial spectrum. Most of it dwells on the moral virtues of expansionism: its challenging effects on British manhood; its invigorating therapy for a nation in danger of becoming supine with success; its provision of visible proof that Englishmen were chosen to conquer and rule; its value as a secular religion in the service of which young men could exercise their idealism, duty, ambition, and near-Arthurian devotion to a cause. One such young man was Lord Lugard, who 'had the lasting habits of Christian training. These merged with his more conscious standards which were those, he claimed, of an English Gentleman, derived immediately from his family, public school and army training, and ultimately, perhaps, from the code of the medieval Christian knight ... the code of noblesse oblige.'[6] The close interweaving here of the ethos of public school, chivalry, army, church, colonial service, and empire is recurrent in the activist verse of the 1890s and inspires the protagonists of many a Boer War poem.

The immediate ancestry of these heroes of imperial derring-do can be traced to a number of proto-imperial texts, both in prose and in verse, of the middle of the century. At the time of the Boer War Tennyson, for instance, was seen as a major proponent of imperialism, and reviewers of activist verse regularly invoked Tennyson's patriotic poetry as archetypal.[7] We would now regard most of this verse as topical doggerel, and feel that the vague but powerful sense of mysterious quest which suffuses 'Ulysses' comes much closer to expressing the therapeutic urgencies of Victorian

Peter Duignan, *Burden of Empire* (London, 1968); James Morris, *Pax Britannica: The Climax of an Empire* (London: Faber, 1968); and Max Beloff, *Imperial Sunset*, vol. i: *Britain's Liberal Empire 1897–1921* (London: Methuen, 1969). I am also indebted to the discussions of imperialism as a literary theme in Alan Sandison, *The Wheel of Empire: A Study of the Imperial Idea in Some Late Nineteenth and Early Twentieth Century Fiction* (London: Macmillan, 1967); David Daiches, *Some Late Victorian Attitudes* (London: Deutsch, 1969), and J. A. V. Chapple, *Documentary and Imaginative Literature 1880–1920* (London: Blandford, 1970).

6 Margery Perham, *Lugard: The Years of Adventure 1858–98* (London, 1956), p. 482.
7 e.g. 'The True Poet of Imperialism', *Macmillan's Mag.*, 80 (July 1899), 192–5; and J. A. R. Marriott, 'The Imperial Note in Victorian Poetry', *Nineteenth Century*, 48 (1900), 236–48.

imperialism. Similarly, Longfellow's much-parodied 'Excelsior!', with its haunting devotion to an unnamed cause, suggests more pertinently than most overtly imperialist verse the nature of a Victorian need that imperialist activity partly managed to fill. As early as 1858 Charles Kingsley, in *Andromeda and Other Poems*, placed this activist devotion at the service of military and imperial expansion:

> But the black North-easter,
> Through the snow-storm hurled,
> Drives our English hearts of oak
> Seaward round the world, . . .
> Conquering from the eastward,
> Lords by land and sea.
>   ('Ode to the North-east Wind')

Such sentiments continued to inform Victorian activist verse; we recognize it, at the end of the century, in James Rennell Rodd's 'Frank Rhodes: A Memory' (1905), which pays moving tribute to a number of the poet's contemporaries who had all lost their lives in Africa. The subject of the poem was an elder brother of Cecil Rhodes who had taken part in the Jameson Raid and the defence of Mafeking. His death moved Rodd to reflect nostalgically on the lost masonic brotherhood of empire-builders:

> Young were we still, twelve years ago
> When we went southward, proud to know
> We were of those the sea queen sends
> For witness where her mandate ends.

All became captives of Africa and the mystique of empire:

> What wonder if I hear the call
> Of that far voice that lured them all!
> I cross the sandy wastes again,
> The great mimosa-tufted plain,
> I share the thirsty march, through clear
> Clean mornings, and with eve I hear
> The marsh things crying, see the fierce
> Short sunsets, the large stars that pierce
> The tangled tent of tropic green,
> And all the wonders we have seen
> In that grim world of gloom and gleam,
> Where evermore, across my dream,

> Pervading all, I still behold
> The kind worn face, so young, so old,
> The lifted chin, the deep-set eyes
> At once so merry and so wise,
> The never-failing helpful smile
> That haunts all ways from Cape to Nile.[8]

Another proto-imperialist writer was Carlyle, and once again one can trace, as Jacques Gazeau did at the time of the Boer War in *L'Impérialisme anglais* (Paris, 1903), a direct genealogy from Carlyle to certain late-Victorian imperialist thinkers and poets. His excessive respect for the heroic leader, for instance, was easily transmuted into the notion that the British race itself was marked out for leadership:

The Commander over men; he to whose will our wills are to be subordinated, and loyally surrender themselves, and find their welfare in doing so, may be reckoned the most important of Great Men. He is practically the summary for us of *all* the various figures of Heroism; Priest, Teacher, whatsoever of earthly or of spiritual dignity we can fancy to reside in a man, embodies itself here, to *command* over us, to furnish us with constant practical teaching, to tell us for the day and hour what we are to *do*.[9]

By the end of the century the Carlylean ethic of leadership had been blunted down to statements such as the following:

We happen to be the best people in the world, with the highest ideals of decency and justice and liberty and peace, and the more of the world we inhabit, the better it is for humanity.   (Cecil John Rhodes)

I believe that the British race is the greatest of governing races that the world has ever seen.   (Joseph Chamberlain)[10]

These notions proved fatally attractive for poets such as Alfred Austin, W. E. Henley, and Swinburne. In their poetry the extravagant and already shrill statements of politicians touched off a particularly hysterical and unpleasant note: 'Who dies for England, sleeps with God', intoned Austin's 'Spartan Mothers'

[8] *The Violet Crown* (London: Arnold, 1913).
[9] *Sartor Resartus, and On Heroes, Hero-Worship, and the Heroic in History* (London: Dent Everyman, 1908), p. 422.
[10] Rhodes quoted in Morris, *Pax Brittanica*, p. 124, and Chamberlain in Faber, *The Vision and the Need*, p. 64.

in the *Graphic*, 6 January 1900, and in *Songs of England* (1900) he claimed a kind of special creation for England:

> In the Beginning when out of darkness,
> The Earth, the Heaven,
> The stars, the seasons,
> The mighty mainland,
> And whale-ploughed water,
> By God the Maker
> Were formed and fashioned,
> Then God made England.
>
> ('Alfred's Song')

This and many other poems by, particularly, Austin and Henley remind us that imperialist notions deriving from Carlyle's writings frequently also drew sustenance from the ideas of Darwin. 'Social Darwinism' found its way into the structure of late-Victorian political and imperialist thinking at several points, and two all but conflicting attitudes to imperialism, both traceable to Darwinian thought, emerged: on the one hand, a doctrine of racial conflict and domination presented as essential for the biological and intellectual improvement of the human race; on the other, an argument that the civilized and superior races had a responsibility to spread sweetness and light to those peoples still living under a nature red in tooth and claw. The latter view is clearly that of John Buchan; the former found its champion in the prominent mathematician, linguist, and geneticist, Karl Pearson: 'History shows me one way and one way only, in which a high state of civilization has been produced, namely the struggle of race with race, and the survival of the physically and mentally fitter race.'[11]

Pearson and Buchan adumbrate the themes of many imperialist poems of the Boer War period. While Austin, Henley, Swinburne, and their followers stridently insisted on the supremacy of the British race and empire, Robert Buchanan and William Watson, though conceding the possibly beneficial qualities of empire, regarded the Boer War and the jingoism to which it gave currency as a gross misdirection of the imperial cause. 'The True Imperialism' claimed Watson in a poem of that name in *For England* (1904) —a title surely meant as a reply to Henley's *For England's Sake*

[11] Quoted by Himmelfarb, 'Varieties of Social Darwinism', in *Victorian Minds*.

(1900)—was of the spirit, not territorial. It eradicated ignorance and fear, not peoples:

> Vain is your Science, vain your Art,
> Your triumphs and your glories vain,
> To feed the hunger of their heart
> And famine of their brain.
>
> Your savage deserts howling near,
> Your wastes of ignorance, vice, and shame,—
> Is there no room for victories here,
> No field for deeds of fame?

Poems expressing approval of the war may conveniently be divided into the following groups: those imbued with the activist fervours of the 'Henley School'; those suffused with the exalted public school verities found in Sir Henry Newbolt's verse; and those declaiming a crusading, vitalist doctrine of war, particularly imperialist war, as the panacea for all social and spiritual ills. Below this level one can assemble a further group of more or less bovinely jingo popular ballads, music hall songs, and newspaper doggerel which mushroomed all over the empire during the three years of the war.

The Boer War came at the end of William Ernest Henley's life and brought to a head the obsession with national and cultural degeneracy that activated him during the 1890s.[12] Yeats (like Conrad and Kipling one of the many writers launched by Henley into the literary world of late-Victorian London) pin-pointed Henley's chief fetish of these years: 'Pre-Raphaelitism affected him as some people are affected by a cat in the room, and though he professed himself at our first meeting without political interests or convictions, he soon grew into a violent Unionist and Imperialist.' Richard Le Gallienne, an aesthete successor to the Pre-Raphaelites, put it more sharply: 'W. E. Henley ... was beating the big drum of Imperialism, supported by a band of brilliant young literary swordsmen.'[13]

The deep-seated antipathy between the activists and aesthetes

---

[12] See Jerome H. Buckley, *William Ernest Henley: A Study in the 'Counter-Decadence' of the 'Nineties* (Princeton: Princeton University Press, 1945), for a more extensive discussion of Henley and late-Victorian imperialism.

[13] W. B. Yeats, *Autobiographies* (London: Macmillan, 1955), p. 125; and Richard Le Gallienne, *The Romantic '90s* (London: Putnam, 1926), p. 104.

of the 1890s was not merely one of style and aesthetic theory. For Henley and his followers the *Yellow Book* and the *Savoy* represented a decline in the quality of British civilization which was becoming all too noticeable in the wider field of international, commercial, military, and imperialist competition as well. In these years British trade relative to that of the United States and Germany declined, unemployment and labour unrest increased, Britain's naval superiority was seriously challenged, and the continued hegemony of the empire became problematic.[14] The Boer War confirmed some Englishmen's worst fears when the might of an imperial army failed to contain two tiny farming republics, 60 per cent of British recruits had to be turned away as physically unfit, and the colonies showed, in spite of much popular flag-waving, a strong unwillingness to become embroiled in England's war. Canada's hasty decision to send troops split Laurier's administration, while Richard Jebb, touring the colonies at the time of the war, found Australians strongly opposed to giving aid.[15]

As the real superiority of Britain over her rivals dwindled, so a neurotic desire for self-assertion became more voluble, until there existed what Élie Halévy has described as 'a species of Darwinian philosophy expressed in a mythical form . . . a moral code, chaste, brutal, heroic, and childlike' (*Imperialism and the Rise of Labour*, p. 21). By its very nature volatile and tending to self-destruction, the cult rose to a pitch at the time of the Diamond Jubilee (1897), hovered precariously for a few years, flared up dangerously over minor international crises like the Fashoda incident (1898), exploded in the first few months of the Boer War, and expired in the bonfires of Mafeking Night (18 May 1900).

It inspired statesmen and intellectuals as much as it did music hall jingoes. George Wyndham, Under-Secretary of State for War at the outbreak of the Boer War and a highly cultured product of Eton and Sandhurst ('I should like to review a book now and then of Elizabethan literature, French poetry, Arthurian and other

---

[14] See Halévy and Beloff, *passim*, and particularly Guy Chapman, 'The Economic Background', in Edith C. Batho and Bonamy Dobrée, *The Victorians and After*, 3rd revised ed. (London: Cresset, 1962); and David Thomson, *England in the Nineteenth Century*, The Pelican History of England 8 (Harmondsworth: Penguin, 1950), pp. 194–220.

[15] Recruiting figures quoted in Robert Cecil, *Life in Edwardian England* (London, 1969), p. 98; information on Canadian and Australian reactions from Beloff, p. 67, and Richard Jebb, *Studies in Colonial Nationalism* (London: Arnold, 1905), pp. 190–202.

legends,' he wrote to the *Outlook* in 1897), took a boyish delight in
bellicose statements about the war: 'It was most essential to show
Europe that we could fix up South Africa and remain "as good as
new",' he wrote to his brother Guy in Ladysmith. 'We are both
eaten up with the war, not for itself, but because the British officer
(and man) restores one's joy in the race,' exclaimed Sir Walter and
Lady Raleigh, while Richard Garnett, Keeper of Printed Books
at the British Museum, wrote vitriolic sonnets on President
Kruger and William Watson.[16]

The activism of the time had a savage, materialist imagery all of
its own: 'This dependence of progress on the survival of the fitter
race, terribly black as it may seem to some of you, gives the
struggle for existence its redeeming features; it is the fiery
crucible out of which comes the finer metal.'[17] Thus Karl Pearson
condoned the Boer War, and images of 'fiery crucible' and 'finer
metal', redemption, and 'relentless law' recur in the verses of
Henley and his imitators, expressing not merely an aberrant
literary fad, but much that was central to cultured British thought
at the time:

> In wild hours,
> A people, haggard with defeat,
> Asks if there be a God; yet sets its teeth,
> Faces calamity, and goes into the fire
> Another than it was. And in wild hours
> A people, roaring ripe
> With victory, rises, menaces, stands renewed,
> Sheds its old piddling aims,
> Approves its virtue, puts behind itself
> The comfortable dream, and goes,
> Armoured and militant,
> New-pithed, new-souled, new-visioned, up the steeps
> To those great altitudes, whereat the weak
> Live not. But only the strong
> Have leave to strive, and suffer, and achieve.[18]

Similar themes and images of a brutal race mystique flourished in

[16] George Wyndham, *Letters*, ed. Guy Wyndham (Edinburgh: Constable, 1915):
26 Dec. 1897 and 27 Oct. 1899; Sir Walter Raleigh, *Letters*, ed. Lady Raleigh
(London: Methuen, 1928), vol. i: 14 Nov. 1899; and Richard Garnett, *The Queen
and Other Poems* (London, 1901).
[17] Quoted in Himmelfarb, *Victorian Minds*, p. 320.
[18] Henley, 'Epilogue', *Hawthorn and Lavender* (London: David Nutt, 1901).

verse all over the empire, as in the ecstatic nonsense of Clive Phillips-Wolley from Canada:

> Can ye beat steel from iron in the sun;
> Or crown Earth's master on a bloodless field?
> As Abram offered to his God—his son,
>   Our best we yield.

> And God gives answer. In the battle smoke;
> Tried in war's crucible, washed white in tears,
> The Saxon heart of Greater Britain woke
>   One for all years.[19]

That the war did not go at all well for Britain during the first four months of its duration, tended to feed rather than allay the imperial neurosis. *The Times* published Swinburne's inflammatory 'Reverse' (7 November 1899) and Austin's 'Inflexible as Fate' (2 November) just as the war was beginning to seem disastrous for Britain. At the height of 'Black Week', December 1899, when the British forces had suffered three major defeats in quick succession, Sir Lewis Morris was stirred to sing:

> Though her generals may blunder, though her bravest sons are slain,
> Though her best blood flows like water, and the sacrifice seems vain—
>   *Chorus*: Still cheer for noble Britain . . .[20]

Only a profound and pervasive cultural insecurity, affecting public and literary men of the time alike, can explain such gross over-reaction to a war 6,000 miles away—a war which, as John Buchan put it, really 'affected only those who had kin in the fighting ranks' (*Memory Hold-the-Door*, p. 98).

To what extent Henley created the literary cult of imperialist tub-thumping or was himself the victim of it, is hard to say. He seems to have been genuinely concerned with keeping up a Tennysonian standard of meaningful literary culture against the avalanche of mass-literacy and the popular press on the one hand, and what he regarded as the introspective nihilism of his 'decadent' contemporaries on the other. His 'Book of Verse for Boys', *Lyra Heroica* (1892), which had reached a sixth edition by the time of the Boer War, inspired a host of similar patriotic, activist anthologies,

[19] 'Our Testament', in *Poems and Songs on the South African War*, ed. J. D. Borthwick (Montreal: Gazette Pub. Co., 1901).
[20] 'For Britain: A Soldier's Song', *Harvest Tide* (London: Paul, Trench, Trübner, 1901).

and probably represented the main contact with poetry that most of the men of South Africa had ever had. The *National Observer*, which he edited from 1888 to 1897, launched or encouraged writers like Haggard, Kipling, Yeats, Conrad, Wells, and Barrie, and aimed at a forceful, anti-decadent appeal.[21]

Hence an active desire to shock and to react against decadence must no doubt bear some of the blame for verse which now strikes us as merely outrageous. Jerome H. Buckley evokes the image of a fiercely independent Henley, who articulated an admirable lust for life out of the harrowing personal experiences recorded in his 'Hospital Sketches' (1875), but it is clear from his subsequent work that the attempt to turn a personal triumph over illness into a national directive was disastrous. By 1892, in *The Song of the Sword and Other Poems*, dedicated to Kipling, Henley had come to preach a gospel of sheer blood-lust. The title poem sanctifies the sword as the instrument whereby God separates the weak from the strong and establishes the right and might of the superior races over the inferior:

> Sifting the nations,
> The slag from the metal,
> The waste and the weak
> From the fit and the strong;
>
> .   .   .   .
>
> Arch-anarch, chief builder,
> Prince and evangelist,
> I am the Will of God:
> I am the Sword.

For England's Sake: Verses and Songs in Time of War (1900) and *Hawthorn and Lavender* (1901), which contain most of his Boer War verse, marked a further deterioration. Some of the poems in *For England's Sake* were written before the war, like the highly ambiguous 'The Man in the Street', dated October 1892. It appears to owe something to the hooligan streak in Kipling's 'Loot' and 'Belts', published in *Barrack-Room Ballads* the same year. Glorifying the purblind excitement of 'Death in the right cause, death in the wrong cause', it elevates the morals of a street

[21] See Bernard Muddiman, *The Men of the Nineties* (London: Henry Danielson, 1920), prologue, *et passim*.

brawl ('For you've had your will of a new front door, and your foot on the mat inside') to a model for national policy:

And if, please God, it's the Rag of Rags, that sends us roaring into the fight,
O, we'll go in a glory, dead certain sure that we're utterly bound to be right!

Possibly the poem was meant to be an ironical attack on jingoism, but this seems unlikely when one puts it next to 'The Bugles of England', which invites us to warm to sentiments such as the following:

> What if the best of our wages be
> An empty sleeve, a stiff-set knee,
> A crutch for the rest of life—who cares,
> So long as the One Flag floats and dares?
> So long as the One Race dares and grows?
> Death—what is death but God's own rose?

The reckless and bloody disregard for the sanctities of life displayed here becomes particularly macabre when one reflects that Henley was an amputee.

He found the initial setbacks of British arms in the war incredible. 'Remonstrance', written during the 'Black Week' of December 1899, insists that British destiny ('blood and star') is surely to rule and not to rue. Borrowing a phrase from Swinburne's 'The Transvaal', which had appeared in *The Times* the day after war broke out and had, in turn, found its inspiration in Henry Purcell's 'Britons, strike home!' of 1695, he urges England on to bloody and righteous execution:

> So front the realms, your point abashed;
> So mark them chafe and foam;
> And, if they challenge, so, by God,
> Strike, England, and strike home!

Henley's mawkish Darwinism comes out most strongly in 'The Choice of the Will', quoted in Chapter I, and in the 'Prologue' and 'Epilogue' to *Hawthorn and Lavender*:

> That race is damned which misesteems its fate;
> And this, in God's good time, they all shall know,
> And know you too, you good green England, then—
> Mother of mothering girls and governing men!
>
> ('Prologue')

c

The 'Epilogue', though premature in its celebration of a peace which did not come until 1902, presents an untypically sombre and thoughtful vision of England. She is still 'the strong', but has maintained her right over the weak only at the cost of great sacrifice, humiliation, and a new realization of the austerity of purpose that world-rule demands. Anticipating Kipling's 'The Islanders' and 'The Lesson', Henley depicts 'a rich deliquium of decay' which had beset a too-humanitarian and reposeful England before the war:

> In a golden fog,
> A large, full-stomached faith in kindliness
> All over the world, the nation, in a dream
> Of money and love and sport, hangs at the paps
> Of well-being, and so
> Goes fattening, mellowing, dozing, rotting down
> Into a rich deliquium of decay.

The war, he hopes, has provided the crucible from which a nation 'New-pithed, new-souled, new-visioned' will have risen to fulfil its conquering destiny: 'only the strong/Have leave to strive, and suffer, and achieve.'

Henley inspired not only many of his associates (the 'Henley Regatta') to extravagantly activist statements in both prose and verse on the Boer War, but also a host of minor poets all over the empire. G. W. Steevens, whose *With Kitchener to Khartum* (1898) and *From Capetown to Ladysmith* (1900) are still two of the most readable accounts of these campaigns, was an ardent protégé. His war books grew from his correspondence for the *Daily Mail* and are noticeable for the same unsentimental, clear-eyed depiction of horror and action that marks Henley's 'Hospital Sketches'. So, for instance, he captures the skirmish at Modder Spruit, in the early weeks of the war, in a sharp, cinematic vignette: 'In a twinkling the first line was down behind rocks firing fast, and the bullets came flicking round them. Men stopped and started, staggered and dropped limply as if the string were cut that held them upright' (p. 53). The description rises to a delirious crescendo—'subalterns commanding regiments, soldiers yelling advice, officers firing carbines, stumbling, leaping, killing, falling, all drunk with battle, shoving through hell to the throat of the enemy.' Then Steevens ends on a typically Henleyist note: 'It was over—twelve hours of march, of reconnaissance, of waiting, of preparation, and half an hour of attack. But half an hour crammed with the life of half a lifetime.' Shortly after this, Steevens found himself trapped in the Siege of Ladysmith. To him it was a weariness extreme: 'you squirm between iron fingers' (p. 133), and: 'At first, to be besieged and bombarded was a thrill; then it was a joke; now it is nothing but a weary, weary, weary bore. We do nothing but eat and drink and sleep—just exist dismally. We have forgotten when the siege began; and now we are beginning not to care when it ends. For my part, I feel it will never end' (p. 125). He spoke more accurately than he knew, for within a month he had died of typhoid fever. Henley included his epitaph in *Hawthorn and Lavender*, after improving the facts somewhat:

> We cheered you forth—brilliant and kind and brave.
> Under your country's triumphing flag you fell.
> It floats, true Heart, over no dearer grave—
> Brave and brilliant and kind, hail and farewell!

Henley's thoughts found echoes in strange quarters. Joseph Conrad, whose *Heart of Darkness*, written at the time of the Boer War, has become the classic exposé of one kind of imperial futility and absurdity, harboured oddly Kurtz-like ideas about the Boers. In a letter dated 26 October 1899 he speaks with apparent admiration of the 'deep-seated convictions of the [British] race—the expansive force of its enterprise and its morality', and argues for an aggressive singleness of purpose in the war: 'The victory—unless it is to be thrown away—shall have to be followed by ruthless repression.'[22] Kurtz's dilemma in *Heart of Darkness* lies very close to the surface of Conrad's own thinking here.

Francis Thompson, an alcoholic and opium addict and pre-eminently a writer of the mystical, orientalist verse that Henley abhorred, nevertheless had great admiration for Henley. It appears in an exclamatory desire for a virility he seems to have been incapable of: 'Oh, that I were a *man* again! ... The very streets weigh upon me. These horrible streets, with their gangrenous multitudes, blackening ever into lower mortifications of humanity!', he wrote to Winifred Meynell on 19 July 1900.[23] One

---

[22] Quoted in G. Jean-Aubry, *Joseph Conrad: Life and Letters* (London: Heinemann, 1927), i. 284–5.
[23] *Letters*, ed. John E. Walsh (New York: Hawthorn Books, 1969); and see Buckley, *Henley*, p. 149.

escape from this depression was to write activist occasional verse. His 'Ode for the Diamond Jubilee of Queen Victoria, 1897' combines reasonably well the mysticism of the aesthete with the vigour of the activist. From an opening phrased in the muted weird tones of the symbolists—

> Night; and the street a corpse beneath the moon,
> Upon the threshold of the jubilant day
> That was to follow soon;
> Thickened with inundating dark
> 'Gainst which the drowning lamps kept struggle; pole
> And plank cast rigid shadows; 'twas a stark
> Thing waiting for its soul,
> The bones of the preluded pomp—

the poem mounts to a final exhortation in which the voice of Henley is clearly heard:

> Thou, whom these portents warn but not alarm,
> Feastest, but with thy hand upon the sword,
> As fits a warrior race:
> Not like the Saxon fools of olden days,
> With the mead dripping from the hairy mouth,
> While all the South
> Filled with the shaven faces of the Norman horde.[24]

The oblique reference to a continental invasion in the last line reminds us that Thompson, like so many other thinkers of the period, failed to appreciate that the fears of European war and the reiterated claims that an expansionist British Empire would enforce peace, were hardly compatible. In his 'The Nineteenth Century' the ambivalence becomes outright contradiction. Taking its cue from Darwin—'every water-drop a-sting with writhing wars'—the poem applauds European conquest of the East and Africa, yet laments the century's constant warfare:

> The growl as of long surf that draweth back
> Half a beach in its rattling track,
> When like a tiger-cat
> The angry rifle spat
> Its fury in the opposing foeman's eyes.

Another poet who shared this blind spot with Thompson was

[24] All the verse is quoted from Thompson's *Poems*, vol. ii (London: Burns & Oates, 1913).

Lawrence Binyon. His 'Europe MDCCCCI—to Napoleon' at once records the sad fact that

> These groaning armies Europe fill,
> And war's red planet hath not set;

yet urges Britain to shape the world in an Anglo-Saxon mould:

> Take up thy task, O nobly born!
> With both hands grasp thy destiny.
>
> .   .   .   .
>
> Turn from the sweet lure of content,
> Rise up among the courts of ease;
> Be all thy will as a bow bent,
> Thy sure on-coming like thy seas.[25]

One only has to multiply these notions by the number of armies and parties with nationalist and imperialist aims all over Europe to see how the tinder was laid that set the world on fire in 1914.

Thompson wrote two odes on the Boer War, 'Cecil Rhodes' and 'Peace: On the Treaty in South Africa in 1902'. Once again they dwell on the prophylactic virtues of action and war, invoking Henleyist terms of the knife, fire, and cautery to justify the conflict:

> If thou wilt crop the specious sins of ease,
> Whence still is War's increase,—
> Proud flesh which asks for War, the knife of God,
> Save to thyself, thyself use cautery.

'Cecil Rhodes' is the more attractive of the two and conveys something of the mystique that contemporaries saw in this ambivalent man of gigantic visions and ruthless politics. For Thompson he achieved the near-impossible: an exalted dreamer who controlled a world of action:

> In dreams what did he not,
> Wider than his wide deeds? In dreams he wrought
> What the old world's long livers must in act forego.

The extravagant view of Rhodes as 'a visionary vast' is perhaps no longer shared by most historians, but the poem bears ample witness to the large imaginative grip that men of action had on the poets of the nineties. The theme recurs in Stephen Phillips's 'A Man!' (*New Poems*, 1908), written at a time when the South African campaign, and the War Office in particular, seemed

[25] *The Death of Adam and Other Poems* (London: Methuen, 1904).

remarkably directionless. Phillips was another poet launched by Henley's *National Observer* (Buckley, *W. E. Henley*, p. 196), and we recognize the family likeness:

> O for a living man to lead!
> That will not babble when we bleed;
> O for the silent doer of the deed!
>
> . . . .
>
> Sirs, not with battle ill-begun
> We charge you, not with fields unwon
> Nor headlong deaths against the darkened gun;
>
> But with a lightness worse than dread;
> That you but laughed who should have led,
> And tripped like dancers amid all our dead.

Alfred Austin was a poor shadow of Henley—indeed, on Austin's appointment to the laureateship in 1896, Henley, who no doubt saw himself as a better choice, dismissed the poet elect as 'such an ape' (Buckley, p. 199). They nevertheless beat, politically, to very much the same pulse, and Henley probably escaped the grotesqueries of Austin's laureate verse only by not being given the chance to write them. His first official effort was the notorious 'Jameson's Ride' on the ill-fated 'invasion' of the Transvaal by Dr. Leander Starr Jameson and his 500 men in December 1895. Mark Twain called it a 'poet-laureatic explosion of coloured fireworks which filled the world's sky with giddy splendours'.[26] Like most of his Boer War verse it is now more notable for the many parodies to which it gave rise than for its own achievements. In his attempt to clothe himself in the robes of Tennyson, Austin became merely ludicrous and acquired the vacuousness exhibited in 'Inflexible as Fate', published in *The Times*, 2 November 1899:

> When for a passing hour Rome's manly sway
> Felt the sharp shock of Cannae's adverse day,
> Forum and field and Senate-House were rent
> With cries of nor misgiving nor lament,
> Only of men contending then who should
> Purchase the spot on which the Victor stood.
>
> . . . .
>
> Not less resolved than Rome, now England stands,
> Facing foul fortune with unfaltering hands.

[26] *More Tramps Abroad* (London: Chatto & Windus, 1897), p. 455.

A parodist in the *Daily Chronicle* (whose editor, Massingham, was soon to be dismissed for his pro-Boer sympathies) asked how 'England "faces" Fortune with her "hands",' or how a flag could be 'inflexible', and concluded that the insensitivity of a culture like Austin's was a greater threat to the quality of English civilization than any Boer:

> Poor England, 'mid disaster and despair
> Finds (in the *Times*) she's something worse to bear:
> Jejune as dust, insensible as Fate,
> The dismal twaddle of her Laureate.[27]

But Austin was undaunted. Victory and disaster alike called forth verses which usually appeared in *The Times* and were afterwards collected in the third edition of *Songs of England* (1900), or in *Sacred and Profane Love* (1908). Most of it was in a pseudo-Tennysonese delightfully and regularly parodied by Owen Seaman in *Punch*. The close of the war, which found Hardy and even Henley in sombre mood and produced Kipling's deeply pensive 'The Dykes', found Austin in a quite different frame of mind. He saw fit to produce 'If They Dare!' (*Sacred and Profane Love*), which solemnly equates the triumphant England with God:

> She is lonely as the breeze,
> Lonely as the stars or seas,
> Lone, unreachable as these,
> Lone as God!

A note to the poem explains that it was not published at the time of writing 'because it was thought it might aggravate mischievously the popular emotion'. The coyness was both uncharacteristic and too sanguine.

Another poet whom the Boer War discovered in a sad decline was Algernon Swinburne. His six poems on the war, shrill and vicious, confused in thought as well as execution, were published in *The Times* at regular intervals during the war and were afterwards collected in *A Channel Passage* (1904). 'The Transvaal' (*The Times*, 11 October 1899) set the tone for all the rest:

> Speech and song
> Lack utterance now for loathing. Scarce we hear
> Foul tongues that blacken God's dishonoured name
> With prayers turned curses and with praise found shame

[27] Here quoted from the *South African News*, 25 Nov. 1899.

> Defy the truth whose witness now draws near
>   To scourge these dogs, agape with jaws afoam,
>   Down out of life. Strike, England, and strike home.

It called forth a strong letter of protest from Frederick Courteney Selous, famous big-game hunter and explorer, who knew the Boers well though he did not share their politics: '[I] read with feelings of intense disgust a poem lately published in your columns by Mr. Swinburne, which seems to me to have been written with the sole object of embittering feelings in this country against the South African Dutch.' (*The Times*, 20 October 1899.) But Swinburne could generate even more poison. 'Storm, strong with all the bitter heart of hate,' he wrote on the surrender of the Boer commander-in-chief, General Cronjé, on 27 February 1900, and continued in the same vein for the rest of the war.

The lines of Austin and Swinburne would not warrant quoting were they not illustrative of the culture of violence which accompanied the imperialist ideologies of the time, and were they not symptomatic of a profound insecurity and lack of focus in the imperial dream itself.

The ambivalences and neuroses that mark the poetry of Henley, Austin, and Swinburne were noticeable, too, in a group of poems that appealed more or less explicitly to the *mores* of the public school. A poem by James Rhoades in the *Daily News*, 1 November 1899, ' "Dulce et Decorum Est" ', distinguishing between the kinds of heroism to be expected from the officer of public school origins on the one hand, and the common soldier of more lowly background on the other, is typical of the attempts that were made to isolate and cultivate the stoic mystique of a warrior class:

> We, nursed in high traditions,
>   And trained to nobler thought,
>   Deem death to be less bitter
>   Than life too dearly bought:
>   Sharp spurs have we to honour,
>   But ye without their aid
>   Rush on the deadly breaches,
>   And storm the barricade.

'High tradition', 'nobler thought', 'sharp spurs to honour'—these are some of the strands on which public school, empire, army, and colonial service were tightly interwoven at the end of the nineteenth century.[28] The oddly diverse elements of missionary Christianity, celibate discipline, superior gamesmanship, physical endurance, racial arrogance, and a stoic cult of leadership combined to produce generations of imperial soldiers and administrators whose ideals are sanctified in the rich religiose glow of Matthew Arnold's 'Rugby Chapel' and its late-Victorian derivatives, such as Newbolt's 'Vitaï Lampada' and 'Clifton Chapel':

> To set the cause above renown,
> To love the game beyond the prize,
> To honour, while you strike him down,
> The foe that comes with fearless eyes;
> To count the life of battle good,
> And dear the land that gave you birth,
> And dearer yet the brotherhood
> That binds the brave of all the earth.[29]

The clipped but nebulous aphorisms employed here convey a sense of ardent confusion common to many public school poems, an impression of inadequate reasons and aims behind the crisp front of decisive manhood and simple moral rectitude. Essentially such poems share the *naïveté* of *Tom Brown's Schooldays*, *Westward Ho!*, and the novels of G. A. Henty. They project the image of what W. E. Winn has called 'the huge British hero who always fought victoriously and who spread the doctrines of the English Church. He extolled the merits of massive unconscious goodness as exemplified by the scions of the English squires.'[30]

It is hard to distinguish between the facts and fiction of Victorian public schools. Schools like Eton gave rise to a whole literature of histories, reminiscences, poems, novels, and magazines, which they, in turn, had to emulate. Indeed, as England's real imperial supremacy declined in the 1890s, so did public school myth-making increase. L. S. Amery claimed in later years that his 'manly conception of personal life, of public duty and public

---

[28] For exhaustive discussions of the relationships between public school and empire, see Edward C. Mack, *Public Schools and British Opinion since 1860* (London: Methuen, 1941); Rupert Wilkinson, *The Prefects* (London: Oxford University Press, 1964); and Lochhead, *Young Victorians*.

[29] *Poems New and Old* (London, 1912).

[30] '*Tom Brown's Schooldays* and the Development of "Muscular Christianity"', *Church History*, 29 (1960), 64–73. See also Robert A. Huttenback, 'G. A. Henty and the Imperial Stereotype', *Huntington Lib. Q.*, 29 (1965), 63–75.

policy' had been inspired by the 'poetry in the highest sense of the word' of the Harrow school song, 'Forty Years On' (*My Political Life*, i. 38).

The myths and memories of public school training provided a ready set of attitudes and reactions that could be invoked in time of stress and elation alike. Eventually there existed a body of clichés, based on the terminology of games and on cults of stoic indifference to suffering, that often obscured genuinely harrowing conditions or led to startlingly inappropriate responses. The Boer War provided striking examples of such reactions. So, for instance, a lancer's account in *The Times*, 13 November 1899, of the 'excellent pig-sticking which ensued' after the battle of Eland-slaagte—'the bag being about sixty'—caused a furore in humanitarian circles in England, and so did a sentiment from Baden-Powell's *Aids to Scouting* (1899), quoted in the *Ethical World*, 13 October 1900: 'Football is a good game; but better than it, better than any other game, is that of man-hunting.' J. B. Lloyd, an Inns of Court volunteer, was carried off in schoolboy raptures at the sight of shells bursting among the enemy: 'This was sport with a vengeance, better than seeing Aston Villa's left forward scoring the winning goal, or W. G. hitting three successive boundaries from the best Australian bowling.' Trooper Frank Cornwell Rogers noted laconically in his diary, a week before being killed at Waggon Hill: 'I have broken my duck at last with a fine fat Dutchman at 400 yards.'[31] Norman Bennet's *The Little Bugler and Other War Lyrics* (1900), dedicated to 'the Public Schoolmen at the Front', is only one of many such volumes depicting schoolboys in uniform, 'their gallant hearts aflame', but apparently oblivious of the slaughter around them:

> The cries of wounded comrades as they lie upon the plain,
> The groanings of the dying, the moan of those in pain,
> The blood-bespattered khaki . . .

A less obnoxious feature of some war poems of the public school stamp is the frequent casting of officers in the role of idealized prefects. Indeed, some poems from the front paid moving tribute to such men. One of them was Captain the Hon. Raymond de Montmorency, a V.C. of the Sudan campaign who

---

[31] J. B. Lloyd, *1,000 Miles with the C.I.V.* (London: Methuen, 1901), p. 154; and Frank Cornwell Rogers's diary (Manuscript privately owned).

formed around him the Montmorency Scouts during the Boer War. He was killed at Molteno in the Cape Colony on 25 February 1900. A poem on the event by one of his corporals, Eric McDonald, tells of the charismatic qualities required of a leader of such an élite group:

> We heard him when he first did call
> For men to follow his brave course,
> And foremost did obey that call.
> Since when we watched his little force
> Grow greater as the days rolled by;
> All men expert to ride and shoot;
> Aye weeding with a leader's eye
> His corps of all who would not suit.[32]

Another captain, Cecil William Boyle of the Imperial Yeomanry, killed at Boshoff in the Orange Free State on 5 April 1900, called forth a similar tribute from a school friend, T. Herbert Warren, in the *Spectator*, 12 April 1901:

> Dear hero, you of school's ideal day . . .
> The lion's heart, the panther's lissom grace
> Were your inheritance from a generous line;
> A leader born, your character and face
> Ruled as with right divine . . .
> Captaining men as once you captained boys.

The leading exponent of the image of the public school soldier was, of course, Henry Newbolt. *The Sailing of the Long Ships* (1902) contains a number of poems in which Newbolt brings his ethos of exalted dedication and sacrifice to bear on the events of the Boer War. We will not now agree with the *Academy*, 16 December 1899, that 'The Volunteer' was the best poem the war produced, but it certainly epitomizes the public school hero's selfless, reckless devotion to a vague yet ideal cause:

> He leapt to arms unbidden,
>   Unneeded, over-bold;
> His face by earth is hidden,
>   His heart in earth is cold.
>
> 'Curse on the reckless daring
>   That could not wait the call,
> The proud fantastic bearing
>   That would be first to fall!'

[32] The whole poem is reproduced in Johannes Meintjes, *Stormberg: A Lost Opportunity* (Cape Town: Tafelberg, 1969), pp. 136–8.

> O tears of human passion,
>   Blur not the image true;
> This was not folly's fashion,
>   This was the man we knew.

'The Schoolfellow' and 'The School at War' are as typical as their titles suggest, paler versions of the author's more famous 'Vitaï Lampada', though the first-mentioned poem captures a hint of the wistful, emblematic significance of the soldier that we normally associate with Housman:

> 'To-morrow well may bring', we said,
>   'As fair a fight, as clear a sun.'
> Dear lad, before the word was sped,
>   For evermore thy goal was won.

'April on Waggon Hill'—the title refers to a desperate attempt to break out of Ladysmith—is even more reminiscent of Housman:

> 'Twas the right death to die, lad,
>   A gift without regret,
> But unless truth's a lie, lad,
>   You dream of Devon yet.

Newbolt's more famous poem on the above engagement of the Devons outside Ladysmith on 6 January 1900, 'Waggon Hill', rises sharply out of the roseate glow of the other poems in *The Sailing of the Long Ships*. Tight and evocative in construction, lilting in rhythm, it carries a sense of muted excitement and disaster that few other poems of the war surpassed:

> Valour of England gaunt and whitening,
>   Far in a South land brought to bay,
> Locked in a death-grip all day tightening,
>   Waited the end in twilight gray.
> Battle and storm and the sea-dog's way!
> Drake from his long rest turned again,
> Victory lit thy steel with lightning,
>   Devon, O Devon, in wind and rain!

The poem remains a striking celebration of the conspicuous, Elizabethan valour—the reference to Drake is not accidental—of the late-Victorian public school warrior.

It is also something of a monument to the passing of chivalrous codes of warfare. A comparison of the poem with eyewitness

accounts of this and other battles around Ladysmith shows us to
what extent the traditional display of reckless chivalry on the part
of officers was becoming a dangerous anachronism in modern
warfare. Donald Macdonald noticed on these occasions an
ominous feature that was to become a tragic flaw of officers in the
first months of the Great War: 'He has no rifle, no cover. With
his useless sword in hand he strides bravely on, pointing the way,
a conspicuous target for every sharpshooter on the ridge above
him. It is the correct thing to do. It is the caste of the officer as
compared with the man—and it is magnificent.'[33]

Magnificent or not, the British officer was immune to neither
modern weaponry nor criticism. H. C. Macdowall's 'The English
Officer', quoted in the previous chapter, was one reply to the
many serious criticisms levelled at officers and their public school
training during the Boer War. 'The English officer', wrote
A. H. H. Maclean in *Public Schools and the War in South Africa*
(1903), 'is uneducated, he is "stupid". Hence our many "mishaps". He was brought up on games. He is over-addicted to polo.
He does not read military history. He drags mahogany mess
tables, pianos and other luxuries after him on his campaigns. He
does very well against savage or coloured races, but pitted
against white men, he breaks down. More officers of the studious
type are needed. The right sort cannot be got from the public
schools.' G. G. Coulton, in *Public Schools and Public Needs* (1900),
argued that Colenso and Magersfontein had been lost on the
playing fields of Eton. Criticism of this kind, coupled with the
innovations and reforms which they heralded and the changed
physical aspect of war that Macdonald noticed, were to destroy
the basis for war poetry of Newbolt's variety.

The simple verities of Newbolt's public school heroes often still
have a poignant attraction; the fanaticism of those poems which
attempted to justify the war on religious grounds now probably
has none. Three arguments recurred in the many pious verses
(along with many sermons and pamphlets) that the war provoked.
War was a scourge for a godless people; it was an antidote to the
ease, sloth, and luxury of peace; it was the means whereby Britons
acted out their role as God's chosen people. All three views were

[33] *How We Kept the Flag Flying: The Story of the Siege of Ladysmith* (London: Ward,
Lock, 1900), p. 64.

expressed at all levels of society, from Will Roughton's music hall hymn, 'Onward Tommy Atkins!' (1900), sung to the tune of 'Onward, Christian Soldiers',[34] right up to what is one of the most extraordinary poems of the war, William Alexander, Archbishop of Armagh's, 'Is "war the only thing that has no good in it"?' (*The Times*, 31 October 1899), in which the primate sets out to refute the classical Christian injunctions against war:

> They say that 'war is hell', the 'great accursed',
> The sin impossible to be forgiven—
> Yet I can look beyond it at its worst,
> And still find blue in Heaven.

War can be a purifier of spirit, a test of integrity, a teacher of heroism and of sorrow nobly borne. One is appalled not so much by Alexander's arguments as by the refined savagery of his imagery:

> Methinks I see how spirits may be tried,
> Transfigured into beauty on war's verge,
> Like flowers whose tremulous grace is learnt beside
> The trampling of the surge.

Indeed, the lure of his metaphors makes it impossible for Alexander to see what death on a battle-field is really like. His soldiers are not shot to pieces; they merely lie down to sleep:

> They who marched up the bluff last stormy week—
> Some of them, ere they reached the mountain's crown,
> The wind of battle breathing on their cheek,
> Suddenly laid them down,
> Like sleepers—not like those whose race is run—
> Fast, fast asleep amid the cannon's roar;
> Them no reveille and no morning gun
> Shall ever waken more.

As reward they are vouchsafed 'a great presentiment/Of high self-sacrifice'; for them

> The ascending earthquake dust of battle frames
> God's picture in the skies.

The popularity of Alexander's travesty of Christ militant, reprinted in several ecclesiastical journals around the world—

---

[34] Roughton's broadside appears with ninety-five others in a British Library portfolio, 'The Transvaal War: A Collection of English Songs, Verses, etc. Relative to the Boer War', Cup. 21. ff. 1.

such as the *Southern Cross*, 15 December 1899, at the Cape—needs some explanation. It would seem that as orthodox religious faith waned in the nineteenth century, various surrogates took its place. Hence a stricter domestic and sexual morality, Darwinian racial mythologies, and a vapid, excitable religiosity that could invade all spheres of thought came about. G. M. Young puts it well: 'The Evangelicals gave to the island a creed which was at once the basis of its morality and the justification of its wealth and power, and, with the creed, that sense of being an Elect People which, set to a more blatant tune, became a principal element in Late-Victorian Imperialism.'[35] Just how blatant is shown in a proposition put forward by Cecil Rhodes: 'If there be a God, I think that what he would like me to do is to paint as much of Africa British-red as possible and to do what I can elsewhere to promote the unity and extend the influence of the English-speaking race.' A story in a juvenile magazine showed Christ surveying the British Empire, saying: 'That is well; I am Christ, I have come now to conquer; let all who own My Father rally round this Union Jack.'[36] It is therefore not surprising that in the popular mind (and even in the mind of an archbishop) a deep-seated confusion should exist between the Church militant and the army of the empire.

The Boer War provoked many belligerent statements from bloodthirsty clerics, several of which are collected in Alfred Marks's *The Churches and the South African War* (1905). The war was one of 'light against darkness, a war of liberty against injustice', according to the Bishop of Chichester; Canon Newbolt expressed a preference for the 'horrors of war' to the 'horrors of voluptuous peace'; for Dean Farrar war was 'a moral tonic necessary to the health of nations', or 'a fraction of that Armageddon struggle described in the Apocalypse, in which the son of God rides forth at the head of all his saints to subdue the machinations of the Devil and his angels'.[37] To all of these a blistering

---

[35] *Victorian England*, p. 4. See also Daiches, *Some Late Victorian Attitudes, passim*; and G. Kitson Clark, *The Making of Victorian England* (London: Methuen, 1962), p. 284, *et passim*.
[36] Rhodes quoted in Faber, *The Vision and the Need*, p. 71; and Christ by the Revd. Arthur Harrie in a series of articles, 'Children and Peace Principles', which appeared in *Concord* during 1902.
[37] All quoted by Marks, except Farrar, who is quoted in G. Smith, 'War as a Moral Medicine', *Atlantic Monthly*, 86 (1900), 735.

satire in the Sydney *Bulletin*, reprinted in Stead's *War Against War*, 29 December 1899, replied in kind:

> Now that War is in the air, e'en the parson in his lair
> Is seized with wild desirings for the sight of spurting blood.
> And he pitches it so strong to his sanctimonious throng
> That they almost hear in fancy bodies falling with a thud. . . .
> Be upon them with the sword—'tis the mandate of the Lord—
> And expose your neighbour's vitals to the healthful atmosphere;
> Do not misapply your skill to the doct'ring of his bill,
> But just cleave him through the skull with a gash from ear to ear.
>> Don't put water in his milk,
>> Nor mix cotton with his silk,
>> But just bash him like a Christian-Brother dear.

In Ladysmith, on the day after a Boer shell took off a corner of the church, the archdeacon preached a fiery sermon on Britain's heaven-appointed task to scourge the Boers. 'Very sound, but perhaps a thought premature,' noted G. W. Steevens (*From Capetown to Ladysmith*, p. 116).

But most of the poets in the empire would appear to have been on the side of the archdeacon. Aubrey Mildmay, in *In the Waiting Time of War* (1900), equated death in battle with salvation:

> Death on the veldt! It is angel-attended;
> Sweet is the sound of a nation's 'Well done!'

Sidney Lysaght, in *Poems of the Unknown Way* (1901), prayed that war should not cease:

> From ease that sows corruption and disease,
> From increase paid for in the soul's decrease,
>> Good Lord deliver us, and send us war!

The Revd. R. S. Routh wrote pious jingles on the war every week to please his Stockbridge congregation (*Lines on the War*, 1900), while an alarming number of verses, often the more inflammatory ones, in J. D. Borthwick's Canadian collection of *Poems and Songs on the South African War* (1901) were written by housewives and parsons.

Nearer the actual theatre of war, a poet in the *Cape Times*, 31 January 1900, assured his readers:

> You are doing the Will of the Lord on High,
> You are waging those battles for him,

while the Revd. George Kett (who claimed the spurious title of 'Poet Laureate of South Africa') bombarded his audience with 'The Lyddite Shell to South Africa':

> Then rose the war-cloud—red,
> And the rousing war-trump sang,
> The cannon gave His message mouth,
> And the shriek, and the groan outrang—
> 'Ears so gross as such ears', said He,
> 'Will be deaf to all gentler minstrelsy.'[38]

Or be deafened by Kett, one might add. But it was in Cape Town, too, that an appeal to troops for cathedral building funds brought forth a scathing reply in the *Owl*, 19 October 1900:

> They left him wounded, in the lurch—
> The Priest and Levite, sleek and fat;
> Now they build themselves a Church,
> So send him round the earnest hat.

There was, indeed, considerable opposition throughout the empire to pious war propaganda. If early-Victorian evangelicalism nourished messianic imperialism, it also created a growth-culture for organized opposition to imperialism: the humanitarian, radical ideologies and Christian socialism of late-Victorian England had their roots in the religious fervours of the beginning of the century, too. Hence, according to Peter d'A. Jones, 'one area of public policy—imperialism and war—did arouse deep and widespread radicalism (strong dissent with official British policy, merging into pacifism) among Christian socialists. Most of them bitterly opposed the Boer War at a time when it took great moral fortitude to do so. . . . In fact, Christian socialists preserved more of a united front against colonial war than did British socialists in general.'[39] Conrad Roden Noel, referring to Cecil Rhodes, put it more bluntly: 'The ancestors of such men killed both Jesus Christ and St. Paul.' Noel's fierce tone echoed through publications like W. T. Stead's *War Against War in South Africa* and the pamphlets of the Manchester National Reform Union, collected in H. J. Ogden's *The War against the Dutch Republics in South Africa* (1901). These and other humanitarian, radical, and socialist publications,

---

[38] *Lyrics of Empire* (Privately printed, n.d.).
[39] Peter d'A. Jones, *The Christian Socialist Revival 1877–1914* (Princeton: Princeton University Press, 1968), p. 9; Noel is quoted on p. 247.

such as *New Age*, *Brotherhood*, *Coming Day*, *Concord*, and *Daylight*, carried many anti-war and anti-imperialist verses based on religious scruples. Their Christian-humanitarian gist was aptly summarized in a letter that one John Hunter wrote to *Saint Andrew*, 26 October 1899:

While it is sad enough to find at the end of the nineteenth century of Christianity that war is still possible between professedly civilised and Christian people, it is surely unspeakably humiliating from the point of view of the Christian teacher, to discover that it is still possible to glorify war, to get up enthusiasm about it, and to invest its heroes with a lustre which philosophers, prophets, poets, painters, philanthropists cannot win.

James Jeffrey Roche's bitter 'Hymn before Action' appeared in the *Century Magazine*, December 1899, and was widely reprinted in the anti-war press; for instance, in *War Against War*, 22 December 1899:

> When the volleys of hell are sweeping
> The sea and the battle plain,
> Do you think that our God is sleeping,
> And never to wake again? . . .
> We may swing the censer to cover
> The odour of blood—in vain;
> God asks us, over and over,
> 'Where is thy brother, Cain?'

Fierce old Robert Buchanan, in the last two years of his life, wrote several raw satirical ballads, collected in *The New Rome* (1900), against the jingo-commercial exploitation of pious sentiment. 'The Image in the Forum' is a grotesque caricature of the capitalists whom Buchanan held responsible for the war:

> Not Baal, but Christus-Jingo! Heir
> Of Him who once was crucified!
> The red stigmata still are there,
> The crimson spear-wounds in the side;
> But raised aloft as God and Lord,
> He holds the Money-bag and Sword.

'The Ballad of Kiplingson' accuses Kipling of debasing the empire's religion as much as its language:

> For the Lord my God was a Cockney
> Gawd, whose voice was a savage yell,
> A fust-rate Gawd who dropt, d'ye see,
> The 'h' in Heaven and Hell!

The irony of this aspect of the war is that the Boers were, if anything, even more adamant than the jingoes that God was on their side and would pay them his undivided attention. John Runcie's 'The Jock's Prayer', in *Songs by the Stoep* (1905), puts it one way:

> The Boer is chosen, so he cries;
> He kens Thee like an open book.
> It's nae for us to criticize,
> Nor meet Thy awful Holy look,
> Nor gie advice; but this we ken—
> Ye micht hae chosen ither men.

In a London clerical newspaper, the *Guardian*, 20 December 1899, M. Bramston caught something of the sadder irony in this utter conviction of righteousness on both sides of the fray:

> In veldt and farm, in camp and town, two warring prayers arise on high,
> Briton and Boer, each gasps his prayer to the same Lord for victory;
> The one falls grimly in his lair, the other charges on to die.
>
> ('Warring Prayers')

But it was left to Hardy to encapsulate the startling contradictions contained in all war between so-called Christians. His 'Christmas Ghost Story' first appeared in the *Westminster Gazette*, 23 December 1899, at a time when the patriotic temperature ran high. It provoked much criticism in the press, but Hardy retained it, in expanded form, in *Poems of the Past and the Present*:

> South of the Line, inland from far Durban,
> A mouldering soldier lies—your countryman.
> Awry and doubled up are his gray bones,
> And on the breeze his puzzled phantom moans
> Nightly to clear Canopus: 'I would know
> By whom and when the All-Earth-gladdening Law
> Of Peace, brought in by that Man Crucified,
> Was ruled to be inept, and set aside?
> And what of logic or of truth appears
> In tacking "Anno Domini" to the years?

Near twenty-hundred liveried thus have hied,
But tarries yet the Cause for which He died.'

Many saw the problem the way Hardy did; more, however,
shared the view of the archbishop of Armagh, a view not
materially different from that of the music hall and popular press.

III

The Muse Rampant and the Lion's Whelps

> From English pavement, Irish bog,
> Welsh valleys, Scottish braes,
> The puny bards are all agog
> Themselves to don the Bays!
> > Dum-Dum, 'To Arms!', *At Odd Moments* (1900).

BEYOND Henley, Austin, Swinburne, Newbolt, and the fairly distinct groups of poems discussed in the previous chapter, stretches a vast, largely unexplored territory of Boer War verse which appeared in periodicals, newspapers, music halls, broadsides, and slim volumes all over the empire, from Cape Town to Calcutta and from Wellington to Winnipeg. Most of it, however, was produced in England:

> Where are the dogs agape with jaws afoam?
> Where are the wolves? Look, England, look at home

suggested W. H. Colby in Swinburnian parody in the *Echo*, 13 October 1899, and he did not overstate the case. By 1 September 1900 the *Academy*, reviewing Edgar Wallace's *Writ in Barracks*, spoke despairingly of 'these khaki-coster rhythms, these music-hall sentiments, and this extremely facile vein of brag'. Pointing out that the war was not a glorious combat with a traditional enemy like France, but one of the 'dull, stern, burdensome tasks of empire', the reviewer suggested that the poetry of the war should reflect something of this solemnity. Reading through the scores of volumes of poems that the war produced, one sympathizes with another reviewer, this time in the *Athenaeum* (31 August 1901), who exclaimed: 'It is difficult to understand how any one of these writers could have been persuaded, or could have persuaded himself, that he had any justification for ushering the fruit of his leisure moments into a world already more full than it can hold of better poetry.' The *Literary World* (2 November 1900) found the reason in the fact that 'we live in what we may christen the Tin Age of Poetry', but G. K. Menzies found that the editors of popular magazines were clamouring for this 'Tin Age' verse:

> 'Give us', they cry, 'the rattle
> Of rifles and the battle
> Of Boer and Briton—that'll
> Be something up-to-date.'[1]

Some poets tried to rise to the heights of solemn occasion demanded by the *Academy* and produced ambitious, if preposterous, epics on the war. Henry Bate published a sixteen-page 'First Canto' of his *Transvaal War* in April 1900 and promised that five more would follow at monthly intervals. No trace of them survives; perhaps a blessing. Anthony Shipway Docking (incredibly, the name is not a pseudonym) published his 150-page *The Great Boer War 1899–1900*, in laborious rhymed couplets, in 1902. A few lines on the Boer camp after the surrender at Modder River will suffice:

> Now see the burnt out waggons; now see the gowns and goats—
> While swiftly past the river banks enteric fever floats.
> Half buried are the slaughtered, upon the Modder's brink;
> There is death upon the waters, and fever in a drink.

William Gerard attempted an involved allegory in Spenserian vein, *Una: A Song of England in the Year Nineteen-Hundred* (1900), in which Cecil Rhodes acquires Arthurian dimensions, while Gilbert Highton brought forth *The Siege of Mafeking: A Patriotic Poem* (1900) in Miltonic measures.

Not only literary ambition but also downright ignorance about conditions in South Africa led poets to these assaults on the muse. Descriptions of Mafeking as a 'city', of President Kruger on a 'tyrant's throne', and of 'foemen launched upon the deep' become comic when one considers the heap of tin shacks that formed Mafeking, Paul Kruger with pipe and spittoon on his stoep, and the land-locked position of the Transvaal. Dr. Edward Coyle, in *The Empire: A Poem* (1905), was quite convinced that the 'scowling Boer, in selfish greed', planned to rob England of her empire,

---

[1] *Provincial Sketches and Other Verses* (Paisley: Alexander Gardner, 1902).

while a local bard of Uitenhage in the Cape Colony (*Uitenhage Times*, 20 October 1900) considered that

> Herculean Right will cleanse the stables
> Augean Kruger heaped with wrong.

Similar infelicities of phrase make havoc, too, of A. G. Butler's assurance, in *The Choice of Achilles* (1900), that

> They may tell us we are sinking, that our sun is nearly set,
> But they haven't seen the bottom of the old country yet

or of Sydney E. Auchinleck's description of the horrors of war in *For the Honour of the Queen* (1900):

> The battle had been fierce and long, and fearful was the slaughter,
> Our hands were still all stained with gore, for there was lack of water.

But none of these snatches of bathos can rival the stoic nonchalance of J. C. M. Duncan's 'Bugler Dunn' (Borthwick, *Poems and Songs on the South African War*), who urged his company on,

> Till—what an honour!—a screeching shot from a sudden awakening hell,
> Shattered the arm of the bugler-boy and down on his bugle he fell;
> He fell—the first in that fearful fight, but his soul shrank not with the pain:
> 'Thank God,' he said, 'I've still my left arm, I can hold my bugle again.'

Most of the loyalist verse that the war provoked was of the above kind, but occasionally a poem that can still command our attention would rear itself from the miasma of doggerel. One of these is Post Wheeler's crisp ballad, 'The Trooper', in *Poems* (1905):

> 'Soldier, soldier, out of the South,
> Bring you mourning for my mouth?
>   Your face is sad, your eyes are dim;
>   Where in the blue veldt laid ye him?'
>
> 'Mother, mother, oh, we were few!
> Out in the wide veldt, bare and blue,
>   Where an hundred helmeted troopers fell,
>   There in his blanket he sleeps well!'
>
> 'Soldier, soldier, give me your hand!
> Fought he well in that stubborn land?
>   Here at home he was wild and bad;
>   Rode he well for the Queen, my lad?'

'Mother, mother, he spurred between
And gave me his body for a screen.'
'Thank God, Soldier! Never gave he
His body between the world and me!'

Another is W. G. Hole's 'The Road to Ladysmith', from *Poems
Lyrical and Dramatic* (1902):

Gentle herdsman, tell me, pray,
Unto the town of Ladysmith
Which is the right and ready way?

The way is easy to be gone,
Although to use but lately won;
And though across the thirsty waste
And o'er the veldt but faintly traced,
For scarce yet green, on either hand,
Are graves that mark in that new land
The long lone way to Ladysmith.

Edward Sydney Tylee published a number of war poems in the
Spectator which were afterwards collected in *Trumpet and Flag*
(1906). 'The Drummer', which appeared on 30 December 1899,
has an infectious rhythm that captures the high patriotic spirit
aroused by the disasters of that month. It pictures a 'dwarfish
Drummer', marching down a village high street:

A war-worn ancient, travel-stained,
Beating a weird tattoo,
Whose cunning lilt its hearers chained
And caught them, ere they knew.

Responding to the lure of the drum, men drop their occupations
and fall in behind him:

Ere the slow priest his blessing said,
The bridegroom left the bride.
The mourner left the cherished dead
His love had watched beside.
Pressed close and fast through lane and street
The ever-thickening throng;
All stepping to the measured beat
That marshalled them along:
Rataplan!
The teasing, tripping measure that led their lines along.

Tylee, too, was one of the few loyalist poets who appreciated that President Kruger was no mere 'mad old burgher man', and his country not simply the home of boorish brigands; his 'Paul Kruger' acknowledges the pathos and genius of Kruger's leadership in a clash that the Boers could neither avoid nor win:

> So rough a scabbard leaves unguessed
> How keen the blade inside;
> The trenchant will, the subtle brain,
> So strangely doomed to wage
> With climbing Fate's resistless main
> The hopeless war of age.

Poems such as Tylee's must be set over against a sub-culture of jingo jingles which, in the form of pamphlets, broadsides, music hall songs, and newspaper poems, pervaded the lower orders of literature at the turn of the century. A bound volume of ninety-six ephemera in the British Library reveals something of the range and tenor of these products of the backroom muse.[1a] 'Sons of the British Empire', 'How Britain's Call was Answered', 'A Soldier's Elegy', 'We'll Give Them What They Ask For', 'How Kruger Lost his Sweetheart', and 'The Absent-Minded Butcher' are some of the stirring titles. Here we read that Sarah Swain's

> New Year's song sent up to God
> Was VICTORY!! DEATH!! and BLOODY SOD!

and that the author of 'Arm! Arm! against the Invader' apparently confused Kruger with William the Conqueror:

> The foeman's foot is on England's soil
> Our homes to pillage, our lands to spoil.

The two greatest purveyors of these sub-literary appeals to patriotism were the press and the music hall. Jessica Sykes describes the situation in *Side-Lights on the War in South Africa* (1900):

One is almost smothered by unceasing Press issues, and deafened with exaggerated tales of slaughter, shouted in triumphant tones by their vendors. The theatre and the music-hall are equally devoted to clap-trap sentimentality, and exhibitions of so-called patriotism taking the form of perpetual brag and boast as to our superiority over other nations, these claims being based on the fact that we are 'English men'.

[1a] See above, p. 60, n. 34.

A whole range of papers and periodicals deliberately exploited the more or less refined jingoism which could be found among all classes of readers, from those who took *The Times* and liked the sumptuously leather-bound volumes of the *Anglo-Saxon Review* (edited by Lady Randolph Churchill and defunct before the war was over), to those who enjoyed the middle-brow humour of Owen Seaman in *Punch*, or, lower down the scale, paid their penny for Harmsworth's *Answers*, or *Ally Sloper's Halfholiday*. Harmsworth's papers encouraged imperialist versifying among their readers. The *Daily Mail*, founded in 1896 and dedicated to 'the supremacy and the greatness of the British Empire', was a veritable clearing house of partisan doggerel. Within a month of the outbreak of the war it reported (20 November 1899) the receipt of over 700 poems, 'the handiwork of all classes of the community —of schoolboys and old soldiers, of clergymen, coal miners, doctors, Lancashire factory hands, commissioned officers in the Army and Navy; the mothers, brothers, sisters, wives, and sweethearts of "the absent-minded beggar" at the front'.

Often these newspaper pieces were Kiplingesque in style and diction, though usually a good deal coarser in sentiment and execution than anything to be found in Kipling. Several efforts by George Griffith in the *Daily Express* were typical, particularly 'Play the Game' (2 July 1900), provoked by the guerrilla tactics of the enemy:

> Come out of it, Dutchy, or chuck it—kopje an' krantz an' pan—
> Lick us, or take your lickin' like a proper fightin' man.
> You gave us socks at Nicholson's Nek—Modderfontein as well;
> Colenso too, and Tugela, and Spionkop—O 'ell!
>> But, Brother in Peace or Foeman in War—
>> To us it's about the same—
>> If you wanted a fight to a finish,
>> Why didn't you play the game?

Sometimes, but only rarely, a deeper note of compassion, or a sharper awareness of the realities of war would break through this screen of chauvinism, as in the following lines from Rachel S. Robertson's 'The Soldier's Wife':

>> Neighbours come sometimes and talk together
>> Of the war, and oft they disagree;
>> Ah! my heart; I cannot reason whether
>> We should fight the Boers or let them be.

'An Appeal', from another anonymous cutting, is a piece of satire almost worthy of Sassoon. It exposes British manufacturers who were supposed to have sold arms to the Boers:

> When evil-minded scandal brings
> Its rumours o'er the sea, Tommy,
> You won't believe the nasty things
> Traducers say of me, Tommy?
> I'm ever your devoted friend;
> And rapturously stand on end,
> And wildly shout and drain the cup
> At dinners, when your name is up.[2]

The poem continues in this vein, but concludes in withering self-exposure:

> And if at last you're finished by
> A shell supplied by me, Tommy,
> I promise you I'll simply cry
> Until I cannot see, Tommy:
> To compromise the sad event
> I'll hand your widow one per cent.
> Of profits netted from the foe—
> And advertise my doing so.

The influence of newspapers and periodicals as carriers of easily digestible imperialist ideologies was widely recognized and lamented by 1900. Wilfrid Scawen Blunt noted on 16 September 1899 that the editor of *The Times*, Buckle, was 'one of the gang acting with Rhodes, and . . . the Jameson Raid was concocted, so to say, in *The Times* office'.[3] In *The Psychology of Jingoism* (1901) J. A. Hobson argued most convincingly that the whole war had been engineered by a group of financiers through their monopoly of the press in both South Africa and Britain.

There was a large number of correspondents at the front, eager for news, often risking their lives to get it, and not always beyond manufacturing it. F. W. Unger claimed, in *With 'Bobs' and 'Kruger'* (1901), that of fifty-eight correspondents who accompanied the main British forces, forty were killed, wounded, or imprisoned at some stage or other during the war. On the other hand, Reginald Auberon tells how maps, accounts of battles, and other

[2] Both in the Pera Muriel Button Collection of newspaper cuttings of the South African War, iii. 42 and 138, Library of Parliament, Cape Town.
[3] *My Diaries* (London: Secker, 1919), i. 405.

material 'from our special correspondent at the front' were 'often concocted at home and out of sheer fantasy',[4] while an editorial in the *Morning Leader* on 11 June 1901 complained that 'journalists at the front . . . invent for us victories that have no foundation in fact'.

The role of the press in creating an excited public involvement in the war was therefore immense, with a consequent effect on popular verse. Every victory, every blunder, every excessive statistic of expense or casualty was reported, analysed, and be-rhymed, usually to the chagrin of the War Office and the commanders in South Africa. As a couplet in the *World* (29 November 1899) put it:

Do heroes fall? By 9 a.m.
Next day you read their 'Requiem'

or *Blackwood's* in February 1900: 'Had Wellington fought with a mob of correspondents and a telegraph-wire at his back, he would never have survived Torres Vedras' (p. 285). The press created around the war an aura of vicarious excitement and immediacy, and a body of myth often in excess of the facts. The siege of Mafeking, as Brian Gardner's *Mafeking: A Victorian Legend* (1966) has shown, was an outstanding example of this process, distance acting as an optic glass which selected only the glamour and Boy Scoutish resourcefulness of Baden-Powell's men.

Poetry was an integral part of the daily fare of most newspapers. Not only were poems frequently used as 'liveners' to war news—we shall see some of these in a later chapter—but some correspondents also turned out to be poets, like A. B. Paterson of the Sydney *Morning Herald*, A. G. Hales of the London *Daily News*, and Edgar Wallace, who represented the *Daily Mail*. It was the great era of the newspaper and magazine poet; Reginald Auberon reports how quite successful poets, like Stephen Phillips, would offer him a sonnet for half a guinea, 'or three for thirty shillings' (*The Nineteen Hundreds*). Several 'little magazines' traded exclusively in ephemeral verse of a patriotic variety. A 'Grand Patriotic Number' of *Poet's Corner* (No. 8, Winter 1899) offered readers such items as 'The Dying Soldier's Dream':

The battle raged at Nicholson's Nek:
An English soldier lay,

[4] *The Nineteen Hundreds* (London: Allen & Unwin, 1922).

> Struck down in the dark in the deadly fight
> His life-blood ebbing away.

Thrush, 'A Periodical for the Publication of Original Poetry', mainly neo-imperialist, lasted for one year of the war (January 1901–February 1902) and then withered after the *Academy* referred to it as 'discreditable to literature'. Most of issue No. 10 (October 1901) was taken up by the excruciatingly bad 'The Siege of Mafeking', the work of the editor, T. Mullett Ellis.

Several general magazines appeared under imperialist mast-heads—'For Queen and Empire' was the *Sphere*'s—their contributors providing verse to suit. T. T. Bouve's 'The Last Charge' in the *Idler* (April 1901) is typical of the ferocity that could mark these productions:

> Trumpeter, blow on, terrific and thunderous,
> Blow till thy bugle outrings the wild gales;
> Spare not the wounded that writhe and wind under us,
> Drown in our ears all their piercing death wails.

Several of these loyalist periodicals were as short-lived as the frenetic brand of imperial enthusiasm that gave them birth. The *Empire Review* (*c.* 1900–1), the *Imperial and Colonial Magazine and Review* (December 1900–May 1901), and *King and Country* (1902–3), which all published imperialist verse, thrived on neo-imperialism and collapsed with it. So, too, did a number of lesser penny-spinning jingo papers, like *Under the Union Jack* and *With the Flag to Pretoria*. The star in this category was the *Black and White Budget*. It had fifteen correspondents and illustrators at the front (No. 17, 3 February 1900), who plied readers with sketches, photographs, and stirring stories of the war, as well as a backroom full of versifiers who supplied rousing accompaniment. Fred C. Smale's 'Kruger's Christmas Party', in issue No. 9 (9 December 1899), set the tone for the rumbustious music hall cadences to follow in the next few months:

> So please you, Uncle Paul,
> Light the lantern in the hall,
> We know we're welcome as the flow'rs in May;
> Just keep the pudding hot
> For the lively little lot
> Who are coming up to dinner Christmas Day.

Acts of heroism were celebrated in picture and verse, the poetry frequently indulging in a kind of gory rowdyism. 'Song of the Bayonet' (No. 16, 27 January 1900) is fairly representative of the savage talents of one regular contributor, Walter Ragge:

As it was at Inkerman, so it is to-day;
Steel it is that proves the man, steel that wins the day.
Charge, boys, charge! and drive the foe before us,
Seize their guns and break their ranks and sweep them down the hill.
Cheer, boys, cheer! and shout it out in chorus,
That the good old British Bradawl is the master still.

The next week, however, 'The Song of the Shells' plunged to even greater sadistic and blasphemous depths:

'Where low, dim earthworks wind, I sweep across
And, bursting, ere I reach them, low in air
Scour forward to surprise the grey ants there,
And sow my far-flung, livid, leaden grain
In a red reek of spattered blood and brain.'
    We three! We three!
    Grim Trinity!
The Common and Shrapnel and Lyddite Shell.
    Like a meteor's flight
    On the fringe of the night,
    Shriek over the blue,
    Terrible, true,
With our summons to heaven or hell.

Many of these poems were written in the style of music hall choric ballads and several, in fact, became music hall hits. The magazine kept in close touch with the halls and regularly published pictures of Boer War music hall spectaculars; for instance, Mrs. Beerbohm Tree's lucrative nightly recitals of Kipling's 'The Absent-Minded Beggar' at the Palace Theatre (No. 6, 3 November 1899). Smedley Norton's 'Sergeant, Call the Roll!' (No. 14, 13 January 1900) became one of the great Boer War hits. According to a letter from the *Budget's* editor, reproduced in Norton's *Bramcote Ballads* (1904), 600 applications for public recital of the poem were received. It has no poetic merit, but as a skilful pastiche of sentiment, patriotism, and melodramatic heartache as appreciated by a Victorian music hall audience, it stands as a supreme example of its kind:

For those who strew our battlefields
No passing bell shall toll;
Report the living and the dead,
Sergeant, call the roll!

. . . .

In the hush-tide of the gloaming,
Will there come, amidst the gloom,
The shadows of our loved ones
From that far-off Southern tomb?
Will pictures glow in the embers
With faces fond and true,
Of those who died whilst fighting
For the old red, white, and blue?

As purveyors of popular culture and manipulators of public opinion the music halls were second only to the press. Kipling's 'Absent-Minded Beggar' earned £340,000 (including a sixty-six-acre gift of land in Hampshire), largely from music hall recitals.[5] In *Something of Myself* (p. 81) Kipling tells us how the music hall comic monologue influenced his style and led directly to the creation of the *Barrack-Room Ballads*, but he was not the only poet who fell under the spell of the music hall. There were over fifty halls in London at the time of the war, and they found the vicarious excitement of a far-off conflict the ideal vehicle for their trade in popular sentiment, patriotics, and cockney humour, though for J. A. Hobson their influence was as pernicious as that of the press: 'In ordinary times politics plays no important part in these feasts of sensationalism, but the glorification of brute force and an ignorant contempt for foreigners are ever-present factors which at great political crises make the music-hall a very service-able engine for generating military passion.'[6] A few days after the outbreak of the war, the *Daily Mail*, 16 October 1899, described a music hall pageant of just this kind: a singer in Guards uniform, accompanied by a troupe of Guards, sang 'Up with the Old Flag', followed by 'Rule Brittania', 'God Save the Queen', and a standing ovation from the audience, lasting several minutes, after which the excitement was rounded off with a biograph film of

[5] Col. James Gildea, *For King and Country, being a Record of Funds and Philanthropic Work in Connection with the South African War* (London: Eyre & Spottiswoode, 1902), p. 120.
[6] *The Psychology of Jingoism* (London: Grant Richards, 1901), p. 2; and see John Montgomery, *1900: The End of an Era* (London: Allen & Unwin, 1968), pp. 171–85.

General Buller's departure, 'which had taken place a few hours earlier'. Already the speed of celluloid communication had become miraculous. Popular, too, were Mr. Rossi Ashton's sixty-second cartoons, created on the stage. The *Royal Magazine*, April 1900, reported that the greatest favourite was 'One for Majuba', showing a Highlander bayoneting a pleading Boer, and 'always completed amid howls of enthusiasm'.

Music hall songs and recitations on the Boer War often emulated Rossi's efforts; for example, Charles Tretheway's 'Britain's Sons; or, We Will Bump Old Kruger' (1900):

> We will bump Old Kruger straight,
> Bump the Boer with all our weight,
> Bump him fair, and bump him square,
> Bump, and make him grin, and stare,
> We will bump and make him quake;
> Bump him black, and bump him blue;
> British pluck and steel shall make
> The wretched rebel rue.

The issues of the war were naturally reduced to blunt and simple alternatives, as in Will Dalton and F. J. Willard's 'A Hot Time in the Transvaal To-night':

> There is trouble in the Transvaal,
> And England wants to know
> Whether Mister Kruger or
> John Bull shall boss the show?[7]

Fortunately not all music hall pieces were of the blood-stained or flag-waving variety. *Success*, a penny weekly which regularly recorded the current hits of the halls, published some genuinely amusing pieces, like 'Oh! The Khaki!' (4 August 1900):

> She's trimmed the room with Khaki, and
> Although it seems a shame,
> The chairs have Khaki covers, and
> The table-cloth's the same;
> Her golden hair was natural,
> With pride, she used to hint,
> But now she's dyed those lovely locks
> A brilliant Khaki tint.

[7] One of many in *War Songs*, No. 16 in McGlennon's Standard Series (1901).

George Pollinger's 'My Lulu is Half Zulu and Half Dutch,' Albert Chevalier's 'Mafekin' Night', and W. C. Robey's 'The Pretoria Dinner Party: or, In Walked England' rocked the halls, though 'The Transvaal Hero's Grave' might have done so unintentionally: 'Farewell then he cried, fell back and then he died.' Similar lines may be found in dozens of songs that the war made popular— 'The Vacant Chair', 'Break the News to Mother', 'Bury Her Picture with Me', and the two great favourites of the war, with both soldiers and public: 'Good-bye Dolly, I Must Leave You' and 'The Miner's Dream of Home'.[8]

The importance of these music hall ballads lies, for our purpose, not so much in their small literary merit, or in their more substantial value as cultural history, or even in the influence which T. S. Eliot believed they had on twentieth-century verse forms, as in their formative effect on the literary efforts of many amateur soldier poets in South Africa. The lilt and lyrics of these songs became the vehicle of route march, campfire concert, sardonic song, and homesick jingle for both Tommy Atkins and Brother Boer, as we shall see later. On occasion songs produced by service men found their way back to England, and even became popular. One of these, 'The C.I.V.: or, The British Volunteer', by Harold Hardy, who was a member of that force, casts an interesting light on the lower middle-class composition of both the City Imperial Volunteers and music hall audiences:

> You thought we played at soldiers when we met upon parade,
> You watched us shoot at Bisley with a sneer,
> But the moment you are asking for a soldier ready-made
> You find him in the British Volunteer.
> *Chorus* A something in the City—a shopman or a clerk,
>   A fellow with a pen behind his ear,
>   A journalist, a lawyer, or an idler in the Park,
>   Is the ready-when-he's-wanted Volunteer.[9]

The Boers composed and sang their own patriotic songs of a music hall stamp. 'A Famous Story', now in the War Museum,

[8] See Montgomery, *1900*; Colin MacInnes, 'Soldiers and Sailors', in *Sweet Saturday Night* (London: MacGibbon & Kee, 1967); and M. Wilson Disher, *Winkles and Champagne* (London: Batsford, 1938), for these and many other examples. There is a substantial collection of Boer War music hall songs in the Strange Collection of Africana, Johannesburg Public Library.
[9] Hardy's letters and songs from South Africa are in the National Army Museum, Chelsea, MS. 6901–1/4, 5.

D

Bloemfontein, is a Boer prisoner of war's amusing version of premature British hopes in June 1900 that the war was over:

Lord Bobs went back to England and said the war is o'er
The *Transvaal* and *Freestate* and the boers exist no more
Just fancy his surprise my friend when he stepped on to England shore
To hear those boers had just invaded the Colony once more.[10]

And on at least one occasion Briton and Boer co-operated to produce a song for their comrades, when Lieutenant Harrington Kyle of the Cape Garrison Artillery provided the words and his Boer captive, J. H. L. Schumann, the music for a good old tear-jerker, 'The Boer Prisoner's Prayer', on board the S.S. *Lake Erie* en route for St. Helena:

> I can see the old kraal and the sheep coming in,
> With old Jacob's loud 'hokhok' increasing the din.
> There's the vrouw I can see, but no smile on her face,
> But deep lines of sorrow I sadly can trace.[11]

The cadences of the music hall and the sentiments of the British press echoed through the empire. The attitudes to imperialism we have seen so far often appeared in exaggerated versions in the colonies. Though colonial attitudes to imperialism and the mother country were often ambivalent, popular encomiasts on universal British loyalty did their best to cover the cracks. The ecstatic nonsense of the editor of *An Empire's Greeting* (a supplement to *Good Words* to celebrate Edward VII's Coronation) was typical:

No one in the world had guessed, not even Britain herself, how searchingly the new idea of loyalty had been leavening the whole Empire, and it was not until all of a sudden that cry went up to heaven from under the Northern lights and the Southern Cross, from the Orient to the Isles of the Sea, and the leaping of sword in scabbard ringed the round earth with the clash of eager steel, that the world, astounded, knew, and Britain felt, that her stalwart children were not only proud of the old country and loved it, but were proud of each other's kinship, and jealous of a common honour.

Poems matching this delirium can be found in the files of colonial newspapers around the world. It was, however, two British

---

[10] Copied along with several music hall songs popular among the Boers into an exercise book on St. Helena; now in the War Museum, Bloemfontein, MS. 58/3451.
[11] *Two Songs* (Cape Town: R. Müller, n.d.).

poems, the Revd. L. Maclean Watt's 'The Grey Mother' (*Spectator,* 16 December 1899) and Theodore Watts-Dunton's 'England Stands Alone', that expressed most popularly the spirit of imperial unity. Both poems carried round the globe the fervent hope and assurance that the colonies would, in Watt's words, rally about

> the gray, old, weary mother,
> Throned amid the Northern waters.

This image of an old mother and her children, like that of a lion and its whelps, was a recurrent one in imperial verse. It may have derived from a speech made in the Canadian parliament in 1896— 'the hearts of her children have gone out to the great lone, isolated mother'—or it may simply have grown out of the powerful association of the aged queen and her empire which existed in the popular mind.[12]

Whatever its origin, the image was hardly an accurate reflection of the truth. Many colonials, particularly Australians, thought that their similar backgrounds gave them more in common with the Boers than the British. Henry Lawson wrote, in the *Bulletin*: 'Some of us are willing—wilfully, blindly eager, mad—to cross the sea and shoot men whom we never saw and whose quarrel we do not and cannot understand', and later, in 'The Drums of Battersea', he spoke of 'the far-off foreign farmers, fighting fiercely to be free'.[13] Certainly, it was the colonials who had to teach the British how to beat the Boers at their own game, as Kipling found: 'ye fawned on the Younger Nations for the men who could shoot and ride!' ('The Islanders'). The colonial contingents were, in fact, very small—about 30,000 men in an army of half a million.[14] About double that number was raised in the Cape and Natal, giving the war much more of a fratricidal nature than is commonly realized. It explains some of the extreme bitterness that speaks from so many South African poems on both sides.

But few poets of the empire showed such violent reaction to the war as those of Britain's oldest colony, Ireland. C. A. Parnell's withering attack, already quoted, is only one of many. When the Queen sanctioned the wearing of the green on St. Patrick's day in

[12] Quoted in Christopher Howard, *Splendid Isolation* (London: Macmillan, 1967), p. 18.
[13] *Collected Verse*, ed. Colin Roderick (Sydney: Angus & Robertson, 1967), i. 470.
[14] John Stirling, *The Colonials in South Africa 1899–1902* (Edinburgh: Blackwood, 1907).

honour of the splendid endeavours of Irish troops in the early
battles of the campaign, many poets, including Kipling, seized on
the opportunity to placate Irish nationalism, but nobody was
fooled. In Paris, Maud Gonne and John MacBride continued to
work for the Boer cause and assembled a strong Irish contingent
to fight on the Boer side.[15] When the Queen visited Dublin a
few months later, a striking ballad did the rounds, pointing out
that not long ago people had been shot for wearing the shamrock.
It was called 'A Lament' and was reprinted in *Reynold's Newspaper*
(22 April 1900):

> As I went down by Liffey's side,
>   In meditation free,
> Four ghosts arose upon my path,
>   And barred the way to me.
>
> And three upon their slender throats
>   The hangman's necklet bore,
> And one the headsman's chain of red
>   On his white shoulders wore.[16]
>
> 'And oh!' they cried, 'beneath the ground
>   The dead all restless go,
> And murmur of forgotten deeds
>   And hopes they used to know.
>
> 'They hear the clash of steel to steel,
>   And "Faugh-a-Ballagh" cried,
> And is the old land free at last
>   For whose dear sake we died?
>
> 'For "Ireland", always "Ireland" now
>   We hear the shout go by,
> So joy is with us in the tomb,
>   We cannot peaceful lie.'
>
> 'Go back', I said, 'you murdered four,
>   And slumber in the grave,
> Our hope is quenched, our land forlorn,
>   The land you died to save.
>
> 'You hear the Irish shout—they fight
>   To slaughter England's foe,
> They wear the green that you were slain
>   For loving long ago.

---

[15] Barker, *Prominent Edwardians*, pp. 115–27.
[16] The Manchester Martyrs and Robert Emmet, according to a footnote.

'And Ireland, your lov'd Ireland, goes
  A foreign queen to meet,
Red roses wreathed on her brow,
  The chains upon her feet.'

The *Times of Natal* (24 November 1899) reported that Limerick
Town Council was officially praying for the war to end in disaster
for Britain just at a time when Irish regiments such as the Dublin
Fusiliers and Inniskilling Dragoons were conspicuously valorous.
'The Irish patriots had been joining in prayer for the death of Irish
soldiers', commented the paper.

In other quarters the situation created mirth rather than malice.
An Irish-American, John Gwynne of Milwaukee, wrote an
amusing satire, *Homer 2nd's Bulliad* (1900), on British bungling in
the early months of the campaign, in which he lampooned attempts
to recruit Irish soldiers:

Where are those Irish? Patsy you may wear
The green or any old thing for which you care;
The queen'll be right over you to see;
We'll fly your flag in London—hully gee,
I never, never needed troops so bad!
If you will but be good my bonny lad,
Home rule, lone rule, or good old rule of fist
You'll have if only you will just enlist.

F. W. Reitz, ex-President of the Orange Free State and an accom-
plished comic rhymester, considered that Paddy was a fool:

Ah! yes bedad! the Irish lad
  Full many a fight has won
For Saxon despots, who at home
  Won't trust him with a gun.
For ages long he's suffered wrong,
  And yet he thinks it's right—
Dragged through the mud—to shed his blood
  In every English fight.[17]

Another American ballad, the anonymous 'Battle of Dundee',
gleefully described how the 'English fought the Dutch' in these
encounters:

The sun was sinking slowly, the battle rolled along;
The man that Murphy 'handed in' was a cousin of Maud Gonne,

[17] 'The Wearing of the Green', *Oorlogs en Andere Gedichten* (Potchefstroom: *Het
Westen*, 1910).

Then Flanagan dropped his rifle, shook hands with Bill McGuire,
For both had carried a piece of turf to light the schoolroom fire.
Then Rafferty took in Flaherty; O'Connell got Major McGue;
O'Keeffe got hold of Sergeant Joyce and a Belfast lad or two.
Some swore that 'Old Man Kruger' had come down to see the fun;
But the man they thought was 'Uncle Paul' was a Galway man named
  Dunn.
Though war may have worse horrors, 'twas a frightful sight to see
The way the 'English fought the Dutch' at the Battle of Dundee.[18]

Lady Gregory, in a chapter on 'Boer Ballads in Ireland' in her
Poets and Dreamers (1903), records some of the heartache that the
war caused in Ireland:

On another part of the Echtge hills, where a rumour had come that the
police were to be sent to the war, an old woman said to a policeman
I know: 'When you go out there, don't be killing the people of my
religion.' He said: 'The Boers are not of your religion'; but she said:
'They are; I know they must be Catholics, or the English would not
be against them'. . . . At Galway Railway Station, whence the Connaught Rangers set out for the war, I have heard that wives, saying
good-bye, begged their husbands 'not to be too hard on the Boers'.

She quotes several of the many ballads that were sung all over the
country, most of which, like 'The Song of the Transvaal Irish
Brigade', were much more concerned with Ireland than the
Transvaal. 'The Curse of the Boers on England', however, is a
sombre anathema in Gaelic to which, Lady Gregory assures us,
translation does little justice:

> That Queen that was beautiful
> Will be tormented and darkened,
> For she will get her reward
> In that day, and her wage.
>
> . . . .
>
> Her wage for the bones
> That are whitening to-day;
> Bones of the white man,
> Bones of the black man.
>
> . . . .
>
> Her wage for the white villages
> She has left without men;
> Her wage for the brave men
> She has put to the sword.

[18] Included in an anonymous and somewhat enigmatic collection, *The South African
War: Some Poetry Published in England and the United States* (no imprint, n.d.).

Yeats, in spite of his close involvement with key-figures in the pro-Boer movement, remained comparatively uninvolved, hoping only to 'transmute the anti-English passion into a passion of hatred against the vulgarity and materialism whereon England has founded her worst life and the whole life that she sends us'.[19]

In some parts of the empire the war hardened resistance to closer ties with Britain as much as it called forth protestations of loyalty.

> No power can conquer, no quarrels shall weaken
> The Rose and the Maple, the Wattle and Heather!

wrote Trooper G. Simes in the Bloemfontein *Friend* on 28 March 1900, but things were not that easy. While the war was still on, Australian plans for interstate federation rather than closer ties with the empire came to fruition, and from Canada Goldwin Smith wrote to James Bryce that the war had endangered plans for imperial federation, aroused strong resentment to Britain, and spelt the end of jingoism.[20] Yet it was in Canada that loyalist poets most persistently ravaged the muses. On the day that the Canadian contingent departed, 4 November 1899, the Toronto *Globe* published 'A Page of War Poetry', all of it patriotic doggerel. No doubt the presence of French Canadian anti-imperial sniping kept these bards on their mettle in a way that was denied to, say, Australian poets.

The *Globe* was a typical large, loyalist colonial paper, and its reactions to the war may stand as representative of scores of others. It faithfully followed the progress of the Canadian contingent. On 4 December it reported their safe arrival in Cape Town; on the 5th it starred the Canadians' engagement at Modder River; on the 6th readers were told that the contingent was to be brigaded with the Black Watch and Seaforths—two regiments soon to be involved in a major disaster. By 14 December the first news of the fatal engagement at Magersfontein had come through; the Black Watch had been decimated, but were the Canadians involved? They were not, we are told on the 15th, but the future looks grim for the Empire's forces. The next day a banner headline, 'Yet Another Stunning Blow', recounted the battle of Colenso,

[19] *Autobiographies*, pp. 431–2.
[20] Letter dated 19 Jan. 1900, Bryce Papers, Bodleian MSS. Bryce (English) 16 and 17. See also Goldwin Smith, *In the Court of History: An Apology for Canadians who were Opposed to the South African War* (Toronto, 1899).

followed on the 18th by another: 'The Empire Now at Stake'. Then, on 19 December we have a poem, enshrined on the leader page:

> Once on a time when days were dark,
> And Britain's sons were plunged in gloom,
> A Song that made the mourners hark
> Went tossing upward like a plume. . . .
>   'The meteor flag of England
>   Shall yet terrific burn
>   Till danger's troubled night departs
>   And the star of peace return.'

At the front the Canadians seem to have been little moved by these sentiments. According to one of them, Dr. A. S. McCormick, the men hated the officers, who were all political appointees, and on route marches preferred to sing 'Blow Ye Winds in the Morning' and 'I'll Make dat Black Girl Mine'.[21] Perhaps some of them, too, shared the sentiments of a woman in a Toronto crowd celebrating Kruger's downfall, recorded in John Wilson Bengough's *In Many Keys* (1902):

> But in the crowd, that soft-toned, woman's voice
> Which muttered 'Poor old man, I feel for him,'
> Went deeper than the surface fun.

Compassion for the conquered marks several of the better Australian Boer War poems, too. Australians responded strongly to their Boer enemies' love for and identification with the veld and wild places. One of the most popular poems of the war was John Sandes's 'Death Song of the Boers'. It first appeared in the *Melbourne Argus*, then found its way into several other papers around the world, to end up back in Australia and in Borthwick's anthology under a different signature.[22] Essentially loyalist, it nevertheless expresses, particularly in the last stanza, reproduced here, a fellow-colonial's sympathy for an unhurried, pastoral independence that the Boers could not hope to preserve:

> The old, old faiths must falter; the old, old creeds must fail—
>   I hear it in the distant murmur low—
> The old, old order changes, and 'tis vain for us to rail,

---

[21] 'The Royal Canadians in South Africa' (Akron, Ohio, 1960), mimeographed notes, Royal Commonwealth Society Library 55c 8 Pam.

[22] The peregrinations of the poem are recorded in *Poetry of Empire*, ed. John and Jean Lang (London: T. C. & E. C. Jack, ?1911), where it appears as 'With Death's Prophetic Ear'.

The great world does not want us—we must go.
And veldt, and spruit, and kopje to the stranger will belong,
  No more to trek before him we shall load;
Too well, too well I know it, for I hear it in the song
  Of the rooi-baatje singing on the road.

('Rooi-baatje', i.e. 'red-coat', was the Boer nickname for British troops, dating from earlier conflicts.)

Sandes's poem falls into a genre that is known in Australia as the bush-ballad, the product of a 'lyre strung with horse-hair', as one historian of Australian literature, H. M. Green, calls it.[23] Long in line, leisurely but compulsive in rhythm, and growing out of the horse stories and songs of the outback, these ballads became the vehicle for much of the country's literature in the eighties and nineties. They particularly celebrated, as in Sandes's poem, the attractions of an outdoor life and a rough-hewn independence, fostering by their very nature a healthy scepticism of grandiose political schemes such as federation and empire.

Several of the masters of the bush-ballad were involved in the South African War. A. B. ('Banjo') Paterson, creator of 'Waltzing Matilda', went to the front as a correspondent for the Sydney *Morning Herald*.[24] He published some rousing ballads in the Bloemfontein *Friend*, afterwards collected in *Rio Grande's Last Race* (1902), and expressed the view (*Daily Express*, 23 November 1900) that 'the effect of the campaign on the Australians will be to make them fifty times more English than before. I'm sure that the bulk of our fellows would, after a few months' spell, assist in any other English war, out of a feeling of comradeship.' Nevertheless, he showed a frontiersman's grudging respect for the Boers, his 'Johnny Boer' reading like a descant to Kipling's 'Fuzzy-Wuzzy':

They reckon Fuzzy-wuzzy is the hottest fighter out.
But Fuzzy gives himself away—his style is out of date,
He charges like a driven grouse that rushes on its fate;
You've nothing in the world to do but pump him full of lead:
But when you're fighting Johnny Boer you have to use your head;
He don't believe in front attacks or charging at the run,
He fights you from a kopje with his little Maxim gun.

[23] *A History of Australian Literature* (Sydney: Angus & Robertson, 1961), i. 360.
[24] *The Golden Treasury of Australian Verse*, ed. Bertram Stevens (London: Macmillan, 1912), p. 366. Extracts from verses by A. B. Paterson reprinted from *Rio Grande's Last Race and Other Verses* (1904) by permission of the Copyright Proprietor and Angus and Robertson Publishers.

'On the Trek' must have expressed the feelings of many of Banjo Paterson's countrymen who had rushed to enlist in the imperial cause:

When the dash and the excitement and the novelty are dead,
   And you've seen a load of wounded once or twice,
Or you've watched your old mate dying—with the vultures overhead,
   Well, you wonder if the war is worth the price.
And down along Monaro now they're starting out to shear,
   I can picture the excitement and the row;
But they'll miss me on the Lachlan when they call the roll this year,
   For we're going on a long job now.

Someone who certainly regretted joining up was Harry ('Breaker') Morant. He contributed many ballads to the *Bulletin*, including some on the Boer War, which saw him in an irregular troop of very tough characters, the Bushveld Carbineers. The unfortunate shooting of two Boer prisoners, in which Morant was involved, led to a court martial and the execution of Morant and Lieutenant P. J. Handcock on 27 February 1902, largely to placate Boer feeling in preparation for a peace settlement. The incident led to a furore in Australia and is fully recounted in several books, most notably in *Scapegoats of the Empire* (1907) by Lieutenant George R. Witton, who had been tried with Morant and Handcock.[25] As the title indicates, these Australians were bitterly disillusioned with imperial authorities who failed to appreciate that the tough guerrilla tactics of the Boers demanded harsh and impromptu retaliation. The night before his execution Morant wrote 'Butchered to make a Dutchman's Holiday':

No matter what end they decide—
Quicklime? or boiling ile? Sir,
We'll do our best when crucified
To finish off in style, sir! . . .
And if you'd earn a D.S.O.—
Why, every British sinner
Should know the proper way to go
Is: 'Ask the Boer to dinner!'

[25] See also F. Renar, *Bushman and Buccaneer: Harry Morant, His Ventures and Verses* (Sydney: Dunn, 1902); and F. M. Cutlack, *Breaker Morant: A Horseman Who Made History* (London, 1962). Cutlack claims that the notebook Morant kept in South Africa has 'some extraordinarily vivid and original poems in it'. I have not been able to examine these. Cutlack quotes only 'Butchered to make a Dutchman's Holiday'.

The best-known of these balladists, Henry Lawson, did not go to South Africa, but, judging by his *Letters*, it was not for lack of trying.[26] What he would have done there is not clear, since he was against the war from the start. His 'Our Fighters (From a Worldly Point of View)', published in the *Australian Star* (28 October 1899), soon after an Australian contingent had been suggested, is a highly sardonic treatment of the excitements of battle:

If you get yourself into a mess, cut off in broken ground,
In a red-hot gully, where the foe are firing down all round;
Where the 'burring' bullets smash your heads and the shells cut mates in two;
There's the honour of old New South Wales from a worldly point of view!

This is hardly the Newboltian version of rallying round the flag. Several others followed, such as 'The Blessings of War' in the *Bulletin* (27 January 1900). Shortly afterwards Lawson left for England, which he came to loathe, and where he put his bush-ballad muse to the service of pacifists and social reformers, as in 'The Drums of Battersea':

Where the hearses hurry ever, and where man lives like a beast,
They can feel the war-drums beating—men of Hell! and London East.

Here, too, he wrote a poem which bitterly, but correctly, warned that peace in South Africa would be hollow, temporary, and dependent on force—'As Far as Your Rifles Cover':

Do you think, you slaves of a thousand years to poverty, wealth and pride,
You can crush the spirit that has been free in a land that's new and wide?
When you've scattered the last of the farmer bands, and the war for a while is over,
You will hold the land—aye, you'll hold the land—the land that your rifles cover.

Till your gold has levelled each mountain range where a wounded man can hide,
Till your gold has lighted the moonless night on the plains where the rebels ride;

[26] *Letters 1890–1922*, ed. Colin Roderick (Sydney: Angus & Robertson, 1970), pp. 112–14. All Lawson quotations that follow are from *Collected Verse*, ed. Colin Roderick.

Till the future is proved, and the past is bribed from the son of the
  land's dead lover—
You may hold the land—you may hold the land just as far as your rifles
  cover.

The Sydney *Bulletin*, which published so many of the poems I
have mentioned, was itself strongly opposed to the war.[27]
Socialist and republican, it campaigned for Australian nationalism
under the banner 'Australia for the Australians', though, ironically, many of its contributors wrote in the vein of Kipling, whom
the paper consistently derided. Thus 'The Fat Man and the War',
afterwards collected in *The Bulletin Reciter* (1902), typically exposed
the war as a capitalist plot:

> When the sun has licked the blood up
> An' the brown earth hid the bones,
> His miners will go out seekin'
> For gold and precious stones.

Loyalist verse on the war was scarcer in Australia than anywhere
else. Apart from W. H. Dawson's *War Songs* (1901), W. H.
Robinson's *Australia at the Front* (1903), and the Amazonian
'Thistle' Anderson's *Verses At Random* (1901), which enthusias-
tically lobbied for an Australian women's contingent, there is
only the work of George Essex Evans. Once again a journalist
(on the *Queenslander*), Evans churned out much patriotic and gory
doggerel to accompany news stories. The editor of his *Collected
Verses* (1928), Firmin McKinnon, tells us that ' "The Lion's
Whelps", for instance, was written one hot night in the office of
the old *Darling Downs Gazette*, in the agony and anxiety following
the receipt of a cable announcing the disaster at Magersfontein.
The poem appeared the following morning, side by side with the
news of the reverse. It was thus, in the white heat of passionate
emotion, that he wrote many of his patriotic poems.' It is a rousing,
thumping creation indeed:

> There is scarlet on his forehead,
> There are scars across his face,
> 'Tis the bloody dew of battle dripping down, dripping down,
> But the war heart of the lion
> Turns to iron in its place . . .

[27] Jebb, *Studies in Colonial Nationalism*, pp. 190–202.

Eager as some of the lion's whelps may have been to join the fray, most of them could not leave South Africa soon enough. A more thoughtful poem by Evans, 'At the Base Hospital', wistfully expresses the strained loyalty of some colonial defenders of the empire:

They are bringing in the dying, they are bearing out the dead,
  And I watch the nurses moving to and fro.
In the long, low, white-washed wardroom, I lie dreaming on my bed,
  And it may be that I, too, shall have to go. . . .
I've seen an army moving out a hundred thousand strong,
  I've felt the thrill of battle and the smart,
But I'd barter all the glory for a day at Dandenong
  With the cool hand of the Bush upon my heart.
They say we drove their rifles back like chaff before the wind,
  They say our name and fame have travelled far—
But my heart is full of hunger for the girl I left behind,
  And the old folk by the river at Glenbar.

J. H. M. Abbott, author of *Tommy Cornstalk: Some Account of the South African War from the Point of View of the Australian Ranks* (1902), experienced a similar tug of nostalgia when he came across a row of Australian gum trees in the middle of the veld:

Back, by the creeks in the far-off plains;
  Over the ranges blue;
Out in the West where it never rains;
  We whispered 'good-bye' to you.
We left you alone on the high clay banks,
  On a fringe round the dry lagoon,
Where your white trunks gleam by its empty bed
  In the pale, soft summer noon.[28]

Unfortunately not all those involved in the South African War could pack up and leave after it was all over. After the Australians and Canadians, Jack Tar and Tommy Atkins had departed, the citizens of the two colonies and the two ex-republics had to cope for many decades—indeed, still do—with the legacy of what had really been a civil war. The magnitude of their resentment becomes clear when one looks at the verse that Cape and Natal supporters of the imperial cause produced. These versifiers held, at best, the ideals of the South African League, formed at the time of the

[28] 'Old Friends', Bloemfontein *Friend*, 10 April 1900.

Jameson Raid: 'to support the existing supremacy of Great Britain in South Africa, and . . . to oppose any attempts that may be made to weaken or destroy this supremacy'.[29] At worst, they shared the views of the mayor of Ladysmith, G. W. Willis, who regarded the Boers as 'presumptuous and barbarous invaders who so wantonly surprised and over-ran these territories with the object of conquest and plunder',[30] or the hatred of Arthur M. Mann's *Songs for the Front* (Cape Town, n.d.):

> Throw their flesh to the dogs, and the vulture's foul maw,
> Beyond pity, grace, pardon, or pale of the law.

On the other hand, the same volume of Ladysmith siege diaries that contains Willis's words also quotes a Boer girl's letter found in the trenches after the siege: 'The only thing I want you to bring me from the war is a live Englishman. I want to kill him myself.' However, we shall return to the views and poems of the Boers and their international supporters in later chapters.

English poems from the Cape and Natal were overwhelmingly loyalist. Although editors of country newspapers such as the *Midland News* and the *Uitenhage Chronicle* would at times become impatient with Britain's failure to match the Boers' fighting methods, they all harboured one or more local poets who kept up a flow of patriotic doggerel. These included M. Tuck in the *Uitenhage Chronicle*, Marianne Farmingham in the *Midland News*, W. Stanley Shaw in the *Grahamstown Journal*, S. H. Paddon in some Port Elizabeth papers, and John Paton, W. H. Walker, and Lynn Lyster in various Natal papers. Some colonial versifiers scribbled their lines in the heat of resentment in diaries and on scraps of paper where they can still be found in war museums around South Africa; others rose to the eminence of published volumes, rare little books such as Benjamin Franklin Bates's *The Anglo-Saxon Union: or, Hands Across the Sea* (Cape Town, 1902), A. Cunningham-Fairlie's vitriolic *Glimpses in Rhyme* (Lovedale, 1900), or W. B. Yaldwin's equally spiteful *British and Boer: Satirical and Patriotic Verses* (Port Elizabeth, 1900).

Their interests were many, their abilities uniformly poor, often comically so. Occasionally W. H. Paddon, for instance, could rise

---

[29] Quoted in Robert Crisp, *The Outlanders: The Men Who Made Johannesburg* (London: Peter Davies, 1964), p. 381.
[30] Ladysmith Historical Society, *Siege Diaries*, No. 4 (Ladysmith, 1973).

to lines like the following on the battle of Paardeberg (*Eastern Province Herald*, 28 February 1900):

> About each rocky bed
> The heedless dassies play;
> The desert calm, around the dead,
> Makes endless Sabbath day;

but most of his work justified the especial scorn which the *South African News*, the only substantial pro-Boer English paper in the Cape, reserved for him, as in the issue of 13 October 1900:

> Old Paddon's again on the rampage,
> He's still got Oom Paul on the brain,
> He never turns over a new page,
> But jingles again and again.

The paper then went on to suggest a recipe for verse of this kind:

Commence by alluding to Mr. Kruger as a 'thief'. It at once puts your audience into a good humour, because they know it is real poetry and not Pale Pills or something of that kind. . . . Do not forget to mention the word 'veldt' at least once and do not on any consideration leave out the 't'. It is an absurd affectation on the part of the Dutch to spell it otherwise, and if you were to do so your readers might think you knew another language than your own, and might even doubt your loyalty. . . . If you make your verses scan and rhyme so much the better, but if you make your sentiments gory enough your readers will forgive you a great deal in the merely mechanical way. Wind up with something grand, not to say grandiose.

Yet the Cape and Natal papers faithfully continued to publish verse in this vein. Sometimes a voice of satire or disgust would break through, as in the following two extracts from the Pera Muriel Button Collection of Natal newspaper cuttings in the Library of Parliament, Cape Town. The first, from 'The Queen's Chocolate', purports to be a Boer's comment on the Queen's magnanimity to her troops:

> For you've bled for Queen and country, yet yer life is being sold
> For 'arf a pound of chocolate and a tin. . . .
> And when yer back in England, minus a leg or other limb,
> They'll preach a special sermon and compose a special 'im,
> But you Tommies must be satisfied the Queen 'as 'ad 'er whim,
> As you've 'ad yer 'arf a chocolate and the tin.

The second, from 'The War Demon', represents one of the few outright condemnations of war to appear in these files:

> War! we cried to the Heavens, war! we yelled to the wind;
> The war that makes men devils, and warps the gentlest mind—
> What do we care for justice, or what for mercy or peace? . . .
> Oh! the ping of the merry bullet as it flies for a moment alive,
> Bearing death on its lightning breath, in swift, unerring dive. . . .
> And the land will go a-mourning for the feet that echo not,
> In the horrors of that dawning o'er the brave that we have shot.

In contrast to the Natal papers, two publications in Cape Town maintained critical attitudes to the war: the *Owl* and, much more outspokenly, the *South African News*. A critical weekly conceived along the lines of the *Spectator* or *Outlook*, the *Owl* followed a moderate course, but was nevertheless eventually banned. Side by side with loyalist poems it published items such as 'What does it matter?' (30 March 1900) on Tommy's uncomplaining lot:

So what does it matter to Tommy where the right or the justice lies,
Of the cause for which he is fighting, and for which he so readily dies?

or 'Magnificent Magnanimity' (21 December 1900), which delightfully lampoons an official announcement that all members of the Imperial Yeomanry and Volunteers would be issued with a cheap suit on demobilization:

> His tunic was torn and his putties were ripped,
>   And his helmet had often been hit,
> But the soldier man knows the pursuit of De Wet
>   Plays the dickens and all with his kit.
> He had scarcely a rag of a shirt to his back,
>   Or a bit of a sole to his boot;
> But he laughed, for he knew he was right on the track
>   Of a thirteen-and-sixpenny suit.
>
> And his eye would grow dim and his bosom would heave
>   As he thought with affectionate pride
> Of the beautiful reach-me-downs, short in the sleeve,
>   That his country was going to provide.
> And in fancy he saw himself swaggering round,
>   While with envy comrades were mute,
> For he looked quite the gentleman down to the ground
>   In his thirteen-and-sixpenny suit.

The *South African News* was a much sharper thorn in the Cape imperial authorities' side. Its editor during the war years was C. Louis Leipoldt, who was to become one of the most prominent of the first generation of Afrikaans poets and write some of the best Afrikaans poems on the war.[31] Like the Cape Afrikaner Bond government, which it supported, the paper at first attempted to remain neutral to the war. An editorial on 1 November 1899 encouraged Dutch colonists to remain loyal and claimed that Britain would treat the Republics fairly. But it supported the Boers more and more openly as the war escalated, and the authorities suppressed it in October 1901. It naturally gave great publicity to the pro-Boer movement in Britain and Europe, acted as mouthpiece for Olive Schreiner and her feminist associates, and reprinted the sympathetic poems of William Watson, Alice M. Buckton, and disgruntled soldier poets. On 19 January 1901, for instance, it gave an Imperial Yeoman trooper's reply to reports that had reached South Africa regarding the excessive lionizing meted out to men invalided home:

> Yes, no doubt it's very pleasant, you broken fighting man,
> To exchange into a hansom from a wagon and a span;
> There's many another fellow, though, who hasn't had your luck,
> Who got well rather quickly, too, and so out here he's stuck.

On the same day, too, the paper took lugubrious delight in reporting an Aberdeen (South Africa) undertaker's remarks that 'business done during the year has greatly increased, and the prospects for the future are hopeful'.

The *South African News* shares with several other Cape Town papers the claim to be the earliest publishers of Edgar Wallace, who was probably the best poet Cape Town could boast in those days. But before we look at some of the youthful Wallace's war poems, it is necessary to turn to the work of his avowed master—Rudyard Kipling.

[31] Rob Antonissen, *Die Afrikaanse Letterkunde van die Aanvang tot Hede* (Pretoria: HAUM, 1955), p. 95.

IV

Kipling and Kiplingson

> Time and again were we warned of the dykes, time and again
> we delayed:
> Now, it may fall, we have slain our sons as our fathers we have
> betrayed.
> > Rudyard Kipling, 'The Dykes', *The Five Nations* (1903).

> O God of Battles, by whose fire
> Thy Kipling warms his brain;
> How blest are they who only pay
> While other men are slain!
> > *Justice*, 13 January 1900.

T HE above two quotations suggest that, at the time of the Boer War, a considerable discrepancy existed between what Kipling was thought to be writing and what he actually wrote; the lines from 'The Dykes' register a sense of profound failure, while the epigram from *Justice* sketches a high priest of jingoism. This sharp ambivalence, however, was a typical feature of Kipling's contemporary reputation, and it was not unwarranted. His books of verse published just before and just after the war—*The Seven Seas* (1896) and *The Five Nations* (1903)—show several anomalies in his thinking on empire in these years. The present chapter will attempt to reconcile these discordant elements, assess the achievements of his Boer War verse, and conclude with a discussion of Kipling's imitators.

The facts of Kipling's involvement in the South African War are well known from the contemporary work of Julian Ralph, *War's Brighter Side: The Story of The Friend Newspaper Edited by the Correspondents with Lord Roberts's Forces* (1901), and from his own *Something of Myself* (1937).[1] *Something of Myself*, however, written

---

[1] See also C. E. Carrington, *Kipling: His Life and Work* (London: Macmillan, 1955), and V. C. Malherbe, *Eminent Victorians in South Africa* (Cape Town: Juta, 1972), ch. 4.

during the final period of his life, does not present the complete Kipling of the Boer War. It gives us essentially the man totally disillusioned by empire. The chapter on South Africa is marked by impatience, ill-tempered comments on the country and its people, and an obsession with the folly of the war and its aftermath:

At long last, we were left apologising to a deeply-indignant people whom we had been nursing and doctoring for a year or two; and who now expected, and received, all manner of free gifts and appliances for the farming they had never practised. We put them in a position to uphold and expand their primitive lust for racial domination, and thanked God we were 'rid of a knave'. (p. 166)

The tone here does not reveal the boisterous, almost boyish, Kipling who wrote a music hall hit to collect funds for the war and who, at Bloemfontein, threw his heart and soul into the business of entertaining Tommy Atkins with his newspaper work. 'Oh, how good it is to be at work in a newspaper office again!' he exclaimed (Ralph, p. 132), and again: 'How good it is to be with men who are doing things!' (p. 258.) Both comments reveal someone searching for involvement in events as an escape from ideas. At both Bloemfontein and Cape Town he happily broke through red tape to visit prisoners of war and smuggle supplies into hospitals, and once he came under fire in a lively skirmish at Karree Siding, near Bloemfontein.

The Kipling of these years is sketched more accurately in Edward Dowden's 'The Poetry of Mr. Kipling'.[2] Here we meet a figure whose public stature and political significance had become truly international: 'It was long since a morsel of verse constituted an historical event of importance for two hemispheres; but this, without exaggeration, is what certain short poems of Mr. Kipling have been. They have served to evoke or guide the feelings of nations, and to determine action in great affairs.' Though not a 'music hall jingo', he was nevertheless a 'maker of tribal lays', accurately anticipating and expressing public senti-ments. Dowden spotted the puritanical strain in Kipling's imperial writing: his 'feeling for Empire . . . rises at the summit to a solemn and even religious sense of duty'. At the same time, Dowden stressed, there were other, less spectacular pillars to Kipling's imperial temple: sheer hard work, and a simple sense of adventure. 'He is a poet not of contemplation but of action. . . .

[2] *New Liberal Review*, 1 (1901), 53–61.

The "reigning personage" of Mr. Kipling's creations is the man who has done something, of his own initiative (or of God's), if he be a man of genius; and if not a man of genius, then something which he finds, like the brave M'Andrews . . . allotted or assigned to him as duty.'

Dowden, in fact, had hit on a duality in Kipling's concept of empire—on the one hand, the emblem of the ordinary man doing his job; on the other, an exalted, mystical vision of beneficent rule—which goes a long way to explain both the ambiguity in Kipling's own reactions to empire, and the ambivalence of his reputation as a writer on empire. For it is not always realized that the Boer War came at a relatively early stage in Kipling's career as laureate of empire; that it occurred at a time when the cele-bration of the colourful characters of empire had only just given way in his work to the worship of a vast and ultimately nebulous panorama of imperial ideology. The Boer War provided him with the first real opportunity to put this vision to the test, and to formulate it against a background of intense imperial controversy. I would like to argue, however, that he found the intellectual and theoretical equipment he had assembled by that stage wholly inadequate for the task in hand, and hence that the rude awakening which Britain underwent impinged on Kipling as a personal failure. Like Conrad's Lord Jim, he became obsessed with a failure of nerve; South Africa showed Kipling's empire on the bolt, and his own grandiose concept of empire too brittle to outlast a real imperial war.

Kipling's early writings, up to the Vermont period (i.e. 1892), are markedly un- and even anti-imperialistic in the sense in which the term came to be understood in the late nineties. His Indian stories and poems explored the colourful, the blackguardly, the exotic, the adventurous, the workmanlike aspects of life in rough and far-off places, and mightily whetted the appetite of an urban-ized middle class for literature of the colonies and frontiers.[3] But these works, particularly the poems, are largely scornful about British racial and imperial pretensions; they present Kipling as primarily a journalist, keeping his distance, quick to pick out concrete detail and unusual occurrence, but wary of ideology.

[3] See Amy Cruse, *After the Victorians* (London: Allen & Unwin, 1938), for a discus-sion of the popularity of 'frontier' literature in the 1880s and 1890s, and of Kipling's part in the vogue.

The very first poem in *Departmental Ditties* (1886), 'General Summary', is as unflattering a picture of English racial presumption in India as one can find:

> We are very little changed
> From the semi-apes who ranged
> India's prehistoric clay:
> Whoso drew the longest bow
> Ran his brother down, you know,
> As we run men down to-day.

This law of the jungle (as distinct from 'The Law of the Jungle', formulated only in 1895) is the controlling principle in the weird happenings, brutal and amorous, mean and heroic, in the *Ditties* and in many of the Indian tales. Like the stories of these years, the poetry was materially responsible for the rehabilitation of the soldier in the public's eye, but it did not create a one-sided image of selfless and heroic warriors of empire. 'The Grave of the Hundred Dead', for instance, tells a story, not of officially approved imperial wrath at the sniping of a subaltern, but of the fierce and primitive loyalty of the men of the First Shikaris to their white officer, Lieutenant Smith. The savage revenge they exact for his death demotes the white man and the empire he represents to the level of a tribal chieftain and a reign of terror:

> They made a pile of their trophies
> High as a tall man's chin
> Head upon head distorted,
> Set in a sightless grin. . . .
> For the Burmans said
> That a *kullah's* head
> Must be paid for with heads five score.

The most explicit comment on empire in *Departmental Ditties* is contained in the wry, guarded, Browningesque monologue of Lord Dufferin in 'One Viceroy Resigns'. Lord Lansdowne, his successor, coming east from Bombay, sees 'Enough to frighten any one but me', and is advised:

> You'll never plumb the Oriental mind,
> And if you did it isn't worth the toil.

The out-going viceroy's review of his rule remains throughout underpitched, unflattering of the country, and unencouraging on empire. Lansdowne is told to trust in God, 'if there be a God', and to make the best of 'Princes and Powers of Darkness, troops and trains . . ./Whitewash and weariness, red rockets, dust'.

Barrack-Room Ballads (1892) still shows relatively little enthusiasm for empire in action, and even less for the idea, but by now W. E. Henley's influence (and that of Gatti's music hall, according to *Something of Myself*) was beginning to tell. But if Henley's raucous activism was an influence, so were Mary Kingsley's sanity and scepticism. In *Something of Myself* (pp. 77–8) Kipling pays high tribute to her friendship in these years, and much of his later work on imperial themes shows him moving between the poles of Henley's activism and Mary Kingsley's scornful idealism.

The *Ballads* are concerned with the people, especially the soldiers, rather than the ideas of empire. The dedicatory poem ('Beyond the Path of the Outmost Sun') presents the soldier as the rough-and-ready man of all seasons and trades, whose blasphemous existence is mysteriously sanctified by his devotion to a simplistic but pure sense of duty and comradeship. Like Henley, Kipling tends to overstep the bounds between justifiable activism and sheer hooliganism in 'Cells', 'Loot', and especially 'Belts', but most of the poems are accounts of soldierly pathos, humour, camaraderie, and behaviour under stress.

At the same time, though, imperialism—even a very chauvinistic brand of it—begins to show in a few of the poems. In 'The Widow at Windsor' and 'The Widow's Party' it is unattractively camouflaged as a common soldier's enthusiasm for his queen and flag:

> Take 'old o' the Wings o' the Mornin',
> An' flop round the earth till you're dead;
> But you won't get away from the tune that they play
> To the bloomin' old rag over'ead.

The English Flag', in spite of the wise counsel: 'What should they know of England who only England know?' catches the full-blooded jingo lilt:

> Must we borrow a clout from the Boer—to plaster anew with dirt?
> An Irish liar's bandage, or an English coward's shirt?

The publication of *Barrack-Room Ballads* was followed by four years (till 1896) which Kipling spent largely in the United States,

and which saw the formulation of the naïve but rigidly authori-
tarian 'The Law of the Jungle' in *The Second Jungle Book* (1895).
Edmund Wilson has suggested, in 'The Kipling that Nobody
Read',[4] that Kipling's unfortunate family feuds in Vermont led
him to adopt an ideology of empire that was truculently anti-
foreign, pro-British, and basically anti-democratic. But perhaps
Kipling simply had more time to think and talk about the ideas
and aims of empire now that he no longer had any contact with
the characters and frontiers of empire. Travelling around the
world possibly also led to a naïve conviction that the British
could do it all much better. Whatever the cause, in these years
Kipling fell prey to a simplistic but stupendously idealistic notion
of empire, expressed below in 'A Song of the English', which,
put to the test in a situation of real imperial crisis, could not but
lead its creator to disillusionment:

> We were dreamers, dreaming greatly, in the man-stifled town;
> We yearned beyond the sky-line where the strange roads go down.
> Came the Whisper, came the Vision, came the Power with the Need.
> Till the Soul that is not man's soul was lent us to lead.

Hence the next volume of verse, *The Seven Seas* (1896), though
still containing several ballads of men of action—soldiers, sailors,
engineers—was redolent with a spirit of imperial activism and
racial mission in poems such as 'A Song of the English', 'The
Native-Born', and 'Soldier an' Sailor Too'. Immediately, though,
another, more sombre note, reminiscent of the earlier sceptical
poems about empire, became audible, too. 'Hymn before Action'
is the first of Kipling's famous austere, admonitory poems; it
anticipates the solemn, cautionary tones of 'Recessional' and 'The
White Man's Burden':

> From panic, pride, and terror,
> Revenge that knows no rein,
> Light haste and lawless error,
> Protect us yet again.

Like most of its successors, 'Hymn before Action' is, as a poem,
inferior to the earlier verse. It deals in abstractions, moral
counsels, and chilly pronouncements which simply lack the fire
and wit of the early poems on the men and actions of empire.

[4] *Atlantic Monthly*, 157 (1941), 201–14.

It was the first of the poems that Kipling's admirers most commonly remembered him by, and his modern detractors most readily quote against him—the puritanical, high-minded, and inevitably suspect admonitions to stoic self-control and self-effacement in the service of an ideology that was, after all, political and partisan.

In the few years between *The Seven Seas* and the Boer War, Kipling concentrated on the vein struck in 'Hymn before Action', his greatest success coming with 'Recessional' (1897). Written at the conclusion of the Diamond Jubilee, aloof, stirring, anxious, it made respectable and even sanctified exactly that aggressive mood of Jubilee imperialism against which it was supposed to serve as a warning. It expressed Kipling's anxiety about empire without putting forward any coherent development of his 'Vision'; paradoxically, in turning his attention to the ideas of empire, Kipling had lost sight of the thing itself.

The fundamental change and uncertainty in Kipling's conception of his role as poet just before the war are confirmed by the sudden violence of the reactions he now provoked. Several critics all at once depicted Kipling as prostituting his art to a jingo muse. The first influential piece of iconoclasm was Robert Buchanan's 'The Voice of the Hooligan'.[5] In retrospect, Buchanan found throughout Kipling's work a streak of 'unmitigated barbarism', rising to its crowning glory in *Stalky & Co.* (1899). It is significant that Buchanan should have waited till 1899 to express these views on works which appeared up to a decade earlier and in which no one had detected the viciousness discerned by Buchanan. But similar attacks came from several other sources at the beginning of the war. *Justice* (7 October 1899) called Kipling the 'Bard of Bloodshed' and 'about the most over-rated writer of our own, or of any other, time . . . if he were not an out-and-out Imperialist bloodshedder nobody would pay any attention to his verse'. Two years later the *Rambler*[6] epitomized him as 'a Poet who cannot scan, a Patriot who aims at exposing his Country to Contempt, a Vulgarian who should never have been promoted from the Gutter to bawl even upon the most ephemeral Stage'.

Kipling had changed, in two years, from a popular and uncontroversial figure at the time of the Diamond Jubilee to a highly

---

[5] *Contemporary Review*, 76 (1899), 774-89.   [6] No. 217 (1901), 1314-16.

polemical one. Consequently the outbreak of the Boer War placed him in an intolerable position—he had to vindicate, in the eyes of supporters and detractors alike, a vision of empire as yet untried and all but unformulated. He was trapped in a mould of public expectation that he had allowed to form too easily.

A further major problem was that an ideology nurtured on racial imperialism in India was now put to test in, and invoked to vindicate, a war of expansion against another white race. One can look at this feature of the war in terms of an analogy dear to neo-imperialist writers, including Kipling: the comparison of the British and Roman empires. The analogy of imperial Rome had a powerful and obvious attraction for late-Victorian imperialists as well as their critics. Conrad invokes it in the opening pages of *Heart of Darkness*; William Watson draws a direful parallel between Britain and Rome in his Boer War poem, 'Rome and Another', in *For England* (1904); while Hardy's 'Embarcation', from *Poems of the Past and the Present* (1902), describes England as still in the clutch of Vespasian's ideals of expansionism. These may all be seen as reactions to the frequent invocation of Rome in the imperial writings of, for instance, Lords Cromer, Curzon, and Rosebery.[7]

However, in contrast to this equation of the British and Roman empires, one of the fathers of neo-imperialism, J. A. Froude, had described the Boers in terms of the pastoral simplicity and rectitude of *republican* Rome:

The Boers of South Africa, of all human beings now on this planet, correspond nearest to Horace's description of the Roman peasant soldiers who defeated Pyrrhus and Hannibal. There alone you will find obedience to parents as strict as among the ancient Sabines, the *severa mater* whose sons fetch and carry at her bidding, who, when those sons go to fight for their country, will hand their rifles to them and bid them return with their arms in their hands—or else not return at all.[8]

Here was a problem, not merely of imagery, but of the place of the Boers in the imperial scheme. Were they to be cast in the mould of republican Rome or were they an inferior race? The former view

---

[7] See Richard Faber, *The Vision and the Need: Late Victorian Imperialist Aims* (London: Faber, 1966), p. 120, for typical parallels.
[8] *Oceana; or, England and her Colonies* (London: Longmans, Green, 1886), p. 42.

became the exclusive one on the Continent, giving rise to a powerful myth that dominated all response to the Boer War in France
and Germany. In England, however, the dichotomy remained
largely unresolved, and lies at the heart of Kipling's and many of
his compatriots' doubts and agonies about the war. Even socialists
found this aspect of the war objectionable: 'No normal development of the Empire ought to include the conquest of a white
race. . . . The Empire, as a moral Ideal, has never contemplated
so harsh a possibility as that of having to break up a white
nationality, and then to rule it by compulsion,' said Henry Scott
Holland's *Commonwealth* (No. 7, October 1901). The Boers were
clearly not (to use Dilke's terminology) one of the 'cheaper' races,
but one of the 'dearer', and an ideology based on racial imperialism
could not accommodate the subjection of one white race by
another. Kipling's love–hate relationship with the United States
reveals this ambivalence as much as do his ambiguous reference
to 'lesser breeds without the Law' (black or white, savages or
Germans?) in 'Recessional', his prose treatises on the Boer War—
The Sin of Witchcraft (1901) and *The Science of Rebellion* (1902)—
and the Boer War stories and poems. 'The Captive', 'The Comprehension of Private Copper', and 'A Sahib's War' (*Traffics and
Discoveries*, 1904) all turn on points of racial ambiguity, somehow
suggesting that the Boers were worthy opponents but not of quite
pukka stock. Poems such as 'Piet' and 'General Joubert' attempt
to qualify Boer courage as great but not quite British:

> Ah there, Piet! whose time 'as come to die,
> 'Is carcase past rebellion, but 'is eyes inquirin' why.
> Though dressed in stolen uniform with badge o' rank complete,
> I've known a lot o' fellers go a dam' sight worse than Piet.

The disillusion, even panic, that resulted from Kipling's
acquaintance with British official bungling and military ineptitude
in the only war of his experience in which Britain fought another
white race, must account for the shrill abuse of 'The Lesson' and
'The Islanders', the deep melancholy of 'The Dykes', and the
sardonic attempts later, in *Something of Myself*, to cast the Boers in
a mean and inferior role. Indeed, so closely did Kipling identify
with his imperial vision, that its failure was registered as a deeply
personal one. Two poems in *The Five Nations*, 'The Palace' and
' "Wilful-Missing" ', bear this out. The former is the monologue

of a king who has to abandon operations on a magnificent palace for no other reason than that his vision turns out to be incapable of fulfilment. ' "Wilful-Missing" ' expresses a strange sympathy for deserters in the Boer War, dwelling conspicuously on an unexplained sense of personal failure that drove these men to abandon their identities:

> What man can size or weigh another's woe?
> There are some things too bitter 'ard to bear.
> Suffice it we 'ave finished—Domino!
> As we can testify, for we are there,
> In the side-world where "wilful-missings" go.

The argument that Kipling was especially conscious of imperial failure in the Boer War must not be taken to mean that he wrote about nothing else. Because of his sensitivity to the situation, he saw rather more of what was happening and of what was at stake than the majority of his countrymen. Several of the poems in *The Five Nations* continued the quest for a viable vision of empire, and effectively isolated both the strengths and the weaknesses of the imperial engagement in South Africa.

Significantly, Kipling's first contribution to the Boer War effort, 'The Absent-Minded Beggar', was not included in *The Five Nations*. An overhasty pastiche of money-spinning catch-phrases and music hall lilts, it served its fund-raising purpose only at the expense of confirming the critics' worst fears. Kipling's quip, 'I would shoot the man who wrote it if it would not be suicide' (Ralph, p. 113), suggests that he soon recognized the damage the piece had done to him just at a time when his reputation was in the balance and great things were expected of him. In this respect the poem's title could well apply to its author. It earned him the title of the 'jester-jongleur of the hour' in a pamphlet by Marie Corelli, *A Social Note on the War: Patriotism or Self-Advertisement?* (1900): 'We had hoped he would have stormed Parnassus, rather than be content to stand with the mountebanks of rhyme at the foot of the Olympian hill.'

In contrast, many of the poems in *The Five Nations* present thoughtful attempts to place the war against a wider, portentous background of approaching calamity. Often he uses an image of the sea as ominous, powerful, threatening, to suggest the apocalyptic forces surrounding the island-empire: 'The sleek-barrelled swell before storm, grey, foamless, enormous, and growing' ('The Sea and the Hills'). 'The Feet of the Young Men', 'The Explorer', and 'The Burial' (on Rhodes's death) continue, in terms of empire, that Victorian search, started in poems such as Tennyson's 'Ulysses' and Longfellow's 'Excelsior!', for the ultimate, ghost-laying commitment to a stupendous but nebulous cause:

> Dreamer devout, by vision led
> Beyond our guess or reach,
> The travail of his spirit bred
> Cities in place of speech.
>   ('The Burial')

'The Old Issue', dated two days before war broke out, places the conflict with President Kruger's republic in the context of a universal struggle between democratic, constitutional freedom and the tyrannic rule of the autocrat:

> 'Here is nothing new nor aught unproven,' say the Trumpets,
> 'Many feet have worn it and the road is old indeed.
> 'It is the King—the King we schooled aforetime!' . . .
> Sloven, sullen, savage, secret, uncontrolled—
> Laying on a new land evil of the old.

He foresaw quite clearly what would happen in South Africa two generations later if Krugerism were not curbed. While this historical clairvoyance tells us nothing about the quality of the poem, it nevertheless gives 'The Old Issue' a breadth of insight superior to the unpleasant propaganda for the arms race in 'The Peace of Dives' or the shrill tub-thumping of 'The Islanders'. 'The Settler', too, improves on the nebulous qualities of the other gnomic poems on empire by looking steadily at a real and demanding situation—the need to 'repair the wrong that was done/To the living and the dead'.

But the most striking poem in this group is 'The Dykes'. The resonance of its commanding, tightly-controlled sea-image contrasts sharply with the jingly self-righteousness of 'The Lesson', which shares its theme, namely the exposure of England's weaknesses during the Boer War. Reminiscent of Matthew Arnold's 'Dover Beach', it expresses a similar mood of self-doubt and stress both personal and national:

Far off, the full tide clambers and slips, mouthing and testing all,
Nipping the flanks of the water-gates, baying along the wall;

Turning the shingle, returning the shingle, changing the set of the
  sand . . .
We are too far from the beach, men say, to know how the outworks
  stand.

The fifteen 'Service Songs' in *The Five Nations*, in the style of
Barrack-Room Ballads, are inferior to their predecessors. Instead of
the racy, hard-bitten soldier ballads in many moods of a decade
earlier, these are mostly thinly camouflaged eulogies of various
branches of the armed services—the Mounted Infantry in 'M.I.',
the Royal Artillery in 'Ubique', and so on. A few rise to greater
significance. 'Chant-Pagan' marks a major development in the
social and political self-consciousness of the soldier; it suggests
why neither war poetry nor public awareness of war could ever
be quite the same again after the Boer War:

> Me that 'ave been what I've been,
> Me that 'ave gone where I've gone,
> Me that 'ave seen what I've seen—
>   'Ow can I ever take on
> With awful old England again,
> An' 'ouses both sides of the street,
> And 'edges two sides of the lane,
> And the parson an' 'gentry' between,
> An' touchin' my 'at when we meet—
>   Me that 'ave been what I've been?

'Stellenbosch', too, gives a fair premonition of the poetry Sassoon
was to write fifteen years later:

> The General got 'is decorations thick
> (The men that backed 'is lies could not complain),
> The Staff 'ad D.S.O.'s till we was sick,
> An' the soldier—'ad the work to do again!

'Bridge-Guard in the Karroo', though not among the 'Service
Songs', deals with the role of the common soldier in the imperial
cause, and it is the best poem in the volume. It first appeared in
The Times, 6 June 1901, under the epigraph,

> 'and will supply details to guard the Blood River Bridge'.
> *District Orders—Lines of Communication.*

That the Blood River took its name from an earlier conflict for
supremacy in South Africa (Boer against Zulu) is no doubt a

deliberate addition to the poem's meaning. Based on the monotonous life of those left out of the excitement of the main conflict, the poem also takes its place in the Victorian mini-genre of railway poems. When Samuel Smiles died in 1904, the *Athenaeum* (23 April) wrote: 'He saw the rise of the railways and he shared the common belief that the lines which fell on the pleasant places of England secured prosperity for the population ... and that mechanics meant the millennium.' The obituarist neatly expressed the enormous imaginative significance that the railways acquired in Victorian times. The building of railway lines all over the empire turned this visible symbol of progress and unity into something of a cult. Rhodes's dream of a line from Cape to Cairo; the enormous sacrifices in human life that went into the building of the Uganda Railways and the Beira–Rhodesia line; Conrad's wry description of derelict rolling stock in *Heart of Darkness*—all are as much part of this mystique of imperial communications as North American ballads on the Pacific Railroad and, during the Boer War, numerous poems on guarding the lines.

Hence the simple activity of sentry duty on a railway bridge becomes, in Kipling's poem, part of the process of ordering chaos and the unknown. The sentries are placed against a magnificent but hostile African panorama—the desert is a 'raw glare', the mountains are 'Ramparts of slaughter and peril'. It is, however, a 'Royal ... pageant', awesome but imperial, the mountains are also 'the thrones of kings', and the guards' apparently minor function in the imperial process is proportionately enlarged. Their activity represents a modest victory of civilization in this great emptiness. At the end of the poem, after the lighted train has brought

> a handful of week-old papers
> And a mouthful of human speech,

darkness flows back into their world, and they have to guard as much against it as against the Boers:

> And the darkness covers our faces,
> And the darkness re-enters our souls.

By then, however, we have been told that a whole universe is defined and held between the girders of a man-made bridge:

And the solemn firmament marches,
And the hosts of heaven rise
Framed through the iron arches—
Banded and barred by the ties.

The limited and small actions of the sentries (they 'slip' and 'stumble on refuse of rations,/The beef and the biscuit-tins') become part of a larger process, beyond their recognition, in which they have an assigned role:

We take our appointed stations,
And the endless night begins.

As in 'The Dykes', the use of a key-image with considerable resonance allows Kipling to escape from the confines of versified imperial journalism so obvious in some of the other poems.

In conclusion, then, one can point to a small harvest of poems in *The Five Nations* that offers Kipling's answer to the challenge he faced at the outset of the war. Poems like 'The Dykes' and 'Bridge-Guard in the Karroo' pass beyond the abstractions of imperial visions and glories, the thumping-out of military and racial propaganda, into the realm of an archetypal conflict between shape and shapelessness, order and chaos, man's institutions and awesome immensities. As in his earliest poems, human beings and their artefacts once more become more valuable than ideologies, and imperialism a viable if limited way in which man can order his world into meaningfulness. Kipling, in other words, coped with his distress at the failure of imperialism only by turning imperial endeavour into a metaphor for a much profounder human activity.

Unfortunately, few of Kipling's critics looked beyond the jingles to the complex moods of his best poems, hence the attacks found in journals like *Justice*. Part of the problem was that most of Kipling's imitators, too, stopped short at the obvious attractions of the 'barracky' style. A host of Kiplingesque versifiers created a veritable sub-culture of ballads on Tommy Atkins and his doings. Indeed, the man in khaki exploited this new voice as much as anyone else. Julian Ralph found in Bloemfontein that Kipling's effect on the ranks was enormous: 'So deeply has Kipling stirred the Tommy's heart with those verses which treat of or appeal to the soldier that—not to exaggerate ridiculously—one fancies that every tenth man in the ranks aspires to be regarded as a disciple of this inspired and inspiring master.'[9]

The pages of the Bloemfontein *Friend* provide ample evidence of this effect of Kipling on the khaki muse. By no means all of it was complimentary to Kipling, as is clear from the following unflattering recipe of 'Rudyardkiplingese' (Ralph, pp. 342–3):

> The man that writes a poem
> In praise of our Tommy A.'s
> Ain't got no call to study
> Their manners, nor talk, nor ways,
> 'E's only to fake up something
> What's Barracky—more or less—
> And civilians don't know as it's rubbish and so
> The Ballad's a big success.

'The Absent-Minded Beggar's Apology' (1900), the work of J. Sheldon Redding of the King's Own Yorkshire Light Infantry, was one of many poems in which soldiers objected to Kipling's condescending appeal for charitable hand-outs to their dependants:

> And if they're left in poverty you must not blame him for that,
> For he hadn't any railway scrip to sell;
> And a working man and family can't prosper and grow fat,
> And put money in the Three per Cents. as well.

'Mrs. Tommy Atkins on the Situation', purporting to come from a soldier's wife, made a similar reply to Kipling—

> Let me have my Tommy's pay in a decent sort of way,
> And not depend on charity for bread—

and also contained a telling vignette of the working man's indifference to the imperial issues of the war:

> 'I'm for off,' says he, 'a hunting of the Boer.'
> He would stand for hours debating
> With his mates in the canteen,
> Till 'is ale was growing stale from sheer neglect,
> And he don't seem to mind the suzerainty of the Queen,
> 'Cause he don't tumble to it, I expect.[10]

[9] *At Pretoria* (London: C. Arthur Pearson, 1901), p. 189.
[10] Newspaper cutting, Pera Muriel Button Collection: The South African War, vol. iv, Library of Parliament, Cape Town.

" He is out on active service,
Wiping something off a slate "—KIPLING.

Tommy Atkins—the worship of the common soldier *à la* Kipling. (See p. 27.)

Three generations of Boers under arms.

Literacy at the front. (See pp. 3–5 and 157.)

Kruger, an abandoned monument, sheltered by Queen Wilhelmina of the Netherlands. (See pp. 242 and 262.)

General C. R. de Wet. (See p. 243.)   President S. J. P. Kruger. (See p. 242.)

Cape rebels—men of Lotter's Commando. (See p. 238.)

Magersfontein—the Boer trenches in the light of day. Note the device which caught the British completely by surprise: the trenches were *in front of* the hill, not on top.

Magersfontein—the charge of the Black Watch as imagined in England. (See pp. 195–7.)

Paardeberg—after General Cronjé's surrender.

Paardeberg—the Boer laager from the British ranks.

Only a pawn! (See p. 187.)

A small library of Kiplingesque verse grew out of the Boer War. Several poets found that the outspoken vernacular verse made popular by Kipling's poetry was an ideal vehicle for satire and social comment. The best of these were: Harold Begbie, *The Handyman and Other Verses* (1900); 'Coldstreamer' [Harry Graham], *Ballads of the Boer War* (1902); T. W. H. Crosland, *The Five Notions* (1903); 'Mome' [Captain G. Murray Johnstone], *The Off-Wheeler Ballads and Other Verses* (1910); and Edgar Wallace, *Writ in Barracks* (1900).

All these volumes contain some dead wood of 'bloomin'' ballads which are no more than raucous music hall propaganda for certain arms of the services; for instance, Wallace's 'The Naval Brigade' or Begbie's 'Liberty Jack' and 'R.A.M.C.' But Begbie could also rise to the terse inevitability of 'An Incident', a sentimental but realistic ballad on the Everyman-figure of the war. I quote the first and last stanzas:

In his uniform soaking and draggled, with the blood in his sleepless eyes,
Hungry and dirty and bearded, he looks at the morning skies,
He feels for his pipe in the blanket, he calls to his chum for a light—
When a bugle sounds on the chilling air, and he stands in his boots upright. . . .

In his uniform soaking and tattered he lies with the mist in his eyes,
The sun has set and the air is still, but he looks no more on the skies;
The lips of the cannon are frothless, there is rest in the worn brigade,
And the only sound on the stricken field is the noise of his comrade's spade.

Harry Graham, who was a captain in the Coldstream Regiment, hence his pseudonym, wrote a number of infectious popular recitations on the war, some in a vein of grim comedy. In 'The White Flag' a reluctant Tommy is ordered to surrender:

Well, I was a-feeling mortal bad,
An' 'ere was this hinsubordinate lad
As wouldn't be wise, nor wouldn't obey,
But was throwin' 'is bloomin' life away.
Once more I ordered 'im, 'Stand up, there,
And wave your 'andkerchief in the h'air!'—
Then 'e stood, an' waved—but they shot 'im dead.
'Thank Gawd,' says 'e, 'as my 'andkerchief's red!'

E

Underneath the banter, however, Graham managed to convey a considerable amount of criticism of army institutions and organization. 'The Blockhouse' (another variation on the theme of Kipling's 'Bridge-Guard in the Karroo') describes some of the 'comforts' supplied to Tommy Atkins:

> Last week we'd a sack o' papers,
>   An' what do you think *h'I* got?
> A copy o' *Punch* (as I can't abide,
>   'Cos they 'ides the jokes so far inside
>   That I misses the blooming lot)

while 'The Army Chaplain' slates a certain variety of padre:

> We're 'miserable worms', says 'e,
>   An' earth's a blooming 'vale o' tears'.
> (I ain't no worm, an' seems to me
>   This h'earth's no worse nor it appears;
>   It may be bad, h'or it may not,—
> But it's the h'only one we've got.)

T. W. H. Crosland, editor of *Outlook*, produced a regular column of verse commentary in his magazine, much of it à la Kipling. He published two volumes of outright parodies of Kipling, *The Absent-Minded Mule* (1899) and *The Five Notions*, of which even the lay-out and typography were carefully copied from *The Five Nations*. Much of the contents consists of ephemeral skits on Kipling, but some of it could hit hard. The title poem conveys Crosland's comments on what he regarded as Kipling's remarkably naïve concept of what the war was all about:

> 'E 'ath a notion that the War
> Was a Imperial beano, gave
> By a 'eroic people for
> A people twenty times as brave.
>
> .   .   .   .
>
> Ar—you might think from Rudyard's lines
> That Cecil went about in white:
> 'E never owned no dimon mines,
> 'E drank no fizz with Verner Beit!

He played havoc with Kipling's imperial sanctities and solemnities; *his* 'The White Man's Burden' is a corrosive complement to Kipling's poem, filling in the parts of the picture of empire that Kipling left out:

Take up the White Man's burden,
    Descend his reeking shafts,
Gasp in his red-hot workings
    And get your air in wafts:
And since there is no telling
    How soon you may be dead,
Remember, that fat White Man
    Is shooting overhead!

Crosland's real achievement, however, was to produce one of
the most moving of all poems on the Boer War: 'Slain'. It
appeared in *Outlook*, 11 November 1899, and must have been
written at a very early stage of the war. He included it in *The Five
Notions* and again among the 'War Poems' in his *Collected Poems*
(1917), where one likes to think that it might have been read by
Wilfred Owen, with whose work the poem has much in common:

'Dulce et decorum est pro patria mori'
    You who are still and white
        And cold like stone;
    For whom the unfailing light
        Is spent and done;

    For whom no more the breath
        Of dawn, nor evenfall,
    Nor Spring nor love nor death
        Matter at all;

    Who were so strong and young,
        And brave and wise,
    And on the dark are flung
        With darkened eyes;

    Who roystered and caroused
        But yesterday,
    And now are dumbly housed
        In stranger clay;

    Who valiantly led,
        Who followed valiantly,
    Who knew no touch of dread
        Of that which was to be;

    Children that were as nought
        Ere ye were tried,
    How have ye dared and fought,
        Triumphed and died!

        .   .   .   .

> Yea, it is very sweet
> And decorous
> The omnipotent Shade to meet
> And flatter thus.

In its ironic use of Horace's epigraph and the phraseology of Wordsworth's Lucy poems ('still and white/And cold like stone'; 'on the dark are flung/With darkened eyes'; 'dumbly housed/In stranger clay'), 'Slain' seems to show more than a chance anticipation of some of Owen's poems, notably 'Futility' ('Was it for this the clay grew tall?'), 'Anthem for Doomed Youth'—

> No mockeries now for them; no prayers nor bells;
> Nor any voice of mourning save the choirs—

and, of course, 'Dulce et Decorum Est':

> My friend, you would not tell with such high zest
> To children ardent for some desperate glory,
> The old Lie: Dulce et decorum est
> Pro patria mori.[11]

Whether or not the poem had any direct influence on any poetry of the Great War may be beyond proof, but it bears striking witness to the way in which Boer War poems sometimes anteceded qualities which have come to be regarded as peculiarly those of First World War verse.

Begbie and Crosland had no direct experience of the war. They wrote essentially as journalists moved by the issues of the war and the new popular compassion for the common soldier. G. Murray Johnstone and Edgar Wallace, however, were like Graham involved in the South African conflict. Johnstone took his pseudonym, 'Mome', from the the battle of Mome Gorge in the Zulu Rebellion of 1906, in which he took part after the Boer War. He later served as a captain in the South African forces in the First World War, and produced *The Avengers and Other Poems from South Africa* (1918), a collection fairly pale in comparison with the verse of *The Off-Wheeler Ballads*. The Boer War volume contains several nondescript 'barracky' ballads, but among them is the striking title poem. In spite of its sensationalistic qualities and a somewhat brutal concept of the demands of duty, it is a harrowing

---

[11] *The Poems of Wilfred Owen: A Selection*, ed. D. Hibberd (London: Chatto & Windus, 1973).

piece, reminiscent of Kipling's 'Snarleyow' (*Barrack-Room Ballads*).
In both poems a driver has to take a gun carriage over a fallen
horse in order to save his gun; both exploit the peculiar rhythm
of the genre to create a sense of excitement and urgency:

We was racing hard for safety when he crossed his legs and fell,
And he bust the bloomin' traces and we jammed,
And the bullets they was falling—Lord, how them bullets fell!—
So we took the gun across him and be damned!

Johnstone's two outstanding poems on the war are 'Christmas,
1899' and 'The Front', both of which develop a tension between
compassion and sardonic comment. In the first poem the stark
depiction of a dead soldier against the sky-line invites a comparison with the Christ-figure suggested in the title:

Something 'uddled 'gainst the sky
Some poor devil dead,
And our squadron riding by
Cursed his gaping 'ead—
Just a man and nothing more,
Smudged across with red. . . .

Something 'uddled 'gainst the sun.
What's the odds or why?
Some poor devil's work is done—
Might be you or I—
We wondered if it 'urt him much
When 'e come to die.

This particular analogy was to become almost a cliché in the
poetry of World War I, Sassoon's 'The Redeemer' offering the
most striking treatment of the motif. In 'The Front' Johnstone
turned a more ironic eye on martial glory and produced an
abrasive compound of pity for the soldier and disgust for
authority:

A bit of a scrap on a bit of a plain,
And somebody shot in the head;
A bit of a row at the front again,
And a bit of the map that's red.
And somebody pulling the wires at home,
Whilst somebody's son lies dead.

> What is it all about? Good Lord!
>   We at the front don't know;
> But somebody's paid to wear a sword,
>   So somebody's got to go
> A-chewing biscuits and eating sand
>   Whilst the poor old bugles blow.

Edgar Wallace was a perfervid imitator of Kipling. The out-break of war found him a medical orderly at Simonstown, revelling in the title of the 'Kipling of Cape Town' and in the fairly rapid fame which his contributions to the local press had brought him. The notebooks and commonplace books Wallace kept during these years reveal a somewhat naïve young man who did not quite know how to handle his obvious penchant for spinning out Kiplingesque cockney verses, and who liked to see his work in as many papers as possible. Hence Wallace's poems can be found scattered through a dozen or more South African and British publications (for instance, the *Owl*, *Cape Argus*, *South African News*, *South African Review*, *Cape Illustrated Magazine*, *Spectator*, *Daily Chronicle*, and the *Simon's Town and District Chronicle*) during the years 1898–1900, often under pseudonyms such as 'James', 'Mars', 'Review Poet', 'Lobile', and 'Dennison Joe', and with titles different from those under which they were eventually collected in *Writ in Barracks* (1900).[12]

He arrived in Cape Town in 1896 and first caught the public's attention with his 'Welcome to Kipling' ('Tommy to his Laureate' in *Writ in Barracks*), published in the *Cape Times* on Kipling's arrival in January 1898. A word of encouragement from the master himself and favourable notices in the local and British press (carefully preserved in the notebooks) led him to become 'a frank imitator of Kipling' (*Edgar Wallace by Himself*, p. 106). Another influence was the activism of Henley in its popular aggressive form as found in, for instance, Arthur Conan Doyle's *Songs of Action* (1898), crossed with the sensationalistic naturalism

[12] Four journals and notebooks (lots 353 and 354) were auctioned on 17 July 1972 at Sotheby's, where I had the opportunity of examining them. They are now in the South African Library, Cape Town, and have been described by Dr. A. M. Lewin Robinson in the *Quarterly Bulletin of the S.A.L.*, 28 (1973), 2–10 and 53–4. I am also indebted to Mr. John A. Hogan of High Wycombe, an ardent Wallace collector and researcher, as well as to Wallace's autobiography, *Edgar Wallace by Himself* (London, 1932), and Margaret Lane, *Edgar Wallace: The Biography of a Phenomenon* (London: Heinemann, n.d.), for information about Wallace's activities in South Africa.

of war correspondents such as G. W. Steevens, whom Wallace was to succeed as a representative of the *Daily Mail* during the Boer War.[13] Out of this strain Wallace produced war poems of a crude, clipped immediacy that marked a new departure in the genre. Drafts of 'Army Doctor', 'After!' ('Cease Fire' in *Writ in Barracks*), and 'War' appear in the commonplace books as early as 1898, suggesting that Wallace, like Stephen Crane and Kipling, could exploit the journalistic techniques of the day to produce effective renditions of war without ever having seen action:

> A tent that is pitched at the base:
> A wagon that comes from the night:
> A stretcher—and on it a Case:
> A surgeon, who's holding a light.
> The Infantry's bearing the brunt—
> O hark to the wind-carried cheer!
> A mutter of guns at the front:
> A whimper of sobs at the rear.
> And it's *War*! 'Orderly, hold the light.
> You can lay him down on the table: so.
> Easily—gently! Thanks—you may go.'
> And it's *War*! but the part that is not for show.
>
> ('War')

One has to concede the power of Wallace's description here, even while suspecting, partly on the evidence of the context provided by the notebooks, that these poems were carefully created to exploit a local vogue for Kipling and a mounting war fever. The ambivalence is particularly striking in 'Cease Fire', a compulsively narrated ballad on a young soldier's search for his brother after a battle. One of the commonplace books contains several discarded drafts of the final stanza, as Wallace sent his character along various routes to arrive at the most horrific ending:

> They're layin' out our dead just now,
>   He can't be—, no, that—that ain't sense,
> An' when he comes there 'll be a row!
>   A-keepin' me in this suspense!
> 'Tis here our line of killed commence,
>   I'll sorter look—for make-pretence!

[13] See Steevens's *With Kitchener to Khartum* (London: Blackwood, 1898) and *From Cape Town to Ladysmith* (London: Blackwood, 1900).

> Pretendin' some one's here I know—
> I'm half inclined to turn aback—
> But one by one, along I go,
>   And see the crimson clottin' black. . . .
>   *His troop was first in the attack!*
> What! Jack! Is this—this Thing our Jack?

As well as writing war poetry, Wallace produced much political verse at the Cape. In his autobiography he claims to have shared the conciliatory attitudes of General Sir William Butler, who resigned as Commander-in-Chief of the British forces in South Africa three months before war broke out, but this moderation is not very evident from the regular columns of topical satire he contributed to a number of papers, consisting largely of lampoons on Kruger, the Boers, and the Afrikaner Government of the Cape Colony. In his earliest independent publication, *The Mission That Failed* (1898), most of the verse is of this kind. The title poem is a skit on the abortive Jameson Raid, but 'The Sea-Nation' exhibits a resounding jingoism:

> We lived, and live! The world shall see
> An inextinguishable flame.
> The nations fade; but we shall be!
> When Gaul and Teuton are a name!
> For us the seven seas in one:
> For landlocked hordes—oblivion.

Like Kipling, he was spell-bound by Rhodes's vision and wrote 'Cairowards':

> Going up—and all by one man's will!
> Untrodden lands shall echo with our roars,
> Our engines' wheels shall break the mountains' still,
> Uncharted rivers see us by their shores;
> And where the lions drink, and panthers prey,
> Shall lie the ballast of our iron-bound way.

When war boke out, Wallace was quick to seize the opportunity. He collected some of his war verse to hand in a threepenny pamphlet, *War! and Other Poems* (Cape Town, n.d.), which was to be the first in a series called 'Poems for the Period'. Only one further selection appeared, titled *Nicholson's Nek!* (Cape Town, n.d.), purporting to be by 'Dennison Joe'. As all these poems were afterwards included in *Writ in Barracks*, one can only surmise that Wallace must have felt that his readers would like a little more variety in their poets than Cape Town could offer, and so continued to play Box and Cox, as he had done with his magazine verse.

Wallace now resigned from the Medical Corps, went to the front as correspondent for, successively, Reuter and the *Daily Mail* —his *Unofficial Despatches on the Boer War* (1901) covers this period —and after the war became the founding editor of the *Rand Daily Mail*. His war verse continued to exploit the Kipling cult, celebrating various branches of the services ('The Naval Brigade', 'The Armoured Train'), or aspects of Tommy Atkins's chequered career as hard-bitten tin-tack philosopher ('T.A. in Love', 'Tommy Advises'), but without adding any new dimensions to the verse he had already produced.

Like Kipling and the other poets I have mentioned, Wallace soon lost interest in South Africa—he left in 1903. Eleven years later the greater catastrophe of world war finally nudged the Boer War into the back pages of history as essentially a parochial conflict. The war in South Africa, however, had by then played a vital part in the changing formulation of imperial concepts (Empire was becoming Commonwealth), while Kipling and his acolytes had created a body of war poetry that gave some inkling of what a great war might produce.

V

Protests and Pacifists

Ah! were Byron living now, what satire scathing
He would pour out on the man whose crime or blunder
All South Africa in blood and tears is bathing—
He would crush the wretch with song's avenging thunder!
D. F. Hannigan, 'The Dying Century', *Westminster Review*,
December 1899.

THE Boer War gave aim and form to the anti-imperialist and
pacifist forces that had been mustering in Britain and Europe
during the last decade of the nineteenth century. Though the
Hague Peace Conference, which ended only a few months before
the start of the war, was marked by hesitation and suspicion
among the delegates and by scepticism and dismissal among the
world's governments, the war forced men of all shades of opinion
to declare themselves on the issues of war and empire. It brought
into the open the confused thinking of organizations such as the
Fabians on these matters, and it provided a centre of action for
others that had high ideals, such as the Ethical Movement, but
few commitments as yet.[1]

All over Britain—indeed, all over the western world—liberal,
radical, socialist, humanitarian, feminist and religious leaders and
groups were stung into militant pacifism. Organizations such as
the Transvaal Committee, the Stop the War Committee, the
National Reform Union, and the South African Conciliation
Committee gathered an enormous momentum of publicity (if not
of influence) which filled the English press for at least the first
year of the war, led to blows at several public meetings, came to a
climax during the Khaki Election of October 1900, and left its
traces in the form of thousands of pamphlets.[2] Through the

[1] For discussions of the pro-Boer movement, see A. P. Thornton, *The Imperial Idea
and its Enemies* (London: Macmillan, 1959), ch. 3; B. Porter, *Critics of Empire*
(London: Macmillan, 1968); and Stephen Koss, ed., *The Pro-Boers: The Anatomy of
an Antiwar Movement* (Chicago: Chicago University Press, 1973).
[2] John S. Galbraith, 'The Pamphlet Campaign of the Boer War', *J. of Mod. Hist.*, 24

agency of men such as Montagu White, Consul-General of the South African Republic in London and a keen propagandist, the English pro-Boer movement kept in close touch with its continental counterpart as well as with Kruger's Government and his Brussels-based minister plenipotentiary, Dr W. J. Leyds, with the result that a great deal of anti-war, pro-Boer material was made freely available to the British public and press.[3]

The war threw the Liberal Party into especial confusion and accentuated the malaise that had existed in the party ever since the departure of Gladstone and its pettifogging performance over the Jameson Raid in 1896.[4] Liberal attitudes to empire covered a complete spectrum from vociferous acceptance to total rejection. On the one hand Joseph Chamberlain, ex-Liberal, Colonial Secretary, and one of the chief engineers of the war, had much support among Liberal Imperialists; on the other hand virulent opponents of war and empire, socialists and radicals such as John Burns and Lloyd George, still regarded themselves as Liberals. John Ramsbottom's 'A Letter on the Crisis', which appeared in the *Spectator* just before the war (30 September 1899), lightly but neatly pinpointed some of the moral and strategic conflicts Liberals were going to have to resolve in the course of the war:

> Supposing now that we are wrong
> With Kruger, just because we're strong,
> I guess again that those are right
> Whom he's oppressing with his might. . . .
> My friend—'tis John I mean—protests
> Against financial interests,
> And cunning men of greedy mind
> Who have a private axe to grind.
> Does he deny there're others who
> Have axes in Pretoria too?

(1952), 111–26. See Koss, pp. xxiv–xxv, for the finer distinctions between the aims and methods of the various anti-war committees.

[3] See the Montagu White papers in Rhodes House, Oxford, MSS. Afr. s. 116; and the Leyds Collection, State Archives, Pretoria.

[4] See Jeffrey Butler, *The Liberal Party and the Jameson Raid* (Oxford: Clarendon Press, 1968). I am also indebted to Halévy, *Imperialism and the Rise of Labour*, and D. A. Hamer, *Liberal Politics in the Age of Gladstone and Rosebery* (Oxford: Clarendon Press, 1972), in the discussion of Liberal reactions that follows.

Three groups emerged within the Liberal Party and among its supporters in the course of the war. A powerful section under Lords Rosebery and Grey formed the Liberal Imperialists and to all intents and purposes supported Chamberlain. A second, smaller group under the guidance of the Party's nominal leader, Sir Henry Campbell-Bannerman, supported by writers such as W. T. Stead, G. K. Chesterton, and Hilaire Belloc, did not oppose imperialism in principle, but argued that it had miscarried badly in South Africa. Thirdly, a small, impressive, but ultimately powerless group, shading off into the rapidly growing socialist and labour movement and represented by the radical Henry Labouchère, John Morley, Lloyd George, John Burns, and J. A. Hobson, opposed imperialism root and branch. Their views about war and empire were those of international socialism as set out by Tolstoi in a letter he wrote to the *Revista Popolare* of Rome at the outbreak of the war, and as adumbrated by James Sims, President of the Labour Church Union, in the *Ethical World* (6 October 1900), during the Khaki Election:

We have a Government in power likely to land us into war even further than it has done, and apparently only waiting a favourable opportunity to increase its military power at home; ... a House of Commons (likely to be returned again) the obsequious and willing servant of the landlord, the capitalist, and brewery magnates; ... a National Church giving its blessing to wholesale murder and rapine; teaching the honour and glory of war in its schools; drilling its youth with mimic guns, and familiarizing them to instant obedience to the word of military command.

Each of the Liberal groups had a sizeable daily and periodical press. By 1900 mass-literacy was well-established, and if we were to believe with J. A. Hobson that the war had largely been engineered by financiers controlling the press, we would also have to accept that opponents of war managed to put their case more volubly, more insistently, and to a much larger audience (particularly among the working classes) than in any previous war. In this paper campaign verse was front-line ammunition on both sides, but was perhaps used more adroitly by anti-imperialists than by their opponents. Sometimes it served no further purpose than to provide mnemonic emphasis to a slogan, or to phrase a catchy version of a complex argument. On 29 October 1899, for instance, *Reynold's Newspaper* embellished the news of the Queen's

distress at the first casualties in South Africa with a poem by
W. Hipp:

> Just think of the 'glory' of losing a leg,
> An eye, or an arm (or even a head);
> Such trifles as these are only a part
> Of the pain which is felt by your Queen's 'bleeding' heart.

On 12 November an epigram (anti-Semitic, as so often in these
papers) punctuated an analysis of the financial interests benefiting
from the war:

> Oh, Tommy, Tommy Atkins,
> My heart beats sore for you,
> To be made the bloomin' catspaw
> Of the all-pervading Jew.
> And when you're back in England
> Invalided, full of care,
> You'll find you've drawn the chestnuts
> For the multi-millionaire.

Much of the Boer War verse campaign was conducted on this
level.

Moderate Liberals who opposed the war were frequently ambivalent about imperialism. They seemed to harbour an uneasy conviction that, while universal British rule was perhaps still the
greatest blessing that Britain could bestow upon the world, late-
Victorian imperialism had become too tainted with 'the tactics of
the company promoter and the morals of the mining camp'
(Young, *Victorian England*, p. 183). Consequently, since their
avowed aim was to shake the gold-dust of South Africa off their
feet, they had to repudiate imperial extortion even while up-
holding an ideal of British imperial mission that could not readily
be separated from the more seamy aspects of expansionism. An
early version of this dichotomy appeared in Olive Schreiner's
Trooper Peter Halket of Mashonaland (1897), in which the soon-to-be
bitter opponent of war and imperialism still subscribed to the
vision of a *moral* Greater Britain, objecting only to the more
blatantly commercial ventures of Cecil Rhodes and his like.

During the Boer War one of the leading figures in this operation
to salvage Britain's moral greatness from the murky waters of a
stockbroker empire was G. K. Chesterton. In 'A Song of Defeat'

(*Poems*, 1915) he does it by separating the 'financiers' from the main current of English life and by describing them as racially inferior:

> When the mongrel men that the market classes
> Had slimy hands upon England's rod,
> And sword in hand upon Afric's passes
> Her last Republic cried to God.

The same moral aloofness marks 'Africa', though in this sonnet we find a greater willingness to shoulder the blame as well as a more sharply phrased indictment:

> A sleepy people, without priests or kings,
>   Dreamed here, men say, to drive us to the sea:
> O let us drive ourselves! For it is free
> And smells of honour and of English things.
> How came we brawling by these bitter springs,
>   We of the North?—two kindly nations—we?
> Though the dice rattles and the clear coin rings,
>   Here is no place for living men to be.
> Leave them the gold that worked and whined for it,
>   Let them that have no nation anywhere
>   Be native here, and fat and full of bread;
> But we, whose sins were human, we will quit
>   The land of blood, and leave these vultures there,
>   Noiselessly happy, feeding on the dead.

Chesterton's lifelong associate, Hilaire Belloc, wrote in much the same vein. 'The Leader' (*Verses*, 1910) depicts Britain's imperial destiny as an armed and fleeing figure, challenging the torpid money-grubbers of the moment:

> The sword fell down: I heard the knell;
> I thought that ease was best,
> And sullen men that buy and sell
> Were host: and I was guest.
> All unashamed I sat with swine,
> We shook the dice for war,
> The night was drunk with an evil wine—
> But she went on before.

'Verses to a Lord' explains that those who opposed the war objected to its speculators, not its soldiers, and tries to lay the blame for the war at the feet of Jewish financiers.

That some kind of diabolical capitalist conspiracy lurked behind the war was a widespread belief. The most prominent exponent of the theory that both war and imperialism were inherent in capitalism was J. A. Hobson. In three successive works which appeared during the Boer War he elaborated the theory that 'the economic root of Imperialism is the desire of strong organized industrial and financial interests to secure and develop at the public expense and by the public force private markets for their surplus goods and their surplus capital. War, militarism, and a "spirited foreign policy" are the necessary means to this end.'[5] Thus, he argued, the so-called grievances of the 'Uitlanders' in the Transvaal and the question of British suzerainty in Southern Africa were merely red herrings dragged in by a capitalist-controlled press in order to precipitate a war that would ensure tighter control of the mines for Rhodes and his associates. Furthermore, he repeatedly stressed 'the absurdity of spending half our financial resources in fighting to secure foreign markets at times when hungry mouths, ill-clad backs, ill-furnished houses indicate countless unsatisfied material wants among our own population' (*Imperialism*, p. 86).

Hobson's theories were cogently argued and widely accepted in the socialist, anti-war press. 'From the first', wrote *Reynold's Newspaper* (29 October 1899), 'we have told our readers the plain truth—that the Outlander grievances were made the pretext for a war on the Transvaal to seize the mines and weld them into a gigantic syndicate, just as was done with the diamond mines at Kimberley.' Stead's *War Against War* (16 March 1900) put Hobson into verse:

'Whom Rhodes deceives is well deceived,' the story will be told—
And faith, you've been colossally deceived.
For they've run a little factory of falsehoods and of Gold,
And whatever lie they've fashioned you've believed.

On Christmas Day, 1899, the *Daily Chronicle* published Richard Le Gallienne's somewhat unsubtle but fierce contrast between the blood of the slain and the festivities of the rich:

And you, ye merchants, you that eat and cheat,
Gold-seeking hucksters in a noble land,

[5] *Imperialism* (1902; 3rd ed., revised, London: Allen & Unwin, 1938), p. 106. Hobson's two other books on the war were: *The War in South Africa* (London: James Nisbet, 1900), and *The Psychology of Jingoism* (London: Grant Richards, 1901).

> Think when you lift the wine up in your hand
> Of a fierce vintage, tragically red,
> Red wine of the hearts of English soldiers dead,
> Who ran to a wild death with laughing feet.

These views were bound to appear at the front as well. Major
C. G. Dennison found it difficult to refute his elderly Boer captor
who argued: 'You and I . . . cannot help these things. We are not
the cause of the war; it is Rhodes's war, it is a war caused by the
capitalists of the Rand. We only must do our duty, though we
suffer for it, you for your side, I for mine.'[6] Both sides treated the
'Rand refugees', the polyglot commercial inhabitants of Johannesburg who fled to the coastal cities on the outbreak of war, with
equal and undisguised contempt. Donald Macdonald, who witnessed their departure from Johannesburg, described them as
'human garbage'; Lionel James, who saw them returning a year
later when the Golden City was safe once more, launched a
virulent attack against this 'mass of degraded manhood' whom he
dubbed the 'Mount Nelson Light Horse' after the famous Cape
Town hotel which formed the city's social centre during the war.[7]
The Christmas 1900 number of *Truth* developed James's attack
into caustic satire:

> Go to the front, forsooth! Not they;
> The streets of Cape Town they invaded,
> Held the hotels in mighty force,
> And all the drinking-bars blockaded. . . .
> Above the popping of their corks
> They cannot hear the sounds they dread—
> The shrieks of sorely wounded men,
> The sound of shrapnel overhead;
> Above their conversation's hum
> The roar of lyddite does not come.

One of the more delightful poems on the incongruities of
imperial ventures which involved public patriotism as much as
private gain was Grant Allen's 'The Bold Buccaneer', written at
the time of the Jameson Raid but frequently resurrected during
the Boer War. A bard—clearly a caricature of Alfred Austin—

---

[6] C. G. Dennison, *A Fight to a Finish* (London: Longman, 1904), p. 153.
[7] Macdonald, *How We Kept the Flag Flying*, p. 40; Lionel James ('The Intelligence
Officer'), *On the Heels of De Wet* (London: Blackwood, 1902), p. 120.

overwhelms a returning raider with a paean of praise, quite
heedless of the latter's attempt to tell the true story:

> The poet, he heaved a quiet sigh.
> 'Yet still, 'twas a glorious cause', he cried,
> 'For your country's sake you strove to die.'
> The bold buccaneer, he stepped aside.
> 'You don't understand finance,' said he;
> "T was the glorious cause of £. s. d.'[8]

If J. A. Hobson provided the intellectual centre for the pro-
Boer movement, W. T. Stead was its main propagandist, with
one important reservation: Stead was not anti-imperialist. Indeed,
as late as 1895 Olive Schreiner could write about him: 'When
you discuss Rhodes with him he always says "Ah but think of the
noble work for Jesus and Civilization he is doing in Mashonaland." '[9] He remained throughout a supporter of enlightened
imperialism, particularly imperial federation, and though Rhodes's
complicity in the Jameson Raid shook his unbounded admiration
for the Colossus, it was against Chamberlain and his own former
colleague on the *Pall Mall Gazette*, Alfred Milner, that he directed
his voluminous scorn during the Boer War, rather than against
Rhodes.

His main arguments, repeated ad nauseam in editorials in his
Review of Reviews and *War Against War*, were that the South
African imbroglio dissipated the strength of Britain; laid her
possessions open to the predatoriness of empires that did not share
Britain's enlightened aims; and, by compromising Britain's
diplomatic *bona fides*, jeopardized the role she chould play in
establishing international machinery of arbitration that would
obviate all future wars (*Rev. of Reviews*, January and March 1900).
He was an ardent pacifist and played a major part in convening
the Hague Peace Conference.

In this amalgamation of imperialism and pacifism Stead
exhibited exactly that curious dichotomy we have already seen in
poets such as Binyon, Thompson, and even Kipling: the inability

---

[8] *Morning Leader*, 16 Feb. 1900; *Clarion*, 24 Feb. 1900.
[9] Letter to the Revd. G. W. Cross, Grahamstown, *ca.* 1895, now in the Cory Library
for Historical Research, Rhodes University, MS. 14,462. See Warren S. Smith, *The
London Heretics 1870–1914* (London: Constable, 1967), pp. 265–70; and Joseph O.
Baylen, 'W. T. Stead and the Boer War: The Irony of Idealism', *Canadian Hist. Rev.*,
40 (1959), 304–14, for discussions of Stead's Boer War activities, and Koss, pp. xxiv–
xxv, for the view that Stead did more harm than good.

to see that peace and the interests of competing empires, however humane, made conflicting demands on international politics. Another poet with this particular blind spot was George Barlow, whose *To the Women of England* (1901) reads like versified Stead. Barlow believed that empire should have higher aims than mere conquest:

> To widen Empire to earth's furthest bound
> Is not to rule, to triumph, to succeed.
>
> ('Leaderless')

But, like Stead, he did not find his vision of a civilizing, pacifist empire incompatible with the argument that Britain would have to fight for her possessions one day and was now wasting her resources in South Africa:

> Each warrior wasted in a worthless quarrel,
> Means one sword less when England's strife begins. . . .
> Who shall atone for the countless corpses, rotten
> On those far plains that England's blood makes red?
>
> ('England's Choice')

In *Vox Clamantis* (1904) and *Songs of England Awakening* (1909) Barlow continued these dire warnings, aiming them ever more clearly at the German threat. He died, however, in 1913, without witnessing the catastrophe to which the demands of competing empires inevitably had to lead. Stead had died the year before, in the *Titanic* disaster.

Throughout his career Stead was a prolific journalist. As editor of the *Pall Mall Gazette* (1883–90) he inaugurated the 'new journalism'—sensational, commercial, repetitive, and easily digestible.[10] At the time of the Boer War he often turned out 12,000 words a day, a prodigious output that went into numerous book-length pamphlets attacking the Government's, especially Chamberlain's, handling of the war. *The Candidates of Cain, Shall I Slay my Brother Boer?*, *Methods of Barbarism*, and *Joseph Chamberlain: Conspirator or Statesman?* were some of the thumping titles through which Stead spoke to the nation. His books cannibalized one another or were nourished by the *Review of Reviews* and *War Against War*. All gave extensive coverage to pro-Boer items appearing in the continental press, to stories of atrocities committed in South Africa, and especially to news from soldiers and

[10] Montgomery, *1900*, p. 154.

correspondents at the front sickened by the war. *The Candidates of Cain*, for instance, is a compendium of stories such as the following, culled from the *Manchester Guardian:*

In ten miles we have burned no fewer than six farm houses; the wife watched from her sick husband's bedside the burning of her home a hundred yards away. It seems as though a kind of domestic murder were being committed. I stood till late last night and saw the flames lick round each piece of poor furniture, . . . and when I saw the poor housewife's face pressed against the window of the neighbouring house, my own heart burned with outrage.

Every week *War Against War* published, within heavy black margins, 'Mr. Chamberlain's Butcher's Bill', consisting of the week's casualty list and Chamberlain's comment in the House of Commons on 25 October 1899: 'I still find myself absolutely unrepentant.'

Stead's publications formed the main pabulum of the anti-war movement and the poetry that formed part of it. *War Against War* must have inspired many an indignant rhyme, and in turn it not only reprinted the war poems of established poets, such as Hardy and William Watson, but also published the work of numerous obscurer versifiers. W.H.H.'s 'Our Willidge', which appeared on 27 October 1899, was one of the more touching of the many which the first few weeks of the war produced:

> Owd Snooks, wot druv the carrier's cart,
> 'E browt the news from Sat'dy's mart,
> In a London piper as 'eld the list
> Of kilt an' wownded, lorst an' miss'd;
> So Joey the ploughmin, 'is tears they run,
> F'r 'e's seed the last of a gallant son.
> (' 'Ard times, this winter')

Mary A. M. Marks's 'The End of the Century' (29 December 1899) was a more than usually competent poem on the sad realization that the Victorian era's great hopes of liberty and progress were collapsing in war and bloodshed:

> Not thus we deem'd 'twould be, long, long ago . . .
> But now . . .
> Pale hate, red-eyed revenge, stalk fierce and grim
> In all the dreadful panoply of War:
> While upon the hill and valley-side afar
> The dead lie cold beneath the Southern Star.

In a rare moment of self-parody the paper reprinted 'The Wandering Pro-Boer' from the *Morning Post* (23 March 1900), a delightful skirmish, in imitation of 'The Ancient Mariner', at some future date between an aged pacifist pregnant with good speech and an unwilling auditor:

> 'With bursting heart from town to town
> I wandered, and to each
> I offered on my hands and knees
> To make that single speech.
>
> 'On hands and knees I humbly went,
> To plead the cause of Peace,
> In vain, in vain! I ever left
> Escorted by police.' . . .
>
> I waited while he mouthed his speech—
> Wild, wild the words and rash;
> And at the end my aged friend
> Had crumbled into ash.

Several other Liberal writers as well as a substantial section of the Liberal press supported Stead's anti-war campaign.[11] The *Star*, the *Manchester Guardian*, the *Westminster Gazette*, the *Morning Leader*, the *Daily Chronicle*, and the *Daily News* regularly gave space to verse, often thoughtful pieces such as Meredith's unflattering view of history, 'At the Close', in the *Chronicle*, 16 November 1899:

> So in all times of man's descent insane
> To brute, did strength and craft combining strike,
> Even as a God of Armies, his fell blow;

or his scathing exposure of the treatment of the common soldier in the *Westminster Gazette*, 18 February 1901—'Atkins':

> Yonder's the man with his life in his hand,
> Legs on the march for whatever the land,
> Or to the slaughter, or to the maiming,
> Getting the dole of a dog for pay. . . .
> Exquisite humour! that gives him a naming
> Base to the ear as an ass's bray.

---

[11] See Koss, pp. xxix-x, for the vagaries of the Liberal press during the war. The *Daily Chronicle*, for instance, became imperialist; the *Daily News*, anti-imperialist.

Among periodicals Henry Labouchère's *Truth*, T. W. H. Crosland's *Outlook*, the *Speaker*, the *Pall Mall Magazine*, and the *Westminster* and *Fortnightly Reviews* either took a pro-Boer stance, or at least adopted, in the words of Crosland's biographer, an attitude of 'reasonable imperialism', campaigning for 'a cleaner, brighter, and saner England' rather than expansion abroad.[12] All published verse which, like Crosland's columns of 'Outlook Odes' or *Truth*'s editorial satire, regularly pounced on current blunders of army or empire. Rhodes's statement that the Union Jack was 'the greatest commercial asset in the world' sent reverberations in rhyme through *Truth*, and so, too, did reports of incompetent generalship (12 April 1900):

> Small use it is for 'Tommy', brought to bay,
> To fight until he's not another cartridge,
> If those who lead him show of common sense
> No more than moves the average driven partridge.

S.G.O.'s 'An Ovation', in the *Speaker* (8 June 1900), drew an even less forgiving contrast between commander and commanded:

> For him the gilded coronet,
> This man of sombre enterprise;
> For us and for our sons the wet
> Wide fields of carnage 'neath the skies.

Crosland's 'Outlook Odes' were not particularly sympathetic towards the Boers, but *Outlook* nevertheless published some of the war's most compassionate poems, possibly because of the editor's own poetic concern with the war. His 'Slain' appeared here, and so did Henry de Vere Stackpole's 'The Dead Warrior' on 10 February 1900:

> He flung his life away
> Just as he flung his pay;
> His pence to the canteen,
> His life to serve the Queen.

Crosland celebrated the end of the war with a striking anonymous poem, 'May 31, 1902', which paid a deft tribute to the Boers' honourable defeat after two years of guerrilla warfare:

> Beleaguered in the hills,
> Grim Winter will not yield;

12 W. S. Brown, *The Life and Genius of T. W. H. Crosland* (London: Cecil Palmer, 1928), p. 69.

Behind an ice-bright shield
A braggart blast he shrills.
And though, by day, the hot besieging sun,
Searching his dizzy berg with far-flung fire,
May melt its crystal ramparts one by one,
By night, the work's undone;
Frost, moon, and stars conspire,
And morning sees new bastions pilèd higher.
Until the waxing days
The dwindling eves outwear,
And nights may scarce repair
Walls that fierce noons will raze.
Then, grandly beaten, in unbroken pride,
The rebel heeds the trumpets of the King,
And hies him down the sounding mountain-side;
Torrents all round him sing
And race to lowlands wide,
Scented and gemmed with sweet bright flowers of Spring.

Much of the poetic effort of the Liberal press went into satire, lampoon, and caricature. The epigraph to this chapter quotes D. F. Hannigan's appeal to the spirit of Byron, but it was to Lewis Carroll rather than Byron that most of the popular lampoonists turned for inspiration, producing works such as *The Westminster Alice, Clara in Blunderland* (1902), and *Lost in Blunderland* (1903). *Clara in Blunderland*, by 'Caroline Lewis' (in fact, Harold Begbie and others), contains some sprightly parodies, such as 'You are old, Father John' and 'Porlokrocky' (on Kruger):

They packed their Milner to the Cape;
Long time they drawled on this and that—
So footled they on the dum-dum lay,
And piffled as they sat.
And as in snifty mood they piffed,
The Porlokrock, with soul aflame,
Came slimming through the spruity drift,
Pom-pomming as he came!

Sir Wilfrid Lawson, Liberal M.P. and clever comic rhymester, co-operated with a *Westminster Gazette* cartoonist, F. C. Gould, to produce the amusing *Cartoons in Rhyme and Line* (1905) which inveighed against the prevailing 'blessed "Rule Britannia" brag'. It was only one of many works of verse provoked by the cheap jingoism and aggressive expansionism of the time, though not all were marked by Lawson's sense of humour. Anthony George Shiell's *Pro-Boer Lyrics*, for instance, was shot through with a near-pathological hatred of empire.

Compared to the earnest doggerel of many such verse-makers, the work of William Watson takes on a compelling quality. His *For England* (1904), subtitled 'Poems Written During Estrangement', continued a theme started in *The Purple East* (1896) and *The Year of Shame* (1897): a lament for the failure of Gladstonian liberalism and the advent of the febrile new imperialism. The inevitable accusations of anti-patriotism that these works provoked he described, in a dedicatory letter to Leonard Courtney in *For England*, as 'odious to one who has prided himself on being peculiarly English in his sympathies and sentiments, and who comes of many generations of such Englishmen as fought indomitably for faith and commonweal'.

Inspired by the political sonnets of Milton and Wordsworth, especially the latter's 'Poems Dedicated to National Independence and Liberty', Watson took upon himself the solemn task of chastising his country for the scandalous dereliction of its liberal traditions:

> Friend, call me what you will: no jot care I:
> I that shall stand for England till I die.
> England! The England that rejoiced to see
> Hellas unbound, Italy one and free;
> The England that had tears for Poland's doom,
> And in her heart for all the world made room.
> ('On Being Styled "Pro-Boer" ')

Several of the poems in *For England* first appeared in the *Speaker*, the *Fortnightly*, and other liberal publications, and became the stock-in-trade of the pro-Boer press, a fact which gave them the unfair reputation of being no more than versified journalism. Watson, however, was concerned with larger issues. His rejection of military imperialism and his regard for England's pre-industrial, rural simplicity led him to an idealized view of the Boers' pastoral and independent existence. Hence 'The Enemy' reads as a crisp epitome of the rural myth woven round the Boers which affected most of Europe during the war:

> Unskilled in Letters, and in Arts unversed;
> Ignorant of empire; bounded in their view

By the lone billowing veldt, where they upgrew
Amid great silences; a people nursed
Apart—the far-sown seed of them that erst
Not Alva's sword could tame: now, blindly hurled
Against the march of the majestic world,
They fight and die, with dauntless bosoms curst.

After Kitchener introduced his 'burnt earth' and concentration camp policies in order to contain the Boers' guerrilla campaign, Watson warned—quite correctly—that the resentment inspired by the suffering of women and children would merely ensure the Boers' eventual domination of the whole sub-continent:

We thought to fire but farmsteads: we have lit
A flame less transient in the hearts of men. . . .
Redder from our red hoof-prints the wild rose
Of freedom shall afresh hereafter spring,
And in our own despite are we the sires
Of liberty, as night begets the day.

('Achievement')

'Calamity makes them great', he wrote in 'The Unsubdued'. He saw, too, that ultimately the grave made Briton and Boer indistinguishable, that it pronounced their quarrel meaningless and their deaths more noteworthy than their cause:

Already is your strife become as nought;
Idle the bullet's flight, the bayonet's thrust,
The senseless cannon's dull, unmeaning word;
Idle your feud; and all for which ye fought
To this arbitrament of loam referred,
And cold adjudication of the dust.

('The Slain')

If Liberalism came near to grief over the Boer War, the rapidly growing Labour movement cut its teeth on the same issues. The Boer War debate made an important contribution towards the isolation and definition of socialist as against traditional liberal objectives, particularly on the issues of war and empire. Organized socialism was forced, for the first time, to make up its mind about imperialism, and the initial effect was one of confusion.[13] Socialist

[13] I rely in this discussion of socialist responses to the Boer War on: Bernard Semmel, *Imperialism and Social Reform 1895–1914* (Cambridge, Mass., 1960); Brian Simon, *Education and the Labour Movement 1870–1918* (London, 1965); Richard Price,

thinking about empire covered an enormous spectrum, from the 'social imperialism' of the Tories to the outright rejection, on the part of early communists, of everything that smelt of capitalism. The aggressive appeal of racial imperialism had obvious attractions for a working class from whose ranks most of the men in the army were drawn and who shared with the lower middle classes the jingo nourishment of a cheap press and the music hall. 'They would like a bloody battle twice a day, so that breakfast and supper might have a relish, and ennui be chased away,' wrote George Sturt about the response of villagers and farm labourers to the war.[14] At a higher level of theoretical socialism, Shaw and the Fabians voted, after much debate, for imperialism and support of the war, though H. T. Muggeridge's review of *Fabianism and the Empire* (1900)—largely Shaw's work—in the *Ethical World* (13 October 1900), gives some measure of the fierce reaction that this decision provoked among fellow socialists: 'A more inept misconception of the nature of the opposition of the Socialist party to the present phase of Imperialism it would be impossible to conceive.'

For other socialists, inspired by the kind of argument seen in Hobson's writings, the war was a 6,000-mile distant irrelevancy drawing attention from the pressing social issues at home:

We are spending £100,000,000 in slaughter, in order to soothe the offended pride of Englishmen in the Transvaal who were making millions if they were capitalists, and earning £1 a day if they were workmen; meanwhile, 55,000 children are driven every day hungry and underfed into the public [i.e. charity] schools of London. (*Stop the War Committee's Publications*, No. 13.)

For some, indeed, the war was concerned with issues which even in South Africa had little relevance, and, with the benefit of hindsight, the modern reader may well be amazed that so few socialists bothered themselves with the point H. M. Hyndman made in *Justice* (20 July 1901): '[The war is] a struggle between two burglars. . . . The country belongs neither to Boer nor to Briton. . . . The future of South Africa is, I believe, to the black man.'

An Imperial War and the British Working Class (London: Routledge, Kegan Paul, 1972); and Ian Henderson, 'The Attitude and Policy of the Main Section of the British Labour Movement to Imperial Issues', B. Litt. dissertation, Oxford 1964.
[14] *Journals*, 24 Oct. 1899.

No doubt shrewder socialists also recognized that their opposition to war was inspired by a class distinction. If, as I suggested
in Chapter I, the heroic view of war and imperial conquest was
appropriate to an upper class reared in public schools and
accustomed to command, then the iconoclastic view of war as
unheroic and socially disruptive was probably inevitable among
at least the spokesmen of those classes who had been under
command in the past but were now finding a voice of their own.
A story of a Labour meeting in Battersea during the Khaki
Election of 1900 illustrates how working class flirtation with the
imperial fervour of the day could be cut short very peremptorily.
John Burns, sitting radical M.P. for Battersea, managed to turn a
hostile crowd of 5,000, full of the joys of Mafeking Night, into an
audience of enthusiastic supporters within a few minutes, simply
by playing off working class needs against Government expenditure on the war. Here is the *Ethical World*'s description of the
scene:

The man who came to howl the speaker down and to create riot by
shouting premeditated insult, remained to listen and support. The
khaki-clad soldier invalided home, and who was to be one of the chief
instruments in securing the reactionary triumph, stands on the edge of
the crowd, and punctuates with approving cheers and comments the
denunciation of the war and its authors. . . . Unskilled labourers, with
brothers or cousins in the Transvaal, called out as Reservists, hand up
to the platform letters disclosing the needless sufferings of our troops
or containing a eulogy of the character of the Boers. . . . It is proof of
how shallow the whole movement for military conquest has been.
(22 September 1900.)

In this way the Boer War came to establish firmly what may be
called the working class view of war, in which the soldier is seen
primarily as bread-winner and not, in the first place, as patriot
(the middle class view), or as dashing professional (the upper class
view).

In spite, then, of some initial confusion about the appropriate
socialist reaction to the war, the majority of socialists eventually
came down firmly in condemnation of the war, if not always of
empire itself. The lasting image a present-day reader derives from
the files of contemporary socialist papers, and particularly from the
polemical verse in them, is one of a fiery and unanimous con-

demnation of the war, based almost invariably on the notion of a capitalist conspiracy at the working man's expense.

Verse as a medium of anti-establishment propaganda had a vigorous Victorian ancestry. Popular ballads of the sort recorded in John Ashton's *Modern Street Ballads* (1888) formed one branch of this tradition:

> For your most gracious Majesty
> May see what wretched poverty
> Is to be found on England's ground,
>   Now you are Queen of England.
>   ('Queen Victoria', 1837.)

'Except the Crown, no institution is safe from ridicule in the ballads of the people,' wrote Michael MacDonagh in the *Nineteenth Century*, 54 (1903), 458–71, and his one reservation can be easily disproved. The balladry of the socialist press revelled in iconoclasm, and the monarchy enjoyed no particular sanctity. Another branch of socialist verse can be traced back to the humanitarian concerns of Shelley's 'Queen Mab', quoted by Keir Hardie in the *Labour Leader* on 18 November 1899; Elizabeth Barrett Browning's 'The Cry of the Children' (1844) and 'A Song for the Ragged Schools of London' (1862); and Thomas Hood's 'The Song of the Shirt' (1843):

> Oh God! that bread should be so dear
> And flesh and blood so cheap.

Ernest Jones's *Battle-Day* (1855), Alsagar Hill's *Poor Law Rhymes* (1871), William Morris's *Chants for Socialists* (1884), and the verse of Harriet Martineau, W. H. Mallock, and Roden Noel continued this tradition of socialist protest poetry imbued with apocalyptic fervour.

The Boer War produced an epidemic of such work, much of it already quoted in these pages. *Reynold's Newspaper*, *Justice*, and the *Labour Leader* led the way in the verse campaign, with smaller papers, such as the *Clarion*, *Echo*, and *Daylight*, providing supporting fire. *Reynold's* quoted Longfellow's powerful 'The Arsenal at Springfield' at the outbreak of the war, as well as Dickens's exposure (in *The Uncommercial Traveller*) of the treatment of sick soldiers after the Indian Mutiny, and warned eager volunteers that they would end up, like their predecessors, in the workhouse.

It dubbed the mine-owners 'Randlords' and 'Ooflanders', and cleverly juxtaposed news from Cape Town about the gay life of 'refugees' with accounts of anxious throngs at the War Office waiting for lists of casualties. Jingo parsons were the paper's especial *bêtes noires* and were dealt with crudely:

> O Lord, Thou knowest our anguish sore
> When Blacks are butchered by the Boer;
> 'Tis our prerogative of yore
> To slaughter niggers;
> Only to make them love Thee more
> We pull our triggers.
> ('Holy Hughie's Prayer', 22 October 1899.)

The *Labour Leader* shared these sentiments, publishing verse such as 'Socialists and the War', by 'Gleaner', on 4 November 1899:

> When grass waves over heroes' graves,
> And reason finds her voice,
> What thoughts the widow's tears shall dry,
> Or orphan hearts rejoice?

Justice, mouthpiece of the most important of late-Victorian socialist movements, H. M. Hyndman's Social Democratic Federation, admitted on 13 January 1900 that the war 'does seem to have occasioned some confusion of thought among a certain number of Socialists', but most of the doggerel in its pages took a fairly obvious line of condemnation:

> Let Rhodes arise, or Kruger fall,
> The wage-slave's portion is the same;
> He gets his hovel, takes his wage,
> And feeds with wealth the vile class game.
> ('A Socialist Prayer to the God of Battles',
> 23 December 1899.)

As we saw in an earlier chapter, the paper regarded Kipling and imperialism as virtually synonymous, so that much of its polemical verse was cast in the form of Kiplingesque parody.

It is impossible to keep socialist-inspired verse separate from the much wider field of poetry cultivated by the ethical, humanitarian, nonconformist, and pacifist movements of the time. These organizations, opposed in a multiplicity of ways to all or some of the establishments of army, state church, and empire, ultimately all derived—like much in socialism itself—from the religious dissent of the early nineteenth century. Hence their publications often cannibalized one another, and their leading figures, such as J. A. Hobson, Bernard Shaw, Havelock Ellis, and Edward Carpenter, were intellectual pluralists, active in dozens of societies and responsible for an enormous output of polemic in numerous journals. Indeed, Shaw's Reverend James Morell (*Candida*, 1895) has all the makings of a caricature of men such as the Revd. Silas K. Hocking and John Page Hopps, who appeared with striking regularity on pro-Boer platforms, under various different banners.

Kitson Clark has pointed out that Victorian England produced the world's first truly humanitarian society.[15] This became abundantly clear in the late-Victorian radical intellectual's reaction to the Boer War, particularly to the 'methods of barbarism' devised to curb the protracted guerrilla campaign—farm burning, concentration camps, the transportation of Boer prisoners of war to distant colonies, and the execution of Cape Colony rebels. And war was not merely physically abhorrent. Its really deleterious effects were seen to be the erosion of man's moral being:

The last evil of war is not its ruin of cities, wasting of homes, or burning of cornfields; not its plague, its famine, or its fire; . . . the peculiar sin [of war] is that it corrupts while it consumes, that it demoralizes while it destroys. . . . The damage it inflicts upon the persons and property of men is trifling beside the damage it inflicts upon the morals; and it is this that is exciting in thoughtful minds a fresh interest in the whole military conception.[16]

These words of Walter Walsh adumbrate the ideas that inspired the work of Emily Hobhouse in South Africa, the editorial policies of a score of periodicals, the activities of numerous anti-war organizations, and the verse of many poets.

Several publications appeared under explicitly pacifist mastheads. Among them were *Concord*, 'The Journal of the International Arbitration and Peace Association'; *Brotherhood*, 'Designed to Help the Peaceful Evolution of a Juster and Happier Social

15 *The Making of Victorian England*, p. 62.
16 Walter Walsh, *The Moral Damage of War* (London: R. Brimley Johnson, 1902), p. 7.

Order'; and the *Herald of Peace and International Arbitration*. All published verse. The *Herald* proposed, in November 1900, a competition for 'a good, rattling Peace song . . . to neutralize the popular [jingo] rubbish', but the results were not inspiring. Pacifist verse was often shrill and hardly peaceful, as in Edward Carpenter's 'Empire', which appeared in *Concord*, July 1900:

> O England, thou old hypocrite, thou sham, thou
> Bully of weak nations whom thou wert called to aid;

or it was simplistic (not to say simple-minded) in the recurrent argument that soldiers were merely passive and pathetic gun fodder, as in B. Paul Neuman's 'The Voice of England', once again from *Concord*, March 1900:

> For brave and simple are the gathering hosts
> Who move like dumb beasts to the shambles led,
> Who hear the word and take their ordered posts,
> Nor know the cause for which their blood is shed.

These faults also flaw much of the verse that appeared in the two most influential humanitarian publications of the period, the *Ethical World* and *New Age*. The former carried regular contributions by writers such as Herbert Spencer, J. A. Hobson, Edward Carpenter, and John Morley, and, during the first few weeks of the war, an influential series of articles by Olive Schreiner, entitled 'The African Boer', which aroused much sympathy for the Boer cause. The paper's stand on war was clear-cut: 'Reduced to its simplest elements, war is the wickedest absurdity ever invented by the human race. That a lot of men should go out into a field, and kill a lot of other men whom they have never seen before, and with whom they personally have not the remotest cause of quarrel, is surely a strange phenomenon,' wrote editor Stanton Coit on 4 November 1899. On 10 February 1900 he published Herbert Spencer's gloomy prognosis—'We are in the course of rebarbarization; and there is no prospect but that of military despotisms, which we are rapidly approaching'—a statement which suggests that pacifists were at times given to as much extravagant fervour as militarists and imperialists.

The *Ethical World* published relatively little verse; *New Age* a great deal, much of it collected in *Songs of the Veld* (1902). It took the lead in various campaigns for radical reform and published several important socialist documents, such as the *Encyclopaedia of Social Reform* (1903), edited by W. D. P. Bliss and counting Sydney Webb, Keir Hardie, and Auberon Herbert among its contributors. The paper's editor, Harold Rylett, was secretary to the Stop the War Committee, and with several anonymous correspondents in South Africa it became something of an unofficial organ for the whole pro-Boer movement in England. It was banned in South Africa, along with several others of the same persuasion.[17]

Most of the verse appearing here took the form of a virulent propaganda against the 'methods of barbarism' practised in South Africa. With the exception of a group of South African poets, whose work appeared in *Songs of the Veld* and will be discussed in a later chapter, none of the *New Age* poets could base their work on first-hand knowledge. Stead, Hobson, the socialist and humanitarian press, and particularly the revelations contained in Emily Hobhouse's *Report*, published in June 1901 and circulated by pacifist journals like *Commonwealth*, provided almost the sole source for verse of such apocalyptic extravagance as the following:

> Woe is my country, woe!
> For the worst is fallen
> That e'er befell
> The greatest of the great!
> She hath left her high,
> Her fair estate
> For a garbled cry
> And a thirst for gold:
> And darkness—darkness manifold
> Hath led her to the gate,
> The gate of shame.
> (A.B., 'Lament'.)

The wrongness of such verse is not merely attributable to its badness as poetry. These poems were apparently widely read and were reprinted, along with scores of others, in *Songs of the Veld* as a result of many requests from *New Age*'s obviously intelligent readership. One explanation for the wide acceptability of such doggerel is that it was part of a general over-reaction to the waning of Gladstonian liberalism. Two decades earlier liberals had

[17] See *New Age*, 8 May 1900, for mention of the correspondents, and the *Midland News*, 26 June 1901, for a list of publications banned in the Cape Colony.

believed that freedom was a political absolute in the especial custody of Britain; it did not have to remain an approximate ideal, but could inform practical and even imperial politics. The realities of the first Boer War (1880–1), of the conflict over Irish Home Rule, and then of the second Boer War proved that this was not so, hence the anguish of radicals and humanitarians in their reiterated laments for the passing of a partly fictitious Liberal golden age. In *Songs of the Veld* these are clearly the sentiments that inform, for instance, S. Hancock's 'The Day of Dishonour':

> Where is thy boast of freedom? Where thy wealth
> Of liberty, which once thou didst bestow
> Upon the lesser peoples? Where that glow
> And sweep of thought, that beating pulse of life,
> Full trumpet-call to all heroic strife,
> Which, like the rough and sounding winds that sweep
> Across thy steadfast isle from deep to deep,
> Bred scorn of tyrants?

A recurrent theme—again of classical Liberal origin—in the humanitarian periodicals was that evolution should have made war obsolete by the end of the nineteenth century. *Brotherhood* carried 'Evolution' in its masthead and published poems such as Ernest H. Crosby's 'The Bugler in the Rear: to Kipling' (January 1900), which argued that Kipling's martial clamour was

> harking back to times out-worn,
> A-bugling in the rear.

Crosby's own *Swords and Ploughshares* (1903) has much more to say on the theme that 'War is hell, because it makes men devils'. In the *New Century Review*, February 1900, Charles E. Byles's 'To a Preacher of War' framed a curt response to the Darwinist argument that war was essential to man's evolution:

> Vain emulation! If by war alone
> Mankind be hewn into the higher type:
> And human nature but to rot grow ripe.

At the end of the same year it gave a grim sketch of the process of devolution that had laid South Africa waste: 'All of the wide fighting arena is desolate, the progress of a decade has been torn from the history of South Africa and its place taken by the sullen race-hatred of unborn generations' (December 1900).

The same editorial stressed that war invariably does most harm to those most helpless, another recurrent notion in Boer War pacifist verse and one which confirmed a different kind of evolution, mentioned in Chapter I: with the Boer War the world came much closer to twentieth century civilian warfare, as against the largely professional conflicts of earlier times. Obviously, women and children had suffered before, but they now became a strategic object for the British forces in South Africa—indeed, had to, if the guerrilla war was ever to end. It was a sad new truth for poets to consider:

> If the stroke of war
> Fell certain on the guilty head, none else;
> If they that make the cause might taste th'effect,
> And drink themselves the bitter cup they mix;
> Then might the bard, though child of peace, delight
> To twine fresh wreaths around the conqueror's brow; . . .
>   But alas!
> That undistinguishing and deathful storm
> Beats heavier on th'exposèd innocent.[18]

In England, too, there was now a much stronger awareness of the suffering of the soldier's wife and child, a development no doubt partly dependent on the articulation of feminist views generally. In *For England* (1900), for instance, the authoress, Lady Caroline Lindsay, is clearly torn between the traditional patriotic feelings of her class—according to the *Dictionary of National Biography* all the titled Lindsays were army officers—and her even stronger feelings as a woman. As befits a woman of her status, the young bride in Lady Caroline's poem sees her husband off to the Transvaal with little show of emotion, but at the end of the poem she ponders that

> war is as a cloud of blood
> And swarth the year when strife and death prevail,
> And nations rise in ireful mood.
> Then, through the din, our women sob and wail,
> And, in your midst, the wan and wild-eyed widows press,
> And, cold and hungry, cry the fatherless.

The point here is not that musings of this kind were being articulated for the first time—they had appeared before—but that they were now expressed with such regularity.

[18] Crowe (?), 'For Christmas Time: An Appeal', unidentified press cutting, War Museum, Bloemfontein, File 1637.

F

Feminists played an important part in the pro-Boer movement and in the organization of anti-war meetings, activities which confirm that the emancipation of women and the resultant release of many ideas hostile to the activist conceptions of a masculine world must have deeply affected traditional attitudes to war. Indeed, some ladies acquired a rather extravagant notion of their new usefulness. At one anti-war meeting a feminist proposed that a contingent of women should go to South Africa and take up position between the firing lines:

> We'll go and stand firm as a rock
> Wherever battle thunders loudest
> Whichever side stands victory-proudest:
> Right in between the battle-shock
> And its advance defiant block.[19]

By now, too, several periodicals with specifically feminist intentions existed, such as the *Englishwoman's Review* and the *Humanitarian*, edited by Victoria Woodhull Martin and Zula Maud Woodhull. They occasionally published verse which looked at the soldier's death from a woman's point of view, as in 'Found on the Field', which observes the 'two silent dreadful eyes' of a soldier fallen in battle and meditates on the last desperate attempt he may have made to communicate with a loved one in England:

> What came? what went? what stays?
> That subtle fluid thread,
> Through the unending maze,
> What yearning message sped?
> Did *she* know, in the north,
> When flashed that message forth?
>
> Did the gurgle of the spruit—
> A little mocking trill
> Just like an elfin lute—
> A fourth dimension fill,
> And fall upon her ear
> In cataracts of fear?
>
> And sitting in her place,
> Felt she upon her face

[19] H. V. Storey, 'Women and War', *Britannia Poems* (Oxford: Clarendon Press, 1910).

> A fleeting icy breath,
> A swift and sudden pain
> That tore her heart in twain
> With hate of death?[20]

If feminist poets voiced their disaffection for war more clearly now, some male poets found themselves, true to the times, caught between the conflicting attractions of a martial life and a humanitarian disavowal of it. Richard Le Gallienne's *New Poems* (1910) contains several poems inspired by the seductive but censured excitement of the Boer War:

> And yet how sweet
> The sound along the marching street
> Of drum and fife, and I forget
> Wet eyes of widows, and forget
> Broken old mothers, and the whole
> Dark butchery without a soul. . . .
> O snap the fife and still the drum,
> And show the monster as she is.
> ('The Illusion of War')

Another poet who responded strongly to the magnetism of military pomp even while condemning war as outdated and inhuman, was Thomas Hardy. Man's urge to destroy himself in a posture of fruitless heroism and to submit his life to the exciting roulette of blind chance spoke particularly forcefully to Hardy out of the eagerness and ado with which troops set off for the Boer War. Half of the 'War Poems' in *Poems of the Past and the Present* (1902) are concerned with departure, and they all suggest that Hardy observed his country's commitment to this war with a sad but fascinated and ironic resignation. Still engaged on *The Dynasts* (1903), he must have seen in the Boer War a real counterpart to his fictional panorama. He watched the departure of the 73rd Field Battery from Dorchester Barracks on 2 November 1899, and composed 'The Going of the Battery' in an unsuccessful Kiplingesque lilt:[21]

> Gas-glimmers drearily, blearily, eerily
> Lit our pale faces outstretched for one kiss,

---

20 *Humanitarian*, 16 (1900), 283.
21 Florence E. Hardy, *The Life of Thomas Hardy* (London: Macmillan, 1962), p. 305; and J. O. Bailey, *The Poetry of Thomas Hardy: A Handbook and Commentary* (Chapel Hill: University of North Carolina Press, 1970), pp. 114–25.

While we stood prest to them, with a last quest to them
Not to court perils that honour could miss.

He cycled down to Southampton to watch the troops set out, and
wrote 'Embarcation', 'Departure', and 'The Colonel's Soliloquy',
all dwelling on the tension between muted excitement and profound hopelessness that informed these occasions. It is made most
explicit in 'Departure':

> While the far farewell music thins and fails,
> And the broad bottoms rip the bearing brine—
> All smalling slowly to the gray sea-line—
> And each significant red smoke-shaft pales,
> Keen sense of severance everywhere prevails.

Watching the 'long tramp of mounting men', he demands:

> Must your wroth reasonings trade on lives like these,
> That are as puppets in a playing hand?

Like Tennyson's Ulysses, Hardy's colonel responds with
bemused awe to the fatal attractions of a voyage from which he
might not return, but, unlike Ulysses, he cannot adopt an un-
ambiguously epic stance:

> And where those villains ripped me in the flitch
> With their old iron in my early time,
> I'm apt at change of wind to feel a twitch,
> Or at a change of clime.

In 'The Souls of the Slain' the returning shades discover that they
are remembered not for their 'glory and war-mightiness', but for

> Deeds of home; that live yet
> Fresh as new—deeds of fondness or fret;
> Ancient words that were kindly expressed or unkindly,
> These, these have their heeds.

In contrast to 'The Sick Battle-God', which expresses a wooden
and didactic pacifism that cannot be extrapolated from the other
poems in the group, Hardy's finest Boer War poem, 'Drummer
Hodge', is a full and profoundly moving record of the humanitarian response to war. Drawing once again, like T. W. H.
Crosland's 'Slain', on the concepts and imagery of Wordsworth's
Lucy poems, Hardy's poem presents a highly ambivalent picture
of an unknown, unglamorous soldier who nevertheless becomes

the involuntary subject of a cosmic apotheosis: Hodge's fellow men (note the emphatic but impersonal 'They') merely throw him in, but the Southern landscape harbours him as something precious:

> They throw in Drummer Hodge, to rest
> Uncoffined—just as found:
> His landmark is a kopje crest
> That breaks the veldt around;
> And foreign constellations west
> Each night above his mound.
>
> Young Hodge the Drummer never knew—
> Fresh from his Wessex home—
> The meaning of the broad Karoo,
> The Bush, the dusty loam,
> And why uprose to nightly view
> Strange stars amid the gloam.
>
> Yet portion of that unknown plain
> Will Hodge for ever be;
> His homely Northern breast and brain
> Grow to some Southern tree,
> And strange-eyed constellations reign
> His stars eternally.

Hodge's story is an existentialist paradox: he is totally unimportant in the proceedings of a war as big as the Boer War, yet he is the representative hero of an unwritten human epic in which the Boer War itself is only a small episode.

Although socialism and humanitarianism grew in late-Victorian times in proportion to the waning of interest in orthodox religion, much of the impetus behind resistance to the Boer War was still explicitly religious in nature and origin. We saw such responses in discussing (Chapter II) the reactions that the jingo piety of the time elicited. The interests and activities of nonconformist Christians often overlapped with those of Labour, the Fabians, and the Ethical Movement, since the ethics of late-Victorian socialism, 'the religion of humanity', were to a large extent an outgrowth of the evangelicalism of the century's early decades. Hence the Christian Socialists, who combined all these interests, presented the remarkably united front to the Boer War which

Peter d'A. Jones comments on in *The Christian Socialist Revival 1877–1914* (1968).

The majority of religious publications that carried anti-war verse came from a background of Dissent. Samuel E. Keeble's *Methodist Weekly* kept up a barrage of anti-Boer War propaganda after a previous editor, the Revd. Hugh Price Hughes, had turned imperialist and had drawn the fire of *Reynold's Newspaper* in 'Holy Hughie's Prayer', quoted earlier. The Quaker *Friend* regularly inveighed against war, as on 12 May 1900: 'If we think of the British wars in Africa during the last thirty years we shall have to admit that land-hunger, the "narrowing lust for gold", the love of power, have been the prime factors in all or most of them, rather than philanthropic or missionary zeal.' It published some clamorous anti-war poems, indistinguishable from those which appeared in Henry Scott Holland's Christian Socialist monthly, *Commonwealth*, Dr. R. P. Downes's *Great Thoughts*, or the Revd. John Page Hopps's *Coming Day*:

> Hark! the booming of the guns,
> Slaying fathers, slaying sons;
>   They call it glory:
>   I call it hell.
>
> 'Peace on earth, good will to men'?
> Close your churches! odious when
>   Their path is gory:
>   Hush the bell![22]

The themes of these poems were all too predictable: the dichotomy between a gospel of peace and a warlike Christian nation; between prayers for peace and prayers for victory; between the Christian demand for humility and assumptions of the enemy's unrighteousness:

> In the prayers of a million women
> A merciful God is besought
> That He spare the life of the smiter—
> Though the smiter himself spare naught,

wrote S. R. Elliott in the *Temple Magazine* in March 1900. George Ives adopted an even more vatic strain in his *Eros' Throne* (1900):

> Both have transgressed,
> And now they call on Heaven,

[22] J.R.G.G., 'Glory?' *Coming Day*. April 1900.

> With folded hand
> That raised the red-stained thongs, . . .
> And thousand-voiced
> Unite in one proud prayer;
> But they appeal unto the fiend of war:
> And he is come.

The 'fiend of war' stalked through many an anti-war poem of the period, possibly straight out of the thirty-ninth stanza of Canto 1 of *Childe Harold's Pilgrimage:*

> Lo! where the giant on the mountain stands,
> His blood-red tresses deep'ning in the sun,
> With death-shot glowing in his fiery hands,
> And eye that scorcheth all it glares upon.

These were also the latter years of the Symbolist painters, when the grotesque and nightmarish conceptions of Henry de Groux's 'Cataclysm' (1893), Jean Delville's 'Satan's Treasures' (1895), and Arnold Böcklin's 'The War' (1896) still occupied the foreground of Europe's imagination.[23] Their influence can be clearly seen in numerous Boar War poems presenting a horrifying or apocalyptic vision of the terrors of war, such as B. Paul Neuman's 'The Shrine of the War-God'—

> Splendid, upon a bare and blasted plain,
>   It rose before me in the sunset light,
> Vast, many-towered, like some majestic fane
>   With one great cross of gold to crown its height.

> And then I looked within; a poison-breath
>   Sickened me, and I saw the temple's Lord
> Stalk up and down his festering house of death,
>   A naked savage with a dripping sword—

or Arthur Stringer's 'The War Spirit':

> He sat behind his roses and did wake
>   With careless hands those passions grim
> That naught but War and Blood and Tears can slake,
>   And naught but years can dim.

[23] All are reproduced in Philippe Jullian, *The Symbolists* (London: Phaidon, 1973), except for Böcklin, which appears in Heinz Gollwitzer, *Europe in the Age of Imperialism 1880–1914* (London: Thames & Hudson, 1969), p. 177.

> So o'er their wine did Great Ones sit and nod,
>   Ordaining War—as it befell:
> Men, drunk with drum and trumpet, talked of God,
>   And reeled down blood-washed roads to Hell.[24]

Canon H. D. Rawnsley, who, judged by the rest of the poems in his *Ballads of the War* (1900), was by no means a pacifist, nevertheless wrote one of the more macabre pieces on 'The Horrors of War':

> Men talk of battle, pass the time of day
> And buy and sell and feast, as who should say
> 'Pour out the wine and weave the rosy wreath!
> And sing and laugh and toast!' while underneath
> The banquet-board a man uncoffined lay.

G. J. Smith's 'War Clouds' and E. G. Harman's 'War' depict war as haunting and traumatic. The former appeared in *Great Thoughts* (13 January 1900), and dwells on the surprise and disbelief with which a country that regarded itself as secure in peace suddenly found itself at war:

> With lips set stern and flashing eyes, the men
> Took down the sword and trod in martial line,
> While children, wond'ring, learned a strange new game:
> But wives and mothers wept; their tender ken,
> Prophetic, saw the red blood poured like wine.

Harman's sonnet, dated 1902, appears in his *Poems* (1920). It is a striking example of a poem inspired by the anti-war climate of the Boer War that was still felt to be relevant after the greater holocaust of 1914–18. A footnote tells us that the opening lines of the sonnet come from a letter of Napoleon to Josephine:

> A hotel—'5 a.m. It rains. My men
> Are in full march. All my affairs go well.
> I held them baffled, and the day will tell
> The issue. Have no fear. I love you.—N.'
> The battle, closing over field and fen,
> Found them undaunted. Fate ran out the spell
> Of fifty thousand in that game of hell.
> Rotting they lay, recorded by no pen.
> The ragged Victory cheered and took its fill,

[24] Neuman, *Pro Patria and Other Poems* (London: Brown Langham, 1905); Stringer, *Bookman* (N.Y.), 14 (1901–2), 416.

> Pleading necessity which knows no law,
> If plea were meet, or, blind to good or ill,
> With death at elbow, and the earth a field
> For their swords' reaping, what its tilth would yield
> Reaped, and endured the rest. Friend, that was war.

Interestingly, nothing in Harman's First World War verse was nearly as good.

Like Harman's poem, Alfred Olivant's 'Death in Battle', published in *McClure's Magazine* (May 1900), does not relate explicitly to the Boer War, but is nevertheless a product of contemporary thinking. Although it deteriorates into a conventionally mawkish piece about God welcoming the holy warrior at the gates of heaven, the opening of the poem is startlingly out of character with this conclusion. It portrays war as cataclysmic, and reveals considerable tension of movement and richness of vision:

> His hand upon th' Impregnable, he blunders
> Headlong in the Cataract of War,
> Blasted on by flaming-throated thunders,
> Founders in the Deluge; sinks to soar,
> Hugely borne upon Jehovah-handed surges,
> Whose crests out-tower the bulwarks far of Mars,
> Thro' bellowing abysses, till he emerges
> In the still sweet silence of the stars.
> From the roar of ruin'd firmaments and riot,
> He slides into his sleep,
> As a ship into the haven's sudden quiet
> From the clamour of the hungering outer deep.

One reason for the poem's attraction is no doubt that it reminds one of the opening of a later and more famous piece, Owen's 'Strange Meeting':

> It seemed that out of battle I escaped
> Down some profound dull tunnel, long since scooped
> Through granites which titanic wars had groined.

Paradoxically, while contemporary drives towards symbolism and surrealism introduced the horrific into war poetry, the opposite literary and artistic cults of naturalism and realism had almost the same effect. G. G. Somerville's *The Retreat from Moscow*, which appeared in 1899, boasted the sub-title, 'A Poem realistically illustrating the horrors of war'. In this it was typical of many attempts made since the appearance of Zola's *La Débâcle* in 1892, also sub-titled in Vizetelly's translation 'A Story of the Horrors of War', to foreground the gruesome details of battle. The emphasis on brisk and vivid realism in the new journalism made itself felt in war reportage, too, as we have seen in the prose of G. W. Steevens and the verse of Edgar Wallace. Pacifist writers were quick to exploit these possibilities for making war unattractive. Soon after the Boer War broke out, Henry Lawson tried to give his eager Australian compatriots a foretaste of what it would be like: 'When a few shells have made a mess, and left objects that look as if fresh offal from a slaughter-house has been stuffed into dusty uniforms to make dummies, which have been thrown over and have burst—nothing but dust, and heat, and smoke, and dust— and blood-caked objects—fragments of humanity.... etc.' (*Australian Star*, 28 October 1899.) He may have had some effect. Later, in 'I killed a man at Graspan', his countryman, M. Grover, re-created the tale of a returned contingenter haunted by his close-up view of the business of killing an enemy in battle:

> I killed a man at Graspan,
> Maybe I killed a score;
> But this one wasn't a chance-shot home,
> From a thousand yards or more.
> I fired at him when he'd got no show;
> We were only a pace apart,
> With the cordite scorchin' his old worn coat
> As the bullet drilled his heart. . . .
>
> I killed a man at Graspan,
> I killed him fair in fight;
> And the Empire's poets and the Empire's priests
> Swear blind I acted right.
> The Empire's poets and the Empire's priests
> Make out my deed was fine,
> But they can't stop the eyes of the man I killed
> From starin' into mine.[25]

On 20 October 1899 the *Daily Chronicle* announced: 'We do not often publish poems by writers unknown to us, but these lines, in spite of some defects, appear to us to have a character which promises distinction for their author.' The lines which followed

[25] William T. Pyke, ed., *The Coo-Ee Reciter* (London: Ward, Lock, n.d.).

were Herbert Cadett's 'War: Private Smith of the Royals'. The author seems to have remained unknown, *pace* the *Daily Chronicle*, but his poem deserves a better fate. Stark, chilly, unheroic, the effect of its sensational depiction of war is actually enhanced by the apparently inappropriate lilting rhythms and insistent internal rhymes of Kipling's 'barracky' style:

Private Smith of the Royals; the veldt and a slate-black sky,
Hillocks of mud, brick-red with blood, and a prayer—half curse—to
 die.
A lung and a Mauser bullet; pink froth and a half-choked cry. . . .

Private Smith of the Royals, self-sounding his funeral knell;
A burning throat that each gasping note scrapes raw like a broken
 shell.
A thirst like a red-hot iron and a tongue like a patch of Hell. . . .

But Private Smith of the Royals gazed up at the soft blue sky—
The rose-tinged morn like a babe new born and the sweet-songed birds
 on high—
With a fleck of red on his pallid lip and a film of white on his eye.

In 'The Song of Modern Mars', which appeared in *Success* (10 February 1900), Cadett repeated his performance with a poem which, if objectionably bloody in parts, presents a remarkably accurate preview of the sentiments and imagery of some poems of World War I:

Three miles of trench and a mile of men
In a rough-hewn, slop-shop grave;
Spades and a volley for one in ten—
Here's a hip! hurrah! for the brave.
A flash from the front that shames the sun,
The crash of a bursting shell,
And the rat-tat-tat of the Maxim gun—
A machine-made funeral knell. . . .

Infantry dodging from rock to rock,
And gunners from peak to peak,
Rifle-shots playing at postman's knock
And soldiers at hide and seek.
Crimson flecks on a sand-coloured mound,
Like rays of the rosy morn,
And splashes of red on a khaki ground,
Like poppies in fields of corn.

If some of the gory details here upset the modern reader's sense of decorum, it will be helpful to remember that in many quarters the prevalent mood was still to prettify war, as in Aubrey Mild-may's words, quoted earlier:

> Death on the veldt! It is angel-attended;
> Sweet is the sound of a nation's 'Well done!'

or to glamorize it, as in an article which appeared in the *Regiment*, 'An Illustrated Military Journal for Everybody', on 7 January 1899: 'Men in the Egyptian war [were] singing at the top of their voices as they fought hand to hand with the enemy, and some even went so far as to keep time with their bayonet thrusts to the tunes they were singing.' Much else in the same vein can be found in *Regiment*'s pages. In the following chapter we shall see what the men in South Africa had to say about the business of killing.

VI

Poets of Veld and Parlour

> Say, was it worth it, you should train
> The fullness of your heart and brain
> To squander all amid the slain?
> A. C. Kennedy, 'R.H.G. (K.R.R.) Killed at Dundee Fight',
> *Avenged and Other Verses* (1899).

THE men who went to South Africa and wrote poems about their experiences were, like the poets at home, the products of their time. This is a truism, but a necessary one to keep in mind when dealing with statements such as Sir Mark Sykes's, made in 1900:

It would seem as if Lord Salisbury were the last of a long and illustrious line; think of his predecessors. And as it is in politics, so it is in letters. Every war since 1700 has been an accepted opportunity for poets and writers. What can we say of our modern productions? Compare Stead's vapourings with Swift's 'Conduct of the Allies', 'The Absent-Minded Beggar' with 'The Charge of the Light Brigade', Napier's 'Peninsular War' with Winston Churchill's 'London to Pretoria'. . . . In no direction do we seem to shine, nowhere do we see tremendous genius.[1]

In a review in the *Edinburgh*[2] B. H. Holland wrote: 'The latest South African war has been illustrated by countless deeds of valour . . . but it has not, we think, inspired a single poem which is likely to live.' He called Kipling ephemeral, Watson unpatriotic, and Swinburne and Austin 'better forgotten as soon as possible'. The problem, said Holland, was twofold: 'No one of the authors of the later English war-poems which we have quoted, had ever, we think, heard a shot fired or seen a sword drawn in battle'; and at the front itself, 'the actual vision of battle does not seem to inspire poetry . . . the men who fight do not write'. Sykes and Holland were both wrong, and Holland on both counts.

---

[1] Shane Leslie, *Mark Sykes: His Life and Letters* (London, 1923), p. 72.
[2] 196 (1902), 29–54.

Many of the men in South Africa reacted to the war in much the same way as the poets at home. They made use of the popular poetic modes of the time, and they were conditioned by the ideologies of the period. They wrote for war and against war; about imperial glory and about the grisly death of comrades; they prayed for victory for Britain but showed compassion for their foes; they worshipped 'Bobs' and (to a lesser extent) Buller, but wrote cynical verses about their officers. Often, indeed, it is impossible, or not very profitable, to distinguish poems written at the front from those written in England, so that Holland's distinction is really impossible to make. Poets in England *did* write movingly about the war, and the men at the front *did* write vividly about the whole range of their experience.

Who went to South Africa? Two facts are important for our purpose: these men represented a complete cross-section of British society, and they were nearly all literate. The facts behind these phenomena were outlined in Chapter I. Next to regular Tommies, who hailed mostly from the working classes, the middle and upper classes flocked to the war not only as officers, but also, and this is important, as volunteers in the prestigious Imperial Yeomanry and City Imperial Volunteer movements. Geoffrey Cousins, in *The Defenders: A History of the British Volunteer* (1968), states that out of a total army commitment in South Africa of 480,000 troops, only 184,000 had been on the lists of the Home Regular Force before the outbreak of the war. It was, therefore, really a volunteer army on the pattern to be confirmed in 1914.

The experience of rubbing shoulders with men higher up or lower down the class ladder altered the social perspectives of many, and furthered that social mobility in the army which had been implicit in army reform from 1870 onwards. In simple terms, it meant that the individual became more important, and that the ordinary soldier became an even more popular subject for verse than Kipling had already made him. At times it even meant an exaggerated worship of uniformed disreputables, as in R. Ellis Gerrard's 'Drunken Sandy' (*Ballads of Battle and Poems of Peace*, 1914):

> They called him Drunken Sandy; though he soldiered with a will,
> He was either in the guard room, or doin' defaulters' drill,
> He was fat, and he was podgy, and the Sergeant-Major felt
> They should send him as a target for the Boer on the veldt.

He didn't go on furlough, for his people long before
Had turned from him in loathing as a sort of family sore;
So he donned his kilt, and sporran, and gartered up his hose,
And left a dirty lassie, with a snivel in his nose.

Needless to add, Sandy is the man who ends up rescuing his wounded captain.

The very frequency of references to the social mixing taking place at the front confirms its novelty. 'A curious medley of men gathered themselves together there—young and old, high and low, rich and poor, landlord and labourer, all standing on level ground for England's sake', wrote Violet Brooke-Hunt about the recreational institutes she had established at the front, and she quoted the words of a young squire about a fellow trooper: 'He is our second footman, and he would come out when I did; and he is always trying to do little things for me, though I tell him he must remember we are just fellow-troopers now.' A member of the City Imperial Volunteers commented:

We are men of all sorts of conditions,
   'Duke's son, cook's son, son of a belted earl,'
eating, sleeping, and drilling shoulder to shoulder indeed, for there is no room between. Our accents are various, but our dress the same and our duties the same.[3]

He took pride in writing his book 'amid the camp work and surroundings of the ordinary Tommy, not from the comparative luxurious environment of the officers' mess'. Against this hands-across-the-orderly-room affability one must mention E. S. Turner's reminder, in *Gallant Gentlemen: A Portrait of the British Officer 1600–1956* (1956), that at the end of the century 90 per cent of the officers were still public school men, and that between 1898 and 1902 only 136 officers were promoted from the ranks. Clearly, social mobility within the army, upwards as well as downwards, was something very new, and hence all the more likely to stimulate an awareness of human relationships.

The new-found literacy of the Boer War soldier was as frequently commented on as his social diversity. Partly because of the universal education that followed on the Education Act of 1870, and partly because of the educational campaigns that formed an integral part of the social and humanitarian revolution of the late-

---

[3] *A Woman's Memories of the War*; Lloyd, *1,000 Miles with the C.I.V.*, p. 10.

Victorian era, male literacy rose from 63·3 per cent in 1841 to 92·2 per cent in 1900.[4] In South Africa this meant that Miss Brooke-Hunt frequently found 'men eagerly awaiting the train with a beseeching appeal for "an old paper or a bit of anything to read" '. Another result was an avalanche of war memoirs, from the Hon. Sidney Peel's *Trooper 8008, I.Y.* (1901) and the Earl of Rosslyn's *Twice Captured: A Record of Adventure during the Boer War* (1900), right down to R. C. Billington's *A Mule-Driver at the Front* (1901), and, most relevant in the present context, numerous attempts at verse, from therapeutic exercises to powerful records of experience.

If men at the front were voracious for reading matter, so were readers at home, and here we have another remarkable literary feature of the war: it proved a rich new source of exciting narrative material for the enormous popular press of magazine verse and story, and for the Victorian genres of parlour poem and public recitation. Everything soldiers could produce was seized upon, and where they failed the professional ballad writers filled the breach. Anecdotes, real or apocryphal, of the Boer War provided a welcome extension to the activities of the heroes of colonial or military literature made popular by Kipling, G. A. Henty, F. S. Brereton, G. M. Fenn, John Strange Winter, and others. Undiscriminating but eager to read, the mass of 'quarter educated' (Gissing's phrase) formed the larger part of the audience for Boer War verse.

Much of the poetry, therefore, written by or about men at the front falls into the cadences of the popular recitational ballads and music hall tunes of the time. Indeed, a glance through a few of the well-known school-boy anthologies of the period, Henley's *Lyra Heroica* or Langbridge's *Ballads of the Brave*, will reveal the models of most of the Boer War verse produced both at home and at the front.[5] Chief of these was the iambic quatrain of the border ballad, as in 'Sir Patrick Spens', or a simplified version of it, as in Cowper's 'The Loss of the Royal George':

> Eight hundred of the brave,
> Whose courage well was tried,

---

[4] Malcolm Bradbury, *The Social Context of Modern English Literature* (Oxford: Blackwell, 1971), p. 204.
[5] All the poems quoted from in the next two paragraphs appear in either Henley or Langbridge, or in both.

> Had made the vessel heel,
> And laid her on her side.

Developed during the nineteenth century into a veritable cult by the infectious efforts of writers such as Mrs. Hemans ('The boy stood on the burning deck'), the simple narrative ballad was the most readily available mode for Tommy poets. There were also many useful variations. The quatrain, for instance, could become the loping couplet of the rhymed fourteener, as in Macaulay's 'The Armada' or Marryat's 'The Old Navy':

> The captain stood on the carronade: 'First lieutenant,' says he,
> 'Send all my merry men aft here, for they must list to me.'

Another, and very popular, variation was to substitute an anapaestic rhythm for the genre's basically iambic metre, as in Wolfe's 'The Burial of Sir John Moore'—

> Not a drum was heard, not a funeral note,
> As his corse to the rampart we hurried;
> Not a soldier discharged his farewell shot
> O'er the grave where our hero we buried—

or to introduce internal rhyme, as in Macaulay's 'The Last Buccaneer':

> The winds were yelling, the waves were swelling,
> The sky was black and drear,
> When the crew with eyes of flame brought the ship without a name
> Alongside the last Buccaneer.

The anapaest, of course, had other narrative advantages, particularly to create speed and mobility, as in Scott's 'Lochinvar' or Byron's 'Sennacherib':

> The Assyrian came down like the wolf on the fold,
> And his cohorts were gleaming in purple and gold.

Along with the octosyllabic couplet, once again very useful for an extended, easy, and rapid narrative, as in Byron's 'The Storming of Corinth', the anapaestic rhymed couplet served a universal purpose in Victorian popular verse. It formed, for instance, the basis of what A. L. Lloyd calls the 'Come-all-ye' ballad—simple to compose, easy to remember, and full of readily manœuvrable formulae:

> Come all you good people and listen a while,
> I'll sing you a song that will cause you to smile.

Lloyd says of the Victorian perpetrators of these folk styles that they 'carried in their heads a mixed musical baggage of parlour ballads, music hall song, some hymn tunes, a few scraps of opera, [and] a smattering of traditional song'.[6] This was clearly true of many Tommy poets, as may be gathered from the following description of a typical Boer War smoking concert:

These entertainments form a quaint medley. . . . There is no lack of talent. Music hall songs with 'lodger' and 'mother-in-law' complete, are sandwiched between madrigals and Tennysonian recitations, and sparring matches between the Pride of Mile End and the Pet of Drury Lane form a relief to the sentimental ditties with valse refrain such as are beloved of regular Tommies, and good old cavalier marching tunes are contrasted with the lilt of the modern war song, whose triumphant and bellicose words are somewhat marred by the eccentricities of their rhyme.[7]

Other varieties of the ballad were possible and popular, for example, the Australian bush ballad or the American frontier ballad, but one particular form exercised a powerful influence on Boer War poets: the sentimental parlour ballad, as perfected by George R. Sims:

> It is Christmas Day in the Workhouse,
>   And the cold bare walls are bright
> With garlands of green and holly,
>   And the place is a pleasant sight

or:

I stood at eve, as the sun went down, by a grave where a woman lies,
Who lured men's souls to the shores of sin with the light of her wanton eyes.

According to Sims's editor, the above poem ('Ostler Joe') was reprinted in 1,285 papers in the United States alone.[8]

Along with Kipling, Sims was largely responsible, too, for the vogue of vernacular narrative and for the formulæ that went with it: 'Go for a sail this mornin'?—This way, yer honour, please'. Many a Boer War narrative poem was to be introduced after this fashion. Other popular vernacular modes were the pidgin German

---

[6] *Folk Song in England*, pp. 351 and 364.   [7] Lloyd, *1,000 Miles*, p. 25.
[8] *Prepare to Shed Them Now: The Ballads of George R. Sims*, ed. Arthur Calder-Marshall (London: Hutchinson, 1968).

of the music hall—used, for instance, in *Der Junge Breitmann in South Africa* (1900), based on Charles Leland's famous *Breitmann Ballads* of 1876—or a pastiche of Scots. Thus just about every newspaper in the English-speaking world carried a poem about pipes and pibrochs after the decimation of the Highland Brigade at Magersfontein on 11 December 1899. Behind most of them one could detect James Hogg's 'The Lament of Flora Macdonald'.

Finally, to the bits of poetic equipment available to the Victorian popular poet, and to the bard in the ranks particularly, one must add 'the ribald old army songs which had been handed down by ten generations of soldiers from mouth to mouth'.[9] In 'Songs that Soldiers Sing', which appeared in the *Evening Standard* during the war, the compiler found it hard work to locate any ex-soldier 'who could recollect the name, let alone a line or two, of a single patriotic song he had ever heard sung in a canteen'.[10] On the other hand, he found plenty of the following, of which, no doubt, he could only reproduce the more printable portions:

> Away to the old canteen, my boys,
>   Shall be our battle croy,
> Away to the old canteen, my boys,
>   We'll booze before we'll doy

or:

> I ne'er shall forget her,
> That girl of Valetta:
> The first time I met her
>   I thought she was prime.
>
> But I managed to get a
> Peep through her faldetta;
> I saw that I'd better
>   Get out while there's time.

One feature of the new popular literacy which is very relevant to the present discussion and which was responsible for much of the verse dealing with the campaign, was the enormous increase in the importance and number of war correspondents and war artists. It is significant that the standard history of the war, *The*

[9] C. E. Carrington ('Charles Edmonds'), *A Subaltern's War* (London: Peter Davies, 1929), p. 118.
[10] Reprinted in the *Diamond Fields Advertiser*, 30 Jan. 1900.

Times History of the War in South Africa (1900–9), was produced by a group of journalists under the editorship of L. S. Amery, himself a war correspondent. Not only could such correspondents now cable frequent, voluminous, and highly coloured reports to England, thus providing up-to-the-minute, blow-by-blow accounts of events at the front, but the quick sketches by war artists, which often formed the basis for heroic full plates in magazines such as the *London Illustrated News* or the *Sphere*, also provided a visual immediacy for home readers not possible in earlier campaigns.[11] So profitable was the correspondence business that quite a few volunteers signed contracts with publishers or newspapers before setting out for South Africa. One such was Sharrad H. Gilbert: 'Before leaving with my squadron for South Africa, I had arranged to contribute to the Press a series of articles descriptive of the life we should lead, and the varied vicissitudes and adventures through which it would be our fate to pass.' Hostile commentators, indeed, were not slow to pounce on this eager rush to the front in search of gore:

> Of correspondents too, a score or more,
> To chronicle great deeds while cannons' roar
> Scared Kruger's Dutchmen into ague fits,
> And shook the landscape into little bits:
> Knights of the quill migrated far to south,
> Seeking sensation in the cannon's mouth.[12]

Leafing through the contributions of 'Linesman' and 'The Intelligence Officer' (Colonel Lionel James) to *Blackwood's*, or Conan Doyle's *The Great Boer War*, or Donald Macdonald's *How We Kept the Flag Flying*, or G. W. Steevens's *From Cape Town to Ladysmith*, one is frequently struck by the vivid narrative competence of these writers, the eye for exciting, amusing, or sensational detail which could not fail to impress amateur poetic sensibilities at home. In an earlier chapter I quoted some of Steevens's writing; here is James's description of the veld:

We may curse its boundless wastes—curse that endless rise which so often has lain between our tired bodies and the evening bivouac; but the curses will die over the rail of an ocean steamer and with the fading

[11] See A. C. R. Carter, *The Work of War Artists in South Africa* (*Art Journal* Christmas Number, 1900).
[12] Gilbert, *Rhodesia—and After* (London: Simpkin Marshall, 1901), preface; Gwynne, *Homer 2nd's Bulliad*, p. 3.

lights of Cape Town, while the memory of the exhilarating air, the freedom, the stirring adventure lurking in every dip and donga of that wind-swept, sun-dried, war-racked expanse of steppe, will live with us forever. Who can forget those autumn mornings, when the horse, influenced by the same exhilaration as his rider, races across the spongy soil; playfully shies at a half-hidden ant-heap; with cat-like agility avoids the dangerous bear-earth; when all seems strong, and young, and full of life; when war is forgotten, until the rocket-bird falls slanting across your path, and its plaintive note calls back to your memory the whine of the Mauser bullet! (*On the Heels of De Wet*, p. 52.)

In a passage which seems to refer to the original of the American machine-gun tout, Laughton Zigler, in Kipling's Boer War story, 'The Captive', Donald Macdonald etched a coolly sardonic portrait of the operator of a new Colt automatic:

It is an American invention, proved to be very deadly in the late war with Spain, and was brought out to Natal purely as a speculation. One of the men connected with it is said to be a well-known socialist leader, whose projects for levelling the masses have evidently taken a new turn. The company sent out an expert, who was eagerly waiting a chance to try the weapon under new conditions, and this is surely the most up-to-date development of the commercial traveller. On Sunday morning that soldierly bagman was calmly refilling his feeding belt. (*How We Kept the Flag Flying*, pp. 194–5.)

Macdonald also articulated a common awareness that the Boer War marked a radical change in the nature of war:

In Natal war was divested of absolutely everything that once lent it meretricious glamour—no bright uniforms, no inspiring bands playing men into battle, no flags, no glitter or smoke or circumstance of any kind, but just plain primeval killing, without redemption, and with every advantage taken that international law allows. The loss in artistic effect was prodigious. The war artist had to presuppose, the war correspondent to imagine, much. (p. 149.)

As an aid to imagination, Macdonald and his host of colleagues produced many a stirring description of bayonet charges and death in battle.

Several correspondents went a step further and produced poems as versified editorial comment or 'liveners' to news stories. One thinks of Edgar Wallace of the *Daily Mail*, A. G. Hales of the

Daily News, or B. Fletcher Robinson of the *Daily Express*. The most prolific of the correspondent poets was probably A. B. Paterson, some of whose Boer War productions we met in Chapter III. His *Rio Grande's Last Race*, however, contains several other catchy ballads about the war, among them the spirited 'Driver Smith'—

So Driver Smith he went to the war a-cracking his driver's whip,
From ambulance to collecting base they showed him his regular trip.
And he said to the boys that were marching past, as he gave his whip a
   crack,
'You'll walk yourselves to the fight,' says he—'Lord spare me, I'll
   drive you back.'—

as well a rollicking account of General French's cavalry dash to Kimberley and an amusing piece about exaggerated rivalries at the front:

> Most of the troops to the camp had gone,
> When we met with a cow-gun toiling on;
> And we said to the boys, as they walked her past,
> 'Well, thank goodness, you're here at last!'
> 'Here at last! Why, what d'yer mean?
> Ain't we just where we've always been?
>   Right in front of the army,
>   Battling day and night!
>   Right in front of the army,
>   Teaching 'em how to fight!'
>   Correspondents and vets. in force,
>   Mounted foot and dismounted horse,
>   All of them were, as a matter of course,
>   Right in front of the army.

Naturally, most of the verse about the campaign not written at the front must have been based on newspaper reports, but it is possible to relate some of it to specific news stories. Walter Earle's *Home Poems* (1900) are all of this kind; the melodramatic incidents in Edith Horsfall's *Great Britain* (1911) derive mostly from specific reports in the *Black and White Budget*; and Mrs. E. S. Macleod's *For the Flag: Lays and Incidents of the South African War* (1901) is headed throughout with extracts 'from the public press of the period'. F. J. Hamilton and Canon H. D. Rawnsley must have spent much of their time combing the war press and writing poems about suitable incidents. An example from Hamilton's *Sunbeams through the War-Cloud* (1900) will show how these transmutations worked. He quotes a report of two men of the Connaught Rangers risking their lives to carry their wounded colonel off the battle-field, then deftly reshapes this plain account into a stirring ballad suitable for public recitation:

> They carefully lift him to bear him from dangers,
>   'Mid the whistling of bullet and screaming of shell;
> When a shot from a Boer gun strikes one of the Rangers
>   Who carry the leader that led them so well.
>
> 'Who's hit?' says the Colonel, with anxious concern.
>   'Begorra! it's me, sir,' replies Livingstone.
> 'Stop, boys! lay me down, and let me take my turn
>   With the rest of the wounded to perish or moan.'

Both, of course, refuse and are severely wounded in the final effort to bring the colonel in:

> Brave Livingstone faints, for his blood's freely flowing,
>   And his comrade lies covered with war-dust and grime;
> But 'tis well! since a halo of glory is glowing
>   Round their simple devotion, their courage sublime.

Another incident that attracted Hamilton along with several other poets was an occurrence at Ladysmith after the battle of Wagon Hill. As the British were carrying their wounded off the field and burying the dead, a party of Boers arrived who helped care for the suffering and prayed over the graves of their enemies. The story appeared in an Army Medical Officer's letter home, reached the press, and circulated widely in a pamphlet of the South Africa Conciliation Committee. Out of it Hamilton devised his appropriately lachrymose 'The Boers' Prayer over English Graves', Robert Morgan submitted 'Boers at the Burial of Our Dead' to the *Liverpool Express*, and Rawnsley, mistaking the place, wrote 'A Graveside Memory at Colesberg'.[13]

Canon Hardwicke Drummond Rawnsley, a founder of the National Trust, was a shining example of the late-Victorian public man of many interests who habitually expressed his response to the nation's affairs in verse. A canon of Carlisle cathedral, 'he was on endless committees and was particularly happy arranging public meetings and raising funds for worthy objects. . . . He

[13] Robert Morgan, *Poems* (Liverpool, 1900); Rawnsley, *Ballads of the War*.

could produce a sonnet for almost any occasion at short notice. . . . He would compose a hymn for Ruskin's funeral or for the Grass-mere Rushbearing with equal facility.'[14] Small wonder, then, that his *Ballads of the War* (1900; 2nd, enlarged ed., 1901) dealt with almost every noticeable incident of the campaign: 'The Wounded Piper at Elandslaagte', 'The Dead Boy and the Dying Boer', 'How They Saved the Wagon Bridge at Bethulie', and dozens of others. All were accompanied by relevant quotations from news reports. His most trenchant effort was 'The Last Question', based on an incident reported by Dr. (later Sir) Frederick Treves:

> The curse of battle has its antidote;
>   His were brave words, heart-medicine to give,
>   Who dumb, because his face was shot away,
> Took pencil in his dying hand, and wrote
>   Not—'Doctor, have I any time to live?'
>   But—'Doctor, did we win the fight to-day?'

Most home poets, however, gave no indication of the sources behind their war poems, and one frequently suspects that the campaign simply provided topical settings for largely fictitious acts of derring-do. Quite effective ballads could be woven out of the twin strands of impressionistic news stories and the well-tried techniques of popular recitational verse mentioned earlier. So, for instance, Thomas Rowley's 'The Relief of Ladysmith' (*The Maid of Malta and Other Poems*, 1913) owed as much to Mrs. Hemans's 'Casabianca' as to recent history:

> The general stood by the river's bank,
>   And thus he harangued his men:
> 'It is yonder, the town—where, in circling rank,
>   The hilltops watch and frown;
> Where the thundercloud is lowering dark,
>   And the quivering flash is seen,
> Which may gleam on the faces cold and stark
>   Of some who our brothers have been!'

Sir William Allan's 'In the Front Rank' (*Songs of Love and Labour*, 1903) relies even more shamelessly on the sure-fire effects of the anapaest:

> A tempest of lead from the foemen entrenched,
>   Swept over the African plain,

[14] Bruce Thompson, 'Canon Rawnsley: "The Guardian of the Lakes" ', *National Trust News*, No. 14 (1972).

> But never an eye of a soldier was blenched,
>   Who faced it with British disdain;
> Unflinching and steady the front rank advanced,
>   Though many a brave comrade fell,
> The river of death lay before them and danced
>   To the fiery music of hell.

The emblematic 'river of death' was in this case a real one—the
Modder. It reappears, this time as the Tugela, in Percy T. Ingram's
'Colenso' (*Songs of the Transvaal War*, n.d.), a poem whose debt to
'The Charge of the Light Brigade' is unambiguous:

> Over the river, the river of death,
>   Over the rush of the river,
> Of guns half a score reached the opposite shore,
>   The forward assault to deliver;
> But caught by the fire of a deep ambuscade,
> Like swathes from the sickle the gunners were laid,
> Back, back through the river fell Hildyard's brigade,
>   Back through the rush of the river.

Ingram could keep up this skein of loosely woven but no doubt
effective recitational verse almost indefinitely, as is clear from his
150-line 'French's March to Kimberley':

> The hollow drums have beat tattoo;
> Who's riding at night through the falling dew,
> With creaking harness and loose flung rein,
> And the jingling song of the snaffle chain,
> And the rumble and rattle of battery guns,
> Over hill and dale as the ox trail runs?

The public recitation has now virtually disappeared from our
social scene, but in late-Victorian times it was a staple ingredient
of amateur entertainment. Musical at-homes, impromptu concerts, smokers, social gatherings of school, church, working-
men's clubs, and temperance societies created an insatiable demand
for verse suitable for public declamation. It would be tedious to
rehearse here all the Boer War pieces created for this market,
since there were hundreds, but one should at least look at their
range. Mrs. Clement Nugent Jackson's *Gordon League Ballads* (2nd
series, 1903), prefaced with a lengthy treatise on the art of public
recitation, was aimed primarily at temperance society audiences,

hence the ballads are all designed to exhibit the virtues of her teetotal hero, Harry,

> Him that won the Queen's Cross in Egypt,
> And stands over six-feet-one!

In 'Shot on Patrol' (a rubric tells us it is 'Suitable for Any Audience') it is Harry's turn to be rescued, at Colenso, by a comrade of the same abstinent persuasions, Johnny Lee:

> He was pious-like, and quiet,
> Didn't smoke, or joke, or play.

The poem has a predictably inspiring conclusion:

> 'Shelter yourself, lad,' gasped Harry,
> 'Leave me . . . before it's too late!'
> 'Never alive!' rang his answer. And the Boers came up to the bend:
> Like a young lion he faced them standing over his friend.

The rigours of teetotalism were called upon to sustain other Boer War heroes. In Harriet A. Beavan's *The 'Bobs' Reciter for Bands of Hope, Temperance Societies and Sunday Schools* (?1901) 'Brown, of Battery 6', fatally wounded, is offered a drink of brandy by the surgeon:

> Brown pushed the draught from his parched lips,
> With the hand that was torn and red,
> 'No brandy, for I'm teetotal,
> So, doctor, don't force,' he said.

Robert Buchanan, whom we have already met among anti-imperialist poets, also had designs upon his listeners with *Pat Muldoon* (n.d.), a broadside published by the International Arbitration League. The poem is set in the first Boer War (1880-1) and deals with a fifteen-year-old wounded drummer boy's rescue by a kindly Boer and his return to health under the Boer family's care:

> O the rest, and O the calm, in that quiet upland farm,
> Where Jack was nurst through them long summer hours!
> To watch in a half dream, while the sleepy old mill stream
> Lay sprawling its fat fingers through the flowers!

In a dramatic revelation it transpires that the boy is none other than the narrator himself, Drum-Major Pat Muldoon, now dispatching recruits to South Africa once more and warning his charges that 'It's a noble foe you'll find across the Say!' Such melodrama was, of course, characteristic of the genre. Roland Hill's *Voices in Dreamland* (1900) is full of stern episodes in which nurses come across their own wounded husbands but stoically carry on with their duties, or wives make up letters from their slain husbands in order to conceal the tragic news from a mother-in-law.

Mostly, however, these recitational ballads had no further aim than that of rousing, dramatic entertainment, expressing the patriotic excitement of the hour or reflecting the vogue for soldierly stories. Frederick Langbridge, editor of the popular *Ballads of the Brave* (1889; 4th ed., 1911), stirred to emulation by the many spirited examples under his hand, composed 'Pat at Glencoe' (*Ballads and Legends*, 1903):

> 'Twas hail on the dropping forest then,
> But the hail was death and the leaves were men.
> A jerk of the arms and a face turn'd white,
> And the boy at your side was out of sight.

Still among the Irish, W. Copeland Trimble's *Inniskilling Fusiliers at the Battle of Inniskilling Hill* (?1901) was a lavishly produced folio of one of the most declamatory of Boer ballads:

> A hail of front and flanking fire swept thro' the surging flood,
> Yet not a warrior faltered, though weak with weltering blood,
> And step by step shot, stroke, and thrust the sullen foe obey'd,
> And darkness fell—yet no supports our jaded men to aid.

Fire and blood, thunder and smoke sweep through most of these poems with awesome regularity, but rarely more stunningly than through Ada Bartrick Baker's lines on the battle of Paardeberg, in *A Palace of Dreams and Other Verse* (1901):

> In a pit of fire and blood,
> Thunder and smoke and flood,
>   Rebels still—they lay;
> And our tearing shot and shell
> Thickly upon them fell,
> Hot as the mouth of hell,
>   Day after day.

Not all pieces designed for recitation were lengthy and robust exercises in the popular ballad measures of the time. P. S. Clay's

Ode to Lord Roberts (1900), for instance, is one of several stiff-
jointed examples of an ambitious Drydenesque 'high style' still
occasionally favoured for such narratives:

> The bristling batteries point their gaping jaws
>   Towards the rocky bastions of the foe;
> The regiments of the line, with never a pause,
>   On their heroic errand cheerly go;
> And our illustrious Chief doth calm proceed
> To seize the laurels for his brow decreed.

On the other hand, a short poem, 'Relieved', reprinted in the *Times
of Natal* on 20 June 1900, shows what effects could be achieved
in a brisk eight lines, and comes as something of a relief amidst
the mass of mythopoesy that surrounded the siege of Mafeking:

> Said he of the relieving force
>   As through the town he sped,
> 'Art thou in Baden-Powell's horse?'
>   The trooper shook his head,
> Then drew his hand his mouth across,
>   Like one who's lately fed.
> 'Alas for Baden-Powell's horse,
>   It's now in me,' he said.

So far we have looked at verse which, written in England, largely
expressed traditionally heroic attitudes to war which, on the
whole, would justify the complaints of Mark Sykes and B. H.
Holland quoted at the beginning of this chapter. There was,
however, another body of verse, also written in England, but
witness to more compassionate thinking about war and ignored
by Sykes and Holland. The reasons for the existence of this
poetry were discussed in Chapter I, and are adumbrated in
Conrad's Preface to *The Nigger of the 'Narcissus'*, written two years
before the Boer War began. Conrad called his tale 'an unrestful
episode in the obscure lives of a few individuals out of all the
disregarded multitude of the bewildered, the simple, and the
voiceless'. These words have a much wider application than
Conrad may have intended, since they not only articulate a growing
theme in the literature of the 1890s, but particularly express the
deepening concern of most lasting war poetry from this time
onwards.

Certainly, there is ample evidence among Boer War poems of a more clear-eyed consideration of that fine balance between folly and fame which characterizes all war. Again and again poets speculated on the war as an emblem of the common man's insignificance in the midst of cataclysmic events; the soldier became a symbol of helpless man acting out a relentless destiny to the noble or pathetic best of his abilities. Hardy's war poems immediately come to mind, but he was not alone. In contrast to the extravagant heroics of much Boer War verse, a considerably cooler view of the soldier emerges from Alfred Cochrane's 'The Colonel' (*Collected Verses*, 1903):

> He long has found that war's romance
> Is but the issue of occasion,
> Since deathless fame requires the chance
> Of deathless onset or invasion.
> So, never glittering in the fight,
> And cutting no sensational capers,
> He serves his Queen, a faithful knight,
> And knows his work and signs his papers.

The departure of troops 'to their hopeless wars' struck other poets as it did Hardy. Ella Fuller Maitland mused on the incongruous pageantry of the occasion in 'Through the Streets' (*Spectator*, 2 December 1899):

> Through the dim London morning
> The soldiers rode away,
> The crowd, in sable, round them;
> The sky above them grey.
>
> Two strains of music played them—
> One mournful and one glad.
> It was the mournful music
> That sounded the least sad.

A similar mood appears in Alfred Noyes's 'Rank and File' (*The Enchanted Island*, 1909), which may not refer directly to the Boer War, but could not have been written long after it:

> See the gleam of the white sad faces
> Moving steadily, row on row,
> Marching away to their hopeless wars:
> Drum-taps, drum-taps, where are they marching?

> Terrible, beautiful, human faces,
>   Common as dirt, but softer than snow,
>   Coarser than clay, but calm as the stars.

In Jane Barlow's blank verse one-acter, 'Ghost-Bereft', published in the *National Review*, 36 (1900), 273–85, the heroine reflects on the departure of her husband for the front a year earlier. Amidst the undeniable signs of the advancing seasons she comes to accept, almost with timid relief, that she must at last give up all hope of his return:

> Last time I came here frost lay on the grass
> Along the borders, and the air was cold,
> So cold, I thought how it would be warm and bright
> Where Gerald was; and then I seemed to hear
> The bullets shrieking in it. And now all day
> It is warm and bright. I only hear the birds
> That wake me singing. It will be a long, long time
> Before the days are quiet and dark again. . . .
>   Half glad he was, I know,
> Half glad to go, even when he said good-bye,
> And said: 'Don't let those rhododendrons blossom
> Till I come back to see them.' There they are,
> The white ones glimmering low upon the edge,
> Too steady to be foam. They are early.

Some poets attempted to re-create the quality of the soldier's experience in South Africa not in a heroic mode, but in a manner closer to actuality. In Kaufmann C. Spiers's 'To the Fallen' the soldier struggles on 'Beneath that burning barrenness of blue', a phrase which Harriet Childe-Pemberton expands into a full chord:

> Oh, Friend! that veldt
> Stretching eternally, is fit to melt
> The very heart out of a soldier's hope!
> Sometimes, when fever gives my fancy scope,
> I dream that hell is like the veldt,—a waste,—
> A changeless desert, wherein who be placed
> Against invading madness must keep guard,—
> Arid, monotonous, despairing, hard![15]

---

[15] Spiers, 'To the Fallen', *Guido and Veronica* (London: David Nutt, 1903); Childe-Pemberton, 'Men, Women, and a War', *Love Knows and Waits* (London: John Long, 1906).

Walter C. Casselton's 'The Sentinel', on the other hand, sketches a more restful moment in the soldier's life—

> Bright glow the tents, where upon tent-poles swaying
> The lanterns flicker;
> Till day's last bugle-notes, with long drawn sigh,
> Hush song and laughter—lights fade out and die.—

while 'Moonlight on the Veld', by R. S. Craig, is a sombre aquarelle of his final encampment:

> The night wind lingers where the dead are lying,
> By dreaming homesteads and deserted towers,
> Where lonely night-birds by the burns are crying,
> By slumbering waters and by folded flowers.[16]

In Beatrice Allhusen's 'A Northerner', however, the soldier's strangeness in his harsh environment makes rest impossible:

> They buried me, who loved the sea,
> In an unwatered land,
> Where for all shade, the savage thorn
> Pierced the red arid sand. . . .
> But underneath that ardent sun my body could not lie,—
> Even in death there was no peace for such a man as I.

Only once his restless spirit has made its way back to a familiar world can it accept death as final:

> 'Neath old familiar stars at length,
> Lightening a wind-swept sky,
> I watched, where circled overhead
> The seabird's mournful cry. . . .
> I heard the beat of wind-swept waves upon the silent shore,
> And I knew that I had passed beyond and was dead for evermore.[17]

Death in battle had become, for a number of poets, a matter of considerable ambivalence. Still seen as an act of high sacrifice and as a test of manhood, it was incontestably also a tragic waste and a disturbingly blunt reminder of the terror and mortality that lurk beneath the surface of life. The dice is loaded against man, even

---

[16] Casselton, *Verses* (London: Grant Richards, 1903); Craig, *In Borderland* (Hawick, 1899).
[17] Beatrice M. Allhusen and Geraldine Robertson-Glasgow, *Verses* (Hampstead, 1905).

if the game is of epic proportions, and most especially against the soldier, as Meredith suggests in 'Before the Storm':

> They stand to be her sacrifice,
> The sons this mother flings like dice.

In such a context, ask the stars in B. Paul Neuman's 'Vox Militantis', why squander one short life with such prodigality?

> Cold, calm, and brilliant, from that awful height
> They ask: 'Were ye so weary of the light?
> Ours the slow aeons, yours the flying day,
> Why reckless fling its noon and eve away?'

For Ethel Clifford national glory could not offset the loss inflicted on a single bereaved one. The celebrations in her 'A Song of Peace', inspired by the events of 31 May 1902, are punctuated by the refrain:

> My soldier is sleeping still,
> Under the hill

and in 'A Song of Victory' the clash between public jubilation and private sorrow is even more marked:

> 'Ring out the bells for Victory,
> The glorious message tell!'
> 'How strange that for a victory
> They ring the passing bell.'[18]

The soldier's death made itself felt to Frederick G. Bowles with a startling if crude immediacy in 'A Dead Man's Rifle' (*Songs of Yesterday*, 1902), a poem apparently inspired by the disastrous battles of December 1899:

> I touched its hot metallic lip,
> Black with his deadly fellowship—
> God! how the bullets spin and rip
> In the dark days of December.
>
> And stark and yellow now he lay,
> With wide eyes to the burning day;
> The warm wet veldt had rolled away
> In the dark days of December.

[18] Meredith's poem, apparently uncollected, appears in *Pro Patria et Regina*, ed. William Knight (Glasgow: James Maclehose, 1901); Neuman, *Pro Patria*; Ethel Clifford, *Songs of Dreams* (London: Bodley Head, 1903).

Although F. Norreys Connell's 'Before the Battle' is pre-Boer
War—it appeared in *Pearson's Magazine* in August 1899—it is
typical of many contemporary poems, simple and balladic in form,
which attempted to express the soldier's own sardonic conception
of his gamble with fate:

> Eternity isn't a pill
> You want when you're not feeling ill.
> At dawn, safe and sound, at night underground;
> Whist! Matey, the mornin' is chill!

A similar theme, handled with an elusively naïve but powerful
bluntness, appears in two more ballads: John Huntley Skrine's
'Digging the Grave (After Magersfontein)':

> Shovel and pick, and a moonlight broad
> On the soil of the veldt up-heaven.
> Pillow and bed for a dreamless head—
> Comrades nine times seven. . . .
>
> Sixty and three were the lads at dawn,
> Lusty and light were they.
> What is he whom the moonbeams see?—
> Four arms' burden of clay

and the extraordinarily foreshortened 'Sniped', by Arthur
Maquarie, here given in full:

> Last night I heard a sob
> Beside me as I lay;
> I turned and fell asleep,
> I woke and it was day.
>
> The bugle called to arms,
> We rushed and worked the gun,
> Ten hours we fought unscathed,
> But we were lacking one.
>
> At night we bathed our heads
> And laid us down to rest;
> The one we lacked was there
> With blood upon his breast.
>
> A little patch of black
> With pink around the rim—
> We cursed our sniping foes
> And dug a grave for him.[19]

[19] Skrine, *The Queen's Highway and Other War Lyrics* (London: Elkin Matthews, 1900);
Maquarie, *The Voice in the Cliff* (London: Simpkin Marshall, 1909).

G

If the soldier's death proved an evocative theme in these years, the man himself often served as a figure of the perplexed everyman, a symbol resonant with undefined heartache. In this role he impinged on the imagination of Herbert Trench, in 'I heard a Soldier' (*New Poems*, 1907):

> I heard a soldier sing some trifle
> Out in the sun-dried veldt alone;
> He lay and cleaned his grimy rifle
> Idly, behind a stone.
>
> 'If after death, love, comes a waking,
> And in their camp so dark and still
> The men of dust hear bugles, breaking
> Their halt upon the hill,
>
> 'To me the slow and silver pealing
> That then the last high trumpet pours
> Shall softer than the dawn come stealing
> For, with its call, comes yours!'
>
> What grief of love had he to stifle,
> Basking so idly by his stone,
> That grimy soldier with his rifle,
> Out in the veldt, alone?

A poet to whom this view of the soldier could be expected to appeal was A. E. Housman. The loss of his brother Herbert at the front gave a sharper and more poignant edge to the gentle melancholy and seductive fatalism which the soldier habitually inspired in him anyway.[20] He published 'Illic Jacet' in the *Academy*, 24 February 1900, and wrote to his sister: 'The function of poetry is to harmonize the sadness of the world.' Certainly, the poem presents the soldier as more than half in love with death:

> Oh hard is the bed they have made him,
>   And common the blanket and cheap;
> But there he will lie as they laid him:
>   Where else could you trust him to sleep? . . .
>
> And low is the roof, but it covers
>   A sleeper content to repose;
> And far from his friends and his lovers
>   He lies with the sweetheart he chose.

---

[20] I am indebted to Norman Marlow, *A. E. Housman: Scholar and Poet* (London: Routledge, Kegan Paul, 1958) for information used in this and the following paragraphs. All verse quotations are from *Last Poems*.

It is difficult to say how many more poems Housman wrote about his brother's death. 'Illic Jacet' appears as number IV in *Last Poems* (1922), the first volume of verse Housman published after a silence of almost three decades: *A Shropshire Lad* had appeared in 1896. According to the 1922 volume's Preface, most of the poems belong 'to dates between 1895 and 1910'. In *A. E. Housman: Scholar and Poet* (1958), p. 18, Norman Marlow claims that, in *Last Poems*, VIII 'Soldier from the wars returning' and XVII 'Astronomy' were inspired by Herbert's death. From internal evidence V 'Grenadier', VI 'Lancer', and XIII 'The Deserter' would seem to refer to the Boer War, too. 'The Deserter' dwells on the same passionate wooing of death in distant lands as 'Illic Jacet':

> Their love is for their own undoing,
>   And east and west
> They scour about the world a-wooing
>   The bullet to their breast.
>
> Sail away the ocean over,
>   Oh sail away,
> And lie there with your leaden lover
>   For ever and a day.

Both poems strongly suggest that the 'volunteer' is no volunteer at all, but is strangely drawn to self-destruction, a suggestion which 'Grenadier' tempers further with a sad, ironic comment on the small rewards of such death:

> To-morrow after new young men
>   The sergeant he must see,
> For things will all be over then
>   Between the Queen and me.
>
> And I shall have to bate my price,
>   For in the grave, they say,
> Is neither knowledge nor device
>   Nor thirteen pence a day.

'Astronomy', reminiscent of Hardy's 'Drummer Hodge', was Housman's most powerful contribution to the poetry of the Boer War. Like Hardy, he strips the soldier's death of all its patriotic

and heroic glamour, and substitutes for it a sudden, stark awareness of a cosmic immensity in terms of which the soldier's death
is of pitifully small importance:

> The Wain upon the northern steep
>   Descends and lifts away.
> Oh I will sit me down and weep
>   For bones in Africa.
>
> For pay and medals, name and rank,
>   Things that he has not found,
> He hove the Cross to heaven and sank
>   The pole-star underground.
>
> And now he does not even see
>   Signs of the nadir roll
> At night over the ground where he
>   Is buried with the pole.

The eternal cycle of constellations both indicates a scale of time
and space in which the soldier's aspirations are absurd, and forms
a gauge of the tragic proportions of his error: *he* makes the
decision to go south, hence sinking the pole-star below the horizon,
but now he is buried beneath the Southern Cross and can 'not
even see' the foreign stars which, by implication, move in sublime
indifference over the folly of his ambition. Few poems have
caught so precisely, and yet with such resonance, the peculiar
dichotomy of late-Victorian imperial military campaigns: the
spectacle of thousands of young men going off to lose their lives
in the remote places of the earth in the service of an ideology only
barely understood.

Poetry on the pity of war was not the only way in which the new,
sharpened concern with the common soldier's lot revealed itself.
Satire, or at least outspoken exposure of the treatment and
leadership to which Tommy was subjected, formed an integral
part of this new war literature. A. St. John Adcock produced, in
Songs of the War (1900), a whole volume of Kiplingesque lampoons
on the contractors, equipment, and generalship that made the
soldier's life harder than it needed to have been. 'Tommy on his
Tack' was written after it transpired that certain contractors had
shipped off to South Africa tinned meat unsaleable in England:

An' off we goes with tons of tins of prehistoric waste,
That's strong enough to overcome the strongest man of taste,
An' 'ave to start subscribin', when the voyage once begins,
To 'elp the widders of the men what opens up the tins!

'An Awakening' lambasts the blissful amateurishness and inferior weaponry with which the War Office expected its armies to win wars:

It's a way we have in England, it's the good old British way,
To leave it all to Tommy, cheaply arm him as we may,
To dream that if he's sent to win, no matter how or where,
Though death and hell should bar the road—he'll still get there.

Another failure of the War Office, this time its inability to match Boer tactics in the early months of the war, inspired *Punch's* Owen Seaman to write:

'Tis an old truth, but very sound—
You get to swim through being drowned;
And this, I feel, is what a war
Is ultimately useful for. . . .

We heard that [they] had got some guns,
But only very little ones;
We also heard of mounted forces,
But never dreamed they rode on horses.

With more brutal directness, these sentiments also inform T. S. Omond's 'February, 1902':

Not theirs the doom, your dupes, who, nothing loath,
Sprang forth like heroes, wrought and bled like men,
Tricked, foiled, deceived, yet fighting to the last.[21]

One aspect of Tommy's treatment that caused some controversy was the amateur nursing to which he was subjected. It became fashionable for women who regarded themselves as fairly emancipated, particularly among the titled set, to go to South Africa as nurses. No doubt there were numerous devoted women among the many who went to South Africa for this purpose, and Kipling pays a feeling tribute to them in 'Dirge of the Dead Sisters' (*The Five Nations*). But it also soon became clear that the scene of war had become a fashionable rallying point for society

[21] Seaman, unidentified press cutting; Omond, *Scattered Verses* (Tunbridge Wells: R. Pelton, 1904).

ladies with vaguely charitable intentions and little useful knowledge. 'The place is swarming with women, and they are driving
the people at the Castle crazy with bothering them so', wrote
Violet Brooke-Hunt on her arrival in Cape Town (*A Woman's
Memories*). The Christmas 1900 issue of *Truth*, which throughout
the war kept an argus eye on military mismanagement, pounced
on revelations such as Miss Brooke-Hunt's. Describing the scene
after a fierce battle in which

> The wounded lying
> Are vainly trying
> To scatter the flies around them flying,

and many are

> Hopelessly maimed
> For life or lamed
> With a bullet through the spine,

the editorial poet turns his full scorn on the 'nurses':

> But who are these
> Taking their ease
> At this end of the crowded tent?
> Who chatter and laugh,
> And merrily chaff,
> In an atmosphere charged with scent?
> My Lady Fitz-Vere
> Is certainly here;
> And Mrs. Maccaw,
> And my Lady Daw,
> For we've seen these dames before;
> And adjusting a curl
> With a kittenish twirl
> It is! it is Anastasia Gore!

The chapter of the war that produced perhaps the greatest
amount of adverse commentary was General Sir Redvers Buller's
incompetent handling of the Natal campaign. Failing repeatedly
to get his forces across the Tugela in order to relieve Ladysmith,
he eventually sent General Sir George White, commanding the
defending forces, a somewhat cryptic heliographed message which
in effect, advised White to surrender: '. . . make the best terms
possible with the general of the besieging forces, after giving me
time to fortify myself on the Tugela'.[22] When this story reached

[22] See Kruger, *Good-Bye Dolly Gray*, p. 143, and Holt, *Boer War*, pp. 279–80.

the press and the War Office, Buller was slated, reprimanded, and recalled to the relative obscurity of the Aldershot command, from where he emerged in October 1901 to defend, in a sensational public speech, his odd advice to White. He explained that he had not meant to tell White to surrender, but had 'spatchcocked' into the message a passage that would allow White to do so if he wished. The outcome of the resultant furore was Buller's enforced retirement on half-pay and a crop of exuberant satires on the spatchcocking general. Hector Munro, in *The Westminster Alice* (?1901), depicted Buller as Humpty Dumpty:

> I sent a message to the White
> To tell him—if you *must*, you might
> But then, I said, you p'raps might not
> (The weather was *extremely* hot).
> This query, too, I spatchcock-slid:
> How would you do it, if you did?
> I did not know, I rather thought—
> And then I wondered if I ought.

An anonymous poem in the National Army Museum, Chelsea, elaborates the lampoon, this time in parody of Browning:

> There lay the Boers; here we. You know my bluff,
> Blunt, bulldog, brutally British sort of way;
> So I went at 'em, like a bull at a gate;
> When—what should turn up but a river between.
> Just my luck. What's worse, it had a bank—
> The very bank on which the wild *Times* blows;
> Rank luck again—and so we lost the guns.
> I did my best, and no man could do more;
> It follows, none could have done more than I.
> I telegraphed: 'White plays. Mate in three moves.
> I'm beat, as sure as two and two makes four.
> Colenso's Primary Arithmetic.'
> Then I just patched, despatched, or spatchcocked in
> (In the middle of a line) '*Chuck up the sponge.*'
> But, Lord, *I* knew my man. And he knew me.
> I can't think clearly when the weather's hot;
> And this despatchcocked cock-and-bullergram
> Was just my fun, to cheer him up a bit.
> And pull his gallant leg.[23]

---

[23] 'The Cock and the Buller', typescript, National Army Museum 6302-48-7.

While poets in England guarded over Tommy's interests and articulated his finer (and not so fine) sensibilities, what did the man himself have to say about it all? One complication, as I suggested earlier, is that it is not always possible to distinguish between poems produced at home and poems written out of personal experience of the war. Some of the pieces already used in this chapter may very well have been soldiers' poems. However, working from those pieces clearly identified as the work of men at the front, we can answer the question in several ways. In the first place, the soldier was for the most part blissfully unaware of the tragic role in which poets such as Hardy and Housman cast him. Secondly, *pace* B. H. Holland, he certainly did not hesitate to write down his own poetic thoughts, which ranged from staunch patriotic convictions and pious jingles (see, for instance, the many which appeared in *Forward!*, the monthly journal of the Soldiers' Christian Association), to comic songs, long narrative ballads, and poignant lyrics on the death of comrades. According to Julian Ralph, every Tommy harboured a poet in his breast: 'In the ease with which [he] pumped his muse, and the abundance of the results, we early came to know that the British army is an organized host of poets' (*At Pretoria*, p. 189).

Among the examples of such verse which have survived in manuscript or print, one readily detects the influences and popular modes of verse discussed earlier. On 25 January 1900 the *Cape Times* published a batch of soldier poems, somewhat apologetically, but no doubt with patriotic intentions. The formulaic opening of a contribution by a ranker of the First Loyal North Lancashire regiment is typical of the rest:

> Kind friends, if you will listen,
> A tale I will unfold
> About the Transvaal Crisis,
> And our soldiers brave and bold.

Similar batches appeared in the *Diamond Fields Advertiser* during the siege of Kimberley, where one contributor lampooned the host of siege bards as follows:

> I just get the words to rhyme,
> Without ripple, without chime,
> Never caring about metre, or the sense.

Here, too, may be found the work of a prolific soldierly master of
the parlour tear-jerker, Private H. Shepherd, again of the Loyal
North Lancashires. The *Advertiser* published his 'The Soldier's
Last Farewell', a competent pastiche, on 11 January 1900 and
several more subsequently. The close similarities between one of
them, 'Sad Memories: A Story of the Anglo-Boer War in Verse',—

> A soldier lay on the battlefield,
> His young life ebbing fast,
> That day he'd fought a stubborn foe,
> Fought nobly to the last—

and Louis H. Victory's 'The Dying Soldier's Dream'—

> The battle raged at Nicholson's Nek:
> An Irish soldier lay,
> Struck down in the dark in the deadly fight,
> His life-blood ebbing away—

show that both writers, one at the front and one in England
worked to well-established formulae, irrespective of what their
experiences may have been.[24]

However, even when clearly concerned with recording personal
experience, the Tommy poet would fall back on traditional
patterns. I have mentioned his fondness for the cadences of
Kipling, but there were other modes that inspired him. Tony
Cooper, for instance, started his *Let 'Em All Come* (broadside,
n.d.), on the siege of Mafeking, with a whole stanza of balladic
space-fillers—

> A song I'll sing to you my friends without the slightest doubt,
> It's on the siege of Mafeking, the truth you'll soon find out,—

and Corporal M. Riley, of the King's Liverpool Regiment,
liberally peppered his otherwise racy and accurate account, *Siege
of Ladysmith* (broadside, n.d.), with the catch phrases of the genre:

What! Tell you about the Siege, Sir? It makes my blood run cold,
To think how we defended Ladysmith, against those warriors bold.
For one hundred and eighteen days, Sir, without a flinch of tire,
We kept those brutes at bay, not heeding their heavy fire. . . .

[24] Shepherd, *Sad Memories: A Story of the Anglo-Boer War in Verse* (Klerksdorp,
1901); Victory, *Imaginations in the Dust* (London, 1903), vol. i.

Now south of our Garrison is Wagon Hill, I remember well the date,
The Boers came on us in thousands, Sir; here brave Cunningham met
   his fate.
Sixth of January, 2.30 a.m., in the sanger back to back,
Seventy of us held our own, Sir, when they made their fierce attack.

There was rifle, Mauser, and Maxim fire whistling o'er our head,
And when the guns commenced to play the sound near woke the
   dead.
The fight went on 17½ hours in the blinding hail and rain;
It was here the brave Devonshire lads earned themselves a name.

To call the Boers both 'warriors bold' and 'brutes' in the same
stanza did not apparently strike the corporal, so careful otherwise
of his facts and figures, as at all odd. Another Ladysmith poet,
trooper Frank Cornwell Rogers of the Imperial Light Horse,
wrote little ditties to the tunes of popular music hall songs such
as 'The Man Who Broke the Bank at Monte Carlo':

> As we piddle along in Ladysmith with an independent air
> You can see the Dutchmen stare
> And murmur 'Vat markair?'   [What's wrong?]
> You can see them scoot wherever we shoot
> And though the buggers are awful cute
> Yet we had them all on toast at Elandslaagte.[25]

Tommy's convictions were normally as orthodox and unexceptionable as his verse. The regimental magazines of the period
(their rapid increase during the 1890s was in itself evidence of the
soldier's growing literacy) carried many loyalist outpourings from
the ranks, such as Bugler Noble's 'Ready, aye Ready!' in the Royal
Marines' *Globe and Laurel*, March 1900:

> We are waiting for our orders to repair to Afric's shore,
> We want a rub at Kruger, we want to join the war
> To avenge our comrades' slaughter, to fight for Queen and
>   country, too,
> To take our place in the firing line and try what we can do.

On the other hand, I have not come across any campaign verse
that reproduces the strident patriotism of the more clamorous
doggerel written at home. The soldier simply did not look at himself from a perspective so untouched by irony or hardship.

[25] Manuscript Diary in private hands.

The most common type of poem written at the front was the straight narrative, often too long, laborious, and toneless, but at least genuine and ambitious in the attempt to convey experience and personal response. So, for instance, the execrable verse but strong feelings of Private A. Butler's 'Lines on the March of the Oxfordshire Light Infantry across the Orange Free State' found many echoes:

> War, war! what hast thou done for me,
> And thousands more besides,
> Who've had to leave their dear old homes,
> Their children and their wives? . . .
>
> We fought throughout [the] Sabbath day
> With neither food nor drink,
> And who did to the river stray
> Was shot upon its brink. . . .
>
> Of course some tradesmen stayed at home,
> And well they let us know it;
> Their prices nearly struck us dumb,
> But of course we had to buy it.[26]

William Corner's 'A Ballad of the 34th', Private E. H. Pollard's 'One Hundred Lines on the 6th Division', and Bugler G. C. Edwards's *The Relief of Ladysmith* (broadside, n.d.) are all examples of such rough-cast balladry.[27] Others may be found in the many crudely produced campaign papers (the *Cossack Post*, *Grouse*, *Gram*, *Orcana Oyster*, and *Pavonia Piffler*, to mention only some) which came out of the war, as well as in a number of siege papers, such as the *Mafeking Mail Siege Slips*, the *Ladysmith Lyre*, and the *Ladysmith Bombshell*. The *Lyre*, particularly, was a spirited if somewhat unsubtle production, edited by G. W. Steevens and W. T. Maud of the *Graphic*.[28] It kept up a stream of banter, in both prose and verse, in an attempt to keep its readers' minds off their predicament. The calibre of the verse in both the *Lyre* and the *Bombshell* may be gauged from 'The Poet under the River Bank'

[26] Typescript in the Royal Green Jackets Museum, Winchester. I am indebted to Major H. P. Patterson for permission to quote these verses.
[27] Corner, *The Story of the 34th Company (Middlesex) Imperial Yeomanry* (London: Fisher Unwin, 1902), app. V; Pollard's typescript poem is in the Royal Green Jackets Museum as well.
[28] See Lionel James, *High Pressure* (London, 1929), p. 138; and James Scott, *Souvenir of the Siege of Ladysmith* (Pietermaritzburg, 1900).

(*Lyre*), which refers to the joys of the bombshelters dug out of the steep banks of the Klip River—

> Wake, for above Umbulwana the coming day
> Lights up the signal for the guns to play;
> How sweet to know 'tis but a living tomb
> Awaits you, and there's time to creep away—

or from the sceptical view of Buller in a noisy song sung to the tune of 'There was an Old Nigger' (*Bombshell*):

> So saddle up your horses, keep your rifles clean,
> Sling your cartridges around your manly chest:
> Buller's men will do their share, but it's easy to be seen,
> That our garrison will have to do the rest.

No wonder that when Army Schoolmaster W. N. Gilbert surveyed his own poetic efforts on the siege, he exclaimed: 'What do you expect on ¼ lb. bread a day? I'm not a Chatterton!'[29]

Soldiers, however, also produced more ambitious verse, clearly meant for public delivery and hence informed with more obvious narrative intent and sense of occasion. These poems normally relied on the received patterns of the recitational verse we saw earlier, as in *John, the Swell: A Poem Founded on an Incident at the Battle of Spion Kop* (1900), by Corporal Drake of the Scottish Rifles:

> Was I at the war, Sir? Why yes, see this 'ere scar?
> I got that on Spion Kop, Sir,—no,—we didn't get a bar,
> God knows the fight was hard enough,—some said 'twas worse than hell,
> I ain't been to *that* place, so of course I cannot tell.

The facility with which soldiers could produce this sort of thing is suggested by a note attached to a poem which appeared in the *Household Brigade Magazine*, written by Private L. McHugh of the Coldstreamers: 'I hurriedly traced the enclosed lines whilst on outpost duty a few days since. Heidelberg, 22 October 1900':

> You all remember the Modder,
>   And the fearful carnage there,
> When every man had his work cut out
>   And bravely did his share.

---

[29] Manuscript Diary, National Army Museum 6309-114.

> The Guards were there from the morning
> Till the last red gleam of the sun,
> Through shot and shell and the thirst of hell,
> Till the field was fought and won.

In the same magazine appeared Lance-Corporal Murray's 'The Unknown' (July 1901), a magnificent vignette of Victorian melodrama:

> A ring of empty cases
>   A rifle splashed with red
> Tightly clasped in an ashen hand,
>   In the last strong grip of the dead.
> A silent, grey-clad figure
>   In the straggling grass laid low,
> And the tale is told of a hero bold
>   And an overwhelming foe.

Such incidents were the delight of war artists and their magazine audiences. Another one that attracted several poets and illustrators was the story of a wounded soldier accidentally left on the field. Before his death, he took out a pocket chess set and carefully placed a single pawn on the board. C.B.'s 'Only a Pawn!', which appeared in the 2nd Battalion Argyll and Sutherland Highlanders' *The Thin Red Line* (June 1901), makes explicit a sense of outrage absent from other, more romantic treatments of the story:

> He gnashed his teeth as he madly thought
>   Of how many blunders had been the same;
> Entrapped like children by those they sought,
>   And who, he wondered, would bear the blame?
> He wept with rage till his eyes were blind,
> At the thought of all he must leave behind.
> And the red sun sank in a crimson ball,
> Veiling the earth in her nightly pall.

A most prolific producer of campaign narratives was Mark Walter West of Thorneycroft's Mounted Infantry, on the Natal front. Mr. Horace W. E. Green of Johannesburg has sent me sixty typescript pages of West's poems covering the battles of Colenso, Tugela, and Spion Kop. All are shaped in a loose, loping weave of couplets or alternate rhyme which are too uneven to hold the reader's attention for any length, but they contain brisk moments of action or tension, such as the experience of shell fire on Spion Kop:

> And I oft' see that wall go shivering,
> All good hard honest rock,
> Like iron 'neath a flash-jet crumbling,
> With its blighting, melting shock. . . .
> I crouch and crawl through cover,
> Then 'tween some boulders spurt,
> When a shell bites through my breeches,
> Leaving my legs unhurt.
> And oh! the mangled soldiers,
> Whose tortuous forms lie dead,
> And the wounded crawling to cover,
> If but to hide the head.

The realities of being under fire attracted numerous soldier poets. R. P. Kent wrote his 'Memories of Magersfontein' in the trenches on the banks of the Modder River in 1900:

> The Guards' fierce charge,—the maxims' fire,
> Again I see and hear,
> Whilst Lyddite's thunder, rising higher,
> Fills every breast with fear:
> And men lie stricken, blanched, and curled
> In death's deformity,
> And foes by scores are swiftly hurled
> Into Eternity.[30]

Lance-Corporal J. McLoughlin's *How the Lancashires Took Spion Kop* (broadside, n.d.) is a particularly harrowing piece, revealing a finer sense of contrast than one finds in most of these pieces:

I'll ne'er forget the anguish all through that awful day,
The groan of the wounded soldier—'Will no one take me away?'
His cry of 'Lord deliver me out of this living hell',
But only to be finally despatched by a merciless pom-pom shell. . . .
That night the pale moon rose and shone around the mountain top,
And kissed the cold pale lips of the soldier lads who fell at Spion Kop.

An uncommon poem was J.A.E.B.'s account of a night attack on sleeping Boers at Frankfort, Orange Free State, which appeared in the Royal West Kent regiment's *Queen's Own Gazette*, April 1901. The poem is unusual on several counts: it is in blank verse,

[30] Three manuscript poems, belonging to and quoted by permission of Mr. M. Kent, Port Elizabeth.

it shows much sympathy for the victims of the attack, and, most
unusually, it attempts to pass comment on the politics of the war:

> The startled men
> Rush from their tents in terror. While, from countless mouths
> Fire and lead are hurled, ripping the tent to ribbons,
> And the sleeping forms within are riddled through.
> Soon all is silence, save the groans of dying,
> Or the moans of some poor miserable wretch with leg
> Or arm destroyed. Old men and boys, who by their President
> Have been compelled to fight for his own ends,
> Now left alone, not e'en a man whose generalship
> Might be relied on. . . .
>
> Call you it victory? Alas! 'tis war's illfortune that the strong
> And weak alike must pay the penalty of greed.

If verse narratives constitute the biggest single group of campaign
poems, complaint and satire must come a close second. Tommy's
protest verse ranged from the simplest levels of rhymed 'grouse'
to substantial satire and caustic comment on all aspects of the
soldier's life, from the food—

> Flies in the butter,
> Flies on the ham,
> Flies on Bobby Graham's face
> Walking in the jam,
> Flies buzzing round your ears
> And in your nose and eyes,
> But we're having such a jolly time,
> We don't mind flies—

the landscape—

> Land of deceitfulness and lies,
> Of dirt and vermin, dust and flies,
> Whose rivers, save it rains or snows,
> Are beds in which no water flows,
> Why call them rivers—goodness knows. . . .
> Thou, land with no good thing whatever,
> I leave thee now, I trust for ever—

and the cold—

> John, here am I, half dead, and sittin',
> Shakin', shiverin', hoastin', spittin',

> Wi' my puir voice like weasles squeakin',
> And wi' my marrow bones a'creakin',
> While melancholy clouds the spirit
> O' your afflicted poet laureate—

to military splendour itself—

> The grand romance of ancient war
> Sounds well in song or story,
> But what is fame to broken hearts?
> Oh! where is all the glory?—

and the callousness of commanding officers:

> As I knelt by the ghastly, blood-stained clay
> That had been my life-long friend,
> When the sounds of our chasing guns grew faint
> And that red day neared its end:
> There fell on my ears a mocking laugh,
> Though my dimmed eyes none could see,
> 'Lord love you! what does it matter, lad,
> If the Colonel is made C.B.'[31]

Soldierly 'grouse' verse could take on a corrosiveness which confirmed a general level of outspokenness new to the annals of war. Thus a bombardier recuperating in a Kimberley hospital exclaimed:

> War! War! what is it?
> You talk in a mighty way,
> As if you knew all about it,
> When you read what the papers say.

A New Zealand captain, reflecting on the British disaster at Bothasberg, levelled a steady aim at the ordnance suppliers—

> For they fell upon us tooth and nail once they started,
> And our gun fired eighty rounds and then got jammed;
> And twenty-six of ours this life departed,
> And the man who made that gun, I hope he's damned—

---

[31] Hedley V. Mackinnon, *War Sketches* (Charlottetown, 1900); 'An Australian's Farewell to South Africa' (1904), typescript, sent by an anonymous correspondent; Ayrshire Policeman's verse letter quoted in Major W. Steel Brownlie, *The Proud Trooper: The History of the Ayrshire Yeomanry* (London, 1964), p. 147; 'Where is All the Glory?' *Thin Red Line*, 8 (July 1902), 46; and Centurion, 'Audi Alteram Partem', *Ante-Room Ballads* (London: Routledge, Kegan Paul, 1905).

while an anonymous poet who claimed that most of his verses 'were scribbled in note books during the war in South Africa', rid himself of some unambiguous sentiments about this experience:

> I must remain in this cursed land
> Till K. says 'The War is o'er',
> And all for an inch of ribbon dear:
> Why, a penny would buy far more.[32]

At other times these sardonic comments on life at the front took the direction of comedy, reaching a level of superb nonsense verse in a lengthy ballad, 'A South African Dream', ascribed to 'A Cavalry Subaltern' and reproduced in Sir George Arthur's *The Story of the Household Cavalry*, Volume ii (1909):

> It gives me pleasure to report
> That Kruger and that Steyn
> Are in nine different places
> All ending in -fontein;
> That Botha has surrendered and
> Is fighting to the death,
> And De la Rey is either well
> Or dead from want of breath.
> A British general has destroyed
> A non-existent force,
> And storm'd a place that wasn't held
> With most terrific loss.

Much of this type of verse was produced and recited or sung around the campfire or at 'smoking concerts'. Parody and burlesque were favourite modes. P. T. Ross's *A Yeoman's Letters* (1901), 'composed of letters written to a friend from South Africa . . . to represent a true picture of the every-day life of a trooper in the Imperial Yeomanry', contains several pieces of this kind. So, for instance, a popular item of music hall pathos, 'Somebody's Darling', became a fairly iconoclastic review of the soldier's life, while 'The Ballad of the Bayonet', apparently the result of a

---

[32] G. H. Oatey (4th Battery, Royal Field Artillery), *Comrade Jim: A Story of the War* (Falmouth: Edwin T. Oliver, 1900); Capt. John Tombleson, *Bothasberg and Other Verses* (London: Walter Scott, 1910); and Centurion, 'Vain Regrets', *Ante-Room Ballads*.

group effort, is a delightful burlesque of both music hall heroics and the recitational ballad. It starts unexceptionably enough—

> Did I ever use the bayonit, sir?
> In the far-off Transvaal War,
> Where I fought for Queen and country, sir,
> Against the wily Boer.
> Aye, many a time and oft, sir,
> I've bared the trusty blade,
> And blessed the dear old Homeland, sir,
> Where it was carefully made—

but what follows would not have moved hearts of oak to anything but hilarity:

> You ask if it e'er took a life, sir?
> Aye, I mind the time full well;
> I had spotted him by a farm, sir,
> And went for him with a yell.
> He tried to escape me hard, sir,
> But I plunged it in his side,
> And there by his own backyard, sir,
> A healthy porker died.

Camp song and concert must have had a considerable part in encouraging and perpetuating the dominant rhythms and easy flow of Tommy's campaign verse. As C. E. Carrington has remarked, the 'folk-art of the late-Victorians was the popular song with a strong melody, a simple rhythm, and a chorus, and is now almost extinct. Everyone joined in, and everyone knew some dozens of songs'.[33] To the universality of the popular song one must add the ubiquity of the banjo, with its strident tones and tempo. Kipling pays tribute to the instrument's power in 'The Song of the Banjo' (*The Seven Seas*), and in Ladysmith Donald Macdonald found: 'The banjo is king out here. Where the foreloper leads the banjo follows; it is the music of the veldt, of the transport riders, the Rand miners, and the heretofore unenlisted legion who volunteered against the Boer.' (*How We Kept the Flag Flying*, pp. 76–7.) Hence the insistent regularity, even monotony, of so much of Tommy's verse should not too readily be put down to uninspired craftsmanship, but to the fact that it is inspired by camp song: it is 'banjo verse', plain and simple.

---

[33] *A Subaltern's War*, p. 228.

On the lonely march from Beira through Rhodesia to relieve Mafeking, the 65th Squadron of Imperial Yeomanry joined feelingly in the extempore songs of Corporal J. B. McCartney, who must have spoken for them all in his complaint about the squadron's obscure role in a side-show of the war:

> Robbed of every chance of glory,
>   To a soldier always dear;
> Robbed of every joy and comfort,
>   Worst of all—their chance of Beer.
>
> Never mentioned in the papers,
>   Lost to friends and light as well,
> Dragging out a dread existence
>   In a veritable H-l.[34]

In Rigby Wason's collection of *Some Volunteer Verse* (1905), J. B. Lloyd, whose book on the war we have already met, wrote about his own contributions:

> We were born among the outposts,
>   We were nurtured on the tramp,
> In a barrack-hut at Shorncliffe,
>   In the guard-tent of the camp.

Among many such pieces in the volume are the songs of Captain J. R. Bailey of the Grenadier Guards, all produced at concerts in Pretoria. It was in Pretoria, too, that Violet Brooke-Hunt's Saturday night sing-songs became so popular that she had to take over the local theatre, where all ranks no doubt participated in the noisy chorus of:

> She banged upon the tambourine,
>   And shouted to the lot,
> 'We're marching on to Glory!'
>   Says I, 'You're marching on to What?'[35]

And one would like to know where and by whom was composed a song which has remained popular in South Africa to this day: 'We are Marching to Pretoria'.

The considerable evidence of such campfire camaraderie must not, however, be allowed to obscure the tensions which existed among men at the front as well. It is clear, for instance, that at

[34] Quoted in Gilbert, *Rhodesia—and After*, p. 224.
[35] Mrs. J. D. Leather-Culley, *On the War Path: A Lady's Letters from the Front* (London: John Long, 1901).

times a very strained relationship existed between regulars and volunteers. The reader will recall that almost two-thirds of the men in South Africa could be regarded as volunteers. Many, of course, had joined regular regiments, but many had joined true volunteer units such as the City Imperial Volunteers, and thus enjoyed privileges unknown to Tommy, such as earning five shillings a day as against thirteen pence. Under these circumstances the extravagant praise meted out to the C.I.V., especially on their return home, galled the regular man in the ranks considerably. In the *Natal Mercury* (27 September 1901) Private Carmichael of the Argyll and Sutherland Highlanders published a bitter poem on the C.I.V. from 'One of the Fighting Line'. A similar poem, 'Our Gallant C.I.V.'s', appeared in the *Green Howards' Gazette* in December

> We were on the march to Komatipoort,
>   To the land of the Portuguese,
> To the fever-stricken vale of death
>   Where they took no C.I.V.'s.
>
> For they wanted only regular corps
>   And scorned the kid-glove ten
> And took on the march through the fever swamp
>   Only seasoned fighting men.
>
> We did not wither away like flowers
>   That died from want of rain,
> Though we lost more men in a single fight
>   Than they did in the whole campaign. . . .
>
> But we are the sons of fighting Sires,
>   We fought with sword not pen,
> We have no friends on the London Press,
>   For we are only common men.

Captain Harry Graham's *Ballads of the Boer War* contain several in this vein, notably 'The Press' and 'The Regiment'.

One of the most excoriating of all Boer War soldier poems that I have come across expresses a tension of a different kind, an animosity that the common soldier could not have expressed in print in earlier wars: his distrust of incompetent commanders. Indeed, the strange metamorphosis which this particular work underwent may very well illustrate a general fate of products of the ranks that were regarded as too outspoken. It deals with one of the war's most notable catastrophes.

The disaster of Magersfontein, where the Highland Brigade lost over a thousand men and the prestigious Black Watch was reduced to half its strength, was a classical example of a conservative commander (Lord Methuen) sticking to the book against all dictates of experience, circumstance, and terrain (Kruger, *Good-Bye Dolly Gray*, pp. 126–35). With inadequate reconnaissance and across open, level veld, Methuen threw 4,000 men in close formation against a superbly fortified Boer position. Compared to the slaughter of fifteen years later, Magersfontein may be regarded as a skirmish, but in December 1899 it was a blow from which an empire reeled and recriminations flashed. 'The Highlanders believed that they had been sent to certain death—"taken into a butcher's shop and left there," said one—and that Methuen had done nothing to relieve them all day.' (Kruger, p. 135.)

In the Strange Africana Collection, Johannesburg, is a typescript copy of an anonymous ballad of twenty-five quatrains, 'The Black Watch at Magersfontein' (S Pam 821 BLA). A slightly different and shorter manuscript version is to be found in the Cape Archives, Cape Town (Acc. 411). A rubric to this copy states: 'The following Verses were written by a Private of the 2nd Black Watch on the Field of Magersfontein 13 December 1899.' The poem is an impassioned, raw utterance. It is cast in the manner of popular oral balladry—

> Tell you the tale of the Battle; Well
>   There aint so much to tell.
> Nine hundred went to the slaughter, and
>   Nearly four hundred fell—[36]

yet it contains some vibrant descriptions of the day's action:

> Wire, and the Mauser rifle,
>   Thirst, and a burning sun,
> Knocked us down by the hundreds,
>   E'er the day was done. . . .
>
> Bullets and shells ne'er appalled us,
>   Trenches nor boulder strewn hills,
> But just a few strands of wire fencing,
>   Brought us, nonplussed, standing still.

[36] All quotations from the Strange version.

But the memorable part of the ballad is its final section, an uncompromising attack on the leaders who had failed the soldier:

> Such was the day for our regiment,
>   Dread the revenge we will take.
> Dearly we paid for the blunder of a
>   Drawing room General's mistake.
>
> Where was the gallant General—
>   Three miles in rear out of sight.
> No men to issue us orders,
>   Men doing what they thought right. . . .
>
> Why wer'nt we told of the trenches?
>   Why wer'nt we told of the wire?
> Why were we marched up in column
>   May Tommy Atkins enquire. . . .
>
> Do they know this in old England?
>   Do they know his incompetence yet?
> Tommy has learnt to his sorrow
>   And Tommy will never forget.

It is a short step from here to Sassoon's 'The General':

> 'Good-morning; good-morning!' the General said
> When we met him last week on our way to the line.
> Now the soldiers he smiled at are most of 'em dead,
> And we're cursing his staff for incompetent swine.[37]

The subsequent history of the ballad, however, suggests that the time was not yet ripe for such verse to appear in print. On 26 May 1900 a shortened version of it, pruned of all the tendentious stanzas and attributed to Corporal David McMahon, appeared in the *Simonstown and District Chronicle*, Cape Town. But this was not the final transformation. In November 1901 the *Thin Red Line* published an even tamer version of the poem, now changed into a heroic and patriotic encomium, thus completely reversing the original poem's sentiments:

> And round our well loved chieftain's lips
>   The smile that proudly played,
> Said better far than words could say:
>   I trust my brave brigade.

[37] *Men Who March Away*, ed. I. M. Parsons (London: Chatto & Windus, 1965).

The poem is here ascribed to 'three invalid private soldiers of the ill-fated Highland Brigade'. How many campaign poems were similarly transmogrified on their way from trench to print it is impossible to say, but it may well be that more of the unexceptionable Tommy ballads which found their way into the press had had such caustic origins.

Also among the poems that may not have survived in print, or can only accidentally be known to have originated in the Boer War, are those soldier poems which are not concerned with war at all, poems about daffodils and green fields, quiet studies in which authors tried to find distraction from the dreary, sun-baked veld around them and the boring or harrowing business of the campaign. Captain W. A. Adams ('Auguste Smada') was a cavalry officer trapped in Ladysmith, where he wrote a volume of poems of philosophic and pantheistic reverie, *Rus Divinum* (1900), that contains not a single reference to either the war or South Africa.[38] An even more unlikely body of poetry to have come out of the war, and certainly an odd collection to have survived, is a small cache of poems that passed between Austin Ferrand and the aesthete poet, Lionel Johnson.

Ferrand and his brother, Alfred, had emigrated to South Africa just before the war. Both joined the colonial forces, Alfred being killed at Ladysmith on 6 January 1900.[39] Austin Ferrand kept up a poetic correspondence with Lionel Johnson, who had been a fellow undergraduate at Oxford, and some of these poems found their way into *Outlook*. Ferrand's 'Guard at Night', expressing a passionate relationship in terms redolent of the *Yellow Book*, appeared here on 27 October 1900:

> The three red flecks on your warm brown skin
>   Are three bright gems of Orion's belt:
> They stir my blood with fire and wine;
>   The slow sky wheels o'er the barren veldt
> Till the starlight faints, falls pale and thin.

It is not clear whether the editor of *Outlook*, T. W. H. Crosland, realized that the poem had been dedicated to Lionel Johnson, then in the last stages of alcoholic despair and loneliness—he died in

---

[38] The information about Adams appears in a publisher's note at the end of his *Horae Fugaces* (London: Fisher Unwin, 1902).
[39] I am indebted to *The Complete Poems of Lionel Johnson*, ed. Iain Fletcher (London: Unicorn, 1953), *passim*, for information about Johnson and the Ferrand brothers.

October 1902. From a poem which Johnson addressed to Ferrand in 1887, 'The End', not published in the author's lifetime, it is clear that a strong homosexual relationship had existed between them. When Austin Ferrand, too, was killed in September 1900, *Outlook* published Johnson's farewell to his two friends, 'Brothers', on 8 December:

> Now hath Death dealt a generous violence,
>   Calling thee swiftly hence,
> By the like instrument of instant fire,
>   To join thy heart's desire,
> Thy brother, slain before thee; . . .
> Fair warrior brothers, excellently dead,
>   Your loyal lifeblood shed,
> In death's gray distant land do thou and he
>   Keep any mind of me,
> Of old days filled with laughter of delight
>   And many a laughing night?

At the same time *Outlook* printed another of Ferrand's sonnets written in South Africa, though again with no indication that the recipient was Johnson. Here is the sestet:

> I feel the battery of rushing blood
> Drown us again in the resistless flood
> Of overpowering passion, undenied
> And unregretted. You are by my side,
> Laid on my heart, through all the surging night,
> Till with dawn you fade from touch and sight.

Here the trail ends. There is no entry for Austin Ferrand in the British Library Catalogue or the *Dictionary of National Biography*, and I have come across no further poems of his in the periodicals of the time. It is a pity, since the two poems addressed to Johnson represent a powerful voice which was either unique among campaign poets or, for obvious reasons, suppressed in all other cases.

We are left, finally, with those poems which record that event on the battle-field which is both the most harrowing of all and the most difficult to convey in verse: the death of a comrade. Of the numerous awkward though moving attempts to express such loss, shock, and sorrow, *The Fate of the 14th Battery* (broadside, n.d.),

by Driver W. Gardner of the Royal Field Artillery, may stand as a
fitting example:

> Oh! that day, yes, that dreadful day,
> When my comrades were laid low;
> The shells they crashed and the bullets passed
> With deadly effect from the foe. . . .
>
> Then there came that wretched roll call,
> Which did make my blood quite creep,
> As to the names of half my comrades,
> I couldn't hear a low voice speak.

In more competent, but perhaps more melodramatic verses
J. H. M. Abbott of the Australian contingent paid tribute, in
Tommy Cornstalk (1902), to those of his countrymen whom Africa
had claimed for good:

> Life that we might have lived, love that we might have loved,
>   Sorrow of all sorrows, we have drunk thy bitter lees.
> Speak thou a word to us, here in our narrow beds—
>   Word of thy mourning in lands beyond the seas. . . .
> Spare not thy pity—Life is strong and fair for you—
>   City by the waterside, homestead on the plain.
> Keep ye remembrance, keep ye a place for us—
>   So all the bitterness of dying be not vain.

Two of the most competent poems on the death of fellow soldiers
appeared in Colour Sergeant R. E. Kemp's unpromising *Khaki
Letters from my Colleagues in South Africa* (1901), apparently the
collected edition of a fortnightly magazine published by the Post
Office Telegraphists. Here, unexpectedly, one comes across S. A.
Coase's 'After—!', a poem which, in spite of some ponderousness
throughout, possesses a density and control of imagery well
beyond the capacity of most Tommy verse:

> Before, behind, the sombre Veldt lies still
> While night's advance-guards fast in the pursuit
> Of day come swiftly on: as shadows, mute
> And chilling, they appear. The ragged hill
> Had couched beneath the richest woof the sun
> Could weave with lengthening fingers, but the night
> Has stolen it away, and now the light,
> With all its offspring, flees. The day is done.
> Yet night is not supreme: the starlight falls

Calmly around, revealing man and horse;
The dead; the dying, that with fevered brain
Review the battle through its hideous course;
The charge; the check; the shell; the burning pain;
The swollen tongue, which faint for water calls.
A fitting consummation of a day
To carnage given. The spectacle appals
All else but Death, the prowling shadow there,
Who comes, but not unbidden, from his lair.

One can say much the same about another poem in the volume, 'To Frank Robinson', by R. W. Eglinton of the 24th Middlesex Rifle Volunteers, except that here the wasteland depicted conveys the poet's own disillusion, a conviction that Africa was never anything but a grotesque and thankless milieu for a hero's death:

Not in the churchyard where his fathers sleep
    Beneath the cool, green, daisy-spangled mounds,
Where the sad yew's dark shadows o'er them creep,
    And the merle's evensong their requiem sounds;
Soothed in his slumber by no rippling stream,
    His couch unperfumed by the rose's breath;
And yet he sleeps—a sleep that knows no dreams—
    His lips sealed by the icy kiss of Death.

Upon that once warm heart the cold stones rest,
    Grey, rugged boulders, jealous of their prey,
Amongst whose crevices the lizards nest
    Like the quick thoughts that animate the clay.
And the cicada's loud, shrill monotone
    Sounds like the heart-throb with deep anguish wrung;
And yon dark shade that falls and then is gone,
    Is from the Aasvogel's unclean pinion flung.

For our final and least glamorized view of death in the shadow of the vulture's wing we have to return to the work of 'Mome', Captain G. Murray Johnstone, whose *Off-Wheeler Ballads* we met in Chapter IV. That the soldier's death is a dishearteningly unspectacular affair, ' 'alf an inch of lead with a kopje for your bed', recurs with the force and regularity of something like an obsession in his poems. In 'The Guns',

When it's cold as the winds of the morning,
    And everything's rotten and dead,
And you've opened the fun with the blooming old gun,
    And your pal has been shot in the head,

memories of cheering crowds and blowing bugles become merely a grim joke,

> And you wonder—oh, God! how you wonder—
> Why something's gone wrong in your head.

Even more pointedly, 'A Comrade' offsets the fighting man's hurried burial against the public's colourful concept of a military funeral:

> It was three rounds blank on a shifting sand
>   When we bade him a last good-bye—
> Now he sleeps 'neath the moon where the sand-winds croon
>   And the bones of the dead men lie.
> Then there weren't no woman and there weren't no kid,
>   Nor there weren't no big brass band,
> And there weren't no coffin with a nice black lid:
>   We dug him a hole in the sand.

Ultimately the British left 22,000 men in such South African graves in the sand. The Boers lost only 4,000, but 26,000 women and children died in concentration camps.[40] It is time to turn to Boer responses to the war.

[40] T. R. H. Davenport, *South Africa: A Modern History* (Johannesburg: Macmillan, 1977), p. 142.

VII

Boers and Boer Voices

Theirs is to them a just and sacred cause,
Ours at best is not so just or clear,
But that, however ably pleaded, flaws
Will in our strongest arguments appear.

Bertram Dobell, 'South Africa, 1899', *Rosemary and Pansies*
(1904).

IF the Boer War turned out to be a chastening experience for
imperial Britain, it was a near-annihilating trauma for the Boers.
Never mustering more than a total of 50,000 fighting men at any
time, but encouraged by vociferous international support and
exploiting their superior knowledge of the theatre of war, the
Boer commandos prolonged a conflict that should not have lasted
more than a few months, to two-and-a-half years, until their two
republics were physically destroyed and they themselves morally
devastated. Some would argue that the experience confirmed a
dour, pessimistic world-view which has informed the Afrikaner's
politics, particularly his obsession with self-preservation, to this
day.

In order to break the back of a remarkably resilient guerrilla
campaign, Lord Kitchener instituted his so-called 'burnt-earth'
policy. It involved the destruction of farms, livestock, and crops,
the herding of women and children into 'refugee' or concentration
camps where they could no longer give their menfolk active and
moral support, the trial and public execution of rebels (i.e.
Colonial Boers caught among the belligerents), and the transportation to St. Helena, Bermuda, and Ceylon of Boer prisoners of war.
In retrospect, most military tacticians experienced in the com-
plexities of modern guerrilla warfare (Malaya, Vietnam, Northern
Ireland) would agree that there was little else the British could
have done, but these measures unleashed a storm of protest, in
Britain (as we have seen) as well as on the Continent and in South
Africa. Whether all the stories of atrocities which appeared in the

continental and British pro-Boer press were true or not, or whether the disaster was really as extensive as it appeared to be, matters little. Contemporaries, Boers and pro-Boers alike, believed that accounts such as the following, which appeared in the *Northern Whig*, were literal descriptions of the wasteland South Africa had become, and they responded accordingly: 'a country despoiled of everything save the useless wastage of war, ruined towns, burnt homesteads, barbed wire and block houses, disorganized, depopulated and literally destroyed'.[1]

Among the Boers, deeply immersed in a patriarchal cult of family and national loyalties, and constantly defining their identity as well as justifying their struggle in terms of their physical attachment to their landlocked republics, the destruction of family life and the removal to foreign shores provoked both profound distress and a lasting, smouldering resentment which has never been completely resolved. Emily Hobhouse, whose publications on the concentration camps provided much of the fuel for pro-Boer opinion, foresaw it all: 'I call this camp system wholesale cruelty. It can never be wiped out from the memories of the people;'[2] or, as William Watson put it in 'Harvest':

> A naked people in captivity;
> A land where Desolation hath her throne;
> The wrath that is, the rage that is to be:
> Our fruits, whereby we are known.

Had the Boers been as literate as their opponents, it is possible that they would have produced a powerful and impressive literature of protest and resistance beyond the level of oral folklore. As it was, their extremely simple, even primitive, rural and nomadic existence failed to give them the level of education and the habits of a literary culture necessary for the production of poetry. The best Afrikaans poems on the Boer War were mostly produced during the decade after the war, for reasons we shall see later.

Though Boer campaign poems, then, are rare, a few have survived. Some years ago Elspeth Huxley donated to the South African Library, Cape Town, the translations of a sheaf of Dutch

---

[1] Quoted in John Fisher, *That Miss Hobhouse* (London: Secker & Warburg, 1971), p. 221. See also Ogden, *War Against the Dutch Republics, passim*, for pages of similar reports.
[2] Fisher, p. 129.

poems which her uncle, Major Robert Grant, had found under a
stone on 27 February 1900, near the scene of the battle of Pieters'
Hill. The author was one W. du Plessis.[3] Grant unfortunately did
not keep the originals, which would appear to have been crude
but lively accounts of the feelings and actions of a fairly uneducated man. Lines such as 'We had to fly from our positions,
carrying our kettles on our backs' still attest to an eye for telling
detail. Other Boer campaign poems came to light as the result of a
public appeal which I made in the course of collecting material
for the present study. Mr. W. A. S. Nel of Ventersdorp, Orange
Free State, aged ninety-two in 1971, sent me some of the unpublished verses he had written in the Potchefstroom camp in
1901. Among several striking pieces is one on the winter of that
year:

> Die Suidpool blaas en skep 'n winterlug
> Waarvoor die trekvoël, bang, vroegtydig vlug.
> Sy koue asem swaai om elke hoek
> Om al wat lowergroen is op te soek
> En hulle met die dood te tart,
> Totdat hulle aansyn is in swart.

(The South Pole blows and shapes a wintry blast from which the
migrant bird flees in haste and terror. His cold breath hurtles
round every corner, seeking out all that's green to taunt it with
death, until all is in mourning.)

It would appear from the orthography that Mr. Nel revised his
poems in later years to conform to modern Afrikaans practice.[4] A
namesake, Mr. J. C. Nell, has sent me the work of his father,
Henry J. Nell, written in the course of the campaign. It includes
several lively accounts of skirmishes, such as 'Aanval op Pan
Stasie' ('Attack on Pan Station'). E. E. Meyer, in 'Transvalers
Plicht' ('Transvaler's Duty'), contributed by an octogenarian
brother, wrote touchingly about a young girl's reaction to the
possibility of her lover's death:

> Gebeurt het dat gy moogt sneuv'len
> Zy sal zingen tot uw lof,

---

[3] The typescript copy in the South African Library is unnumbered. There is another
copy in the Strange Collection of Africana, Johannesburg Public Library, S. Pam
968.0436 Du P.
[4] Afrikaans orthography remained erratic right up to the 1940s. Under these circumstances I have considered it safest to quote all Boer poems as they appear in the
sources available to me.

Bloemen plukken op de heuv'len,
Planten om uw rustend stof.

(Were it to happen that you should die, they will sing in praise of you; they will pick flowers on the hills to plant round your still dust.)

One of the most evocative poems that the appeal brought forth is the anonymous 'Oorlogskans' ('Chance of War'), a ballad with a simple urgency and vivid perception of death in battle:

't Morgenrood! 't Morgenrood!
Spelt my alligt een vroege dood;
Als de krygs trompetten klinken
Zal de Stryd my wreed verminken,
My en menig kameraad.

Onverwacht! Onverwacht!
Word myn levensloop volbracht—
Gisteren noch te paard gestegen,
Straks op 't Slachveld neergezegen,
Morgen reeds in 't koele graf.

(Red morrow! Red morrow! It promises me surely an early death when the war trumpets blow, the battle will maim me cruelly, me and many a comrade. So soon! So soon! My life will be brought to its end—only yesterday mounted on horseback; presently fallen on the battlefield; by to-morrow in the cool grave.)

Ons Klyntji, leading Afrikaans cultural periodical of the Boer War period, published a number of poems on the war, some of which may have been written by Boers in action. 'Di Ontset fan Mafeking' (May 1900), for instance, is a vivid and uncomplimentary vignette of the jubilation of inhabitants of Mafeking on the relief of that town:

Di troepe met di wolenteers
Ruk foorwaarts soos 'n leeu;
Hul het gewin; dis tjeers op tjeers;
Dis al een juig-geskreeu.

(The troops and the volunteers storm onwards like lions; they have won; cheers upon cheers; it's one great howl of triumph.)

The magazine was suspended from January 1902 to February 1903, but on its reappearance published further poems relating to the war; for example, P. J. Muller's 'Di O'ergaaf fan Cronjé'

('The Surrender of Cronjé'), which looks again like an unsophisticated eyewitness account:

> Hiir leg een, hy is swaar gewond;
> En daar leg een, hy is al dood;
> 'n Ander leg met ope mond
> En sug om watersnood.

(Here lies one, heavily wounded; there lies one, quite dead; another lies open-mouthed, moaning with thirst.)

Primitive and naïve as these poems were, they were seized upon by continental (particularly Dutch) pro-Boer publications and reproduced as the folk-art of a suffering people. *Antwerpen-Transvaal* (1902), an early coffee-table book published to collect funds 'to make the lives of thousands of women and children locked up in torture camps in South Africa slightly more bearable', contains several such jingles purporting to come from South Africa. Mme D. B. de Waszkléwicz-van Schilfgaarde's *Carmen pro Invictis: Quelques offrandes de poètes aux Républiques Sud-Africaines* (1901) lionized a young Boer poet killed in action, Martinus Schaink. A *de luxe* production on hand-made paper, the volume contained only one indifferent fragment of a poem by Schaink, but enshrined it amidst pages of the enthusiastic and pretentious continental verse and neurotic prose of the period—sonnets by Sully-Prudhomme, a long 'Dithyrambe funèbre' by Paul-Hyacinthe Loyson, and so on.

We shall see more of these continental extravagances in the next chapter; in the meantime we may remain, with some sense of relief, among the simpler work of the Boers themselves.

There were very few Boer newspapers and campaign publications. *De Rand Post* and *De Volksstem* appeared in Johannesburg and Pretoria until these cities fell, and sporadically published poetry. The *Rand Post* carried several strident English poems by L. W. Bradley, enjoining the Boers to

> Pray to God and prime your canons,
> Waver not, nor be dismayed.

His poems ceased rather suddenly round mid-December 1899. The *Volksstem* carried a few lengthy narrative poems by L. van Vuuren, among which was 'De Johannesburg Politie' ('The Johannesburg Police'). It concluded an account of a skirmish near

Colesberg on the fascinating reflection that Boer superiority was the result of dependence on God and mutton as against the British trust in cannons and corned beef! More of that ilk may be found in *De Brandwacht* and *Jong Transvaal*, fugitive hand-produced papers issued on campaign and now in the Preller Collection, State Archives, Pretoria.

It is also worth noting that more Dutch, Afrikaans, or pro-Boer papers were published in the Cape Colony than in the two republics. Most of them were suppressed in the course of the war, but while they lasted they published numerous poems, ranging from tear-jerkers such as ' 'n Treurige Geskiedenis' ('A Sad Event') in *De Graaff-Reinetter*, 16 December 1899, on the inevitable theme of a father having to leave an only son on the battle-field, to quite caustic satire, such as the monologue of a Rand speculator in *De Zuid-Afrikaan*, 16 January 1900:

> Ek mors mijn tijd drie maande al
> In 'n hotel.
> Di kos en puddings en tsampijn
> Is goed en wel,
> Mar kijk tog net di kanse wat
> Ek kwijt raak in di goue stad!

(For three months I've been wasting my time in a hotel. The food and puddings and champagne are all very well, but just think of the chances I'm missing in the Golden City!)

Considering how persistently incensed later Afrikaner reaction to the war has been, it is remarkable how many contemporary Boers responded to the comedy rather than the pathos of their experience. Sometimes, as in Melt J. Brink's many little volumes of comic narratives, their poems merely exploited the broad peasant farce of seeing Tommy in sticky situations, but others had a sharper sense of satire and irony. The Revd. J. F. Naudé, who wrote *Vechten en Vluchten van Beyers en Kemp* (1903) about his experiences as chaplain to Generals Beyers and Kemp, composed a few brisk epigrams on, for instance, British failure to capture De Wet:

> De groote Generaal C. R. de Wet
> Was steeds te klein voor een Khaki-net.

(The great General C. R. de Wet was still too small for a khaki net.)

H

Naudé also provides a timely reminder that by no means all Boers were semi-literate or ignorant of a wider culture. Reflecting on the policy of farm-burning, he quotes a telling passage from Tennyson's 'Locksley Hall Sixty Years After', and after the battle of Colenso on 15 December 1899 he reflects on the appositeness of Longfellow's 'Christmas Bells', written during the American Civil War:

> Then from each black accursed mouth
> The canon thundered in the South,
> And with the sound
> The carols drowned
> Of peace on earth, good-will to men.

'Yet,' he remarks laconically, 'we celebrated Christmas.'

The best-known exponents among the Boers of both satire and literary bilingualism were the members of the Reitz family. F. W. Reitz, ex-President of the Orange Free State and Transvaal State Secretary during the Boer War, produced numerous comic and satirical verses on the conflict, and did so in English, Dutch, and early-Afrikaans with equal facility. Later collected in *Oorlogs en Andere Gedichten* (1910), several remained popular recitation pieces for a generation. Among his many poems lampooning British commanders and reverses, one of the most successful was 'The Proclamation or Paper Bomb', a neat demolition of Kitchener's attempts to frighten Boers residing in newly occupied territories into submission by declaring them rebels:

> *Whereas* I with a quarter-million men,
> Can't beat you, though you're only one to ten,
> And flying columns answer just as well—
> Or just as little—as a lyddite shell . . .
>
> *Whereas* my horses ridden to and fro
> But serve to feed the vulture and the crow,
> And that in spite of all my plans and schemes,
> Ending the war is harder than it seems . . .
>
> Now, therefore, come up Burghers one and all,
> 'Tis for the sake of Peace I make this call;
> Oh! come to me and then you'll quickly feel
> How a Boer's neck fits to a British heel.

On the loss of the British guns at Colenso he reflected, punningly: 'Yes, Lord Roberts of Kandahar [= "can there" in Afrikaans] is not Lord Roberts of Can-here.' P. R. de Villiers, another member of the Transvaal government during its final nomadic and fugitive existence, has left an account, among his papers now in the Transvaal Archives, of how Reitz would compose his verses, on horseback, for the entertainment of his comrades. Often these would be translations or renderings of songs popular among the Tommies, too; for instance, 'Tramp! Tramp! Tramp! The Boys are Marching' became 'Draf! Draf! Draf! So Ry ons Mense'.

Five of Reitz's sons took part in the war. Of these, Hjalmar Reitz wrote a documentary novel, *De Dochter van den Handsopper* (1903), and Deneys Reitz, later a minister in Smuts's cabinet, produced the Boer War classic, *Commando* (1929), both of which create a vivid picture not only of the Boer campaign, but also of the highly cultured and educated Reitz home, where the works of English poets were prominent and much read. Joubert Reitz, imprisoned on Bermuda, seems to have written all his poems, with the exception of 'Kamppraatjes' ('Camp Chats'), in English. The latter work is a racy piece of nonsense in the tradition of the ballad of comic hyperbole. The results of a Boer raid, for instance, appear as follows:

> Twee honderd Long Toms en een pijp
> Een bandolier en roer
> Een bottel 'Schotch'—jy ken die 'brand'—
> Het hulle meegevoer.

(Two hundred Long Toms and a pipe, one cartridge belt and rifle, a bottle of Scotch—you know the brand—they brought along with them.)

The enormous popularity of the ballad is attested by its frequent appearance in the commonplace books of Boer prisoners of war in the War Museum, Bloemfontein, and the Transvaal Archives.[5]

Joubert Reitz's English poems could be poignant and caustic. Several appear among the P. R. de Villiers papers, including 'The Searchlight', once again a poem that was widely copied and preserved by Boer P.O.W.s:

> And I think of things that have been
> And happiness that's past.
> And only then I realize
> How much my freedom meant,

[5] Here quoted from F. W. Reitz's *Oorlogs en Andere Gedichten*, where it appears with 'The Searchlight'.

> When the searchlight from the gunboat
> Casts its rays upon my tent.

His 'What were your thoughts?' is one of the war's most unrepentant and uncompromising poems. Dismissing the pious image of the warrior as champion of God, justice, and fatherland, he captures the reality of the soldier's thoughts in the midst of battle:

> No! I think if you'll remember all the things you thought of when
> You were fighting like a demon, you will find that your thoughts then
> Were not quite so pure and holy as they should be when you stand
> At death's door, which might be opened now for you at God's command.
> Oh no! You were but as a brute, and thought but that to slay
> Was your especial mission, be the chances what they may;
> You had but become a savage wishing to avenge the blood
> Of your dead and dying comrades lying down there in the mud.

Satire came readily to Joubert Reitz. His 'Bermuda' is wrought with a deflating irony that suggests he may have been familiar with Marvell's 'Bermudas':

> What matters it if Paradise be lost and devastated?
> There's not a soul who cares enough to grieve,
> For they know that even Adam, when he left, was quite elated
> Because he had Bermuda up his sleeve.

The most abrasive of all the Reitz poems is a mock obituary, entitled 'Cecil John Rhodes'. Again from among the P. R. de Villiers papers, it is not clearly ascribed to either father or son, but the virulence of the attack would suggest Joubert:

> On famed Matopos his remains repose,
> And wherefore should profane non-Jingoes chortle
> That in his will himself his trumpet blows?
> He's paid for it, and therefore is immortal. . . .
> [Go] softly, oh, thou multimillionaire,
> And may thy mighty ashes rest in peace
> On the Matopos, waiting grandly, there,
> For others who my country dear shall fleece.

These poems are the more remarkable when one considers that Joubert was only eighteen when captured and sent to Bermuda.

He seems to have produced no further verse, and died, after a wanderer's life, in the German South-West African campaign of 1914.[6]

If the Boers produced little poetry, they loved to sing, and once again the songs were often English. In *The Boers in War* (1900) Howard C. Hillegas tells of an incident near Thaba N'chu in the Orange Free State, where the Boers and their British prisoners tramped from the battle-field singing 'Soldiers of the Queen'. Donald Macdonald (*How We Kept the Flag Flying*, p. 24) describes a similar combined concert after the battle of Elandslaagte. The latter event is all the more remarkable when one considers the lasting resentment with which the charge of the Lancers during that encounter was to be remembered by the Boers. Dutch or early-Afrikaans versions of popular music hall items circulated widely among the Boers, as is clear from their commonplace books. So, for instance, 'Just Before the Battle, Mother' became 'Voor de Slag, mij Liewe Moeder', while 'A Boer Cavalier Sat under a Tree' clearly reveals its non-Boer origins. In Deadwood Camp, St. Helena, J. H. L. Schumann composed typical music hall sentimental songs, such as 'They Will Miss Me' and 'The Boer Prisoner's Return', and sold them to his fellow prisoners.[7]

Like Cromwell's armies, the Boers indulged in much hymn singing, and there are several accounts of English soldiers being unnerved by the haunting, powerful melodies coming from the enemy lines at dawn and dusk. But according to Lieutenant William Home the Boers' singing became a less fascinating experience once they were behind barbed wire: 'The monotonous hymn-singing, which went on almost incessantly day and night within the laager, tended to lull the sentries to sleep, and to counteract this they were required to hail one another every half-hour throughout the night.'[8] Home was referring to the Green Point P.O.W. camp, and he may have had in mind an incident that took place there on 30 April 1900, when a young Boer, Philip Cronjé, came too near to the perimeter fence during such a service and was shot. It was afterwards claimed that he could not hear the

[6] Deneys Reitz, *Trekking On* (London: Faber, 1933), p. 111.

[7] The songs appear in a manuscript songbook presented to me by Mrs. M. Lubbe of Pretoria. Schumann's advertisement appeared in a camp newspaper, *De Krijgsgevangene* (22 June 1901).

[8] *With the Border Volunteers to Pretoria* (Hawick: W. & J. Kennedy, 1901), p. 171.

sentry's challenge because of the singing. The story was reported in the pro-Boer *South African News* on 5 May 1900, and gave rise to a brief-lived local myth, issuing in ballads such as 'The Death of Young Cronjé' which circulated in Cape Town in broadside:

> Have you heard of the death of young Cronjé,
> Who was killed on the Green Point Track?
> He was holding the Bible in his hand,
> When the bullet entered his back.

The concentration and prisoner-of-war camps produced a noticeably larger crop of verse than did the campaign itself. Possibly they provided the leisure and opportunity for self-pity and embittered reflection that could lead to verse-making; possibly it was the humiliation and frustration of these facets of the war that really caught the Boer imagination. Whatever the case, the War Museum in Bloemfontein is full of the albums, commonplace books, and journals containing the literary efforts, humorous as much as pathetic, that record this chapter of Afrikaner history. Much of it was obviously therapeutic in origin, and must be treated on a par with the model ox-wagons, carved napkin rings, and other *objets* that abound in the museum: fascinating, resourceful, eloquent of their makers' preoccupations, but of little aesthetic merit. Among these one could number the numerous rambling narratives, usually in crude balladic form, of the long sea voyages (a totally strange experience for almost all Boers) and the hardships of camp life. Many camp poems must have been recited frequently or must have circulated widely in manuscript, since several appear in a number of different collections, often with substantial variations or ascribed to different authors. Joubert Reitz's 'The Searchlight' is one of these, and so are a few comic boasting songs, such as 'Khoekha-Khaki', sung to the tune of 'Daisy'. Curiously, 'Sarie Marais', usually thought of as a Boer War song and as emblematic of South Africa as 'Waltzing Matilda' is of Australia, does not appear in any of these collections.

One of the most original of the poems on the sea voyage is 'Op Nieuwe Jaar 1901' ('On New Year's Day 1901'), which appears in a collection made by C. D. Oberholzer on Bermuda. It has a raciness and an awareness of narrative situation that distinguish it from the rest. It starts with a rumour spreading through the Green Point P.O.W. camp on New Year's Day to the effect that

the men are going to be released. When the order comes for them
to fall in with all their belongings, they can no longer contain
their excitement:

> Ons denk ons gaan nou na die huis,
> Ons bind die bondels oor ons kruis.
> Om een uur kom ons bij die hek;
> Ik dog die mense wordt nou gek:
> Hulle lag en praat, huil deur mekaar,
> Mij hart word zeer, dit was te naar.

(We thought we were going home, so we tied our bundles across
our backs. At one o'clock we went to the gate; I thought the men
were going crazy: they laughed, chattered, wept all at once. My
heart ached, it was too terrible.)

The lines form up and they march out, but instead of turning
towards the station, the front of the column wavers for a moment,
then swings towards the docks. The men realize they are to be
deported. The author reveals a fine sense of telling contrast at this
point: in the first flush of their excitement they sing the Transvaal
anthem and notice the pretty girls along the route; once they have
realized what is happening to them, they become aware of the
Cape Coloured onlookers shouting taunts at them: 'Boer, where's
your pass?' Oberholzer's collection also contains 'De reis van
Afrika naar Bermuda' ('The Voyage from Africa to Bermuda'), a
sprightly song sung to the tune of 'So Early in the Morning'. It
describes the food on board with an understandable strength of
feeling:

> Omtrent die kos als julle wil weet:
> Kerrie rijs en troepe zweet,
> Bitter koffie met zuur brood;
> Vreet jij die vlijs is jij een jood.

(As far as the food is concerned, if you really want to know:
curried rice and troops' sweat, bitter coffee and sour bread; only a
Jew can stomach the meat.)

Compared to Oberholzer's 'Op Nieuwe Jaar 1901', most of the
other voyage poems are fairly pedestrian, linear narratives about
the normal mishaps and occupations of men aboard ship. In the
anonymous 'Onze reis als Krijgsgevangenen van Durban naar
Trichinopoly naar Zuid India' ('Our Voyage as Prisoners of War
from Durban to Trichinopoly in Southern India') the author

uses an amusing combination of early-Afrikaans and English to describe the impact of the Boers' arrival in India:

> The bastard Boers are coming,
> Al wat leeft is op de been—
> Ladies Gentlemen en Koelies,
> Allen schaart zich om ons heen.[9]

(The bastard Boers are coming, every living thing is on the move—ladies, gentlemen, and coolies, all are crowding round us.)

'Hy was Zeesiek' ('He was Seasick'), included in the reminiscences of Gideon J. van Riet in the War Museum, uses the same device of linguistic farce in the course of its broadly ironical description of the voyage:

> Myn breakfast en myn dinner is
> Al lang al in die zee,
> En morge gaat ik ook daarheen
> In zakke toegedraai,
> Met yzers aan myn voete vast
> Als voedsel voor een haai.
> Jij moet tog aan jou mama zê
> Hoe zwaar ik het gekrij
> En hoe ik voor mijn land en volk
> Tog bitter het gelij.

(My breakfast and my dinner have been in the sea some time, and tomorrow I'll be following—wrapped in sacks, with iron bars tied to my feet—to feed the sharks. Do tell your mama what a hard time I had, and how bitterly I suffered for my country and my people.)

Once in the camps, the Boers gave expression to a wide range of reactions, from bitter resentment on Burtts Island, Bermuda (reserved for Cape rebels serving a life sentence), to positive enjoyment of the lotus-lands of Ceylon and Southern India. They produced a number of camp papers, most of which carried verse of sorts—*De Krijgsgevangene, De Prikkeldraad, De Strever* (all in Diyatalawa, Ceylon), *Kamp Kruimels* (Deadwood, St. Helena), the

[9] Quoted here from a manuscript version sent to me by Mr. J. M. Grobler of Somerset West, Cape. In *Ons Klyntji*, September 1903, it is ascribed to J. F. Kastein. Similar voyage poems are J. A. Herholdt, 'De Zeereis en het Diyatalawa Kamp', Orange Free State Archives, Bloemfontein, Acc. 155/140/1; and A. S. Wessels, 'Ondervinding op Bermuda', in a manuscript diary of C. S. Roodt, Preller Collection, State Archives, Pretoria, Acc. 787/63.

Tick (Umbilo, Durban), and the *Skyview Parrot* (Green Point, Cape Town). All reflected on the events they had just been through, and some wrote quite ambitious doggerel, even in English on occasion, as in J.B.'s 'Spion Kop, January 14th 1900: In Memory of the Men Who Fell at Spion Kop', *De Prikkeldraad*, 26 September 1900:

> And midst that hail [of] shot and shell
> > Which fell on every side,
> And seemed as if the gates of Hell
> > Had been thrown open wide,
> Blood splashed to rocks and soaked the ground; . . .
> Yet now and then, 'twixt shot and shell,
> > We heard our General cry:
> Schiet, kêrels, schiet! en sta niet stil,
> > We either win or die.

Mauritz van der Merwe seems to have been Diyatalawa's most poetic inmate; several of his pieces appear in *De Strever* and recur frequently in the collections made in Ceylon. Judged by the number of times it was copied, his most popular poem was 'Iemands Liefling' ('Someone's Darling'), published in *De Strever* on 19 April 1902. Fraught with Victorian pathos, it nevertheless has an effective opening:

> 't Was roerloos stil op 't eenzaam veld,
> Na al 't rumoer en woest geweld
> Van een gevecht zeer zwaar;
> Slechts nu en dan werd er gehoord
> Een angstig zucht, een laatste woord,
> Van iemand stervend daar.

(It was breathlessly still on the lonely veld after the clamour and fierce violence of a terrible fight; only now and then could one hear an anxious sigh, a last word, from one about to die.)

This kind of poem had obvious attractions for prisoners of war. One octogenarian veteran, Mr. Piet Behrens of Eloffsdal, was able to recall it, a few years ago, entirely from memory.

Of the many poems describing life in camp, a surprising number do so in a humorous rather than resentful fashion. This impression may be deceptive, since it is not always clear whether the writers were fully in control of the tonal registers they wished to use. When, for instance, J. H. L. Schumann writes, in *De Krijgsgevangene* (22 June 1901), of the ailments of his friends:

> Een het een rug
> Wat hom laat zug,
> Gevrete trek en krom gaan;
> Een het een kop,
> Met 'n zeer daarop
> Dat hij van pijn soms stom staan;

(One has a back that makes him groan, pull faces, and walk doubled over; another has a head with a sore on it that leaves him dumb with pain;)

his intention, presumably, was not to caricature them, though that is the obvious effect of the primitive Afrikaans of the passage. Other descriptions, however, were clearly meant to be amusing or satirical, such as the sketch of the camp doctor in the anonymous 'Verzen uit het Gevangenkamp te Groenpunt' ('Verses from the Prison Camp at Green Point'):

> Jij hol nou naar die doktor toe
> Om bij hem hulp te zoek;
> 'Ou Bietje Beter' is zijn naam,
> Die vent kan leelijk vloek.
>
> Hij sèh dan net, haal uit jou tong,
> En gee jou dan een drank,
> Daaruit een emmer vol geschep,
> Voor maagpijn, blind en mank.[10]

(So you run off to the doctor to get some comfort; 'Old Little Bit Better' is his name; the fellow can curse most awfully. All he says is: 'Put out your tongue!' And then he gives you a drink, ladled out of a bucket; it's the same for stomach ache, blindness, and lameness.)

Or there was the problem of what to do with a small bowl issued to prisoners on St. Helena:

> En verder krij ons van die verbrande goed,
> Een kommetjie, vrinde, zoo groot als mijn hoed.
> Toe ons hul eerst krij, het ons strij gehad,
> Of ons daaruit moes drink of daaruit moes bad.[11]

[10] The poem found its way to Holland, where it was reproduced in *De Gids*, 65 (1901), 85–98.
[11] From the notebook of C. F. Dirks, kept on St. Helena, submitted by his son.

(And furthermore, friends, we got from this damned lot a little bowl as big as my hat. When first we received them we had a big argument: were they for drinking or for washing?)

The majority of the poems produced in camp were, however, of a fairly morbid cast. In poem after poem passionate patriotism vied with fervid imprecations upon the British, or exhortations directed to fellow prisoners. The opening lines of J. N. Brink's 'De Gevangene van Diyatalawa' (*Recollections of a Boer Prisoner-of-War*, 1904) illustrate the obsessively depressed nature of much of this verse:

> Zijn oog, zoo scherp, beslist, beteeknisvol weleer,
> Is diep gezonken nu, betraand, en gloeit niet meer.
> Zijn bleek en bevend lip, bewogen door het hart,
> Vertelt in stille taal de maat der bit'tre smart.
> 't Gerimpeld voorhoofd toont hoe diep de onheilsploeg
> Zijn vooren trekt en raakt zijn leven nagenoeg.

(His eye, once so sharp, determined, meaningful, is now deeply sunken, tearful, and glows no more. His pale and trembling lip, moved by his heart, mutely tells the measure of his bitter woe. His wrinkled forehead shows how deeply disaster's plough has drawn its furrows and scored him to the quick.)

In Bermuda an anonymous poet put it more succinctly:

> Hier zit ik aan Bermuda's strand
> Met een verbryzeld hart,
> Verbannen uit myn Vaderland.
> O Heer, wat bittre smart.[12]

(Here I sit on Bermuda's shore, with a shattered heart and exiled from my fatherland. O God, what bitter sorrow.)

Songs such as 'Houdt Moed, Houdt Moed, mijn Broeders' ('Have Courage, Have Courage, my Brothers'), ascribed to the Revd. George Thom, imprisoned on Ceylon, and 'Ziet Gij niet die Blauwe Bergen?' ('Do You not See the Blue Mountains?'), had a powerfully therapeutic impact.[13] The latter song appears in

[12] 'Ontboeseming van een Krijgsgevangene', copied in the manuscript notebook of J. C. van Zyl on Bermuda, Bloemfontein War Museum MS. 58/1723. It also appears in the Roodt diary—see above, p. 214, n. 9.

[13] Both appear in numerous manuscript collections and were published, along with several others, in G. H. van Rooyen, 'Kultuurskatte uit die Tweede Vryheidsoorlog', *Huisgenoot* (7 June 1935).

the *Oranje-Vrijstaatsche Oorlogs Liederen-Bundel,* a booklet of songs produced in 1901 by an itinerant Boer printer. This suggests that the piece originated in South Africa and then spread to the concentration and P.O.W. camps, where it was copied in one collection after another. Pathetically wistful, and with a protracted soulful chorus, its success was guaranteed:

> Ziet gij niet die blauwe bergen
> Waar ons vrienden werd verkocht,
> Door die vijanden gevangen
> En zoo verre weggestuurd?

(Don't you see the blue mountains where our friends were sold, caught by the enemy and sent far away?)

Naturally, Boers in favour of some *rapprochement* with the British, not to mention outright renegades, were frequent targets for verse. J. C. van Zyl noted down in a minute book, now in the War Museum, a poem which expresses some sympathy, but much more scorn, for demoralized Boers who joined the 'Boeren Politie', or National Scouts, a Boer force raised by Kitchener during the last stages of the war:

> En menig een verloor den moed,
> Zocht by den vyand heil;
> Verteerd zyn eigen broeders bloed,
> O snoodheid zonder peil.

(And many have lost courage and sought safety with the enemy— have devoured their own brothers' blood. O disgrace without measure.)

On Bermuda Boers who shaved their beards were regarded by their compatriots as currying favour with the British authorities. A fellow prisoner described them as follows, in a poem in G. J. van Riet's collection:

When a Boer cuts off his whiskers, he becomes a different man;
He is loyal to the Khaki and he looks it (if he can),
He claims that Botha and De Wet his troubles on him bring,
And he whistles 'Rule Brittania' and he sings 'God save the King'.

H. O. Wilsenach, in a batch of poems sent me by his granddaughter, lampooned those Boers whose faces showed 'nought but devastation where once waving whiskers grew', and he sug-

gested, with Swiftian mischief, that the British might have some
use for such men:

> You may think it is impertinent to offer you advice,
> No impertinence is meant, you may be sure;
> The suggestion's no less valuable where'er you get it from.
> Just boil 'em down and use them for manure.

> This would be a decent end for them and benefit you, too:
> No coffin would be needed, do it cheap;
> You could grow potatoes on 'em, carrots, anything would do,
> And you'd get back part of what they've cost to keep.

Among all this verse by prisoners of war, the absence of
complaints about British cruelty—indeed, about any real hardship
at all—is striking, and our discussion of the camp poetry would
not be complete without reference to the verse which suggested
that, on Ceylon at least, the Boers' exile was for many quite an
enjoyable adventure. In a farewell edition of *De Strever* (9 August
1902), Mauritz van der Merwe saluted the island as follows:

> Niettegenstaande al dien druk,
> Vond' velen in u groot geluk,
> Ja meen'gen zeggen in den geest:
> 't Was goed te zijn in u geweest.

(Notwithstanding the hard times, many found much happiness
in thee; yes, many a man is saying to himself: 'It was good to have
been here.')

While their menfolk languished on foreign shores, thousands of
Boer women and children found themselves in concentration
camps all over South Africa. This experience only made its real
impact on Afrikaans political and literary culture after the war,
but some verse did come directly out of the camps. Mostly these
poems and songs, such as those collected by Miss Hester Kotze in
the Bethulie camp and now in the Orange Free State Archives,
Bloemfontein, expressed an intense and gloomy determination:

> Door kruit en vuur en hael en lood
> Moet wij nu strij tot in den dood.

(Through powder and fire and hail and lead we have to struggle till
we are dead.)

Here, too, however, it was possible to look on the more humorous
side of the experience. One of the most ambitious of all Boer

poems is a disjointed, episodic narrative of fifty-six stanzas covering life in the Mafeking camp. It appears in two different versions in the Pretoria archives, one ascribed to a Mrs. Hester Magrieta van Zyl, the other to a group of women of whom one was Hester van Zyl.[14] Much of it is clumsy and naïve, but the poem makes a genuine attempt to portray all aspects of camp life, and there are some passages of memorable detail: the frost on their clothes in the morning; the green logs issued for fuel; the shiny new pails filled with putrid water; the battles between anxious but uneducated mothers and health authorities trying to contain epidemics of measles, the greatest killer in these camps. Here are two stanzas, on the scramble for food and the clashes with the camp sister:

> Gaan ons na die versenshuis,
> Daar is 'n groot gedruis;
> Ons moet mekaar daar druk,
> Om kos uit te ruk.
> Ag ons moet staan en kijk
> Tot ons wil beswijk.
> Pertij moet daar blij staan,
> Tot die son ondergaan.
>
> As ons na nirs toe gaan,
> Daar buite moet ons staan;
> Dan laat sij vir ons tolk,
> Sij dink ons is haar volk.
> Hoor nou weer haar triek,
> Sij sê boere asem maak haar siek;
> Sij word vir ons so kwaad,
> Sij laat die huis toe draad.

(When we go to the ration hall there is a great clamour; we have to push and shove to snatch our food. Oh, we have to stand and stare until we feel like death—some have to wait there till sunset. If we go to the nurse, we have to wait outside. She makes us use an interpreter; she thinks we are her servants. Just listen to her latest quirk: she claims Boer breath makes her sick. She is so angry with us that she has had her house fenced in.)

---

[14] Recorded in the manuscript reminiscences of Hester van Zyl by her daughter, Mrs. G. P. Grobler, and in those of Mrs. S. E. Nel by her daughter, Mrs. J. Dippenaar; both State Archives Acc. 951.

Hester van Zyl ended her poem on the couplet:

> Want die kinders wat niks weet,
> Sal alles weer vergeet.

(For the children who do not know, will forget it all.)

But there was little danger of the Boers, or the Afrikaners, as they came to be called more frequently from now on, forgetting the war. The experiences of these two and a half years became the emotional fuel and imaginative core of an Afrikaner political and cultural renaissance over the next two decades. This nationalist drive and its literary counterpart, 'Die Tweede Afrikaanse Taalbeweging' ('The Second Afrikaans Language Movement'), culminated, respectively, in the formation of the National Party in 1914, and the recognition, in 1925, of Afrikaans as one of South Africa's two official languages. 'The war gave to Afrikaners throughout South Africa common victims to mourn, common injuries on which to brood, a common cause in the restoration of republicanism, and, in the tragic figure of Kruger, dead in exile, a martyr around whom myths could be woven.'[15]

The years of reconstruction were not easy, for either Boers or British. Both parties seemed to follow sharply self-divisive policies. On the one hand Lord Milner, now High Commissioner for South Africa, and his 'kindergarten' of mainly Oxford-bred civil servants set out to turn the Orange River Colony and the Transvaal into models of British colonial rule, and attempted a policy of anglicization which Lord Charles Somerset almost a century earlier had found disastrous. No expense was spared to help the Boers rebuild their farms and communities, but the ambit of cultural imperialism in which reconstruction took place was guaranteed to produce the maximum amount of resentment. At the same time, however, pro-Boers in Britain continued to advocate full independence for the ex-republics, with the result that Campbell-Bannerman's Liberal administration of 1905 granted the two territories self-government with almost unseemly haste, and followed it with inevitably Afrikaner-dominated independence for the whole sub-continent in 1910. The Boers could hardly have regained their freedom earlier and more easily, yet Milner's policies had ensured that it was achieved in a spirit of

---

[15] G. H. L. Le May, quoted in *The Oxford History of South Africa*, ed. Monica Wilson and L. Thompson, vol. ii: 1870–1966 (Oxford: Clarendon Press, 1971), p. 367.

dislike and distrust on both sides. J. A. Froude had warned in 1886 that South Africa would become another Ireland (*Oceana*, p. 67), and British statesmen had managed to effect just that in under ten years.

The Boers, on the other hand, were split, too. Ex-Boer Generals Botha and Smuts accepted the spirit of an imperial family of nations in which South Africa could play her part, and, with considerable success, persuaded many Afrikaners to follow their lead into closer co-operation with Britain and the empire. But there were also the 'bittereinders' ('bitter-enders'), who had pledged eternal enmity to all things British. It was mainly around the leaders and heroes of this movement, men such as De Wet, Herzog, Beyers, and Jopie Fourie, that a nationalistic cult of myths and stirring tales was to develop, especially after the rebellion of 1914 when, on the outbreak of World War I, about 10,000 Boers under Generals De Wet, Kemp, Maritz, and Beyers took up arms against the Union Government, thus forcing Botha and Smuts into the distressing necessity of having to imprison and try their erstwhile colleagues for high treason.

The nationalist movement was nourished during the decade after the war by a spate of Boer reminiscences. It was one of the ironies of the war that, because of the educational facilities provided in both concentration and P.O.W. camps, followed up by Milner during reconstruction, more Boers could now read such books than would have been able to before the war. Apart from military memoirs, the most popular of which were De Wet's *De Strijd tusschen Boer en Brit* (1902)—as *The Three Years War* (1902) it ran to several editions—and General Ben Viljoen's *My Reminiscences of the Anglo-Boer War* (1902), a small library of works on the experiences of women and children came off the press.[16]

These works kept alive a response of outrage among Afrikaners, and it is significant that the literature, particularly the poetry, devoted to the war over the next two decades was almost exclusively concerned with the experiences of women and children or with the execution of Cape rebels, hardly ever with the main

---

[16] Among the most popular were: Emily Hobhouse, *The Brunt of the War and Where It Fell* (London: Methuen, 1902); W. R. Vis, *Tien Maanden in een Vrouwenkamp* (Rotterdam, 1902); Mrs. J. H. De la Rey, *A Woman's Wanderings During the Anglo-Boer War* (London: Fisher Unwin, 1903), an English translation of the undated Dutch original; Johanna van Helsdingen, *Vrouwenleed* (Amsterdam: HAUM, 1904); and Johanna Brandt, *Het Concentratiekamp van Irene* (Amsterdam, 1905).

campaign. It is equally noticeable that whereas poems produced during the war occasionally dwelt on the humour of the situation, post-war works never did. Literary consciousness, like the nationalist temperament of the 'bittereinders', became obsessed with the suffering of the innocents. It turned out that 26,000 women and children had died in these camps, not because of active maltreatment, but because of ignorance on both sides regarding the control of disease in such environments.[17] The preoccupation with civilian suffering came to a head during the highly emotive inauguration of the Vrouemonument (Women's Monument) in Bloemfontein in 1913, an event not unconnected with the formation of the National Party and the rebellion of a year later.

The history outlined in the above few paragraphs should go some way to explain the extraordinary difference in quality between the Dutch and early-Afrikaans verse produced during the war, and the Afrikaans poetry written over the ten years after it. The combination of these political, cultural, and ethnic drives, all centring on the Afrikaans language as both medium and symbol of national unity, generated a supercharged literary atmosphere which caused a veritable explosion of the imaginative and intellectual capacities of the Afrikaner people. Hence, whereas all of the Boer verse produced during the war was written in a non-indigenous Dutch or in the phonetic and unliterary Afrikaans of the pre-1900 period, the work of the new poets, Eugène Marais, Jan F. E. Celliers, J. D. du Toit, and C. Louis Leipoldt, appeared in a suddenly impeccable Afrikaans, almost a new language, supple, evocative, and taut with new energies.[18]

In a sense the poems thrown up by this eruption are not war poems, since they were highly coloured by sensibilities that emerged only after the conflict. Yet they remain fruits of the war, and some of them are amongst the most pungent that the war produced. Often, too, their authors had been involved only marginally in the campaign—indeed, only Celliers served on commando for the duration of the war. Leipoldt edited the *South African News* and attended some of the rebel trials in the Eastern

---

[17] Kruger, *Good-Bye Dolly Gray*, conclusion; and Davenport, *South Africa*, p. 142.
[18] See Antonissen, *Afrikaanse Letterkunde*, pp. 53–9, for a perceptive discussion of this period and of the forces at work. In the analysis that follows, I am indebted to Antonissen, pp. 78–107, for much of my factual information.

Cape; Marais was studying medicine in London for most of the war (though he tried to smuggle arms to the Transvaal); and Du Toit, after a few months on commando, left for Amsterdam to write a dissertation on Methodism. Here, however, was also an asset: all these men were highly educated, often widely read in English, Dutch, and German literature, and trained to a sensitivity to language and an objectivity to experience that were not possible for their compatriots in the field.

The first poem of the new movement to be published, Marais's 'Winternag' ('Winter Night'), in *Land en Volk*, 1905, represented an all but incredible leap from the kind of verse we have seen so far.[19] Explicitly it says nothing about the war, and the information that it was originally meant to introduce a longer poem on the loneliness of a sentry comes as almost incidental. Yet in eighteen short, delicate lines Marais caught the infinitely sorrowful mystery of his country's physical ravishment and its people's spiritual denudation. I quote it in Guy Butler's translation:

> O cold is the slight wind
> and sere.
> And gleaming in dim light
> and bare,
> as vast as the mercy of God,
> lie the plains in starlight and shade.
> And high on the ridges,
> among the burnt patches,
> the seed grass is stirring
> like beckoning fingers.
> O tune grief-laden
> on the east wind's pulse
> like the song of a maiden
> whose lover proves false.
> In each grass blade's fold
> a dew drop gleams bold,
> but quickly it bleaches
> to frost in the cold![20]

[19] The dating of early Afrikaans poetry is a major problem. See, for instance, E. Lindenberg, *Onsydige Toets* (Cape Town, 1965), pp. 20-5, for a discussion of the pitfalls as far as Marais is concerned. Marais's first published volume appeared only in 1925; Leipoldt did not publish the poems written during the war for ten years; Celliers, Du Toit, and Leipoldt continued to revise their poems for many years. Under the circumstances I have relied on generally accepted dates and on the earliest editions available.

[20] In *Afrikaans Poems with English Translations*, ed. A. P. Grové and C. J. D. Harvey

Ironically, as editor of *Land en Volk* before the war, Marais was a strong opponent of Krugerism and supported General Joubert's policy of making concessions to the Uitlanders. The point supports one's impression that 'Winternag' was not motivated by the rights and wrongs of the conflict, but by a complex mood of which the state of the nation was a part, and for which it could serve as a metaphor. Marais wrote little else on the war. His sole volume of poems, *Versamelde Gedigte*—not counting an unauthorized edition of 1925—appeared only three years before his suicide in 1936. It contained a few more poems on the war, but they were fairly pedestrian occasional pieces. 'Winternag' remained a bolt of lightning in his work, just as it was in Afrikaans literature.

Celliers's concern with the war was both more extensive and more persistent. The title poem of his *Die Vlakte en Ander Gedigte* (1908), ('The Plain'), inspired by Shelley's 'The Cloud', is a magnificent rendering of the moods and views of a Karoo landscape. It confirmed the capacities of Afrikaans as a literary language which 'Winternag' had suggested, but, like that poem, it rose somewhat monolithically from its surroundings. Most of the Boer War verse in the volume reads like the old-fashioned productions we saw earlier, and Celliers was to acknowledge later that melodramatic pieces such as 'Ou Oom Willem, aan zij Verslete Ou Baatjie' ('Old Oom Willem, to his Worn Old Jacket') had been written on campaign.[21]

Nevertheless, Celliers's first volume contained, apart from 'Die Vlakte', a few poems that revealed a talent considerably superior to those of the camp poets. In 'Oorlog' ('War'), a cycle of fifteen poems, he rises to moments of sharp vision—

> O, die lippe wat bleek
> om 'n waterdronk smeek,
> —wonde wat brande!
>
> Ongehoor, ongeag
> menig kermende klag
> waar die woelende slag
> dreun oor die rande—

(Oh, the lips that bleakly beg for a drink of water,—wounds that

---

(Cape Town: Oxford University Press, 1962). All the translations in verse that follow are, with a few indicated exceptions, from this collection.
[21] In an autobiographical piece quoted in *Afrikaanse Skrywers aan die Woord*, ed. P. J. Nienaber (1947), pp. 17–41.

burn! Unheard, unheeded, many a sorrowful cry sounds where the turmoil of battle thunders across the hills)
and, like Marais in 'Winternag', to a sensitive depiction of his country's mood of desolation:

> Dit is die winterwind wat waai,
> al wenend deur die lange nag,
> al wenend om die verre dag;
> die twijge swenk die takke swaai,
> dit is die winterwind wat waai. . . .
>
> En winterwinde sing die lied
> van eensaamheid en stil verdriet;
> en sonder weerklank sterf die klag
> op wije velde in die nag,
> al sugtend deur die gras se saad,
> en verre is die dageraad.

(It is the winterwind that blows, wailing all night long, wailing for the far-off day; the branches toss, the boughs sway, it is the winterwind that blows. . . . And the winds of winter sing a song of loneliness and silent sorrow; echo-less their lament dies away over the empty veld in the night, sighing through the grass seeds, and dawn is far away.)

In 'Dis Al' ('That's All') Celliers produced what has come to be regarded as another early gem in Afrikaans literature. Compact, incantatory, it etches into the posture of a single Boer returned out of exile the complex variables of a whole history of sorrow and stress. It seems worth quoting it in both its original form and in Guy Butler's translation:

> Dis die blond,
> dis die blou:
> dis die veld,
> dis die lug;
> en 'n voël draai bowe in éensame vlug
> —dis al.
>
> Dis 'n balling gekom
> oor die oseaan,
> dis 'n graf in die gras,
> dis 'n vallende traan
> —dis al.

Gold,
blue:
veld,
sky;
and one bird wheeling lonely, high—
  that's all.

An exile come back
from over the sea;
a grave in the grass,
a tear breaking free;
  that's all.

Later, after World War I, Celliers was to exploit this epigrammatic style further and produce, in poems such as 'Generaal de Wet' and 'Kruger', powerfully adzed sculptures of the great Boer leaders. Here is part of 'Kruger':

Soos 'n berg, ongebuk,
breed en bonkig van stuk,
  dis hy!
Die gelaat, hap vir hap
uit die kranse gekap,
elke kerf, elke knou
harde noodlot se hou;
elke moet, elke merk
vryheidsvyand se werk,
  dis hy![22]

(Like a mountain, unbowed, broad and block-built—that is he! The face, blow by blow hacked from a cliff; every nick, every bruise the stroke of harsh fate; every notch, every mark freedom's enemy's work—that is he!)

In sharp contrast to Celliers's angular and vigorous response to the stimuli of great men, wide spaces, and telling gestures, the Revd. J. D. du Toit (commonly known by his pseudonym, 'Totius') tended to ruminate on the metaphysics of God's will as revealed in the Boer struggle. The poems in his first volume, *By die Monument* (1908)—the title, 'At the Monument', is in itself an indication of Du Toit's concern with the formalized perpetuation of national memory—are, typically, quiet internal monologues, oblique metaphysical allegories in miniature which, in English literature, we would associate with George Herbert. A small

[22] *Die Lewenstuin en Ander Nuwe Gedigte* (Pretoria: Van Schaik, 1925).

thorntree, blossoms in an orchard, a dove on her nest, children in a garden—all readily became subjects for elusively simple, biblical fugues on the theme of national sorrow. In 'Kindergraffies' ('Children's Graves'), for instance, falling petals under fruit trees quietly metamorphose into the graves of children spelling out a fruitless generation:

> Helaas, dat hulle te gou, te gou
>   die wêreld in gekyk het,
> en onverwagte rypnag oor
>   hul ogies neergestryk het. . . .
>
> Nou lê hul almal, almal daar,
>   die bloesems tussen sooie,
> en rus die stille, stille rus
>   van liewe kleine dooie.

(Alas, that they peered into the world too soon, too soon, and that a sudden frosty night closed upon them. . . . Now they are all lying there, all of them, blossoms under sods, and sleep the quiet, quiet sleep of the dear small dead.)

'Vergewe en Vergeet' ('Forgive and Forget') is the most famous of these mini-allegories, but its child-like story of an ox-wagon crushing a little wayside thorntree which recovers and heals its own wounds should not obscure the tenacity of racial memory which the poem propagates, and the almost sinister nourishing of bitterness revealed in the final stanzas:

> Ook het die loop van jare
>   die wonde uitgewis—
> net een plek bly 'n teken
>   wat onuitwisbaar is.
>
> Die wonde word gesond weer
>   as jare kom en gaan,
> maar daardie merk word groter
>   en groei maar aldeur aan.

(And the course of the years wiped out the wounds—only one spot remained as a sign that could not be erased. The wounds heal over as the years go by, but that one blemish spreads and grows larger all the time.)

In *Rachel* (1913) and *Trekkerswee* (1915) Du Toit continued to mythologize Afrikaner history. His work became suffused with a philosophy which idolized the Afrikaners' Calvinist patriarchal and rural culture as against a cosmopolitan, urban, and inevitably English liberalism. His better poems now were those which moved completely away from national themes, but on occasion he could still produce a quietly evocative poem on, for instance, the musings of a Boer exile, as in 'Herinneringe' ('Reminiscences', *Rachel*):

> Dan sweef verneweld aan
> 'n lange, witte, rij
>   gestaltes, lossies-ijl
>   in sluiers toegedraai;
>   sommige klein en vèr
>   nog, andere al nabij.—
>   Deur die gemoed, groot-oop,
>   die wind van weemoed waai!

(Then, nebulously, a long white line of shapes come drifting by, loosely and thinly wrapped in veils; some small and far away, others quite close.—Through the soul, wide open, the gale of anguish blows!)

The last of the 'Big Four' of the Afrikaans literary renaissance was C. Louis Leipoldt, in many ways also the least Afrikaner-bound of the four. Of German parentage, he wrote all his early poems in English, spent the critical years of Boer reassessment (1902–14) in England and Europe, and in later life, when he returned to writing in English, now on World War II, became disillusioned with the Nationalist cause.[23] Nevertheless, he produced, both in quantity and in sustained effort, the most compelling group of Afrikaans poems on the war: *Oom Gert Vertel en Ander Gedigte* (1911). As editor of the *South African News* he attended rebel hearings in the Eastern Cape, on which he submitted poems to *New Age* under the initials F.W.B., acted as correspondent for pro-Boer papers such as the *Manchester Guardian*, *Daily Express*, *Chicago Record*, and *Boston Post*, and collected the material for the poems he began to write now but published only ten years later.

One night in Dordrecht, Eastern Cape, an old man told him the story of how he had helped a local young Boer to join the rebel commandos, and what, when the youth was captured, his feelings were on witnessing the boy's execution. Leipoldt sat down and

[23] See Antonissen, pp. 95–105; Nienaber, pp. 44–55; and J. Kromhout, *Leipoldt as Digter* (Pretoria: Van Schaik, 1954), *passim*.

wrote, first in English and then in Afrikaans, the original version of 'Oom Gert Vertel'('Oom Gert's Tale'). A blank-verse narrative of over 300 lines, the poem did not achieve its final shape until the 1926 edition, as Leipoldt continued to chip away at the poem's obliquely colloquial style and its deceptively under-pitched arc of tension. The result was a dramatic monologue of considerable density and complexity. Because of the poem's modulation between formal and informal registers of diction and syntax, its many apparent digressions and asides, and a taut emotive under-layer which causes sudden veerings in mood—all expressive of the old man's sorrow, guilt, and distress about his own role in the affair—the poem inevitably suffers much in translation and from quotation in extracts. C. J. D. Harvey's translation, however, captures the poem's major nuances well, and I shall use it throughout my discussion.

The poem dramatizes the large moral and emotional dilemma which Cape Boers faced during the war: the harrowing choice between their legal loyalty to the British crown, and their racial affinity with the empire's enemies.[24] Only once does Oom Gert approach the problem explicitly, but it is present throughout the poem. After a brusque opening—'You want to hear the story of our death?'—the narrative apparently slackens as Oom Gert fidgets with minor details, offering his guest coffee, protesting his own ignorance, chasing chickens off the stoep. Involuntarily, however, he reveals the tensions under which he labours and the reasons for his embarrassed sensitivity about the story: the young rebel was his godson, had courted his daughter, and, most importantly, had revealed by his example the older man's ambivalent loyalty to the Boer cause. Oom Gert's claim, 'we/Were all confused and in a state of panic', which refers ostensibly to the declaration of martial law in the town, has a deeper reference to the old man's ethical problem, while his protestations of moral self-assurance reveal, in fact, a continuing and unresolved debate:

> As for me
> I filled the saddlebags with hard-boiled eggs
> And other edibles. For, after all,
> He was my godson, and then Johnnie, too,
> Was old Saarl's son, and Saarl and I were friends.

[24] See Lindenberg, *Onsydige Toets*, pp. 63 ff., for a perceptive discussion of the poem's theme of loyalty.

So nobody could say I acted wrongly,
Although, it's true, I was a British subject.
Could I stand by and see my own flesh suffer
Whilst I had food? No, I was right, my boy,
And conscience since has never bothered me.

Likewise, his avuncular spelling-out of the more obvious message of his tale, right at the beginning—

It is never too late to learn
More about that, if you can use the knowledge,
Especially for you youngsters. Just hold tight
To what we have, stand on your feet and take
Your part in this our nation—

immediately alerts us to the possibility that the tale contains a less welcome moral for himself. Repeated attempts to evade or postpone the actual account of the boy's hanging have the same effect. We are fully half-way through the story before the crucial events begin to take shape, and the narrator touches on much of the final sequence only hurriedly and obviously unwillingly:

Then one day came the news . . . (Wait, here she's back.—
Please, sweetheart, chase the chickens off the stoep.
Look at that rooster scratching up the flowers!)
Right, one day came the news—and what a shock!
Johnnie and Ben had both been captured and
Been slapped in goal. A military court—
You know the rest!

To enhance the preventive effects of these executions, the military authorities usually commanded senior citizens of the town to attend. Revealingly, Oom Gert's only explosion of emotion comes at this point, and is directed not at the British or at the inhumanity of the whole procedure, but at the inappropriateness of English formal phraseology:

That morning the head constable arrived:
'The colonel sends his compliments.' My God,
His compliments!—you hear? You understand?
You understand, boy, *compliments!*
          Oh, no,
Be still, be still my heart, or you'll break too!
Our crosses we must bear whate'er the cost.

The obliquity of attack here is of a piece with earlier attempts in the poem to exonerate the English authorities as such—'Old Smith, the magistrate ... /He always acted like a gentleman'— and to place the blame on a particularly brutal colonel, Wilson:

> A big, fat bloke with yellow-grey moustaches,
> And great, long eye-teeth and a bright red face.

In his account of the day of execution Oom Gert perseveres in this sidelong approach to his subject, his true feelings appearing entirely in terms of projections of the people, objects, and incidents around him. A longish quotation will illustrate this:

> The minister was there, and Albert Louw—
> You know old Cock-eye Louw, Klaas? Yes, of course,
> And Michiel Nel, and Gys van Zyl, and Piet—
> No, you, of course, wouldn't remember Piet;
> He was before your time; but that chap was
> As strong as Samson—gee! but he was strong!
> And just as restive as a scorpion, too.
> But droll, my boy, and one who could laugh even
> When clouds were dark and stormy and the thunder
> Rumbled among the clouds. I know, of course,
> We all of us have faults and I don't really
> Hold it against Piet Spaanspek that he always
> Had to be making jokes, though all the rest
> Of us were feeling queer and sick at heart.
> 'This wind bites shrewdly, Cousin Gert,' he said,
> 'You'd better lend your overcoat to Ben
> In case the weather's bad upstairs!' He laughed,
> But I was glad the minister was there
> To reprimand him on the spot, and, neatly,
> He put him in his place.
>   'Is this the time
> For jokes, Mr. van Ryn?' he asked him coldly.
> 'For shame! For shame! How dare you say such things
> Today, when all our hearts are full, our eyes
> Half-dimmed with tears for our beloved country?'
> (Sweetheart, do chase those chickens out! They make
> The yard so dirty. We can help ourselves.)
> But Piet Spaanspek was never at a loss
> For words and, not put out, he carried on
> His little jokes, although the rest of us
> Pretended not to hear and took no notice.

> I think he felt as sick at heart as I
> But didn't want the rest of us to see.

The actual hanging is dismissed in half a line, 'The colonel nodded; then . . .', and the effect of the whole incident on the community (once more revealing the narrator's inner focus on the problem of loyalty) is registered in the subsequent actions of Cock-eye Louw and the very Piet Spaanspek who had made the feeble jokes:

> That night, though, Cousin Piet and Cock-eye Louw
> Left town and set out for the nearest farm,
> And afterwards they joined up with our people.

There is a tantalizing possibility that Oom Gert's problem was substantially Leipoldt's own, and that his own conflict between English and Afrikaner loyalties is reflected in the tale. In the dedicatory poem to *Oom Gert Vertel en Ander Gedigte*, Leipoldt cryptically but quite unmistakably apologized for contributing no more than a volume of poems to a cause that had claimed so many lives:

> Neem dan, wat ik (die nooit geen kans gehad het
> Die laaste stap te doen uit liefdeplig)
> Als brokkies vir 'n eerbewijs gebouw het—
> 'n Nietig reeks van rijmpies—mijn gedig.

(Accept that which I—who never had the chance to take the last step demanded by love—have built from small fragments into a token of respect: an insignificant series of rhymes—my poem.)

His departure from South Africa, to England of all places, on the eve of peace may account for the strident qualities of another dramatic monologue he wrote there, 'Vrede-Aand' ('Peace Night'):

> It's peace now! Come, man, screech—or are you hoarse
> With laughing? Laugh, then, that's the story's end,
> It's gone and we can whistle for it, friend![25]

Much of the poem is in this vein, and the speaker's hysterical indignation seems to arise as much from self-accusation as from sympathy with his fallen people. One notices, too, that in several other poems on the war which he wrote before going to London he never refers to the campaign itself, and though he strikes

[25] Trans. C. J. D. Harvey, in Grové and Harvey, *Afrikaans Poems*.

vehemently sarcastic blows at the British for causing Boer suffering, these are invariably delivered from a most oblique angle.

The poems are all concerned with the suffering of women and, especially, children, but the cause of their hardship is as much a malicious, unnamed, snickering fate as it is the British. In ' 'n Nuwe Liedjie op 'n ou Deuntjie' ('A New Song to an Old Tune') he rephrases a traditional folksong into a piece of grim and sardonic fatalism:

> Siembamba, Siembamba,
> Mama se kindjie, Siembamba!
> Kinkhoes en tering, sonder melk:
> Bitter vir jou is die lewenskelk!
> Daar is jouw plek, bij die graffies daar—
> Twee in een kissie, 'n bruilofspaar!

(Siembamba, Siembamba, mama's little darling, Siembamba! Whooping cough and consumption, and no milk: bitter for you is the cup of life! There is your place, there among the graves— two in one coffin, a loving couple!)

'In die Konsentrasiekamp' ('In the Concentration Camp'), written after he had visited the camp at Aliwal North in 1901, feelingly expresses the physical agony and mental hopelessness of such an existence—

> Hier sit jij te koes teen die wind, wat daar suie
> Ijskoud deur die tentseil, geskeur deur die haal—
> Jouw enigste skuil in die nag teen die buie;
> Die Junielug stort oor die stroom van die Vaal—
> Jij hoor net die hoes van jouw kind en die luie
> Gedrup van die reendruppeltjies oor die paal—

(Here you sit and shy from the wind that sucks, ice-cold, through the tent's canvas torn by hail—your only shelter at night against the falling rain. The June-chill pours over the Vaal; you only hear the cough of your child and the lazy drip of raindrops on the tent pole)

and then dismisses all thought of forgiveness or stoic acceptance with a harshly ironic quotation from Dante: 'O, pazienza, pazienza che tanto sostieni!' ('Oh, patience, patience that can bear so much!'). The irrational accusations of 'Aan 'n Seepkissie' ('To a Little Soap-Box')—

They made you in England, little soap-box,
To serve as a coffin for our children here:
They found you little corpses, little soap-box,
And I've seen you used as a coffin here[26]—

reveal a sense of outrage in excess of the stimuli, an impression one also gains from the use of 'uitgestamp' ('stamped out') in 'Die ou Blikkie' ('The Little Old Tin'):

Daar in die konsentrasiekamp,
Daar in ons aaklig oorlogsdamp,
  Ag, armsalige ou blikkie,
Daar is hul lewe uitgestamp!

(There in the concentration camp, in the ghastly rot of war— there, oh poor bedraggled little tin, their lives were stamped out!)

These savage reactions to the fate of the children now seem highly exaggerated. Shot through with an unpleasantly emotive use of sarcasm and resentful argument, they suggest to me that Leipoldt was responding here as much to a conflict within himself as to the distress of the Boers.

Afrikaans poetry did not relinquish the Boer War theme with the work of the four poets I have discussed. Indeed, the war remained a powerful source of inspiration till after World War II, and has only lost its emotional grip on the Afrikaner with the latter's political ascendancy and urbanization. Moving poems on Kruger, perpetuating the mythopoesy of the war years, were to come from Toon van den Heever and J. R. L. van Bruggen in the 1920s, and as late as 1950 a leading Afrikaans poet, D. J. Opperman, could produce an impressive monologue, 'Gebed om die Gebeente', on the execution of the rebel commandant, Gideon Scheepers.[27] Part of the poem's intention, however, was not only to consecrate the bones of Scheepers, but also to lay the ghost of the racial hatred and distrust that still lingered in some hearts. One would like to think that even for the Afrikaner the war has by now receded into the national mythology; that it is an occasional source for narrative or metaphor, a cause and an explanation, but no longer an issue.

We have looked, so far, at the verse produced by the Boers or Afrikaners themselves. There was, however, another body of

[26] My translation.
[27] Translated as 'Prayer for the Bones' by Guy Butler, in Grové and Harvey.

'Boer' verse, namely that written by sympathetic English poets in both South Africa and England. In a strict sense these poems form part of the pro-Boer protest verse we saw in an earlier chapter, but there is one important difference. Much of the protest verse was concerned with pacifist and humanitarian issues in which the Boer cause could readily have been exchanged for another, or it criticized the nature of Britain's imperial involvement in South Africa. Most of the poems we are concerned with here, however, purport to be written from the Boer's point of view. They are often more compassionate and less obviously tendentious. Their authors frequently project themselves into the Boer's frame of mind, or attempt to express an awareness which most thoughtful South Africans shared at the time, namely, that the war was really fratricidal.

The attempt to fathom the Boer mind had held some fascination for foreign observers well before the beginning of the Boer War. Most commentators were agreed that the Boers were cultural anomalies, curious Calvinist anachronisms, walking specimens out of a fossilized chunk of seventeenth-century Europe. Froude, as we have seen, cast them in the role of republican Romans; more realistically W. W. Treleaven, writing in the *Manchester Guardian* 30 September 1899), epitomized them as follows:

They are a people wedded to the past, and hate intensely everything that is new. They hoard their money in holes in the wall, in pits in the earth, and in strong boxes under the bed. In religion they are Calvinists of the seventeenth century. They believe profoundly in election and predestination, that the world is flat and stationary, and [that] the sun travels round the earth once in 24 hours. The natives to them are Canaanites—people under a ban, to be either exterminated or enslaved. Altogether the Boers are a simple pastoral people, a unique survival of the seventeenth century, which their isolation and distance from European life have made possible.

Conan Doyle, by no means a pro-Boer, expressed many British soldiers' hard-earned respect for these museum-piece Boers in the opening lines of his popular *The Great Boer War* (1903): 'Napoleon and all his veterans have never treated us so roughly as these hard-bitten farmers with their ancient theology and their inconveniently modern rifles.'

In these and many similar contemporary descriptions—for instance, Mark Twain's in *More Tramps Abroad* (1897) and

Churchill's in *London to Ladysmith via Pretoria* (1900)—one detects a mixture of fascination, awe, and slight condescension which we might now reserve for a rare and impressive, but doomed, species of wild-life. A similar tone appears in some weaker poems which attempted to put across the Boers' point of view. One example was Trooper G. Simes's 'For Freedom's Cause', which appeared in the Bloemfontein *Friend* (2 April 1900), arguing that the war was about a concept of freedom larger than that which the Boers could conceive:

> Freedom you value but hoard as a miser;
> Freedom we value but offer to all.
> But of the conflict now sadder and wiser,
> Blame you not us, but yourself, for your fall.

There was much 'magnanimous' verse of this kind, but we must turn from it to the poems which were fervently committed to the Boer cause and which tried to explain the Boers' case to the world. Chief of these was the work of a group of South African poets whose poems appeared in *New Age* and were afterwards collected in *Songs of the Veld*. Olive Schreiner, though she wrote no verse herself, played a key role in this group. Alice Greene, Betty Molteno, and Anna Purcell, who all submitted their poems anonymously to *New Age*, kept up a voluminous correspondence with Olive Schreiner during her semi-internment in Hanover, Eastern Cape.[28] Her series of articles, 'The African Boer', which appeared in the *Ethical World* (1 September–20 October 1900) provided a profound insight into the Boer mind for readers in England and South Africa alike, as did her public speeches and her anonymous contributions to the *South African News*. Since her husband was attached to the *S.A. News* during the war, she no doubt knew Leipoldt as well. In her Boer War polemical

[28] The anonymous authors of the *New Age* poems are identified in Anna Purcell's copy of *Songs of the Veld*, described in *Africana Notes and News*, 11 (March 1955), 220–1. That Alice Greene was one of the authors is corroborated in a letter from Olive Schreiner to Pethwick Lawrence, October 1905. This letter, as well as most of those from which I quote below, is in the Murray-Parker Collection, part of the Olive Schreiner Collection in the University of Cape Town. I am indebted to Professor André de Villiers and Dr. Richard Rive for drawing my attention to these identifications. The following works were drawn on for further information: Olive Schreiner, *Thoughts on South Africa* (London: Fisher Unwin, 1923); *Letters*, ed. S. C. Cronwright-Schreiner (London: Fisher Unwin, 1924); and S. C. Cronwright-Schreiner, *The Life of Olive Schreiner* (London: Fisher Unwin, 1924).

writings she returned repeatedly to the Boer rural myth, the indomitableness of Boer women, the execution of rebels, and the historic roots of the Boer–British quarrel. All these points recur in the *New Age* poems of her protégées.

She saw the origins of Britain's conflict with the Boers in Lord Charles Somerset's anglicization policies and the so-called Slachtersnek Rebellion of 1815, which had led to the execution of five Boers. She refers to this event in 'The African Boer' and 'The Boer and his Republics' (*Thoughts on South Africa*, ch. 6). Writing to Betty Molteno and Alice Greene in March 1901, she exclaimed: 'I thought we'd had enough Schlachter's Neks [*sic*], but it seems not. Oh, it's such a mistake, such a mistake from the British point of view! Oh if they could only see it.'

She had moved to Hanover in September 1900. During 1901, particularly in March, her letters referred repeatedly to the execution of rebels in neighbouring towns and its effect on the Boers around her. Her appeals seem to have sparked the imaginations of her friends in Cape Town, for it was from the middle of 1901 that their poems began to appear in *New Age*. Anna Purcell's 'The Rebel', for instance, is dated 20 July 1901:

> Only a youth!
> Scarce one and twenty years
> Of summer sunshine and of wintry tears
> Had o'er him passed! . . .
>
> Only a youth!
> His friends in sullen mood
> Around him stood, as once before men stood
> At Slagtersnek!

It is tempting to think that 'The Rebel' refers to the same event as Leipoldt's 'Oom Gert's Tale'. Alice Greene and Betty Molteno became preoccupied with the Eastern Cape executions, too. On 5 September 1901 Commandant Lotter and his commando of Cape Boers were captured near Cradock and brought to Graaff-Reinet for trial. The group consisted largely of so-called poor whites, and was really no more than a marauding gang. Alice Greene, however, saw them, in 'The Last March of Lotter's Commando', as the upholders of a noble cause:

> Then they marched them through the township,
> For their friends and foes to see;

Boy Scouts in arms—Baden-Powell's resourcefulness at Mafeking. Dummies were used to draw Boer fire, and fishing rods to increase the range of hand grenades. (See p. 74.)

British P.O.W.s entertaining their Boer captors at a communal sing-song. (See p. 211.)

War correspondents awaiting the entry of Lord Roberts into Kroonstad, Orange Free State. Note the photographic

Typical war artist's rapid sketch. These were used as cartoons for the more elaborate plates prepared at home, seen earlier. (See p. 162.)

"*Oh! bravo, British Patriot!*"

45

The British Patriot, as seen by F. Carruthers Gould. Note the resemblance to Kipling. (See p. 132.)

Sons of the Blood—an empire in arms. This plate, from the *Illustrated London News*, carefully depicts members of regiments from all over the empire. (See pp. 80–1.)

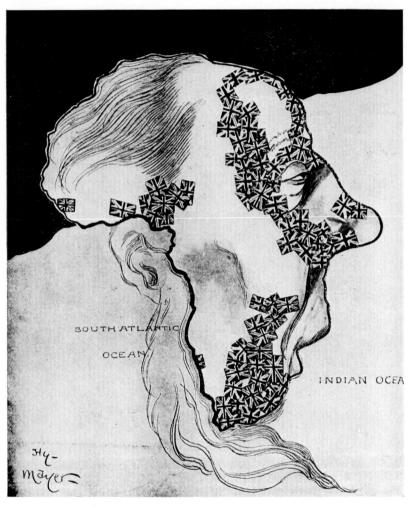

The Empire in Africa; or Kruger's Headache.

One of the most notorious German caricatures. This woodcut was captioned:
'English princesses decorate the youngest soldier in the British army with the
Victoria Cross because he has, though only thirteen years old, already raped
eight Boer women.' (See p. 256.)

The Capitalist Conspiracy. This French caricature of Cecil Rhodes among the dead was captioned: 'Money—that's the blood of others.'

They were 'ignorant bywoners', [squatters]
  Rich in neither land nor fee:
But they marched with head uplifted,
  Men of upland veld and farm,
With their bearded country faces,
  And their air of stately calm.

When another rebel leader, Commandant Scheepers, was captured
about a month later and eventually executed on 17 January 1902,
it was Betty Molteno's turn to write a passionate defence in verse,
called 'Scheepers', a poem until recently ascribed to Olive
Schreiner herself:[29]

So nimble, cool, resourceful, cunning, brave,
His name became a thing to conjure with,
Till 'Scheepers', like old William Wallace, grew
To something monstrous, fabulous, and strange.

The same issue of *New Age* (8 May 1902) that carried the
account of Scheepers's death, by a 'Cape Colony correspondent'
(?Leipoldt, Olive Schreiner), also published Alice Greene's 'The
Four Roads'. It is a powerful ballad, describing four sets of
executions, among them that of Scheepers, who was so ill at the
time that he had to be taken out by ambulance to face the firing
squad:

Four roads lead out of the town,
  And one of them runs to the West,
And there they laid the rebels twain
  With the bullets in their breast.
And the English Commandant laughed low,
  As he looked at the sleeping town,
'Each road shall bear its vintage soon,
  And your feet shall tread it down!' . . .

Four roads lead out of the town,
  And one of them runs to the North,
And there they led the dying man
  In the Red-Cross wagon forth.
And a bullet has stopped the glorious life,
  And stayed the gallant breath.
And Scheepers lies 'neath the road that leads
  To the land he loved till death.

[29] See Johannes Meintjes, *Sword in the Sand: The Life and Death of Gideon Scheepers*
(Cape Town: Tafelberg, 1969), p. 194.

I

Like other writers of the time, Olive Schreiner compared the Boer–British struggle with that of the Dutch against Spain. At the outset of the war she used the analogy in a letter to Mrs. W. P. Schreiner, and at the time of Cronjé's final desperate stand on the Modder River (February 1900) she wrote to Betty Molteno: 'If only they can hold on as the Dutch did in Holland against Spain.' In 'A Song of Freedom' Alice Greene took the idea further, casting the Boers in the heroic mould of Thermopylae, Bannockburn, Haarlem, and the Swiss against Austria:

> And their answer is still the prison grim,
>   And the scaffold ghastly high,
> And the red, red blood which soaks the ground
>   Where 'rebels' calmly die.

In an undated letter written some time during 1901, Olive Schreiner wrote to Betty Molteno: 'England is mad and blind, and driving on to her fate.' Her correspondent remembered the line and in 'Scheepers' it returned as: 'Deaf, dumb,/And stony blind, thou reelest to thy ruin'. The vatic and apocalyptic strain that marks lines such as these—indeed, so many of these poems— is probably traceable to Olive Schreiner's influence as well. Her *Trooper Peter Halket of Mashonaland* (1897) is shot through with oracular pronouncements of imperial doom, and readers of her *Woman and Labour* (1911) will know that she could not avoid a highly excitable style even in professedly expository writing. It may have been to an impassioned harangue in *Trooper Peter Halket*, too, that Betty Molteno owed the grisly analogy for her histrionic 'Ahab', written on Edward VII's coronation:

> Lift up, O King, thy garment's snowy hem
> A little higher. Turn thy head away—
> 'Tis not a pleasant sight to gaze on wounds.
> Thy garment's edge is getting red with blood—
> Step higher, King, still higher,—look not down—
> Step over that red pool and that still form!

So volatile was Olive Schreiner's writing and public speaking during the Boer War, that the loyalist *Graaff-Reinet Advertiser* lampooned her as demented ('Why does Olive Cronwright Schreiner shrilly scream?'). On the other hand, that the distress of Olive Schreiner and her friends at what was happening in the Cape Midlands was no mere quirk, is amply borne out by letters from other loyal English farmers in the area; for example, those of Mrs. Susie Biggs of Brooklyn, Graaff-Reinet: 'I have never anticipated any personal danger from the Boers, for having lived amongst them nearly all my life, I know that they are not what the press represents them to be. I feel quite sure that they will respect defenceless women and children. . . . Five rebels have been put to death in Graaff-Reinet in the short space of a week. They are charged with murder if they have been in an engagement where British soldiers have fallen! I am afraid the Dutch will retaliate and our soldiers will have to suffer for this.'[30]

The concentration camps and the suffering of women and children figure largely in the *New Age* poems. 'Two June Pictures', by F. C. Kolbe, a Roman Catholic priest who influenced Leipoldt greatly in these years,[31] contrasts a pleasant English summer scene ('the lark's mad song' and 'the rich warm scent of hay') with its miserable South African counterpart:

> But blackened rafters, gaunt against the sky,
>   Like grim uplifted fingers, ever seem
> To call down some swift vengeance from on high.
>   Hark! the sad moan, beyond that guarded line,
> Of children wan, pining for warmth and bread.
>   England, behold thy prisoners! All are thine,
> With bareness clothed and on famine fed.

In Alice Greene's 'The Boer Women Camp' and in the unattributed 'The Young Burgher's Mother' the theme returns, with the added force of the women's insistence that the war must go on:

> One image holds my mind from eve to morn,
>   —My boy out there upon the kopjes chill:
> The bare twigs shiver with a cry forlorn,
>   The icy wind blows chill. . . .
>
> Better our folk fall fighting, one by one,
>   Then sleep for evermore in freemen's graves,
> Than that we live, that stern old fight all done,
>   The death-in-life of slaves!

Apart from the *New Age* group, several other English poets, some with South African connections, wrote about the Boers with

[30] Letters to Miss Butler, Plymouth, 1 Mar. and 28 Aug. 1901. Quoted by permission of Professor F. G. Butler.
[31] Kromhout, *Leipoldt*, p. 21.

understanding or admiration. Frequently it was the Boer leaders who were singled out for praise or thoughtful assessment, Kruger and De Wet being the two outstanding figures. Denys Le Febure ('Syned'), who came to South Africa during the war, produced a shrewd study of Kruger in his 'Oom Paul', which appeared in *The Lone Trek* (1908):

> Cast in a rugged shape, an iron mould,
> Untaught, unlettered, and yet strangely wise
> In reading men—their lust for power or gold
> Standing revealed before those shrewd old eyes.
> Knowing the weakness of a stubborn race,
> And with the curb of a long-practised hand
> Guiding his burghers—and in fitting place
> Using the pregnant phrase they understand.

This monumental treatment of Kruger had a peculiar attraction for poets. We saw it in Edward Tylee's 'Paul Kruger' in Chapter III, and in several Afrikaans poets' work. On 8 December 1900 the *Academy*, deprecating Edmond Rostand's high-flown 'A Kruger', which had appeared in *Figaro* on the ex-president's arrival in France, expressed something of the powerful attraction this old man had for contemporaries: 'And yet in the hands of a great poet—wise, tolerant, just—inspired by a large pity for human things ... what a subject for an epic is this passing of a brave nation, this pilgrimage of an arrogant, broken old man, to an ever-receding goal.' That such an epic was never written was not through lack of trying, especially not on the Continent, as we shall see.

On Kruger's death in Switzerland in 1904, followed by the elaborate progress of his body to a state burial in Pretoria, the South African War caught the world's imagination for the last time. Two of the more moving of the many poems written on the occasion were Iver M'Iver's 'To S.J.P.K.' (*Caught on the Wing*, 1911), and F. E. Garrett's 'The Last Trek', which appeared in the *Cape Times* on 14 December 1904. Both poets returned to the heroic, monolithic stature of Kruger as, in M'Iver's words, a

> peasant genius, who, like David, grassed
> Thy father's sheep mid savage liberty,
> Conceiving there imaginations vast
> As those vast solitudes that nurtured thee.

Garrett (who, as editor of the *Cape Times*, had once interviewed Kruger) saw both the massive gesture and the final pathos of his demise:

> Bred up to beard the lion, youth and man
> He towered the great chief of a little folk;
> Till, once, the scarred old hunter missed his stroke,
> And by the blue Mediterranean
> Pined for some brackish pan
> Far south, self-exiled, till the tired heart broke.

The flamboyant escapades of De Wet moved the world's imagination in a different way. Constantly eluding his would-be captors, he appealed to sentiments akin to those of a crowd at a rugby international. The British troops turned their complaints about De Wet into a song:

> Old Christian he comes and he busts up the line
> Whenever he's hard up for scoff,
> He burns up our letters and drinks up our wine,
> And when we arrive he's gone off,[32]

while a contributor to the *Literary World* (31 August 1900) seriously suggested that De Wet should be offered a professorship at Sandhurst after the war was over. Another, in the *Slate* (27 April 1901), argued that De Wet had been allowed to escape so often because, like so many British officers, he was a Freemason. Numerous poems and songs retailing and exaggerating De Wet's will-o'-the-wisp exploits appeared during the later stages of the war. One, by J. M. McKeown, purported to be a series of daily dispatches recording Kitchener's final swoop on De Wet. On Thursday hopes are high:

> De Wet is now caged like a rat, he is fairly in a box,
> Around him grouped are Clements, Cleary, Methuen, French and Cox,

but by Saturday, predictably, the picture has changed:

> A loyal farmer told our scouts that De Wet is trekking east,
> Each man, besides the horse he rode, was leading a spare beast.[33]

[32] In a typescript collection of Boer War poems which Mr. Johannes Meintjes generously gave me.
[33] 'De Wet', reproduced in a Cape Town paper, *Die Burger*, 27 Aug. 1969.

Denis Duval put the same idea even more boisterously:

> They blew him to bits with superior forces—
> When they went to inter him he collared their horses. . . .
> When last seen, soon after his finalest rout,
> He was thumbing his nose with his fingers spread out.[34]

Next to the heroic stature and actions, real or apocryphal, of the Boer leaders, it was the deeper poignancy of the Boers' fierce attachment to their land and the rural, biblical simplicity of their way of life that attracted English poets. Some could write from personal acquaintance with the Boer, such as Kingsley Fairbridge in *Veld Verse and Other Lines* (1909) and Perceval Gibbon in *African Items* (1903). Thus Fairbridge, coming across the body of a Boer marksman on a hilltop above the homestead he had defended to the last,

> The little white-wash'd homestead, the peach trees, and the well,
> Now black, alas! and rooted up,

reflects that the scene spells not defeat, but a confirmation of the very cause for which the Boer had died:

> A brown felt hat, a khaki rag, glint of a rusted gun;
> Rock of the rock It lay upon, blended by wind and sun.
>
> ('The Sniper')

Gibbon's 'Mooimeisjes' contrasts an idyllic pre-war scene of small-town revelry with an incident during the war when the speaker has to participate in the destruction of the same village. Once again the poem laments the passing of a way of life as much as it queries a tragic waste:

> Oh, the little sun-swamped hollow where the little village lay!
> Mooimeisjes, where we were gathered, workers all, to take our play;
> And it lent its patch of purple to our leaden everyday,
> When we rode to Mooimeisjes in the morning.

> But I mind me of a morning that was misty-like and drear,
> When the earth was sick with sadness, and there droned upon the ear
> The rumble and the thunder of the gun-wheels in the rear,
> As we rode to Mooimeisjes in the morning.

> There was Jim and I and Kafir Jack and each one did his share,
> Till we saw the rooftrees blazing where our gentle memories were;
> And I know, despite our handiwork, our hearts were over there,
> With crippled Mooimeisjes in the morning.

[34] 'The Hunting of De Wet', *Back Numbers* (London: Henry J. Drane, 1904).

Poets in England responded as readily as Gibbon and Fairbridge to these aspects of the war. 'If only the English people would try to exercise a little imagination and picture the whole miserable scene,' wrote Emily Hobhouse in January 1901, and many did just that.[35] Information was readily available, in the form of the revelations of *War Against War* or the three and a half million pamphlets circulated by the Stop the War Committee during the first year of its existence (*Annual Report*, 1900). William Watson wrote much of *For England* as part of what seemed to him a one-man campaign to make the British public aware of Boer reactions and attitudes, but he was not alone. One poet who came to his aid was A. G. Shiell, with a volume of very febrile pieces called *Pro-Boer Lyrics* (n.d.). The least strident poem in the volume is 'A Voice from the Veldt', which does manage to give some idea of the desolation and pathetic vacancy of one of these wartorn farms and its inhabitants:

> On all that tumbling plain, or far or near,
> No other homestead shows. Forlorn it looks,
> No bluey spirals from the rustic hearth
> Ascend beneath the cloudless spread of sky.
> Vacant the yards and empty are the pens,
> No sound of bird or beast or man is heard,
> And broods o'er all a silence as of death.

The prolific Canon Rawnsley, who was capable of cheering on both sides, wrote several pieces extolling Boer bravery or perpetuating the archetype of the Boer so prevalent in British minds:

> And presently, propped by a boulder grey,
>   A grey and grizzled old Boer I saw;
> His whole right hand had been blown away,
>   But, quiet and calm,
>   He was reading a Psalm
> From a blood-stained book of the ancient Law.[36]

In 'Old Mortality' he created a more comprehensive and more compassionate image of the Boer. In both mood and insight this description of an elderly Boer sniper's daily routine, witnessed

[35] Fisher, *Hobhouse*, p. 129.
[36] 'After the Battle', *Ballads of the War*.

from the British positions, hovers between humorous observation and a bemused attempt to fathom an enemy so alien and yet so endearing:

> With rifle, bible, luncheon-bag, and pipe,
> We saw him going forth each day to snipe;
> We watched him on the foemen get his bead
> Then fire, then turn his Holy Book to read . . .
> Then could we note how he would luncheon take
> —His bit of biltong and his barley-cake,
> Or sudden sighting scouts upon the hill
> Would lay his rifle true again with skill;
> Then scratch his head and fill his ancient pipe,
> Puff clouds, till chance once more should bid him snipe; . . .
> We called him 'Old Mortality', and came
> Almost with love to think upon his name—
> This Bible-reading, smoking, sniping Boer,
> Whose shots were frequent if his bag was poor;
> And tho' his humour was a little grim,
> We sighed when Death the Sniper called for him.

The outstanding figure among English poets who tried to portray Boer experience was Alice M. Buckton. *The Burden of Engela: A Ballad Epic* (1904) showed a remarkable understanding of the Boer mind, in spite of the fact that she never visited South Africa.[37] She was, however, a friend of Montague White, Consul-General for the Transvaal in England during the war, and as she published some of her poetry in the *Ethical World*, she was presumably familiar with Olive Schreiner's series of articles in that journal.[38] But her real assets were a keen insight into the minds of rural people, and a dramatic ability to capture the characters of her ballad epic in revealing moments. The book tells, in a series of ballads, the story of a Boer family from the night before the men leave on commando to the return, three years later, of the survivors to the burnt-out remains of the farm. Extracts can therefore do little justice to the work as a whole, but the reader will find two of the best pieces, 'At the Garden Rail' and 'At Welbedacht', in Guy Butler's *Book of South African Verse* (1959). The former poem,

[37] See *A Book of South African Verse*, ed. Guy Butler (London: Oxford University Press, 1959), p. 213.
[38] The *S.A. News*, 25 Dec. 1900, reprinted her 'Lament' from the *Ethical World*.

particularly, catches a moving moment during a brief return
of Engela's husband to the farm for the calving season:

> A new-born calf upon his back—
>   He carried it alone;
> The mother followed, licking it,
>   With tender, anxious moan:
> What was there in the sight to make
>   My foolish tears to run?

'At Welbedacht' marks one of the high points in the volume, both
in the course of the narrative and in Alice Buckton's achievement.
Engela is confronted with a British officer commandeering the
last four horses on the farm:

> 'The stallions I must have, good wife! the red one and the brown.
> 'Twill be to your advantage, too, to send them saddled down
> Into the camp to-night; if not, be sure I come at morn!'

That night she goes to the stables and prepares her answer:

> She led to the open manger; she tethered the lantern fast,
> And mixed the ready mash. 'Though it should be our last,'
> She cried, 'we will have to-night our joy of this repast!'
>
> Their lips and nostrils quivered to feel the wholesome corn;
> She combed their massy manes with a comb of yellow horn:
> 'We must be ready, ready to meet the coming morn.' . . .
>
> Four pistol shots rang out in the silence of the night—
> The cow-boy started forth from his hut in sudden fright,
> And met a reeling woman bearing a stable-light.
>
> Two troopers came at dawn, with a sergeant at their head.
> 'Yield us the stallions, woman! the brown one and the red!'
> She gazed as one that wanders: 'Take them,' was all she said.

One by one the men and boys of the household are killed in the
war. 'Geert' recounts the death of Engela's daughter's sweetheart:

> They brought him in at midnight,
>   Across the saddle-bow—
> Geert of the ripe and chestnut hair,
>   Geert of the sunny brow!
>
> She took a covered pillow,
>   And sheets without a fold;
> She laid him on his boyish bed—
>   That bed for ever cold! . . .

> Two men went out in silence,
>   With shovel, pick, and spade,
> And by a lonely koppie-bush
>   A soldier's bed they made.
>
> In sight of home they laid him:
>   And when the morning sun
> Looked down upon the desert-plain,
>   Six horsemen rode alone.

'Face to Face' presents Engela with a death of a different kind: a severely wounded British captain is left on the farm by his comrades, and Engela nurses him for a fortnight:

> And strange it was, but Ouma once I found there, sitting long;
> She liked, it seemed, to speak and hear again the English tongue,
> Taking her back to happier days before the world went wrong.

'Ouma' (grandmother), indeed, turns out to be the poem's main seer and ideologue. In reply to the captain's protestations

> 'Mother, I touch no Politics, however false or true:
> A soldier only knows and does as his country bids him do'

she pronounces what is clearly the main line of thought behind the whole volume:

> 'Conquering is a thing of the mind, no act of fame, or gold,
> And that which once has conquered life will never leave its hold,
> Although it change its name, and place, and treaties damn it, "Sold!" '

At length a passing British column sends a party with orders to pick him up. By now a strong bond has developed between Engela and 'the wounded blue-eyed British scout, a captain of the line', who is fearful of the difficult journey ahead:

> 'Thirty miles on a waggon-track, out under the blazing sun . . .
> You'll find your pains are for a corpse before your task is done.'
> The sergeant fretted around the yard, and counselled with his men.
> 'We've been two days upon the road, and mayn't be near again:
> The column leaves for the North at once: my orders here are plain!'
> He looked at the sergeant—looked at me—he looked at the distant sky:
> I saw a sudden and only tear flash in his fearless eye.
> 'Hoist me cheerily, then, my lads! My generous friends, good-bye!'
> 'Tis four days since they took him back to where the army lay . . .
> And now, they tell, in a new-made grave he lies since yesterday!

Eventually Engela's family is removed to a concentration camp,
where her youngest son dies:

> Under the wild moon
> A rough stone stands,
> Raised too soon,
> Marked by alien hands,
> Glimmering white afar
> In the dead lambs' fold—
>
> 'Jaapie—prisoner of war—
> Ten years old!'

On their return to the farm, it is through the now-blind Ouma that
the family's reactions are recorded and Engela takes new hope:

> Is this the place? Under the bleaching sun
> The land lies desolate, and black and bare;
> The tangled teazles mock the empty fields,
> And scatter wasteful seeds into the air.
>
> 'Lead me, lead me out to the old barn door!'
> Said Ouma, trembling, as she took my hand.
> I helped her from the waggon o'er the heaped
> And broken stones that lay about the land.
>
> The barn was standing roofless; but its walls
> Were solid to the heavens! How could she
> Have known they stood? Her feeble knotty hand
> She passed upon the door-jamb silently. . . .
>
> I led her back. Lo! where the cling-stone peach
> Hung once above the shed, and made a bower,
> The giant aloe of a hundred years
> Had burst its bud, and stood in lofty flower!
>
> And underneath the matted ruined wall,
> Heavy with honey-store of two long years,
> The unmolested hives stood murmuring
> The darkly gathered tale of the flowers' tears!

VIII

A World Astounded

> They stand in the last red ditch and wage an unequal strife.
> But the sound of their barking guns has reached around the
>   world,
> Causing the throng to stop, to wonder, and then to sigh.
> Anon., 'In Victory Defeat', *The South African War: Some Poetry*.

OUTSIDE the British Empire and South Africa the Boer War
aroused surprisingly violent reactions. Like the Spanish Civil War
of a generation later, or the Vietnam War of more recent memory,
it provoked passionate responses from nations not involved in the
war at all, and fired the imagination of poets and the indignation
of intellectuals all over the world.

In order to understand this outburst of (mainly) pro-Boer
sentiment, we have to take note of a remarkable confluence of
international and domestic tensions which affected each of the
countries involved, and made them particularly prone to see the
Boer War both as an analogy for conflicts within their own
societies, and as a final rehearsal for some greater Armageddon.
The turn of the century witnessed not only a fierce stepping-up
of the arms race and imperial rivalry, but also the rapid growth of
a rural myth in industralized societies along with a corresponding
reaction to the 'decadence' of urban culture. The result was that
both in the United States and in continental Europe the Boer War
became a subject for intense debate about the nature and legitimacy
of imperialism. For expansionists the war became an object lesson
in the diplomacy of brute force; for isolationists, liberals, and
anglophobes it was proof of what the inspired republicanism of a
pastoral society could achieve against the decadent empire of an
urbanized one. The situation was ripe for myth-making on a
large scale.

Americans saw in this conflict many parallels with their own
recent excursion into colonial conquest, the Spanish-American
War of 1898. Kipling's dedication of 'The White Man's Burden'

to the Americans on their conquest of the Philippines overtly established a connection between American and British expansionism. The Anglo-Saxon race mystique was as strong in parts of the States as in Britain, and Kipling's widely publicized poem legitimized the right of Americans to invoke the same arguments of a civilizing mission as the British. Activist notions about the rights of the strong to subdue the weak were popular and were elevated, at this time, to an aggressive political platform by Theodore Roosevelt. The official view in the States remained resolutely pro-British during the war.[1]

At the same time there was enormous popular support for the Boers, inspired by a well-organized Boer propaganda campaign. Boer and pro-Boer speakers, such as D. E. van Broekhuizen and Montagu White, undertook lengthy lecture tours through the States, addressing full houses wherever they went. Webster Davis, Republican Secretary of State for the Interior, visited South Africa during the war, became a confirmed pro-Boer, and wrote *John Bull's Crime: or, Assaults on Republics* (1901). The American journalists R. Harding Davis and Howard Hillegas spent time with the Boer forces, too, and wrote highly popular accounts of their experiences.[2]

The reasons for the popularity of the Boer cause were not far to seek. Harold Faulkner has described the 1890s as the watershed between the rural, isolationist frontier-America of the nineteenth century, and the urban, industrialized world-power of the twentieth. Concern for the disappearance of the life and virtues of the frontier gave rise to the myth of an independent, pastoral golden age—'a lost agrarian Eden'. Holders of this view, mainly writers and intellectuals, objected to wars of expansion and imperialism as a betrayal of American republican virtues and the principles of the founding fathers. An articulate Anti-Imperialist League, founded in September 1898, opposed the war with Spain and the annexation of the Philippines, and gathered the support of several American poets, such as William Vaughan Moody ('Ode

---

[1] I am indebted to Harold U. Faulkner, *Politics, Reform, and Expansion 1890–1900* (New York: Harper, 1959), and John H. Ferguson, *American Diplomacy and the Boer War* (Philadelphia: University of Pennsylvania Press, 1939), for information used in this and the following paragraphs.

[2] D. E. van Broekhuizen Collection, State Archives, Pretoria, Acc. 356; R. Harding Davis, *With Both Armies in South Africa* (New York, 1900); and Hillegas, *The Boers in War*.

in Time of Hesitation', 'On a Soldier Fallen in the Philippines'), Edwin Arlington Robinson ('The Field of Glory'), and Bernard Shadwell (*America and Other Poems*, 1899).[3]

American Boer War poetry, therefore, is overwhelmingly pro-Boer, coming noticeably from the Midwest and South, rarely from Anglo-Saxon New England. Some of the pro-British poems, pale loyalist effusions, appear in Borthwick's Canadian anthology; much of the pro-Boer newspaper verse found its way into an anonymous and undated collection, *The South African War: Some Poetry Published in England and the United States*. Vituperation, satire, encomia on Boer leaders, and, of course, harrowing depictions of the plight of women and children form the subjects of most of these poems. From the start the Boers were typecast as upholders of rural sanctities:

> And what though the land was his homestead,
> And within its narrow confines
> Himself and his simple kindred
> Beneath its fig trees and vines
> Led harmless lives, and contented?

Or they were associated with the myths of the American past: the opening up of the West, and the American War of Independence.[4] Anti-imperialist attacks on Britain sank to the dismal depths of J. W. Roddy's *And Britain's Blest with Righteousness?* (1901)—

> Her breath spits famine's putrid slime
> About e'en nature's teeming clime—

or bounced along in Shadwell's 'On the Road to Kimberley', from *America and Other Poems*:

> Do you hear the rifles calling,
>   Cecil Rhodes?
> Brave and honest men are falling,
>   Cecil Rhodes.
> Bursting shell and shrapnel flying,
> Strew the earth with dead and dying.

[3] *Modern American Poetry*, ed. Louis Untermeyer, 4th ed. (London: Cape, 1932), and *War-Time Echoes: Patriotic Poems . . . of the Spanish-American War*, ed. James H. Brownlee (Akron: Werner, 1898).

[4] E. van der Meulen and C. S. Hulst, *An Epistle to Ahab . . . Dedicated to Joseph Chamberlain* (Grand Rapids, n.d.). See also Henry A. Harman, *Freedom's Footprints* (Springfield, 1899); Joaquin Miller, *Chants for the Boer* (San Francisco, 1900); and John F. Sleeper, *The Marion of the Free State* (Sherwood Press, New Jersey, 1901).

> Do you think that you are worth it,
>   Cecil Rhodes, Cecil Rhodes?
> Is their blood upon your conscience,
>   Cecil Rhodes?

Songs of the Veld, the *New Age* anthology, contains more of Shadwell's poems in the same vein, as well as two racy ballads, 'Rebel of the Veldt' and 'De Wet', on the rough vigour of his Boer heroes. The former has an infectious, rollicking cadence—

> Saddle and bridle and girth,
>   Stirrup and crupper and bit:
> Man on the top of a little horse,
>   Shaggy and strong and fit:
> Rugged and bearded face,
>   Ragged old hat of felt,
> Rifle that kills at a thousand yards,
>   And a tight-crammed cartridge-belt—

while 'De Wet' is probably the most evocative of the many poems dealing with the near-mythical elusiveness of this Boer leader:

> Ho, sing me a song both deep and strong,
> Like the thunder of hoofs as they roll along:
> Let the music ride with a swinging stride,
> Like the gallop of steeds in their strength and pride,
> When they reach at their bridles and foam and fret,
> For I sing of a rider: De Wet, De Wet.
>
> Through the black, still night comes a stamp and beat,
> And the dark is a-clatter with horses' feet,
> With the rattle of arms, as they wheel and pass,
> And the dull deep thunder across the grass,
> Who rides by night, when the moon is set?
> And the night owl answers, 'De Wet, De Wet.'

The ballad was a popular vehicle for the vicarious excitement which American Boer War poets attempted to convey. Two of the most effective appear in *The South African War: Some Poetry*: John Jerome Rooney's 'Burgher Smit of the Transvaal', and the anonymous 'Thunder of Hoofs and a Bugle's Cry'. The first was clearly meant as a reply to Herbert Cadett's 'Private Smith of the Royals', which we met in a previous chapter:

Burgher Smit of the Transvaal, alone on the kopje's crest—
Beneath, in the mud, a pool of blood—a ragged hole in the breast—
A groan and a chill—a fever chill—a prayer for a soldier's rest.

The second recounts an event that caught the imagination of several poets, the attempt of eight Boers, at Elandslaagte, to hold back the enemy while their comrades retreated:

> Thunder of hoofs and a bugle's cry,
> And down thro' the veldt came the British horse—
> Down with a rush on the burgher ranks
> With a whirlwind's sudden force. . . .
>
> When, sudden, stepped from the shelter rocks
> Eight burghers—eight in their hero might—
> And there they stood, as a single man,
> To meet the awful fight. . . .
>
> A mighty crash from the charging troop—
> For the burgher eight a sheet of flame—
> And, where they stood, but one was left—
> Sole hostage unto Fame!

The factors which produced excessive American enthusiasm for the Boers were at work in Europe on an even larger scale. Anglophobia and pro-Boer demonstrations, stopping just short of official recognition and intervention, were widespread on the Continent. What W. C. Dreher had to say about Germany was true of much of Europe: 'The attitude of the German public is one of practically unanimous condemnation of England's course toward the Transvaal. No newspaper of influence and no public man of note has come forward in defence of England.'[5] Inspired by envy of the British Empire on the one hand, and by the now popular creed of pacifism and arbitration *à la* The Hague Peace Conference on the other, hatred of Britain and sympathy for the Boers broke out in a rash of 'Burencomités', mass meetings, aid societies, special publications, and, of course, poetry. French, Germans, and Dutch were drawn to the Boer cause not only by racial affinities (the names of the Boer leaders—Kruger, Joubert, De la Rey, Botha, De Wet—proved irresistible), but also by the heroic prospect of two tiny republics opposing the might of a traditional enemy: the British Empire. J. H. Rosny calculated that the war was the equivalent of Holland taking on a country with the population of the whole of Europe, 'et même d'avantage',

5 *Atlantic Monthly*, 85 (1900), 301–8.

while Paul Combes wrote ecstatically: 'Never has history had to witness—not even in those heroic times when the Greek republics struggled against the formidable armies of the Persians—a duel so disproportionate, a scene so barbarous: well-nigh a quarter of humanity united to massacre a small, harmless community.'[6] As in America, the view of the Boer republics through the rosy haze of the rural myth was very attractive, and provided activists with a ready text to preach to a 'decadent' Europe.

Support for the Boers took on many forms, from concerts, petitions, streetsongs, broadsides, villainous caricatures, and the sale of souvenirs of the Boer leaders, to gifts of ambulances and the departure of privately raised contingents of Germans, French, Dutch, and even Swedes to the Transvaal.[7] A pro-Boer meeting in Budapest drew 10,000 people; in Belgium 100,000 petitioners begged the President of the United States to intervene in the war, schoolchildren played at Boers beating the British, and public houses changed their names to Spionkop, Pretoria, and the like.[8] In Paris the estaminets rang to Louis Facq's 'Dix Contre Un' and Louis Catrice's rousing chorus, 'En avant! en avant! en avant! Vaillants Boers, en avant!!' Kruger's Brussels-based minister plenipotentiary, Dr. W. J. Leyds, was in touch with twenty-five major Boer-aid organizations in Europe, the largest of which, the 'Internationale Burenliga', published a voluminous fortnightly magazine, *Der Burenfreund*, and collected over a million marks for the Boer cause.[9]

Caricatures were a staple ingredient of these publications as well as of the many comic weeklies so popular in Europe at the turn of the century. *La Vie pour rire*, *Le Rire*, and *L'Assiette au beurre* in France; *Simplicissimus*, *Kladderadatsch*, *Lustige Blätter*, and *Jugend* in Germany; *Uilenspiegel* and *Ware Jacob* in Holland—these were some of the papers that excelled in wholesale calumny of the British during the war. They showed Queen Victoria crawling round the

[6] J. H. Rosny in the *Revue franco-allemande*, 3 (1900), 33; Paul Combes, *Cent ans de lutte: Les Héros boërs* (Paris, 1901), introduction.

[7] See G. W. T. Omond, *The Boers in Europe* (London: Black, 1903), and G. D. Scholtz, *Europa en die Tweede Vryheidsoorlog* (Johannesburg, 1939).

[8] Philippe Deschamps, *La Reine Wilhelmine: Poésies dediées à sa Majesté la Reine des Pays-bas* (Paris, 1901), p. 283; *Rev. of Reviews*, 21 (1900), 107; and a letter I received from octogenarian Mr. G. P. Baert of Hasselt, Belgium.

[9] Leyds Collection, vol. 801, p. 102; *Burenfreund*, Dec. 1902. Other pro-Boer magazines which published verse were: *Le Cri du Transvaal*, *Op! Voor Transvaal*, *Paris-Pretoria*, *Transvaal*, and *Voor de Boeren*.

mouth of hell, presenting tins of chocolate to skeletons, or decorating bugler boys with the Victoria Cross for raping Boer women. *Les Camps de reconcentration au Transvaal* (1901), the work of a caricaturist on *L'Assiette au beurre*, Jean Veber, was so atrocious (showing, for instance, British soldiers kicking emaciated Boer women) that it was censored by the Préfecture de Police and provoked a British demand for an official apology.[10] Copies nevertheless sold like hot cakes and circulated widely in Germany and Holland, too, under the titles *Das Blutbuch von Transvaal* and *De Boeren-Kampen*. The caricatures of the time may serve to illustrate much of the verse in both subject and tone. Their outrageousness, misinformation, invective, and melodrama were shared by the poems, while they expressed, and helped to form, a hysterical attitude that made a balanced approach to the war unlikely among both magazine poets and their readers.

Another feature of the pro-Boer movement that affected the poetry it produced was its socially limited range. As in England, strong demonstrations of feeling on the war came essentially from the middle classes. If the protest movement made any impact on those in power, it nevertheless brought about no real support for the Boers—indeed, Kruger's arrival in Europe was an embarrassment to every government he approached—and there is little evidence that the war was much of an issue among the working classes. Most pro-Boer organizations carried the stamp of middle-class intellectual pacifism and patriotism, just as most of the numerous publications honouring the Boers were filled with the precious bourgeois fine art and literary efforts of the period. So, for instance, *Der Protest der Deutschen gegen die englische Barbarei im Burenkriege* (1902) contains the effusions in prose and verse of 150 German professors, while *Antwerpen-Transvaal* (1902), the *Leiden-Zuid-Afrika Album* (1899), Nijgh and van Ditmar's *Huldeblad van Nederlandsche Letterkundigen* (1900), and Philippe Deschamps's *Le Livre d'Or du Transvaal* (1901) are just a few of many lavishly produced parlour anthologies in Dutch and French.

Two groups of the bourgeois intelligentsia that were greatly concerned with the Boer War were the pacifists and feminists. The war was both a rallying point and a great disillusionment for

[10] See Omond, pp. 217–18, and Pierre Veber and Louis Lacroix, *L'Oeuvre lithographié de Jean Veber* (Paris: Floury, 1931).

those who had pinned their faith to the Hague Peace Conference. At first regarded as a set-back, the war soon became a test of strength for the newly formed International Peace League: 'The aim of the international League must be primarily to make every effort to put an end to this war imposed on the Boers against all justice and conducted in a manner quite barbarous,' wrote Philippe Deschamps in *La Reine Wilhelmine* (1901), a collection of poems dedicated to the League's chief patroness. But frustration was inevitable. As early as November 1899 Paul Louis wrote in the *Revue socialiste*, 'The Hague conference, its laborious sessions, and all the pomp with which it was surrounded, have been forgotten very quickly by the leaders of the nations.' He went on to argue that the Boer War had simply become an excuse for the major powers to step up the arms race.

Women were much to the fore in the peace movement, and a great deal of the organization of pro-Boer protest devolved on feminist associations. In Holland the impossibly named Mme Douairière B. de Waszkléwicz-van Schilfgaarde headed 'La Ligue néerlandaise des femmes pour le désarmement international' and presented a massive petition to the Dutch Queen (Deschamps, *La Reine Wilhelmine*). In Paris Princess Wiszniewska founded 'L'Alliance universelle des femmes pour la paix', which attracted the effusive support of admiring male poets such as Adrien Blandignière:

> Soyez les chastes Bienfaitrices
> De vos Fiancés ou Maris:
> Soyez les Mères Protectrices
> De vos enfants grands ou petits![11]

(Be the salvation of your Husbands and Fiancés, o virtuous women! And the Protective Mothers of your children, be they men or babes!)

As in England, the articulation of women's opinions on war opened up new and compassionate ways of thinking about war.

The real interest of continental Boer War poetry for the modern reader lies perhaps not so much in what it tells us about the Boers or war, as in its revelation of the mind of Europe at the turn of the century. Again and again the verse suggests that poets were moved by more than mere compassion for two small groups of

[11] *Les Minerviennes de la paix: Hymne* (Monaco, 1900).

farmers 6,000 miles away, and the reader soon finds himself wondering whether the war did not serve as a catalyst and metaphor for conflicts much nearer home. Many contemporary symptoms would support this possibility. A neurotic uncertainty, a proneness to over-react to every challenge or stimulus, was a marked feature of most intellectual, imaginative, and political activity at the time of the war. Barbara Tuchman has described the period as a highly complex one, characterized by doubt, fear, violence, and protest as much as by respectability, complacency, reactionary politics, and an obsession with order (*Proud Tower*, p. xv). The contradictory enthusiasms for pacifism and militarism so prominent in these years was only part of a much larger, fundamental clash between a liberal, humanitarian 'decadence' on the one hand, and a reactionary, aggressive activism on the other. The obsession with national decay, with nations that had become 'too worn out and flaccid to perform great tasks', heralded by Max Nordau's *Degeneration* (1893), was one of the surest signs of a European jitteriness that was ultimately to lead to a world war (Tuchman, p. 33).

France, particularly, seemed to be infected with a disease of morbid self-analysis. Here the optimism and utopianism of the French Revolution and Napoleonic period had steadily declined throughout the nineteenth century. In contrast to Saint-Simon's belief in 1814 that 'the Golden Age is not behind us but in front of us', most commentators at the end of the century were convinced that France had either passed imperceptibly through this golden age or had missed it altogether.[12] Social problems of industrialization; the abortive revolutions of, for instance, 1848; the collapse of older social and religious assurances; the bourgeois trivialization and materialism of the second empire; and, above all, the army's traumatic defeat in 1870–1, produced an acute and contagious pessimism that invaded most spheres of public life.

In reaction to this growth of gloom, some French writers and politicians began to harp on French messianism, 'la gloire' of the Napoleonic years, French military prowess, and colonial conquest. From 1880 onwards the ideal of 'revanche' came to dominate

[12] Quoted in Georg Roppen, *Evolution and Poetic Belief* (Oslo, 1956). I am indebted to Koenraad W. Swart, *The Sense of Decadence in Nineteenth Century France* (The Hague: Nijhoff, 1964); Herbert Tint, *The Decline of French Patriotism 1870–1940* (London: Weidenfeld & Nicolson, 1964); and Henri Brunschwig, *French Colonialism 1871–1914* (London: Pall Mall, 1966), for information used in this and the following paragraphs.

French politics, revanchist publications multiplied, and patriotic organizations such as Paul Déroulède's 'Ligue des Patriotes' broadcast their highly inflammatory anti-republican, anti-democratic, and, inevitably, anti-Semitic message. The reverses of Tangiers and Fashoda just before the outbreak of the Boer War ensured that revanche came to be directed as much against Britain as against Germany. The Dreyfus affair (brought to new life during the Boer War because of this scapegoat's re-trial in 1899) saw the climax to a long rivalry between the forces of humanitarianism and the rule of law on the one hand, and those of chauvinism and military prestige on the other. French reaction to the Boer War was essentially a further chapter in this history of a nation at odds with herself and embittered against her neighbours. Hence the war became a moral and political exemplum for a host of poets and prophets of revanche, decadence, pacifism, and national glory.

French poetry was as much in the doldrums in 1899 as French politics. 'The period from 1900 to 1905 was one of complete anarchy, during which poetry became the victim of the most extravagant makers of word-puzzles and the most blasphemous vulgarizers: a horrible mixture of alchemy and platitudes,' wrote Ernest Raynaud about the frenetic experiments of the time.[13]

One of the period's burning questions concerned the 'mission sociale' of the poet, and Raynaud describes a weird 'Congrès des Poètes' which met at the Sorbonne to assess this on 27 May 1901. The problem boiled down to a choice between the aloof detachment and intense introspection of the symbolists, and a new 'littérature engagée' that might attempt to grapple with France's particular social and political problems. Under the circumstances a strong, if myopic, argument could be made out for such explicit commitment. In *L'Époque 1900* (1951) André Billy describes a whole school of more or less didactic literature that developed from the time of the first Dreyfus trial onwards. He notices particularly the contemporary vogue for literature dealing with war, from the anti-militarist novels that followed on the publication of Zola's *La Débâcle* (1892) to the works of activists such as Jules Lemaître, Ferdinand Brunetière, François Coppée, and Jean Aicard, who formed the militant 'Patrie Française' to 'maintain and encourage love of the fatherland and respect for the national army, and to observe and resist foreign interference and

[13] *La Mêlée symbolistes 1870–1910* (Paris, 1918–20), iii. 61.

propaganda'. P. Daxor's *Poésies martiales* (1900), the Comte du Fresnel's *Rimes d'un soldat* (1903), and Henri Ferry's *L'École et le régiment* (1904) are some of the volumes of poetry expressing this popular military enthusiasm; E. Spalikowski's *Strophes et chansons de la paix* (1903) and Fernando Leal's *Dieu garde le Tsar!* (1899) are some of those espousing pacifism. Obviously, the Boer War would provide ammunition for both sides.

Although I have concentrated on currents of opinion in France, the situation was similar, if less acute, in the two other countries of major pro-Boer response, the Netherlands and Germany. One can trace the same signs of pessimism and morbid self-examination, the same move towards social commitment on the one hand and activism on the other in the Dutch literature of the period as one can in the French. Writers of the leading Dutch literary periodical, *De Nieuwe Gids*, became more and more militantly socialist; Albert Verwey's *Tweemaandelijksch Tijdschrift* propounded activism; *Ons Tijdschrift*, established in 1896, and *Van Onzen Tijd*, established in 1900, represented Calvinist and Roman Catholic anti-socialist reactions to the new direction of the *Nieuwe Gids*. [14] All published poetry on the Boer War.

Germany, as we saw in Chapter I, had throughout the nineteenth century produced a body of literature more strongly committed to social issues, including militarism and pacifism, than any other European country: the evidence is contained in collections such as Helmut Lamprecht's *Deutschland, Deutschland: Politische Gedichte vom Vormärz bis zur Gegenwart* (1969). Historical and patriotic themes were popular in the literature of the 1890s, and so, too, were the rural ideals and preoccupations of the 'Heimat' (home country) movement. Once again the retreat into the German past or countryside was a reaction to industrialization and urbanization, and it is therefore not surprising that one of the most outstanding volumes of Boer War verse in any language, Fritz Lienhard's *Burenlieder* (1900), was the work of the editor of *Heimat*.

There was less doubt and pessimism in Germany than in France; nevertheless the growing insistence from the 1870s onwards on Germany's cultural and military superiority over France and

---

[14] See W. J. M. A. Asselbergs, *Geschiedenis van de Letterkunde der Nederlanden*, ix: *Het Tijdperk van de Vernieuwing van de Noordnederlandse Letterkunde 1885–1950* (Antwerpen, 1951).

Britain became, in the 1890s, a clamorous pan-Germanic cult which actually disguised deep-seated uncertainties about national direction and identity. It became clear that Nietzsche's 'Brutalitätskur', his desire for a universal, cleansing war, had really developed from a pervasive insecurity about German cultural and political integrity after the easy achievements of 1871.[15] It was, significantly, in the 1890s that the most militant satirical weeklies came into being. They directed their corrosive commentary as much at German national life as at Germany's enemies.

German response to the Boer War was bound to be strong. Imperial and naval rivalry with Britain encouraged German interest in the Transvaal to the extent that, as C. D. Penner has argued, the Transvaal became the 'pivot of German imperialistic pretensions' in Africa by the mid-nineties.[16] The Kaiser's famous telegram to Kruger after the abortive Jameson Raid was a highly inflammatory confirmation of this interest, and though by 1899 the Kaiser's enthusiasm for Kruger had cooled considerably, in the popular view Germany still bore a godfatherly relation to the Transvaal. As in France, many observers in Germany realized that the Boer War was the crowning move in the scramble for Africa.

If there is one theme that runs through this brief sketch of late-nineteenth-century Europe, it must be the recurrence of attempts to escape from the growing complexity of modern urban Europe. People looked for clear-cut commitments, clean solutions to murky problems. And as universal as the search was one of the answers: the growing worship of rural simplicity. Albert Samain voiced the desire of a whole age in some lines published posthumously:[17]

> Ah! vivre ici parmi l'innocence des choses,
> Près de la bonne terre, et loin des tristes lois.
> O songe d'une vie heureuse et monotone!
> Bon pain quotidien; lait pur; conscience bonne;
> Simplicité des coeurs levés avant le jour.

(Oh! to live here amid innocent things, close to the good earth,

[15] See Eda Sagarra, *Tradition and Revolution: German Literature and Society 1830–1890* (London: Weidenfeld & Nicolson, 1971), chs. 13 and 15; Ronald Gray, *The German Tradition in Literature 1871–1945* (Cambridge: Cambridge University Press, 1965), ch. 1; and Hermann Boeschenstein, *German Literature of the Nineteenth Century* (London: Arnold, 1969).

[16] 'Germany and the Transvaal before 1896', *J. of Mod. History*, 12 (1940), 31–58.

[17] *Mercure de France*, 36 (1900), 13–15.

and far from unhappy conditions! O dream of a joyful, changeless life! Good daily bread; fresh milk; a clear conscience, and the simplicity of heart in those astir before daybreak!)

There can be no doubt that the immense popularity of the Boer cause resulted primarily from yearnings such as these. French, German, and Dutch poets seized on the Boer republics as two distant, peaceful, rural Utopias, governed by the patriarchal figures of Kruger and Steyn, and now menaced by the imperial arch-rival, perfidious Albion. Six thousand miles away a burning ideal of freedom had survived, a biblical simplicity and heroism of chivalric proportions. The Transvaal and the Orange Free State offered the rural myth as a reality and in a state of timeless preservation. Oversimplified as this view was, it became for many a subliminal vision of a lost European golden age; François Dépasse's editorial in the Epernay *Courier du Nord Est* (1 March 1900) is only one of scores that developed the idea: 'They lived on their own, peacefully, little concerned with the treasures hidden in their soil. They devoted themselves to cultivating the earth, and practised the virtues of the patriarchs. Wise and sane, they made little noise in the world and aspired to nothing but the good fortune of living in peace in their small states.'

Kruger and his generals became for a while the folk heroes of Europe, latter-day exemplars of the ideals and codes of the Arthurian legends and *Götterdämmerung*, fighting archetypal battles against the advent of empire, materialism, and the modern world. In the popular mind, claims Elisabeth Funke, the Boer leaders merged into one impossible heroic figure: 'romantic horseman riding through night and mist; cunning and experienced scout; merciless avenger; and mild, forgiving, magnanimous leader'.[18] When Kruger arrived in France in November 1900, the adulation of the Boers reached its climax. He was at once prophet and saviour; he could raise Europe from lassitude and decay by a mere word. 'Standing on the threshold of the new century, this peasant patriarch to-day represents, on his own, human dignity in its most sublime form,' exclaimed Frédéric Mistral,[19] and Francis Vielé-Griffin apotheosized Kruger as follows:[20]

[18] *Die Diskussion über den Burenkrieg im Politik und Presse der deutschen Schweiz* (Zürich 1964), p. 103.
[19] Deschamps, *Livre d'or*, p. 13.
[20] *Mercure de France*, 34 (1900), 592–5.

Vieillard! quel âge a ta jeunesse?
Ta voix est forte sur la mer;
Il semble qu'on la reconnaisse:
Cloche d'airain, battant de fer!
Ta volonté sur le seuil épique
D'un siècle, vieillard séculaire,
Etend, sans emphase tragique,
Son simple geste tutélaire;
Tu te lèves; nous voici fiers:
Notre âge a surgi de ses hontes
Evoquant la gloire d'hiers
Que sans mots tu racontes.

(Patriarch! How old is your youth? Your voice rings out over the
sea; it seems it has been heard before: a bell of bronze, with iron
tongue! Upon the epic threshold of a century, your will, age-old
patriarch, stretches forth in a simple gesture of protection, without the pomp of tragedy; you rise; and we are present in our
pride: our age has soared above its shame, calling up the bygone
glory you wordlessly bespeak.)

But Kruger's arrival in France was also a signal for a change in
Europe's heroic conception of the war. Up to this point the
continental press had managed to convince itself and its readers
that the Boers would somehow pull off a miraculous victory over
their adversaries, who outnumbered them ten to one. Kruger's
self-imposed exile changed all that, and the verse on the war now
took a sharp plunge from euphoric applause of Boer achievement
to the melodrama of the death of the two republics and the
suffering of women and children in concentration camps. Suddenly, too, old distrusts and hatreds opened up again among the
various nationalities of Boer supporters. Until this moment a
brief honeymoon of common sympathy for the Boers had united
Frenchman and German, so much so that the normally aggressively
Prussian *Deutsches Wochenblatt* had published Adolf Pichler's
'Zeitepigramme' (6 August 1900), urging *rapprochement* between
France and Germany against England:

Schmach, Europa, für Dich! Verlässt Du die tapferen Buren,
Führen sie doch den Krieg, der von den Briten befreit! . . .
Was geschehen, vergiss, o Gallien, schliess Dich an Deutschland!
Was geschehen, vergiss, schliess Dich an Gallien an!
(Shame on you, Europe! Oh, rescue the brave Boers, wage war

to free them from the British! . . . Forget the past, oh Gauls, join up with Germany! What has transpired, forget; join up with France!)

When, however, the Kaiser announced that he would not receive Kruger and left German magazine poets to protest as best they could or to shuffle out of their embarrassment, French writers retaliated with all the old venom. Kruger and the Boers were, after all, only pawns in a much bigger European power game. One of the most bitter poems was Edouard Noël's 'A l'Empereur allemand', a mighty declamation reprinted in Deschamps's *Livre d'or*. It mounts up through a series of more than twenty temporal clauses—

> Alors, quand ce vieillard, que protégeait son âge,
>   S'en allait vers vous confiant,
> Qu'il avait accompli ce périlleux voyage,
>   Armé de la foi du croyant . . .
> Quand il se présentait simple, comme un apôtre,
>   Défenseur d'un peuple opprimé,
> La Bible en sa main droite et vous montrant de l'autre
>   Son flanc par le fer abîmé . . .

to a full-blooded execration of the Kaiser's perfidy:

> Va-t'en! . . . C'est le mot qu'à la bête
> Qui lui mord le pied en passant,
> L'homme dédaigneusement jette, . . .
> Et c'est ce mot cruel, ô Sire,
> Ce cri de malédiction,
> Que vous n'avez pas craint de dire
> Dans un jour d'aberration.
> Avec l'orgueil de votre race,
> Vous le jetâtes à sa face,
> Sans détourner votre regard;
> Dans votre hautaine colère,
> Pour l'étonnement de la Terre,
> Vous l'avez dit à ce vieillard!

(And then, when this aged man, safeguarded by his years, ventured forth to you in trust and hope; when, armed with the faith of the devout, he had made that journey fraught with dangers; . . . when he stood before you in his simplicity, like an apostle, the Defender of an oppressed nation, with the Bible in one hand, and pointing with the other to the gash in his side. . . .

Be off with you! . . . those words are flung in contempt at the
beast which snaps at one's feet in passing . . . and those are
the cruel words, Sire, the harsh curse you felt no qualms
in uttering in a careless moment. With the arrogance of your
race, you flung it in his face and never averted your gaze; in your
pride and anger, to the astonishment of the world, you said *this* to
that old man!)

The range of Boer War poetry in France was considerable—from
street ballads and cabaret songs to the elevated rhetoric of
Academy poets; from Vito Faÿs's waspish revelation that dum-dum
bullets which Britain was frequently accused of using were, in fact,
made in France—

> C'est avec des balles françaises
> Que les carabines anglaises
> Assassinent les Boers! Tant mieux:
> Cette gloire commerciale
> Met à la France glaciale
> Un nimbe d'or délicieux![21]—

(It's with *French* bullets that English rifles slaughter Boers! That's
all to the good: it gives cold-blooded France not only commercial
glory, but also a delightful golden halo of virtue!)

to the sonorous solemnities of the aged Nobel prize-winner,
Sully-Prudhomme, mourning a slain Boer poet:

> Dans la nuit sépulcrale, asile aux murs épais,
> Ne pleure pas l'azur souillé du jour solaire:
> Ta couche fait envie aux vaincus qu'il éclaire,
> Ils survivent debout sans recouvrer la paix.[22]

(In the thick-walled sanctuary of sepulchral night, do not yearn
for the sullied azure of sunny day: thy resting-place is coveted by
the vanquished on whom it shines; they are alive and doing, yet
cannot regain their peace of mind.)

On the whole, the war attracted the wrong sort of poets—
writers eager to produce the 'littérature engagée' demanded by
the occasion, but deficient in the subtlety and visionary powers
required to raise such verse above the level of rhymed polemic.
It was particularly the survivors and revivers of the older school

---

[21] 'Dum-Dum, For Ever!' *Pour les Boërs* (Paris, 1900).
[22] 'Sonnet à un jeune poète boër', in Deschamps, p. 13.

of Parnassiens (Sully-Prudhomme, François Coppée, Jean Aicard), with their fondness for public gesture, literary pose, and rotund phrase, who were inspired by the war, rarely the Symbolists. But it was perhaps natural that the poets who saw the war as a clarion call to France should be the upholders of a more traditional, denotative style of verse composition than could be found in the obliquities of a Mallarmé or a Verlaine.

A striking number of French Boer War poems centre on the idealized image of the two republics as rural utopias. Dépasse's editorial, quoted earlier, could serve as a paraphrase for poem after poem:

> Ils vivaient comme au temps des premiers patriarches:
> Les femmes, l'arme au poing, à cheval dans les marches,
> Défendaient en soldats le bétail au repos,
> Et les fils qu'enfantait cette race de braves
> Grandissaient dans l'horreur des humaines entraves,
>   Coeurs simples, pasteurs de tropeaux.

(They lived as in the days of the early patriarchs: the women, with weapons clenched in their hands, would ride on horseback about the borderlands, defending the peaceful cattle like soldiers; and the sons born of this worthy people grew up simple-hearted, with a horror of human bondage, to be the shepherds of their flocks.)

The Boers were 'grands vieillards farouches et bibliques', and their country had the virtues and fecundity of the golden age.[23] Often this golden age became specifically stoic or pentateuchal, as in Louis de Soudak's *Étapes sanglantes* (1900):

> Un peuple de pasteurs, cœurs naïfs, bras d'acier,
> Vaillants fils du Frison, Boërs, hommes stoïques;
> Emportant avec eux leurs charriots rustiques,
> Le pain de chaque jour et le Livre immortel
> Où l'homme touche à Dieu, sans prêtre, sans autel,
> La Bible du foyer, leur talisman, leur code,
> Source de leur Désert, manne de leur Exode.

(A nation of herdsmen, with hearts of gold and arms of steel, the intrepid sons of Friesland, Boers, stoical men, taking with them their rustic wagons, their daily bread and the Immortal Book through which man comes close to God, with neither priest nor

---

[23] Henri de Veyge, *La Justice des choses: Ode aux Boërs* (Paris, 1900); Lucien Leluc, 'L'Aube', in M. P. Besnard *et al.*, *Au profit des Boërs* (Orléans, 1902).

altar—the Family Bible, their talisman, their law, the water of their Desert and the manna of their Exodus.)

Secure in their moral and material independence, the Boers enjoyed the rewards of a biblical pastoralism, and their country became a land of milk and honey amidst a fallen world:

> Des torrents murmuraient, lointains, dans les vallées,
> Et, dans ces longs déserts, les fermes isolées
> Déployaient des fraîcheurs de molles oasis;
> Leurs étangs reflétaient et figuiers et saulaies,
> Tandis que tout autour, ondoyants jusqu'aux haies,
> Brillaient les clairs frissons des blés et des maïs.[24]

(Distant streams murmured down in the valleys, and, amid those vast desert wastes, solitary farms surrounded themselves with expanses of soft, fresh verdure, like oases; mirrored in their ponds were plantations of fig and willow, while all about them, right up to their hedged boundaries, shone bright fields of rippling wheat and maize.)

In contrast to the Boers, the English appear as restless, puny, predatory:

> Vous êtes des géants. Ils sont des multitudes. . . .
> Les Anglais savent qu'ils devront lutter toujours;
> Leur rage crisse, siffle, gifle, griffe—et mord
> Les semmelles de vos bottes qui les écrasent.

(You are giants. They are crowds. . . . The English know that they will always have to fight; in their fury they gnash their teeth, pant, flail, claw, and bite at the soles of your boots that trample them down.)

France, too, finds herself enervate, lacking in moral purpose and in international prestige:

> Nous avons oublié l'exemple de nos pères,
> Notre passé de gloire et les jours plus prospères
> Où nos soldats, debout, sans haine et sans effroi,
> Vengeant aux quatre coins du monde chaque crime,
> Surgissaient, attendus par tous ceux qu'on opprime,
> Et muselaient la force en déchaînant le droit.

(We have forgotten the example of our forebears, our glorious past and a more prosperous age in which our upright soldiers,

[24] Charles Grandmougin, 'Aux Boërs!' *Pour la patrie* (Paris, 1902).

without hate and without fear, would punish every crime in the
four corners of the globe, arising in answer to the call of all
those oppressed, to trammel force and set justice free.)

To the shame of Europe (and of France in particular) the Boers
preserved strengths and virtues which had been the common
property of their European forebears, the Huguenots especially:

> Fuyant la vieille Europe at leurs persécuteurs
> Par delà les déserts et les lacs de l'Afrique,
> De pauvres paysans huguenots, troupe épique!
> S'installèrent enfin sur ces calmes hauteurs.[25]

(Fleeing from time-worn Europe and their persecutors, traversing
the desert-plains and lakes of Africa, some unfortunate Huguenot
folk—a band of epic stature—finally came to settle in this tranquil,
hilly country.)

Naturally, then, the Boers became superhuman, archetypal
heroes. In battle they were presented as larger than life-size,
capable of enduring staggering punishment. Here is Gabriel
Guiraudon's description of the Boers' legendary stand at Paardeberg, where Cronjé and 4,000 men, with their wives and children,
took eight days of bombardment from Lord Methuen's army of
50,000, before surrendering on 27 February 1900:

> Le feu chassa la nuit obscure.
> De tous côtés tonnaient, ainsi que des volcans,
> Cent bouches de canons sur les fiers combattants.
> Sans repos, sans sommeil, sans répit et sans trêve,
> Que le soleil les quitte, ou que la nuit s'achève,
> Les Boers n'avaient plus de soir ni de matin;
> Sans quitter le combat ils apaisaient leur faim;
> Sept jours, sept nuits durant, dans l'ardente fournaise,
> Ils firent, sur les monts, pâlir l'armée Anglaise.[26]

(Gunfire speedily dispelled dark night. From all quarters thundered
the mouths of a hundred cannons, which, like volcanoes, spewed
forth their contents upon the proud combatants. With neither rest
nor sleep, respite nor truce, the Boers could no longer tell morn-

---

[25] Georges Normandy, 'Espoirs', in *Pour les Boërs*, ed. Fernand Halley (Rouen,
1902); De Veyge, *La Justice des choses*; Léon Riffard, 'La Guerre du Transvaal', *Une
Douzaine de sonnets* (Evreux, 1900).
[26] *Gloria victis: Episode de la guerre anglo-boër* (La Réole, 1900).

ing from evening, whether it was the setting of the sun or the waning of night; they satisfied their hunger without leaving off fighting, and for seven days and seven nights on end, in the blazing inferno, they daunted the English army as they fought in the hills.)

It is no mere battle, but a gigantic struggle for the survival of the race. Men, women, and children all perish in one great sacrifice, and when the victors finally enter the remains of the Boer laager, the accusing eye of a dead woman, still clutching her Mauser rifle, transfixes the conquerors of her people:

> Ce cadavre glacé, resté debout, livide,
> Regardait le vainqueur de son œil fixe et vide.

(That frozen, livid corpse, still on its feet, stared at the conqueror with a fixed, sightless eye.)

The Boers provided ample material for popular myth-making, often of a hyperbolic or macabre variety. Alfred Guenin's 'Les Sept gas' (*La Chanson des Boërs*, 1900) tells of one patriarch's seven sons who went to war and did not return; his 'Pendant la bataille' describes a thirteen-year-old returning to the firing line after a brief rest, with the gay comment: 'I've killed twenty-four of 'em already!' Charles Préseau's *Un Héros* (n.d.) is typical of the many popular melodramatic narratives, inspired by the war, which circulated in broadside. Again a boy, the hero arrives wounded in his father's camp with an urgent message from De Wet to De la Rey. He staggers off his horse, tells his story, hears the general's high praise, then:

> Lorsque soudain celui-ci chancela,
> Je m'élançai et le prit dans mes bras;
> Alors, il parla d'une voix éteinte,
> Et dit, dans une dernière étreinte,
> Merci, mon général, ce me fait plaisir,
> Mais hélas je suis blessé, et me sens mourir.

(When this boy suddenly stumbled, I sprang forward and took him in my arms; then, he spoke in a feeble voice and said, yielding to a last embrace, 'Thank you, General, this gives me pleasure, but alas, I am wounded, and feel death upon me.')

In another broadside, R. P. Davarend's *La Vengeance d'un Boër* (1900), a father revenges the death of two sons in a novel way:

arguing that the English started the war in search of gold, he provides them with it, at a price:

> Lorsque le soir descend, après chaque bataille,
> Vous trouverez toujours, sur le champ de la mort,
> Deux officiers tués avec mes balles d'or.

(After each battle, when evening falls, you will always find among the dead on the field two officers killed by my bullets of gold.)

If Boer sons served as a focus for French mythopoeia, so did Boer women. Like their menfolk, they became near-impossible combinations of Amazonian beauty, matriarchal stoicism, and symbols of undying resistance. Fernand Halley, editor of *La Revue Picarde et Normande*, conducted a Boer War poetry competition, and collected the best entries in *Pour les Boërs* (1902). The volume is a useful gauge of the aspects of the war that interested French readers most, and Boer women were clearly high on the list. One Prigent-Kermillon won second prize with 'Courage, Boërs!':

> C'est la femme boër, c'est l'héroïne antique!
> Elle a vu la mitraille éventrer son hameau,
> La poudre étendre mort son fils dans son berceau,
> Mais son cœur veut avoir sa revanche tragique!

(It is the Boer woman, the heroine of olden times! She has seen her village gutted by shrapnel and her son shot dead in his cradle, but her heart desires its tragic revenge!)

M. C. Poinsot's 'Une Femme' dwelt similarly on the Spartan hardihood of Boer women, but the most forceful poem on the theme was A. Pruvost's 'L'Aïeule', the tale of a grandmother, sole remaining guardian of her farm, whose reaction to the return of her last grandson's body is somewhat staggering in its chilling stoicism:

> Elle dit aux soldats: 'J'avais creusé sa tombe!
> Ce qui vient de mon flanc vit libre ou meurt sanglant!'

(She said to the soldiers: 'It was I who dug his grave! The offspring of my body either lives in freedom or dies a bloody death!')

It is with a sense of relief that one turns to Charles-Adolphe Cantacuzène's quaintly chivalrous admiration for General Botha's attractive wife:

Je ne puis, dame, d'un air beau
Dans les plumes de ton chapeau
Placer une rose suave.

Mais à travers la verte mer
Que domine ton profile cher
—Je t'offre mon sourire esclave![27]

(Madam, I cannot gallantly place a fragrant rose in the feathers on
your hat. But I am your slave, and send you my smile across the
green waters ruled by your beloved profile!)

Stoic acceptance, the black resignation in adversity, was probably the single most remarkable quality that attracted French
poets to the Boers. It brought out exactly that limitless fund of
inner resourcefulness that French commentators missed in their
own nation. Implicit in almost all French Boer War poems, it is
the explicit theme of Lucien Leluc's 'L'Aube', already referred
to. The poem opens on a scene of blank devastation and dismal
languor, reflecting the mood of the Boer who sits dreaming in its
midst:

Les kopjes sont déserts et désertes les villes.
La ruin et la mort, comme des voiles longs,
Enveloppent de nuit la terre. Les sillons
Rayent de traits de sang les plaines infertiles. . . .

Là-bas, les rochers nus sont blancs comme des fresques.
Dans le veld dévasté, seul, immobile, en deuil,
Grand comme un revenant, un Boër rêve, et son œil
S'emplit des visions des combats gigantesques.

(The kopjes are deserted, as are the towns. The earth is wrapped
in great shrouds of death and destruction and darkness. Gory
furrows line the barren plains. . . . Down yonder, the naked rocks
are white as painted walls. In the devastated veld, solitary, still,
bereaved, looming large and ghostlike, a Boer dreams, his eyes
filled with visions of gigantic combat.)

Yet even in the midst of this awareness of immense loss, he awakes
to confidence in the future; the spilt blood has seeded future
peace:

Le sang versé germait sur la terre en moisson
Qu'éclairait le soleil des grandes paix futures.

(The shed blood seeded all over the earth a harvest glowing in the
sun of great peace to come.)

[27] 'Madame Botha', *Sonnets en petit deuil* (Paris, 1901).

K

French poets repeatedly invoked this dour and determined hopefulness of the Boers as a model for their compatriots to follow. Philippe Deschamps's *Le Livre d'or du Transvaal* (1901) is a hefty compendium of ardently rightist statements in prose and verse, dedicated to Kruger, which issued from French writers who were as active in the case of 'revanche' as they were paranoic about French decadence. 'Never, before 1870, would France have tolerated the crime that has been committed against you. Our people are with you with all their spirit and all their sorrow. But defeat has impaired their confidence in themselves perhaps more than it has diminished their power to help. . . . Forgive us,' wrote Jules Lemaître, prominent anti-Dreyfusard, and Henry Houssaye pondered: 'I admire President Kruger all the more because I ask myself what would have happened if a man of this calibre had been in charge of national defence in 1870.' Ernest Daudet, reflecting contemporary French anxiety about self-determination, asked if the future of the Transvaal would be the story of Poland or that of Greece: to be for ever subject to a superior power, or to become mistress of her own fate. But whatever happened, she would remain for France a living symbol of inspired liberty:

> Un symbole vivant et l'immortel exemple
> De ce que peuvent ceux pour qui la Liberté
> Est, après Dieu, l'objet le plus digne d'un temple.

(A living symbol and deathless example of what they can do for whom Liberty is, after God, the cause most worthy of a shrine.)

Another contributor was Théodore Botrel. France's most popular patriotic poet of World War I, he was beginning to make his name now that Paul Déroulède, fierce founder of the 'Ligue des Patriotes', had been banned. Warning France in 'Les Larmes de Kruger' of her supine state, he dwelt lugubriously on greater conflicts to come:

> L'Histoire est là qui vous regarde
> Et compte, à voix basse, les morts:
> Prenez garde, oh! prenez bien garde!
> La coupe est pleine jusqu'aux bords.

(History is there, watching you, and counting the dead in a hushed voice: take heed, oh, do take heed! The chalice is brimming over.)

Both in *Le Livre d'or* and in a further collection assembled by
Deschamps, *La Mort d'un héros* (1901), much of the rightist verse
centred on Colonel Count Georges de Villebois-Mareuil, ex-
Foreign Legionary and flamboyant unofficial leader of the small
group of French mercenaries and adventurers who joined the
Boer side. Prominent in Action Française and convinced, since
the Dreyfus affair, of a widespread, insidious disease in French
national life, he went to South Africa specifically to enhance
French prestige, 'to let a drop of French blood'.[28] Though,
ironically, he was at loggerheads with the Boer commanders for
much of the time and they, in turn, were sceptical of this professional cavalier, his death at Boshoff in the Free State on 5 April
1900 gave French poets a golden opportunity to stake a real share
in the Boer saga:

> Mais la France surtout prend part à tes succès,
> Parce que, combattant pour toi, de grands Français
> Ont trouvé le trépas au milieu de tes plaines

(Why, France in particular shares in your triumphs, because great
Frenchmen have met their death upon your soil, fighting for your
cause), exclaimed Fernand Rouselle (Halley, *Pour les Boërs*). 'The
admirable Villebois-Mareuil has taken it upon himself to represent
us all in the ranks of your little army,' rejoiced Jules Lemaître in
Le Livre d'or, somewhat condescendingly, while cabaret librettist
Léo Lelièvre, for good measure, used the opportunity to claim
General Joubert as a son of France, too:

> Saluons avec déférence
> Joubert! de Villebois-Mareuil!
> Ces glorieux enfants de la France,
> Tous deux tombés avec orgeuil.

(Let us pay our respects to Joubert and Villebois-Mareuil! Those
illustrious sons of France who fell together in noble pride.)

For François Coppée, Villebois-Mareuil was the one noble actor
against the pervasive 'décor de décadence'; in this 'dusk in which
we dream' he became, for Emmanuel des Essarts, the contemporary avatar of earlier French chivalry:

> Ton exemple dément notre apparent déclin.
> Oui! nous avons encore des fils de Duguesclin,

[28] Jules Caplain, *Villebois-Mareuil: Son idée. Son geste* (Paris, 1902). See also a collection
of letters and a pocket book of one of his adjutants, now in the State Archives,
Pretoria, Acc. 1247.

> Espoirs d'une France meurtrie,
>   Résolus contempteurs des vulgaires dédains,
>   Prêts à défendre, avec l'arme des Paladins,
> La liberté d'une Patrie.[29]

(Your example gives the lie to our apparent decadence. Aye! we can yet boast some sons of Duguesclin, the hope of a ravaged France, the men who resolutely reject popular aversions and stand ready to uphold the liberty of a Nation with Crusaders' arms.)

Kruger's arrival in France in November 1900 produced a minor cult of panegyric on the one hand and verbal self-flagellation on the other. From Marseilles, where he disembarked, to Paris, where President Loubet's government came as near as it dared to welcoming him officially, poets lauded the weary old man as hero, patriarch, figure of the world's sorrow, and saviour of France. On to him they projected all their longing for a simple but rock-fast moral and political ethos, all their self-pity, doubt, and profound malaise. Edmond Rostand, native to Marseilles, welcomed the ex-president to his city with the extravagant claim that Kruger's visitation was more conducive to future legend than that of a previous celebrity, Helen of Troy:

> On n'a jamais rien vu de tel que ce voyage!
>   Et la trirème au col sculpté
> Qui jadis vint toucher à ce même rivage
>   Pour nous apporter la Beauté,
>
> N'eut pas les flancs plus lourds de future Légende,
>   N'eut pas plus de sainte grandeur,
> Que ce petit canot d'un vaisseau de Hollande
>   Qui nous apporte le Malheur!

(Nothing has ever been seen to rival this voyage! And the trireme with sculpted prow that once came to berth by this very shore to bring us Beauty, was not more heavily charged with future legend, or more endowed with holy grandeur, than this small dinghy from a Dutch ship that brings us Suffering!)

Deschamps's *Livre d'or*, in which Rostand's poem appears, is full of the verse of a host of minor poets awestruck with Kruger. He

[29] Coppée, 'Après le service funèbre célébré pour le Colonel de Villebois-Mareuil', *Dans la prière et dans la lutte*, 8th ed. (Paris, 1901); Des Essarts, 'A Villebois-Mareuil', *Rev. des poètes*, 3 (July 1900), 19.

was 'sublime pèlerin' and 'héros divin' (Étienne Carjat), and he was indomitable:

> Tu passes parmi nous, fier et vivant exemple
> De l'Héroisme antique adoré dans le Temple;
> Tu fus, tu restes grand—Tu n'es pas abattu. (Édouard Noël)

(You move in our midst, a proud and living example of that ancient Heroism once worshipped in the Temple; you were, and you remain, great—you are indomitable.)

The jaded state of the French intellectual scene on to which Kruger exploded is apparent in L. Baudot's *Salut au Président Kruger* (broadside, n.d.):

> Tu viens, Kruger, éveiller dans notre âme
> Des sentiments qui n'y existent plus;
> L'Europe assiste à ce duel infâme,
> Et tes sanglots, vieillard, sont superflus.
> Va-t-en là-bas, continuer ta tâche;
> Nous ne pouvons rien pour te soulager.
> Ici, vois-tu, l'homme est devenu lâche,
> Il veut jouir et te laisse égorger.

(Kruger, you have come to rouse in our soul feelings which no longer can be found in us; Europe is a party to that squalid contest, and your grief is of no avail, old man. Go back there and carry on your task. We can do nothing to help you. You see, in this part of the world men have become degenerate, and want their pleasures while they allow you to be butchered.)

In a mood of bitter self-accusation, Jean Aicard asked what Kruger hoped for in coming to Europe at all; his world was an anachronism, his faith a subject for mockery:

> Vieillard, tu sors vivant d'une tout autre époque.
> Ton droit? ton Dieu? si tu savais comme on s'en moque!
> La France eut Jeanne d'Arc . . . sais-tu qu'on la brûla?

(Old man, you belong to quite another age. Your ethos? your God? If only you knew how people make fun of them! France once had Joan of Arc . . . didn't you know she was burnt alive?)

François Coppée, leading Orléanist poet and active in several patriotic leagues, shifted the blame from the people of Europe to their leaders, and ended his poem with a splendid gesture of contempt:

> N'accuse que les chefs; les peuples sont pour toi.
> Et le peuple français surtout! Non cette clique,
> Ce parlement pourri, ces ministres tremblants
> Qui, pour ton infortune et pour tes cheveux blancs,
> N'ont pas d'asile en leur soi-disant république! . . .
> Tu passes, grand vieillard, en demandant justice,
> Et l'Histoire écrira que la France a dit non.[30]

(Our leaders alone deserve your blame; the people are on your side. And especially the French people! Not that little group, that corrupt Parliament, those craven ministers who have no shelter for your misfortune and your white hair in their so-called Republic! . . . O grand old man, you come asking that justice be done, and History will write that France said 'no'.)

French Boer War poetry, then, was extremely volatile, a characteristic which appeared nowhere more sensationally than in those poems which attempted to evoke sympathy for the Boers by dwelling on livid and horrific battle scenes. Indeed, as in England, the ready market for such vicarious violence was in itself a symptom of a morbid society. The contemporary naturalistic and journalistic interest in war no doubt encouraged such writing as well, as is clear from Lucien Boyer's gory clinical realism in his broadside *La Balle 'Dum-Dum'* (1899):

> La dum-dum fait tant de dégats
> Que dans les moindres escarmouches,
> Par milliers les pauvres soldats
> Sont tués ainsi que des mouches;
> Et les corps de ces malheureux
> Ne sont qu'une compote étrange
> D'os meurtris, de chair et de fange
> Que des chiens s'arrachent entre eux.

(The dum-dum bullet is so viciously destructive that in the slightest skirmishes, poor soldiers are killed off like flies, by the thousand; and the bodies of these unfortunates are nothing but a grotesque pulp of mangled flesh, bone, and viscous matter over which dogs maul and tear one another.)

---

[30] Aicard, 'A Kruger, en Hollande', in Deschamps, pp. 10–12; Coppée, 'Au Président Kruger', *Dans la prière*.

The versifiers who tried to impugn, often more vituperatively than subtly, British methods in Africa made especial use of this brand of bloody sensationalism. In one of the less clumsy pieces, E. Beaussein's Lucianic satire *Le Songe de Joë Chamberlain* (1901), the Colonial Secretary has a nightmare vision of his troops in Africa. Their portrayal is realistic and moving:

> Pâles, déguenillés, portant sur leurs habits
> Des longs jours de combat les marques évidentes,
> Traînant d'un pas pesant leurs chaussures béantes,
> Le dos voûté, le front bas et les yeux hagards,
> La barbe et les cheveux collés par les brouillards,
> Et conduits par des chefs privés de leur monture,
> Ils défilaient, cachant aux passants leur figure.

(Pale and tattered, bearing on their clothes the obvious traces of long days' fighting, plodding along in their gaping boots with bent backs, bowed heads, and haggard eyes, their hair and beards clammy with fog, and led by unhorsed commanders, they filed past, hiding their faces from onlookers.)

A companion piece is L.A.E.'s *Voyage du Pôle Nord à Cape Town. Poème satirique* (1901), a libellously anti-British narrative which is momentarily redeemed by a glance of pity at the dead and wounded of both sides:

> Nombreux étaient les morts couchés dans la poussière,
> Attendant bien en vain qu'on leur donne une bière,
> Sur ce sol tout jonché de blessés, de mourants,
> De soldats qui n'étaient souvent des enfants,
> Et dans ces durs moments d'angoisse et de souffrance
> Personne n'était là pour prêter assistance.

(Many were the dead lying in the dust and vainly awaiting burial, lying on that ground all strewn with wounded and dying soldiers who often as not were little more than boys; and in those hard moments of anguish and suffering, no one was there to give them aid.)

The war produced a poor harvest of genuine satire in France. Because of the deep level of 'angst' I have talked about, and the resultant inability of poets to see the Boer War as an event which brought out French inadequacies as much as it may have revealed British aggressiveness, much of what had to pass for satire was no more than a mixture of villainous lampoon, lugubrious horror, and dubious indignation in the vein of the caricatures of the satirical weeklies. L. Baudot, for instance, in a poem quoted earlier, accepted without question that Lord Roberts

> fait fusiller les femmes,
> Incendier les fermes, les fermiers,
> Et si l'enfant veut éviter les flammes,
> Un vil soudard le repousse au charnier.

(had women gunned down, and farms set alight, and farmers burnt alive; and if a child tried to escape the flames, an infamous ruffian of a soldier pushed him back into the pyre.)

The charge that women and children had been burnt alive recurred with astonishing regularity. In such an environment Edmond Rostand's 'Ballade en regardant les albums du Jour de l'An', with its poignant contrast between the fancifulness of albums of New Year cards compiled by French children and the actuality of infant experience in the Transvaal, must rank as a complex poem, even if we reject, as we must, its calumnies.[31] The central image of the poem develops neatly from the pretty drawings of the albums, through an acid-etched vignette of children in South Africa, to the stark reminder that the death of the most famous nineteenth-century illustrator of children's books, Kate Greenaway, coincided with her country's war against the Boers:

> Faut-il qu'en des bagnes immondes
> Se glacent tant de petits pieds?
> Au lieu des aquarelles blondes
> De vos gais albums coutumiers
> Pleins de danses sous des pommiers,
> C'est une épouvantable eau-forte
> D'enfants nus jetés aux fumiers!—
> Mais Kate Greenaway est morte.
> *Envoi*
> 'Miss! il faut que vous dessiniez
> Rose, avec des fleurs sur la porte,
> La prison pour ces prisoniers!'—
> Mais Kate Greenaway est morte.

(Must so many little feet be frozen in foul martyrdom? Instead of

[31] 'Ballade en regardant les albums du Jour de l'An'. It appears, with two other Boer War ballads ascribed to Rostand, in an unidentified press cutting in the Leyds Collection, vol. 801.

fair watercolours in your diverting annual albums, full of dancing
under the apple-trees, we have a ghastly vignette of naked children
flung upon heaps of rotting matter!—But Kate Greenaway is
dead. 'Miss! you must draw the gaol for these prisoners in pink,
with flowers growing round the door!'—But Kate Greenaway is
dead.)

Lighter in touch but more sparkling than most French satire on
British imperialism was Arthur Cabuy's *Cause divine de la Guerre
Anglo-Boër* (1900), an amusing skit on the religio-Darwinist
pretensions behind jingoism. Hell, in Cabuy's poem, becomes too
small and Satan applies to God for additional territory. He is
offered the British Empire, with the assurance that the more he can
let it grow, the wickeder it will become. Through Joseph Chamberlain he now sets about convincing Queen Victoria of the advantages of expansionism in a passage of delightful irony:

> Mais la gloire frivole
> Ne sera pas ici notre seule auréole.
> Faire flotter partout notre puissant drapeau :
> C'est poser devant Dieu un acte grand et beau ;
> Accroître et affermir toujours notre puissance,
> Etablir en tous lieux notre prépondérance :
> Çà n'est pas seulement de la nécessité,
> Mais c'est encor bien plus de la moralité.
> Si Dieu appuie toujours l'armée la plus puissante,
> C'est qu'elle est la meilleure et la plus bienfaisante.
> Dieu ne permet jamais le triomphe du mal :
> Le peuple le plus fort est donc le plus moral.

(But in this case, frivolous triumph will not be our only source of
glory. It's presenting God with a great and a noble deed to raise
our powerful flag in every land; why, it is not only essential, but
far more than that, it is *moral*, to continue increasing and consolidating our power, and to establish our dominion everywhere.
If God always takes the part of the most powerful army, it is
because it is the best one, and the one most likely to do good.
God never allows evil to prosper: therefore it's the strongest
nation that's the most righteous.)

The most entertaining and mordant of French Boer War
satire often occurred in street and cabaret songs, the saucy Gallic
cousins of English music hall items. They covered much the same

ground as the more 'serious' verse—the heroism of the Boers, the perfidy of Albion, the pussy-footing of European governments—though often did so with more acid and less rhetoric, were less awed by the trauma of decadence, and were on occasion as irreverent about French *gloire* as about British presumption.

There was, of course, a mighty crop of vociferous patriotic doggerel, corresponding to the jingo jingles of the British press and music hall. Marius Réty, Léo Lelièvre, Léon Lemaire, and Georges Frémin were among the more prolific producers of ceaseless variations on 'Gloire aux Boërs!', 'Vive Kruger!', and 'Le Héros du Transvaal', and managed frequently to interpret the war as somehow either a display of French courage, or a plot 'de morceler notre France en six parts!' Léon Lemaire is of more than passing interest as he appears to have fought with the French contingent in South Africa. A rubric to his broadside *La Mort du Boër*, a tear-jerker about a dying Boer clutching the portrait of 'two little cherubs', claims that the piece was composed and sung in Johannesburg on 10 November 1899.

Perfidious Albion was no new theme in French popular song, and the Boer War provided many variations on old motifs. Children in the street sang

> Monsieur John Bull est mort,
> Chamberlain, Chamberlain, Chamberlain;
> Monsieur John Bull est mort,
> Très noblement tué,

to the tune of 'Marlborough s'en va t'en guerre', and A. Granderye trotted out a well-tried pun on *gale* (scabies, the itch) and *Prince de Galles* (Prince of Wales) in a song about a Highlander's adventures in the war:

> Je suis revenu de la guerre,
> Je n'en ai ramené qu'un bras.
> Un général très . . . militaire
> Un jour m'a demandé, mes gars,
> Pourquoi j'avais le front si pâle,
> De quoi j'avais surtout souffert;
> Je répondis: 'Prince, de Gale,
> Dont tout mon corps était couvert.'[32]

(I've come back from the war, and only brought one arm back

[32] 'La Chanson de Marlborough', *Charivari-Album: Boërs et Anglais* (Paris, n.d.); Granderye, *John Bull en guerre* (Pintenville-les-Nancy, 1900).

with me. One day, chums, a most . . . military general asked me
why my face was so pale, and what had given me the most pain;
and I answered: 'Sir, it's the Prince of Wales rash all over my
body.')

Sick jokes were fair ammunition in this genre.

> 'Tu r'viendras bientôt, je l'espère,
> et si tu n'reviens pas
> tu m'écriras'

('I 'ope yer'll come back soon, and if yer don't, write me a letter'),
remarks Queen Victoria to her departing troops in Vincent
Hyspa's 'Les Dépeches anglaises' (*Chansons d'humour*, 1902). Later
she receives a telegram:

> Nous avons hier
> tout le jour battu la campagne
> où nous avons laissé,
> pour la garder,
> plus de mille soldats
> qui ne s'en iront pas,
> car pour les enlever
> foudrait les déterrer!

(Yesterday we overran the countryside the whole day long, and
to keep it, we left behind more than a thousand soldiers who'll
never leave it, 'cause to get them away you'd have to dig them up
out of the ground!)

Two of the most caustic songs I have come across are, however,
directed at the French rather than the British government.
Dominique Bonnaud's *Le Débarquement de Kruger à Marseille*
(broadside, n.d.) is a witty lampoon on the French authorities'
limp submission to British pressure to ignore Kruger. Here the
British ambassador harangues an apologetic Delcassé, Minister
of Foreign Affairs, on the imminent arrival of Kruger in Marseilles:

> On vous a pardonné Marchand,
> Et crac! voilà qu'vous r'commencez sur-le-champ.
> C'est un' drôl' de manière, oui-dà!
> D'nous faire oublier Fachoda!
>
> De votre insolenc' les Anglais sont lassés,
> Et si c'débarquement s'opère,
> En quarant'-huit heur's, quatre-vingts cuirassés

Jett'ront l'ancre au pont des Saints-Pères.
Ainsi, vous m'avez bien compris:
Pas d'Kruger, ou bien nous viendrons dans Paris,
A grands coups d'torpilles et d'obus,
Couler vos bateaux-omnibus!

(You've been let off over Marchand, and bang! off you go again at once. That's a pretty funny way, it is, to make us forget Fashoda! The English are fed up with your cheek, and if this man's allowed to disembark, eighty battleships will drop anchor, in forty-eight hours, at the Saint-Pères Bridge. So you've understood my meaning, eh? No Kruger, or else we'll come to Paris with heavy fire from our torpedoes and shells, and wreck your river buses!)

An even more sprightly piece of sniping appears in Henri Fursy's *Chansons de la boîte* (1902). Fursy's real name was Henri Dreyfus, and as one of the few popular song-writers to support his namesake, he had to change his name to escape public persecution.[33] He was, understandably, more cynical than most about the real effectiveness and sincerity of the clamorous public enthusiasm for the Boer cause. In 'M. Kruger à l'Élysée' President Loubet is happy to give Kruger 'the assurance that your cause is the most noble in the human race', but when the old man replies: 'No, I would prefer you to get rid of the English for me', he has to hear:

J'trouv' que vous vous fait's trop de bile!
Parc' que la reine Victoria
Vient de vous prendre Prétoria!
Quand ell' prend quelqu' chose à la France,
J'n'y' attach' pas tant d'importance!—
    Moi, j'm'en fous!

Je reste tranquill'ment dans mon trou:
    Ell' nous a pris Fashoda!
Ell' peut prendre c'qu'ell' voudra,—
Pourvu que j'touche, au bout de l'an,
Mes p'tits douz' cent mill' francs.

(I think you're taking it all too seriously! Just because Queen Victoria's gone and taken Pretoria from you! When she takes something from France, I don't think it a bit serious!—*I* couldn't give a damn! I just stay nice and quiet where I am: she took Fashoda

[33] See G. W. Steevens, *Things Seen* (Edinburgh: Blackwood, 1900), 'The Dreyfus Case'.

off us! She can take what she wants,—so long as I get my little
twelve hundred thousand francs at the end of the year.)

After Kruger's departure from France, the pro-Boer fever
collapsed like a straw fire. At the end of the war, in 1902, a few
reflective poets lingered again on the far-off scenes of devastation:

> Les canons se sont tus, rassasiés de sang,
> Et la mort au teint pâle a parcouru le rang
> Des vainqueurs aveuglés par le fléau qui tue.
> Les canons sont sortis de la campagne nue. . . .
>
> Sur le sol dévasté, des cadavres hideux,
> D'un geste menaçant ou d'un rictus affreux
> Redisent le trépas d'un peuple qu'on égorge,
> Et la ferme qui brûle évoque un feu de forge.[34]

(The cannons have fallen silent, sated with blood, and pallid death
has passed through the ranks of the victorious blinded by the
fatal scourge of war. The cannons have left the desolate countryside. . . . On the ravaged earth, unsightly corpses bespeak, with
threatening gesture or appalling, skeletal grin, the death of a
slaughtered nation; and the blazing farmhouse resembles a
smithy's forge-fire.)

But Louis Chollet's gloomy speculations on growing rivalries in
Europe intimated an anxiety that would soon come to occupy
French, and European, poets far more than ever Kruger and the
Boers could:

> L'heure est sombre pourtant. Le Kaiser d'Allemagne,
> De son lourd gant de fer tourné vers la Champagne,
> Applaudit en secret à nos dissentiments,
> Entasse sur le Rhin bataillons, régiments,
> Casernes, arsenaux, canons, cavaleries.
> Poursuivant le succès de ses pirateries,
> L'Anglais, que le Boër trois ans intimida,
> Prépare au coq gaulois de nouveaux Fashoda.[35]

(But this is a dark hour. With his heavy iron fist directed at our
provinces, the Kaiser of Germany secretly rejoices at our dissent,
and on the Rhine he masses battalions, regiments, barracks,
arsenals, cannons, and cavalry. The English, whom the Boers

---

[34] Emmanuel des Hayes, 'Ils ont vaincu', *Mes rêves* (Paris, 1903).
[35] 'La Curée', *Chants de révolte* (Paris, 1904).

kept at bay for three years, are following up their successful piracy and preparing new Fashodas for the Cock of Gaul.)

National pessimism and morbid self-analysis hardly enjoyed the same vogue in Germany as in France. Prussian militarism, German diplomacy, and the Wilhelmine imperial temper were much too confident and successful for that. Nevertheless, the utopian charms of the Boer republics exercised their attractions here, too. The rural myth did not appear as frequently and as explicitly in German as in French verse, but it is often implied, as in the following speech placed in De Wet's mouth in Friedrich Mayer's *Cecil, der moderne Faust* (1905):

> Ein
> Einfacher Landmann bin ich nur, bestelle
> Des Tages meine Felder, oder geh'
> Den Hirten und den Herden nach, und berge
> Sie vor des Sturmes Toben. Abends ruh'n wir
> Am trauten Herd im stillen Haus. Wenn dann
> Der Mutter Nadel sich geschäftig regt,
> Die Kinder spielen um den Tisch, die kleinsten
> Liebkosend mich umhalsen, dann, Mitbürger,
> Vertauschte ich den groben Bauerkittel
> Nicht mit dem goldgestickten Königsmantel.

(A simple farmer only, I cultivate my fields by day, follow my flocks and herds, and protect them from the raging of the storm. In the evenings we rest by the familiar hearth in the quiet house. When the mother busies herself with her needlework, the children play around the table, the little one lovingly embraces me—then, friends, I would not exchange the drab farmer's garb for a king's gold-embroidered robe.)

If the French, via the Huguenots, could claim a share in the Boer alloy, so could the Germans; here, therefore, the war was popularly presented as a test of the mettle of the Germanic race. Bismarck had encouraged the concept of a united Germany as a bulwark in an age of change, hence also the myth of the German people's cultural superiority and world mission. England and France, it followed, had to be materially and morally weak. The epic view of the Boers as Germanic prototypes locked in a struggle for racial survival neatly fitted into and strengthened these prejudices. *Der Burenfreund* published yards of verse which, like

P. Ritter's 'Wir Deutschen fürchten Gott allein, sonst Niemand in der Welt' (a sentiment originally Bismarck's) in Number 22, annexed Boer successes to the annals of Germanic achievement:

> Im Süden tief, ein kleines Volk,
>   entsprossen deutschem Blut,
> In seiner Freiheit Gut bedroht,
> Von seiner Hütten Brand umloht:
> Noch steht's, noch kämpft's trotz bitterer Not
> Mit unverzagtem Mut.

(Far in the South, a small nation, sprung from German blood— their freedom threatened, their homes in flames about them—still stands, still fights with undaunted courage, despite bitter hardship.)

It was particularly the myth of the Boers' heroic activism and sacrifice, the legends of their prowess, cunning, and self-deprivation on the battle-field, that attracted German poets, rather than, as with the French, their reputation for stoic suffering. Hence one finds a preponderance of melodramatic narratives and ballads of action among German Boer War poems, in which the Boers and their leaders typically show a proto-German 'Kriegslust', hold to feudal codes of honour, or are obsessed with racial revenge and survival on a Wagnerian scale. The reverent meditation, for instance, with which Emil Steinweg's Boer commander prepares himself in 'Die Schlacht' (*Burenlieder*, 1901) for the day's battle, followed by an ecstatic determination not to retreat an inch, recalls the commitment of a Teutonic crusader:

> Vielleicht ist's meines Lebens letzte Stunde,
> Und eh' der Thau noch trocknet dieser Nacht,
> Bin ich dem Tod auf seiner düstern Runde
> Begegnet, und mein Tagwerk ist vollbracht! . . .
>
> Ich, euer Führer, schwör' es, hier zu sterben!
> Bis uns zerrissen nicht die Eisenscherben,
> Betritt kein Feindesfuss den heil'gen Ort!
> Umbrüll' uns, Donner der Kanonen!
> Durchheul' die Luft nun, Kugelsaat!
> Den Freien soll ein freies Grab belohnen!

(Maybe 'tis the last hour of my life, and before the dew dries this night I shall have met death on its dark rounds and my task will be finished! . . .

I, your leader, swear that I will die here! Until we are torn apart by shrapnel, no foot of the enemy shall tread this holy place! Roar about us, thunder of cannon! Scream through the air, ye bullets! The free will be rewarded with a free grave!)

In Walter Aigner's *Gedenkblätter an den Krieg in Süd-Afrika* (1903) the scene after battle becomes nightmarish and apocalyptic as beasts prey on human bodies:

> Weit dehnen auf dem Schlachtfeld sich die Leichen
> Von Mann und Ross! Der Mond fliesst mächtig nieder,
> Und lüstern leckt sein Strahl die starren Glieder,
> Als wünsche er die Knochen bald zu bleichen.
> Aus dem Gesträuche schleichen die Hyänen
> Und stillen gierig rings ihr blutig Sehnen.
> Die Walstatt tönt von ihrem Schlurf und Schmatzen
> Und von der Klauen hastig wildem Kratzen.

(The corpses of men and horses lie spread out over the battle-field. Powerfully the moon pours down, and its rays greedily lick their rigid limbs, as if more rapidly to bleach the bones. Out of the undergrowth hyenas glide and satisfy their lust for blood. The battle-field echoes with their guzzling and smacking, and the hurried scratching of their savage claws.)

However, at this moment a group of weary Boers arrive, drawn by ancient codes which demand the honourable burial of those fallen in battle.

The pseudonymous *Cronjés Siegen und Sinken* (1901), by 'Ogilvie', casts the Boer leader in the role of Teutonic folk-hero, 'with glance of falcon and cunning of hyena', and describes the Boer laager as a Germanic tribal encampment:

> Weithin dehnte sich das Lager
> Malerisch am Bergeshang,
> Wie ein Bild aus alten Zeiten,
> Da Germanenscharen sieghaft
> Wogten in den deutschen Landen.

(In the distance the laager lies, spread out picturesquely against the mountain slope, an emblem from bygone days when the Germanic peoples swept victoriously over the German plains.)

Cronjé's last stand at Paardeberg takes on the epic dimensions of Germanic tribal lore, here as well as in Ludwig Thoma's

'Koodoosrand'—'der Nibelungen grimmiges heldenlied'—and
in Countess Louise von Brockdorff-Ahlefeldt's 'Paardeberg':

> Zehn Tage im glühenden Sonnenbrand,
> Zehn eiskalt schauernde Nächte,
> Von der Sonne gedörrt
> Und vom Regen durchnässt. . . .
> Und immer noch singen die Weiber!
>
> Im Kugelregen singen sie,
> Sie singen beim Hall der Geschütze . . .
> Zu uns hinauf dringt kein Hülferuf,
> Nichts als der Gesang der Weiber!—
> Wann werden sie endlich schweigen?[36]

(Ten days under the blazing sun, ten icy shivering nights, parched
by the sun and drenched by the rain . . . and still the women sing!
In a rain of bullets they sing, they sing under shot and shell . . .
To us there comes no cry of help, only the singing of women!—
when will they be quiet?)

In another work of Wagnerian overtones already quoted from,
Mayer's *Cecil, der moderne Faust*, De la Rey in the role of warrior-
priest officiates at a ritual casting of bullets while pronouncing a
solemn anathema on the British:

> Die Kugel treff' die Mörder,
> Geh' hin ein Rachegott,
> Des grauen Hauptes Schänder
> Getroffen sink' zu Tod.

(May this bullet strike the murderers, may it go even as an avenging god; let the violators of grey heads sink, stricken, into death.)

He is specifically described as one of the Teutonic 'Heldenbrüder'
in a collection of *Burenlieder* which purported to emanate from
Cape Town, published by J. F. Lehmann in Munich in 1901.
President Steyn is 'Recht wie ein alter Herzog der Germanen',
while De Wet becomes the exotic outlaw figure of Teutonic
romance, the William Tell of the Free State.

A Natural corollary to the exaltation of Boer heroism was the
constant impugning of British military prowess and ethics. As in
France, such verse ranged from racy street song and magazine
satire in the spirit of contemporary caricature, to middle-class

[36] Ludwig Thoma, ed., *Der Burenkrieg* (Munich, 1900); Louise von Brockdorff-
Ahlefeldt, *Aus dem Burenkrieg: Gedichte* (Riga, 1901).

effusions of righteous indignation and harrowing rehearsals of farm burning and the treatment of women and children. British soldiers commonly appeared as craven buffoons, victims of incompetent blimps and an effete monarchy:

> Tom Jackson der Vater, Tom Jackson der Sohn,
> Die kämpften zusammen für Albion.
> Des Ritterdienstes sich jeder befliss;
> Sie waren voll Eifer für Lady Smith.
> Der Junge griff an und der Alte hielt Wacht;
> Die hatten's sich beide viel lustger gedacht.
> Als am Abend schwieg der Kanonen Gebrumm,
> Sie waren von all dem Dum-Dum dumm.
> Sie sahen im Mondlicht grausig klar,
> Dass Lady Smith keine Lady war. . . .
> Tom Jackson der Vater, Tom Jackson der Sohn,
> Sie hatten reichlich genug davon.
> Man sah sie ganz schweigsam die Strasse ziehn,
> Sie sangen sich heimlich: *God save the Queen.*

(Tom Jackson the father, Tom Jackson the son, are fighting together for Albion. Inspired by noble ideals of service, they are full of ardour for Ladysmith. The youth attacked while the father kept guard, but they had expected a merrier lark.

By the time the cannon fell silent at night, all the dum-dums had turned them dumb. In the grim moonlight they could clearly see that Ladysmith was no lady at all. . . .

Tom Jackson the father, Tom Jackson the son, had had more than enough; one could see that as they silently trod the streets, and sang 'God Save the Queen' under their breath.)

The above ditty appeared in the *Lustige Blätter*,[37] a satirical weekly which also published Jean Veber's *Blutbuch von Transvaal* and, like all its contemporaries, consistently presented the British commanders as inveterate braggarts and liars. 'Englands Zierden', for instance, reported Buller's recall from South Africa as follows:

> Der gute Buller ist gefallen,
> Nicht auf der Ehre blut'gem Feld,
> Daheim in seiner Väter Hallen
> Ist er mit Halbsold kaltgestellt.
> Das ist nicht eben sehr gefährlich

[37] 14 (1899), Number 48.

Für seinen Ruf; er ward gehasst,
Weil er [war] verhältnissmässig ehrlich
Und Ehrlichkeit John Bull nicht passt.[38]

(The good Buller has fallen, but not with honour in bloody battle;
sent home to his ancestral halls, he was docked of half his pay.
But this has not affected his reputation much; he was hated because
he was comparatively honest, and honesty did not suit John Bull.)

Readers were constantly reminded that the British were
'unmilitary'. 'Englischer Brauch' (*Kladderadatsch*, 12 November
1899) professed

Der Krieg ist in der Briten Land
Als kein vornehmes Geschäft bekannt,
Und die als Krieger dort ziehn ins Feld,
Die thun es nur um das liebe Geld—
Der Prinz von Wales bleibt zu Hause.

(In Britain war is not regarded as a worthy pursuit, and those who
sally forth into battle do it only for the love of money—the
Prince of Wales stays at home.)

News of British victories was often suppressed, put down to false
dispatches, or belittled. The inability of the British forces to make
much headway in the early months of the war was a particular
cause of merriment and 'Schadenfreude', as in Ernst Friedrich's
John Bull und die Buren (1900):

Fünfzehnhundert Buren haben
Wir bei Mafeking begraben;
Denn zie wurden in die Luft
Mittelst Melinit gepufft:
Grausig war das Schauspiel! . . .

Und auf Nimmerwiedersehen
Flohn die Buren auf den Höhen:
Ja, das war ein Meisterstück;
Doch wir zogen uns zurück,—
Stets in bester Ordnung.

(At Mafeking we buried fifteen hundred Boers; they were blown
sky-high by means of melanite: a gruesome spectacle it was! . . .
The Boers took off for the heavens, never to be seen again: yes,
that was a master-stroke. But we fell back—in the best order, of
course.)

[38] Reprinted from *Kladderadatsch* in *Lustige Blätter's* collection, *Pfui Chamberlain!*
(Berlin, n.d.).

When the tide began to turn in Britain's favour, especially after the surrender of Cronjé at Paardeberg, 'Die Rache für Majuba' (*Burenfreund*, No. 17) cleverly whittled down Methuen's total victory to a disreputable betrayal of the codes of war.

Reports of British contraventions of the rules of civilized warfare—persistent rumours, for instance, that after the battle of Elandslaagte the Lancers had gone round killing wounded Boers and even prisoners—called forth regular epidemics of febrile magazine verse. The introduction of camps for Boer women and children had the same effect, as is clear from P. Rehman's ballad, Mit-Leiden', in *Burenfreund*, Number 16:

> Es fährt der Wind übers Zeltenlager,
> Wo gefangene Frauen, bleich und hager,
> Hinweggerissen von Heimstatt und Heerd,
> Hinsiechen, von Hunger und Elend verzehrt,—
> Wo, in Nässe und Kälte und Blösse und Not,
> Aus hohlen Augen grinst der Tod;

(The wind blows over the laager of tents where captured women, pale and haggard, dragged forth from hearth and home, languish, emaciated by hunger and misery; where, amid cold and wet and exposure and distress, Death grins out of hollow eyes;)

or from the overwrought *Gedichte* (1903) of Olga Arendt-Morgenstern, who had actually worked in a Boer camp hospital:

> Habt Jahrmarktsbuden Ihr geseh'n
> Bei Regenwetter auf dem Feld
> Im Herbst? Wenn scharfe Winde weh'n
> Die Fetzen von dem nassen Zelt? . . .
> So Zelt an Zelt, nich Wand noch Schutz—
> Kein wärmend Dach—ein enger Raum—
> Verkommend fast in Kot und Schmutz,
> Und draussen—ach, kein Strauch, kein Baum!
> In solchem Leinwandzelte, ach,
> Trefft Ihr die Kinder aus der Farm,
> Die einst so wohl, jetzt krank und schwach,
> So traurig, hungernd—und so arm!

(Have you seen the stalls of an annual fair in a field in autumn rain? When an icy wind rips shreds from the wet tents? . . . So [stood] tent upon tent, without wall or shelter—no warm roof—cramped for space—rapidly collapsing in dirt and squalor; and outside, oh, not even a shrub or tree! In canvas tents such as these, alas, you will find the children from the farm, once so healthy, now ill and weak, so sad, hungry—and so poor!)

Poems of the kind I have been quoting were frequently illustrated with grotesque and villainous caricatures reminiscent of contemporary German ventures into expressionism: those attempts to shock and disturb through the distortion and brutalization of reality. *Der Burenkrieg* (1900), compiled by Ludwig Thoma, editor of *Simplicissimus*, refined these grotesqueries into a malicious art. So, for instance, it reproduced Wilhelm Schulz's 'Der Rotrock', which presents the English soldier as a predatory criminal, below a woodcut showing two soldiers cutting off a wounded Boer's finger to steal his ring. Such productions serve to confirm one's impression that an uneasy but vicious self-righteousness permeated the Prussian imperial and military temper of the time, issuing only too readily in hysterical and melodramatic accounts of British cruelty. Some of the poems and caricatures on concentration camps in particular and on the fortunes of British arms in South Africa in general were resurrected by German propagandists in both World Wars. Nazi apologists, such as the Dutch writer D. Wouters, gleefully reminded their readers that the British had invented concentration camps, and reprinted appropriate Boer War poems to prove it.[39]

A striking number of German Boer War poems appeared in the shape of ballads. The war ballad recurred in German poetry throughout the nineteenth century, and the popular character of the German pro-Boer movement must no doubt have been a further reason for the frequent appearance of this folkloristic genre.

Most of the ballads were simple tales of heroism, loyalty, Boer cunning, or British perfidy, often with a touch of romantic melodrama or Gothic gloom. Less sombre than most was Hans Erdmann's 'Depeschenritt' (*Burenfreund*, No. 16), which works up to a clever anticlimax by exploiting the ballad's potential for raising tension. A British dispatch rider is 'pricking upon the plain':

> Schneller geht es in die Weite,
> Denn Englands Schicksal hängt an seiner Seite.

---

[39] *Na Veertig Jaar . . . Zuid-Afrika en het Lied van de Straat in Nederland* (Nijmegen, 1940), and *Krüger Klaagt Aan* (?Utrecht, 1942).

Von seinem Pferde tropft der blut'ge Schweiss,
Vor seinen Augen tanzt ein roter Kreis.
Nur kurze Zeit—vorwärts! Da kracht ein Schuss,
Fort rast das Pferd, des Reiters Fuss
Fällt schwer vom Kugel, und—dann liegt er still.

(Swiftly he sets off into the distance; England's fate hangs at his side. From his horse drips bloody sweat; before his eyes dances a red circle. Only a few more minutes—onwards! Then a shot rings out. The horse dashes off; the wounded rider's footfall drags—then he lies still.)

His dispatches are brought to De Wet, anxiously opened, and read:

'Lord Kitchener schreibt'—man hält den Atem an,
Voll höchster Spannung drängt sich Mann an Mann—
Da fliegt ein Lachen über seine Wangen—
Er winkt: 'Hier nimm' und eile Dich, mein Sohn,
Bring' die Depeschen schnell zur Poststation . . .
Kinder . . . ich bin schon wieder mal gefangen!'

('Lord Kitchener writes'—they hold their breath, anxiously they crowd around; then a fleeting smile crosses his face—he beckons: 'Take this "dispatch", my boy, and hurry to the post office with it . . . Children . . . I've been captured once again!')

Many ballads kept close to the evocative simplicity of the traditional ballad with its repetitive structures and antiphonal techniques, supplying, as in England, the sentimental narratives so popular in the parlour literature of the time. In 'Das Burenkind' (*Burenfreund*, No. 17) a dying child asks a series of questions of its mother, the answers all telling the same story of pathetic gloom:

O Mutter, liebe Mutter
Wo weiltest Du so lang?
Ich bin so müd' und hungrig
Mir ist so angst und bang?

Lieb' Engel, sei geduldig,
Ich war im Nachbarzelt,
Ich suchte für Dich, Liebling,
Dort Brot und Milch und Geld.

(O Mother, dear Mother, where do you tarry so long? I am so tired and hungry, so anxious and afraid!

Dear angel, be patient; I have been in the tent next door, seeking bread and milk and money for you, my darling.)

Reinhold Fuchs's 'Die Burenmutter', reproduced in S. F. Maurer's *England und Transvaal* (?1901), is a harrowing tale of a dying Boer mother, in hospital, giving a drink to an equally ill British soldier who turns out to be not only one of the troop responsible for burning down her farm, but also, for good measure, the one who had thrown her only son's picture into the flames. One of the most popular ballads of this kind was Otto Heine's 'Die Bur und sein Kind'. It contains, in addition to the untaxing rhythm and rapid development of the ballad in its most workaday form, all the features necessary for a tearful success: a thirteen-year-old boy who insists on accompanying his father to battle; the sorrowful departure from mother and sister—

> Und Pieter liegt in der Mutter Arm,
> Ihre Abschiedsthräne, die netzt ihn warm,
> Eine Feder steckt Antje ihm an den Hut,
> 'Ade, mein Pieter, und ziele gut!'—

(And Pieter, enfolded in his mother's arms, was drenched by her warm farewell tears; Antje stuck a feather in his hat: 'Good-bye, my Pieter, and may it go well with you!')

the fatal battle in which Teutonic courage is laid low by British numbers (the wounded father, with white hair and beard, is 'Ein Urbild alter germanischer Art'); and the predictable death of the boy by the old man's side:

> Er lag als wie im Traume lind,
> Mit seinen Locken spielte der Wind,
> Zur Seite ihm lag sein kecker Hut—
> Und Antjes Feder war rot von Blut.

(He lay as in a gentle dream; the wind played with his curls. Beside him lay his jaunty hat—and Antje's feather was red with blood.)

The pathos of this particular incident in the battle of Elandslaagte attracted a number of poets. Canon Rawnsley made use of it in English, and so did several German poets apart from Otto Heine.[40]

---

[40] Heine's ballad is quoted here from an unidentified press cutting in the Strange Collection of Africana, S Pam 831 HEI. For other ballads on the story, see Dagobert von Gerhardt-Amyntor, 'Der Boerenartz', *Poetische Flugblätter* (1901); Heinrich

Two of the most chilling ballads about Boer fathers and sons came from the pen of Rudolf Presber, who became one of Germany's most active balladists in World War I and who was to write bitterly about some Boer leaders' campaigns against German forces in the later war.[41]

'Der Letzte' tells of a Boer returning home with the body of his son. It served as end-piece to Veber's *Blutbuch von Transvaal*, which may account for its theme of bitter anathema:

> Wir reiten, Pieter, reiten
> Durch unsre kleine Welt,
> Zum letztenmal wir beiden,
> Weils Gott nun so gefällt.
> Doch wo heut Nacht vom Pferde
> Dein Blut herniederrollt,
> Da sei in Fels und Erde
> Verflucht, verflucht das Gold.

(We are riding, Pieter, riding through our little world, together for the last time, because God has ordained it so. But wherever your blood drops down tonight from the horse's back, there let the gold be cursed, cursed in rock and earth.)

'Drei Schüsse' is the even more macabre tale of a sniper who casts three golden bullets every day with which to revenge the death of his three sons. The poem re-creates very effectively, through the use of repetition and bare statement, the brooding obsessiveness of the speaker's hatred, and the cold fanaticism of his resolve:

> Drei Gräber schaufeln sie morgen stumm,
> Drei krächzende Geier kreisen darum.
> Da werden drei Buben, vom Ruhm genarrt,
> Im Herzen mein Gold, in die Erde verscharrt. . . .
> Hab' kein Weib und kein Kind und kein Dach und kein Haus,
> Nur Gold—und giesse mir Kugeln daraus.
> Nur Gold, das in einsamen Bergen lag—
> Drei Schüsse schiess' ich an jedem Tag!

(Silently they dig three graves in the morning; three screeching vultures circle above. There three lads, cheated of their fame, with

---

Offerman, *Die Heldin von Transvaal* (Bonn, n.d.); and Konrad Scipio, 'Bei Elandslaagte', *Türmer*, 2 (1900), 487.

[41] See 'An Louis Botha', *Die Brücken zum Sieg* (?1914). The Boer War ballads appear in *Gedenkblätter aus dem Burenkrieg*, ed. J. Kammerer (Elberfeld, 1903), and, with Dutch translations, in A. Pijnacker Hordijk, *Tegen Haman met Esther en Mordechai* (Naaldwijk, 1901).

my gold in their hearts, are laid into the earth. . . . I have no wife, no child, no roof, no home; only gold—and out of that I cast my bullets. Only gold, which used to lie in the lonely hills. I fire three shots, every day.)

Equally grim and haunting is Anton Renk's 'Es giebt kein Zurück!', which appeared with several other striking ballads in his *Tiroler und Buren* (1901). The title, 'There is no going back!', refers to the (?apocryphal) words of a British officer on the Tugela. He calls for a ferry to take his men across, because 'fate is waiting for us on the other side', but the ferryman who appears is not the one he has expected:

> Hat's ein bleicher Ferge vernommen,
> Der im Felsenwinkel gehockt,
> Ist zum Strande nieder gekommen,
> Hat die Fähre losgepflockt. . . .
> Hat er sie alle aufgenommen,
> Stösst vom Strande das zitternde Boot
> Und es spricht der Fährmann Tod:
> 'Es giebt kein Zurück!'

(A pallid ferryman was seen crouching in a rocky recess; then, coming down to the bank, he untied the boat. . . . He picked them all up, pushed the trembling boat from the shore, and then Death the Ferryman spoke: 'There is no going back!')

The outstanding volume of ballads, however, among German Boer War poetry was Friedrich (Fritz) Leinhard's *Burenlieder* (1900), translated into equally effective Dutch verse by J. F. Sikken as *Boerenliederen* (1900). Vivid, compact, compassionate, these ballads are among the best poems in any language on the war. They were immediately hailed for their 'Echtheit'. A contemporary reviewer described the volume as 'Staunenswerk' (astonishing work) and claimed that war poetry had never been like this before.[42] Much of the volume's attraction for modern readers lies in the atypical absence of didacticism from its pages, even though Leinhard clearly presumes the heroic stoicism of the Boers: he was, significantly, editor of *Heimat* (in fact, founded it during the Boer War) and a prominent figure in the movement to articulate the virtues of rural Germany. The poems exhibit a

[42] Quoted in Paul Bülow, *Friedrich Lienhard: Der Mensch und das Werk* (Leipzig, 1923), p. 238.

striking realism, concentrating on crisply realized moments of action—

> Ganz tot der Berg! Ein rasches Rieseln nur
> Von einem Eidechs, lang und schuppendick,
> Der ins Geröll erschreckend fuhr.
> Und dann ein Pferdekopf, ein leis Gekeuche—
> Ein Hut und Karabiner—Lauerblick
> Ins Thal—und wieder fort—
> Das war ein Bur.

(Dead-still the mountain! Only the quick rustle of a startled lizard, long and scaly, darting in among the boulders. Then a horse's head, a muffled cough—a hat and rifle—a glance into the valley—and gone. That was a Boer.)

or the hyperaesthetic sensations of being under fire—

> Kleingewehrkampf! Auf den Höhen die Kanonenzungen schwiegen.
> Jetzt wie ein Gewitterregen prasselt's aus den Schützenwiegen.
> Prasselt wie von Körnerfalle,
> Rattert wie von Hagelschalle,
> Stäubend durch die Himmelshalle,
> Wo wir hinter Deckung liegen.
> Nein, das sind nicht Prasseltropfen,
> Ist ein drollig Pochen, Klopfen,
> Fast wie auf gespannte Hosen!

(Rifle fire! On the heights the cannons' mouths are silent. Bullets patter from the trenches like rain in a thunderstorm, rattle like a cascade of pellets, clatter like the din of hail, stabbing through the skies to where we lie behind cover. But these are no raindrops; it's like a crazy banging, beating, on taut-strung breeches.)

or the amazed shock and dramatic poignancy of death in battle:

> Mit wilden Fäusten griff er in den Sand,
> Als ihn die Kugel auf das Antlitz schmiss:
> Dann warf er sich herum, und mit der Hand
> An seine Wunde griff er und zerriss,
> Der starke Riese, Wamms und Hemd und Uhr.[43]

(Frenzied, his fists clawed into the sand—the bullet had struck him in the face. Then he spun round, and, with his hand clasped to his wound, the mighty giant clutched and tore at waistcoat, shirt, and watch.).

[43] 'Buren-Patrouille', 'Kleingewehrkampf', and 'Der gefällte Riese'.

As in France, the enormous popular support for the Boers in Germany led, in the end, nowhere.

> Die Freiheitslieder haben sie,
> Jedoch die Freiheit nicht,

(Songs of freedom you have, yet not freedom itself)

remarked Maurice von Stern, and Ludwig Thoma voiced the helpless indignation of many Germans when the Kaiser snubbed Kruger:

> Die deutsche Treue hält nicht in der Not. . . .
> Uns bleibt die Schande, euch ein freier Tod.[44]

(German loyalty fails in time of trouble. . . . Ours is the shame, yours is the freer death.)

It was Thoma, too, who wrote one of the most moving ballads on the end of the war: 'Friede'—

> Über die Heide geht der Wind;
> Es flüstert im Gras, es rauscht in den Bäumen.
> Die dort unten erschlagen sind,
> Die vielen Toten, sie schweigen und träumen. . . .
>
> Wenn die Herrscher versammelt sind,
> Beim festlichen Mahl lasst die Becher schäumen!
> Über die Heide geht der Wind;
> Die vielen Toten, sie schweigen und träumen.[45]

(Over the veld blows the wind; it whispers in the grass, it rustles through the trees. Underneath it the slain, the many dead, lie silent and dreaming. . . .

The conquerors gather—let the goblets foam at the festive board! Over the veld blows the wind; the many dead lie silent and dreaming.)

As one of the smaller literatures of Europe, Dutch writing has always stood somewhat in the shadow of her greater French and German neighbours. This was true during the Boer War, too, even though the Dutch, through the ties of kinship, identified themselves more closely with the distant struggle of the Boers than did any other European nation. Possibly because of this

---

[44] Von Stern, *Gesammelte Gedichte* (Linz, 1906), and Thoma, 'Ohm Krüger', *Grobleiten* (Munich, 1901).
[45] *Neue Grobleiten* (Munich, 1903).

affinity, much Dutch verse on the war is blemished by a rhetoric of such pietistic or vituperative vehemence, exceeding even French and German maledictions, that most of it is unreadable now. The poems collected in, for instance, M. Molenaar's two anthologies, *Nederland en Afrika: Gedichten* (n.d.) and *Transvaal Gedichten* (1902), are unanimous in an anglophobia that one can explain in the case of France and Germany, but which becomes difficult to reconcile with the Netherlands' traditionally friendly relations with Britain. Even the streetsongs were less subtle, less amusing, and more cacodylic here than anywhere else; the best effort of the popular satirical columnist Kees van Ponten was a rather sick pun on 'lance' and 'ambulance':

> Daar schijnen zich weer een paar te roeren,
> Overal Boeren, overal Boeren!
>   Zijn ze gewond?
>   Neen, kerngezond!
> Vooruit met die ambulans—
> 'k Rijg ze pardoes aan mijn lans![46]
> (It seems a few are moving there,
> Boers everywhere, Boers everywhere!
>   Are they hit?
>   No, fighting fit!
> Ahead with the ambulance—
> I'll string them on my lance!)

The rural myth was the most common theme in the war poetry here, since the Dutch consistently looked upon the Boers as preserving the values and ways of life of a bygone Holland. They repeatedly identified the Boers' conflict with that of the Netherlands against Spain three centuries earlier. In 1896, apropos of the Jameson Raid, B. ter Haar complained in *Nieuws van den Dag* that the motto of the House of Orange in the war against Spain, 'Je maintiendrai', had become a mockery, and he urged young Dutchmen to go to the Transvaal:

> Zoekt, jonge mannen, frisch en krachtig,
> Door aanleg, kunde en vroomheid machtig,
> Bij 't volk, aan Neêrland nauw verwant,
> Niet—als de avonturiers, die stroomden naar den Rand—
> Naar goud, met onverzaadbre hand;
> Zoekt daar een tweede vaderland.[47]

[46] 'Ambulance', *Pillen voor Joe* (Amsterdam, n.d.).
[47] *Het Volk van Nederland aan Zijne Broeders in Transvaal* (Nijmegen, 1896).

(Look, young men, strong and healthy, mighty in your ability, skill, and faith—look among that people, closely related to Holland, not—like the adventurers that rushed to the Rand—for gold, with insatiable hand; look for a second fatherland.)

Kruger's visit to Holland brought P. C. Boutens to the realization that the ex-president stood for values no longer recognized or even recognizable in Holland; in contrast to the dim, devalued existence of urbanized Europe, Kruger stood for a moral life-style impressively and sharply defined:

> Hier waar moê slaven in hun schemermijn
> Geruischloos over 't vreugdloos werk gedoken
> Leven en sterven en de onuitgesproken
> Waarheid meêneme' in 't eeuwiglijk-stilzijn,
> Hoe staat hier plotseling de scherpgekante
> Toren van uw slagschaduw, Groote Grijze,
> Eenig massief in 't neevlig-transparante?[48]

(Here, where tired slaves in their dark mine bend quietly over their joyless task, and live and die only to take along the unspoken truth into eternal silence, we suddenly see the sharp-edged tower of your shadow, Great Grey One, uniquely massive in this nebulous opaqueness.)

Idealization of the Boers became a minor cult among the poets of *De Nieuwe Gids*, the most influential Dutch literary periodical of the time. Established in 1885 to reform the Calvinistic dourness of Dutch literature, it was by now equally committed to social reform. Consequently it published numerous poems in which the Boer struggle became either a model of the vitality that could be expected of a healthy nation, or an allegory of rural simplicity contending with capitalist corruption.

> Ging nu voor 't laatst de zon van Holland tanen,
> Die, hoog en stout, in 't verre Zuiden stond,
> Omdat ons ras gerechten strijd aanbond
> Met 't huurlings-rot der diplomaten-vanen?

(Is Holland's sun, which shone so high and bold in the far South, now setting for good, because our race has risked just war with the hireling scum of diplomatic brood?)

demanded Willem Kloos, co-founder and editor, of his readers in May 1900. In 'Drie-zangen' (June 1901) Frederik van Eeden drew

[48] 'Twee Sonnetten Voor S. J. P. Kruger', *Gids*, 65 (1901), 8–9.

a naïve but typical contrast between the Boers and their capitalist
exploiters:

> 't Geldschietersvolk, dat van de boeren leeft,
> Weet met zijn uitgemergeld heer van knechten
> Zich wel joyeus in geplaveide stad
> Den tafel aan te rechten. . . .
> Zie 't Hollandsch huisgezin om blank gedekten,
> spijsrijken disch in kalm en vroom geluk.

(The usurious race which lives off the Boers knows, with its
starved host of servants, how to lay its table opulently in the
paved city. . . . Behold the Dutch family at a clean, well-filled
table, peaceful and pious.)

In a context of *fin-de-siècle* world-weariness, the Boers offered a
new faith in human perseverance. 'I do not know how a century
born at Waterloo could have died at Elandslaagte', wrote Seerp
Anema in *Poëzie* (1903), but Jac van Looy, another regular *Nieuwe
Gids* contributor, was convinced that the Boers had shown
Europe the way to a new vitality:

> Leven verpriegeld niet en niet versentimenteeld,
> Dat 't aan de ziel niet mangelt, niet aan den wortel scheelt.
> Hoor het in 't slaan,
> In 't zingend den dood ingaan,
> Door 't daveren en uit het gefliets:
> Het Leven is alles en de Dood is niets.[49]

(Life not trivialized and not sentimentalized, that doesn't lack soul
nor is without root—listen to it in the clamour, in the singing
meeting with death, through the thunder and out of the flash:
Life is all and Death is naught.)

Herman Coster, a Dutch volunteer who had died at Elandslaagte
and hence enjoyed in Holland something of the fame of Villebois-
Mareuil in France, was enshrined in several poems, for example,
by Jan Veth,[50] as the prototype of a new-found national commitment to noble causes. Indeed, Willem Zuidema could not resist
the temptation in his broadside, *Elandslaagte* (1899), to depict
Coster as superior to the Boers themselves!

Holland was the only European country that gave the Boers
any tangible official support. Queen Wilhelmina was patroness of

[49] 'Een Stem naast een Stem' (1899), *Gedichten* (Leiden, 1932).
[50] *Tweemaandelijksch Tijdschrift*, 6 (1900), 183.

the peace and arbitration movement on the Boers' behalf; she made several personal overtures to Queen Victoria to stop the war; and she sent a Dutch warship, the *Gelderland*, to convey Kruger from Lourenço Marques to Europe.[51] Dutch poets consequently put much self-righteousness into their frequent calls to the rest of Europe to support the Boers' crusade against the forces of darkness:

> Een kruistocht, ja een heil'ge oorlog voor het Recht,
> En dwingt den buiter, die in dienst der misdaad vecht,
> Om af te trekken met zijn horden![52]

(A crusade, yes, a holy war for Justice, and force the exploiter, who fights in the service of crime, to retreat with his hordes!)

Kruger, furthermore, represented in Holland something more than the anti-decadent challenge and stimulus to guilt and self-depreciation he was made to be in France. Here he grew into judge and censor of all the ills of Europe; he was Lear, both victim and scourge of the world's inhumanity and indifference:

> Gij leeft een vreemden tijd—vreemd-sterke man,
> Die Kruger zijt en Lear heet in het spel. . . .
> Over de wereld klimmend gaat uw stap,
> En waar die toeft, pookt uw klankwoord het recht
> Dat in de harten knip-oogt vonkend-uit.[53]

(You live in a strange time—strangely strong man, who is Kruger, but is called Lear in the play. . . . Your footfall mounts over the world, and where it pauses your challenge strikes fire from justice barely glowing in men's hearts.)

Poems on the course and specific incidents of the war often indulged, like their French and German counterparts, in volatile rhetoric about Boer heroism and British perfidy, and demand no further attention here. Quite a few, though, show to advantage the influence of Willem Kloos and the poets of his *Nieuwe Gids* school, who insisted in their new poetry on concrete imagery and the vivid realization of sense perceptions. The result could be war poetry of a striking immediacy or originality of metaphor. Even comic verse might benefit from such an approach, as is clear

---

[51] G. J. Schutte, 'Koningin Wilhelmina en Zuid-Afrika', *Zuid-Afrika*, 49 (1972), 25.
[52] 'Na Cronjé's Capitulatie', in Molenaar, *Transvaal Gedichten*.
[53] A. van Collem, 'Kruger', *Ons Tijdschrift*, 5 (1901), 79.

from Albert Rehm's grotesque description of Buller as 'an obese Phoenix risen from the ashes of Falstaff', in *Verzen* (1901):

> Ik denk, misschien . . . en 'k zie U hergeboren
> In 't beeld van een . . . : korstje—maar geen kaas;
> Twee ooren—maar geen haas; een klokspel—maar geen toren!

(I think, perhaps . . . and I see you reborn in the image of a . . . crust—but no cheese; two ears—but no hare; ringing bells—but no tower!)

In the less successful attempts to capture naturalistic effects the determined attention to detail sometimes led to little more than wooden, melodramatic tableaux, as in Eliza Laurillard's 'Na den Slag' (*Laatbloeiers*, 1904):

> Lijders, dooden, en, daartusschen,
> Hier het fijngetrappeld gruis
> Van een drinkflesch, daar weêr nevens
> 't Afgevallen ridderkruis;
> Hier een speelkaart, daar die bladen
> Van een boek, waaruit ze baden;
> Ginds des krijgers brief van huis.

(Sufferers, bodies, and, in between, here the trampled remains of a water bottle, there again the dropped cross of a knight; here a playing card, there the leaves of a book from which one prayed; over there, a soldier's letter from home.)

But better things were possible. In 'Het Konvooi' (*Verzamelde Gedichten*, 1903) E. B. Koster draws a graphic contrast between the awkward movement of a ponderous British convoy,

> Het schokt en het botst en het dreunt en het trilt,
> De bergdragende aarde schrikt òp en rilt,
> Daar boven de heuwels, daar vliegt het stof
> In bruin-grijze wolken, daar davert het dof.

(It shakes and it bangs and it thunders and trembles, the mountainous earth startles and shivers; above, on the hills, the dust rises up in brown-grey clouds and the echoes rumble.)

and the rhythmic speed of a Boer commando about to ambush it:

> Getrappel al vaartend in dreunende daad,
> De hoeven der paarden slaan bonkend de maat,
> De mannen, breed-hoedig, in rhythmisch gewieg,
> Met de paarden meedeinend in spannend gevlieg.

(Trampling fast, trembling with action, the hooves of horses beat
a bold rhythm; men in broad-rimmed hats, swaying elegantly,
glide in unison with their horses, a taut line of flight.)

Through clouds of high rhetoric Willem Zuidema's *Voor Zuid-
Afrika: Rijm en Onrijm* (1900) allows a few vivid glimpses of the
chaos of battle:

> Kartetsenhagel klettert neêr; de bom braakt gifgas uit . . .
> Boven 't raatlen der zelflader-vuurmonden uit
> En 't gefluit
>
> van het Engelsche lood,
> Zingt de kogel der Boeren zijn knetterend lied . . .
> Kopjes af, velden in—nu koelbloedig en snel!
> Want een hel
>
> houdt heur kaken daar bloot;
> Als een donderwolk dicht vullen bommen de lucht;
> En de slag volgt den slag met verbijstrend gerucht;
> En de regen, die valt, is de dood.

(A hail of shrapnel clatters down; a bomb vomits poison gas . . .
above the rattle of magazine rifles and the whistle of English lead,
Boer bullets sing their crackling song . . . down the hills, over
the veld—calm, cool, and fast! For hell has bared its jaws there;
like a dense thundercloud shells fill the air; crash follows crash
with stunning din; and the rain which falls is death.)

Similar effects may be found in J. P. Vergouwen's descriptions
of the battles of Belmont and Magersfontein in *Gedenkklanken
voor Zuid-Afrika* (1900), but the outstanding poet in this group of
naturalists was Albert Verwey, co-founder of *De Nieuwe Gids*.
By 1899 he had become editor of the *Tweemaandelijksch Tijdschrift*,
in which he now published a series of 'Tijdzangen' ('Songs of the
Time'), dedicated to ex-President F. W. Reitz and afterwards
collected in *Dagen en Daden* (1901). Two of the songs, 'Spioenkop'
and 'De Belegerde Stad', are evocative renderings of the experience of war in South Africa. The first poem captures the ominous
silence, the anxious expectation of ambush which constantly beset
the foreign forces:

> Ginds diep de stroom: de middagzon hing heet
> Op 't rotsge bruin: een ruitertroep daalt steil
> Van de andre zij: veerpont hen over vaart.

L

Doodstilte. Als 't avondt flitst weêrlicht op licht.
Gedempt eers klinkt, van top tot top kaatst dan,
Zang van 't stout volk dat op zijn bergen waakt.
De nacht broeit zwoel. 't Vijandelijk heir hoort bang.

(Over there the deep river: the hot mid-day sun is poised over the rocky brown: a troop of horsemen drop steeply down the opposite bank: a ferry takes them across.

Dead-still. Night falls and lightning flares out, flash upon flash. Hushed at first, then echoing from hill-top to hill-top, a song rings out of a brave race guarding on its mountains. The night is sultry. The enemy host listens in fear.)

'The Besieged City', with its air of oppressive and diseased constraint, its depiction of men burrowing underground like animals, anticipates moods and features of verse of the Great War:

Omsluit in stille liniën
De stad: maak moordend werk:
Met lange ellips en fluiting
Van bom, kartets, granaat,
Die boven 't markplein berst.

Zij kruipen in holen en lachen bleek
Als 't schot boven 't hooft hun de grond doorwoelt. . . .

In donkere gangen ontmoeten elkaar
Wie doelloos drentlen tot de bom komt.
Zij graven hun gangen naar 't veld,
Ontmoeten den vijand die graaft—
Tot een lijk en nog een dien weg spert.

(Enclose the city in silent bonds: make murderous work, with long ellipse and whistling of bomb, shell, grenade, bursting above the market place. They hide in holes and laugh pallidly as the explosion ploughs up the earth above their heads. . . .

In dark tunnels they meet who wander aimlessly until the bomb comes. They dig their mines into the veld, and meet the enemy digging—until a body, and yet another, blocks their way.)

Towards the end of 1900 a striking group of four tightly-woven sonnets, entitled 'Van Sterven' ('Of Death'), appeared over the initials 'Mr. J.P.S.G. v.W.' in *Nederland* (pp. 220–2). They do not deal explicitly with the Boer War, but they are clearly inspired by someone whose life had been cut short in a country far from the

Netherlands, and they invoke the imagery of death in battle. The final sonnet is particularly relevant to our discussion and provides a most suitable point at which to end this discussion of the poetry of the Boer War; it turns on the problem of shaping a fitting memorial in verse for those fallen in battle:

> O, dat slechts één van mijn broze gedichten
> Niet afsleet, doch als monument bestaan
> Bleef voor u, die voor 't oog als ster vergaan,
> Nog na u uwe levensbaan doet lichten.
> 'k Wil bijtlen vers bij vers, totdat daar staan
> Een eerezuil zal voor vervulde plichten,
> Woorden—graniet, dat jaren niet ontwrichten,
> Al zal ik jaren reeds zijn heengegaan.
> Zoo hoopt de krijgsman aan de verre stranden
> 't Geliefde hoofd, geveld door wilden-handen,
> Rotsblok bij rotsblok op met bloedend hart,
> Blij reeds, als sommige niet nederglijden,
> Doch voor de velen, die eens nà hem strijden,
> Een teken blijven, dat de tijden tart.

(O, that but one of my fragile poems would not wear away, but would last as a memorial for you who have sped your life like a shooting star. I want to chisel it verse by verse, until it should stand there, an obelisk in honour of duties done; words—granite, which the years will not dislodge, even when I shall have been dead for years. So, on distant shores, the warrior with bleeding heart piles rock upon rock on the beloved head slain by wild hands, happy that some will not fall down but will remain for those who still fight on, a sign that taunts time.)

Like the memorial built over the fallen warrior, the war poem must both take its meaning from and exist independently of the sorrow and anger of the time and place that occasioned it. It must, in the words of the sonnet, continue to 'taunt time' with its insistence on the complex realities of war. A surprising number of continental Boer War poems have managed to retain this capacity.

Epilogue

Together, sundered once by blood and speech,
Joined here in equal muster of the brave,
Lie Boer and Briton, foes each worthy each.
F. E. Garrett, 'Inscriptions', in *The Centenary Book of South African Verse*, ed. F. C. Slater (1925).

IN 1922, after the greater Armageddon of World War I, Reginald Auberon referred to the Boer War as 'the rumbling clash and clamour of a parochial struggle' (*The Nineteen Hundreds*). It was not only the greater impact of world war that had pushed the South African conflict into a corner of world history. Even while Boers and Tommies were still playing their endless game of hide and seek over the African veld, other events, such as the outbreak of the Chinese Boxer Rebellion in 1900 or the assassination of President William McKinley in September 1901, had edged the Boer War from the front pages of the world press. Simultaneously, the death of Queen Victoria and the federation of Australia, both in January 1901, followed soon by the development of *entente* between Britain and France, confirmed a widespread conviction that the Boer War had marked the end of an era; it had to be the last of Victorian colonial wars, and it had closed a bold avenue to empire that could no longer be safely trodden: 'The empire went to war in 1899 for a concept that was finished, for a cause that was lost, for a grand illusion.'[1]

Peace (31 May 1902) brought forth a crop of wooden odes, among which were Sir Edwin Arnold's 'Peace' in the *Daily Telegraph* and Robert Bridges's 'On the Conclusion of the Three Years' War' (*Poetical Works*, 1912). They added nothing to the sentiments of the poetry written during the war except for a sense of weary solemnity. Much more impressive, and perhaps more faithful to the true feelings of contemporaries, was Robert Service's 'The March of the Dead' (*Songs of a Sourdough*, 1907),

---

[1] Robinson and Gallagher, *Africa and the Victorians*, p. 461. See also Sir Valentine Chirol, 'The Boer War and the International Situation', in *The Cambridge History of British Foreign Policy*, vol. iii, 1866–1919 (Cambridge: Cambridge University Press, 1923).

which painted a horrific picture of a ghoulish army of shades participating in the victory celebrations:

They were coming, they were coming, gaunt and ghastly, sad and slow;
   They were coming, all the crimson wrecks of pride;
With faces seared, and cheeks red smeared, and haunting eyes of woe;
   And clotted holes the khaki couldn't hide.
Oh, the clammy brow of anguish! the livid, foam-flecked lips!
   The reeling ranks of ruin swept along!
The limb that trailed, the hand that failed, the bloody finger-tips!
   And oh, the dreary rhythm of their song!

Apart from this sense of measureless waste, it was the recognition of the brotherhood of the fallen, whether British or Boer, that inspired the more moving verse at this time, rather than the sense of triumph:

> And where the pitted armies met
> Like two fierce waves, the lizard crawls;
> And here and there a violet,
> Shy harbinger of peace, makes fair
> The nameless graves of famous dead,

wrote St. John Lucas in *Poems* (1904).

If, however, the Boer War was the last of the gentlemen's wars, the last old-style colonial conflict, it was also the first of the twentieth century's wars between European colonial empires. The outcome of the Boer War declared Britain the winner in the scramble for Africa, and though France, Germany, and Russia did not clash with Britain physically over the Boer issue, they certainly did so in spirit. The war confirmed the division of Europe into a number of bristling armed camps, and after 1902 alarmist tub-thumping and military breast-beating became ever more strident. In May 1901 the *Imperial and Colonial Magazine*, reviewing the dismal course of the Boer War, demanded that Britain should immediately adopt conscription, introduce military drill in all schools and universities, and require of every man the possession of a certificate of marksmanship. Under Lord Fisher, the Admiralty continued with a scheme, conceived in the 1890s, to build as many warships as the combined fleets of Russia and France, while Germany, in turn, tried to outbid this challenge.[2] Kipling, Laurence Binyon, and George Barlow continued to

[2] Barker, *Prominent Edwardians*, p. 30.

provide an accompaniment of admonitory verse to these military and diplomatic rivalries, and in 1912 Marshall Bruce-Williams, reprinting his *Imperial Sonnets* from an edition first published during the Boer War, proclaimed with renewed emphasis:

> Dream not, O Continent, thy world in arms
> Will ever see Old England on Her knee
> Sueing for peace!

This clamorous paranoia continued to inform the lower orders of European literature until it burst forth in all its aggressive glory in 1914.

Indeed, the outbreak of World War I was a signal for the belated publication of a number of Boer War poems in, for instance, W. H. Draper's *Poems of the Love of England* (1914) and Amy Campbell-Strickland's *A Call to Arms and Other Poems* (1916). One of the earliest of World War I anthologies, John Lane's *Songs and Sonnets for England in War Time* (1914), is largely a collection of the patriotic newspaper verse of several old acquaintances—Adcock, Begbie, Rawnsley, Watson, Newbolt, Kipling, and Hardy. Adcock's own anthology, *For Remembrance* (1918), with its brief biographies of the lesser-known Great War poets, is still one of the most useful of the earlier collections. Some French and German voices of the Boer War period were heard, too. Charles Grandmougin and Théodore Botrel continued to churn out patriotic songs, and in *Die eiserne Zither* (1914) Ludwig Ganghofer complained bitterly of the perfidy of Boer generals now commanding British forces.

But it was not only the patriotic, militaristic view of war which survived in poetry after the Boer War. Alfred Noyes sustained during the interbellum years a vision of war as numbing and disastrous, and published, on the eve of World War I, *The Wine-Press: A Tale of War* (1913), which gave powerful utterance to a type of war poetry then firmly established and about to come to full justice in the verse of Rosenberg, Sassoon, Owen, and others:

> The troop-train couplings clanged like Fate
>   Above the bugles' din.
> Sweating beneath their haversacks,
> With rifles bristling on their backs,
> Like heavy-footed oxen
>   The dusty men trooped in.

It is, however, beyond the brief of this book to pursue the World War I verse of poets of the Boer War any futher, except to mention that little of Hardy's later war verse touched the mastery of 'Drummer Hodge'; that Watson redeemed himself in the public eye and earned a knighthood to boot by becoming one of England's most patriotic bards; and that T. W. H. Crosland's *War Poems by X* (1916) deserves to be much better known. The volume rivals the bite of Sassoon in numerous places.

In South Africa itself it has not been only the Afrikaner who has mulled over the heartache of the Boer War. While Afrikaans poets have pondered the legacy of hatred which the war bequeathed to South Africa, their English compatriots have been drawn repeatedly to the need to question or to make amends for what has increasingly come to be regarded as a historical blunder. In some ways it has been a process of demythologizing, of separating the patriotic gloss from the actuality of imperial conquest:

> They took the hill (Whose hill? What for?)
> But what a climb they left to do!
> Out of that bungled, unwise war
> An alp of unforgiveness grew,

wrote William Plomer in 'The Boer War' (*The Fivefold Screen*, 1932), and behind one of the late-Victorian era's most legendary military disasters, Majuba, Roy Macnab has seen only the mundane reality of a 'five-day sleepless sentry' who 'snored at his post above the wood':

> Only the nibbling goat and the sheep
> Saw how remote were the dead asleep.[3]

In other ways the continuing process has been one of distilling the true myth from the random survival of reminiscence and rumour. Perhaps the most piercing of these distant hindsights is William Branford's 'Trooper Temple Pulvermacher', written in about 1948.[4] Dismissing the 'Unlucky soldiership spent in a bad quarrel', the 'political priestcraft' and 'synthetic humanism', and aware that there is

> No surer provocation . . .
> For loose emotion than the anonymous dead,

[3] 'Majuba Hill' (1952), in Butler, *Book of South African Verse*.
[4] Butler, *Book of South African Verse*. I am indebted to Professor Branford for information on the poem's date.

the poet declares firmly: 'Death itself is your claim to compassion'. Pulvermacher is transformed from just another casualty in a forgotten cause to a part in the stark African myth of ceaseless conflict; he is subsumed in

> The root's comprehension of earth, or the combatant aloe's
> Grasp of essentials.

So, too, the war in which Pulvermacher died has by now been reduced from the trauma of personal agony and memory and from the freneticism of political and racial conflict to the essentials of myth and legend, from where it may continue to inform South African literature from time to time.

Writing in the *Bookman*,[5] a reviewer of 'The Literary Harvest of the War' concluded: 'It is quite possible that some modest but genuine book not properly advertised and pushed, has escaped the notice of critics and readers, and a century hence may be discovered on a bookstall like Fitzgerald's *Omar* and receive its belated homage.' The present study may not have brought such a volume from the bookstalls, but it will have gone some way towards uncovering the poems that might well make up such a volume: poems that serve not merely as dumbshows to the greater tragic act of world war, but also as meaningful statements about war in their own right. After the Boer War, war poetry could no longer be merely a sub-department of patriotic verse.

[5] 22 (1902), 131–3.

Select Bibliography

THIS bibliography is limited to writings either cited in the text or footnotes, or found to be of substantial use in their preparation. It does not claim to be a complete bibliography of Boer War poetry, which may be issued at a later stage. The list is divided into four sections:

A Manuscript material, including collections of newspaper cuttings, miscellaneous pamphlets, and broadsides, as well as unpublished dissertations.

B Published poetry of the Boer War, including all volumes of verse containing some poems on the war, but excluding prose works containing occasional verse (See *D*, below).

C Periodicals and newspapers, largely limited to publications which carried Boer War poems.

D Other sources, including prose works on the Boer War, poetry of other wars, and works of criticism.

A: MANUSCRIPT MATERIAL

ANON. 'An Australian's Farewell to South Africa' (1904), TS. Submitted anonymously.

— 'The Black Watch at Magersfontein', TS. Strange Collection, Johannesburg Public Library, S Pam 821 Bla.

— (Another copy). MS. Cape Archives, Cape Town, Acc. 411.

— 'The Cock and the Buller'. TS. National Army Museum, 6302-48-7.

— 'Onze Reis als Krijgsgevangenen van Durban naar Trichinopoly naar Zuid India'. MS. Property of Mr. J. M. Grobler, Somerset West.

— 'Oorlogskans'. TS. Submitted anonymously.

BAERT, G. P., Reminiscences. MS. Submitted by the author.

BIGGS, Mrs. SUSIE, Letters. MS. Property of Miss Mary Butler, Grahamstown.

Bryce Papers, Bodleian MSS. Bryce (English) 16 and 17.

BUSS, R. W., Newspaper Cuttings. 2 vols. Mendelssohn Collection, Library of Parliament, Cape Town.

BUTLER, A., 'Lines on the March of the Oxfordshire Light Infantry across the Orange Free State'. TS. Royal Green Jackets Museum, Winchester.

BUTTON, PERA MURIEL, The South African War: Newspaper

L*

Cuttings. 6 vols. Mendelssohn Collection, Library of Parliament, Cape Town.

DE VILLEBOIS-MAREUIL, GEORGES, Pocket book and letters. MS. State Archives, Pretoria, Acc. 1247.

DE VILLIERS, P. R., Papers, collection of commando songs, etc. MS. and TS. Vols. 9–10. State Arch., Acc. 284.

DIRKS, C. F., Song book. MS. Property of C. F. Dirks, Vanderbijlpark.

DU PLESSIS, W., Poems in English translation. TS. South African Library, Cape Town.

GILBERT, W. N., Diary and poems. MS. Nat. Army Museum, 6309–114.

HARDY, HAROLD, Letters. MS. Nat. Army Museum, 6901–1/4, 5.

HEINE, OTTO, 'Der Bur und sein Kind'. Newspaper cutting. Strange Collection, Johannesburg Public Library.

HENDERSON, IAN, 'The Attitude and Policy of the Main Section of the British Labour Movement to Imperial Issues'. B. Litt. dissertation. Oxford, 1964.

HERHOLDT, J. A., 'De Zeereis en het Diyatalawa Kamp'. MS. Orange Free State Archives, Bloemfontein, Acc. 155/140/1.

KENT, R. P., Three Poems. MS. Property of M. Kent, Port Elizabeth.

KOTZE, HESTER, Poems and songs collected in Bethulie camp. MS. O.F.S. Archives, Acc. 155/130/1.

LE ROUX, CHARL, Collection of verses from 'Krakoolkamp', India. Roneo copy submitted by Mrs. H. N. du Toit, Middelburg.

Leyds Collection of newspaper cuttings. State Archives, Pretoria.

MCCORMICK, A. S., 'The Royal Canadians in South Africa'. Roneo notes. Royal Com. Soc. Library, 55c 8 Pam.

MEINTJES, JOHANNES, ed. 'Tommy Atkins and Brother Boer: An Anthology of Anglo-Boer War Verse'. TS.

MEYER, E. E., 'Transvalers Plicht'. TS. Submitted by P. J. J. Meyer, Oudtshoorn.

MILLER, MARY RUTH, 'The Crimean War in British Periodical Literature'. Ph. D. dissertation. Duke University, North Carolina, 1966.

NEL, S. E., Reminiscences. MS. State Arch., Acc. 951.

NEL, W. A. S., 'Gedigte uit die Anglo-Boere Oorlog'. MS. Submitted by the author.

NELL, HENRY J., Poems. MS. Submitted by J. C. Nel, Brakpan.

Newspaper cuttings. War Museum, Bloemfontein, 1637.

NOOTHOUD, J., 'De Oorlog en Andere Liederen'. Crude mimeograph. War Museum, 59.

OBERHOLZER, C. D., Song book. MS. War Museum.

Pierson Collection. State Arch., Acc. 63.

POLLARD, E. H., 'One Hundred Lines on the 6th Division'. TS. Royal Green Jackets Museum, Winchester.

Portfolio of press cuttings, poems in MS. and TS., etc. War Museum.

— of pamphlets, broadsides, etc. British Library, 1865 c 8.

Preller Collection. State Arch., Acc. 787.

ROGERS, FRANK CORNWELL, Diary and poems. MS. Privately owned.

ROODT, C. S., Diary and poems. MS. State Arch., Acc. 787/63.

SEAMAN, OWEN, 'Depreciations: Mr. Balfour Apologizes'. Newspaper cutting.

SCHREINER, OLIVE, Letters. MS. Murray-Parker Collection, University of Cape Town.

— Letters. MS. Olive Schreiner Collection, U.C.T.

— Letters. MS. Cory Library, Rhodes University, Grahamstown, MS. 14,462.

Song book. MS. War Museum, 58/3451.

Song book. MS. Submitted by Mrs. M. Lubbe, Pretoria.

'The Transvaal War: A Collection of English Songs, Verses, etc. relative to the Boer War, 1899–1902'. British Library, Cup. 21 ff. 1.

TYE, J. R. 'Literary Periodicals of the 1890s: A Survey of the Monthly and Quarterly Magazines and Reviews'. D. Phil. dissertation. Oxford, 1970.

Van Broekhuizen Collection. State Arch., Acc. 356.

VAN RIET, G. J., 'Herinnering aan mijn Krijgsgevangenschap te Burtts-Eiland, Bermuda'. MS. War Museum, 38.

VAN ZYL, HESTER M., Reminiscences. MS. State Arch., Acc. 951.

VAN ZYL, J. C., Reminiscences. MS. War Museum, 58/1723.

WALLACE, EDGAR, Four notebooks. MS. South African Library.

WEINSTOCK, DONALD J., 'The Boer War in the Novel in English, 1884–1966: A Descriptive and Critical Bibliography'. Ph. D. dissertation. California, 1968.

WEST, MARK WALTER, Poems. TS. Submitted by H. W. E. Green, Johannesburg.

WHITE, MONTAGU, Letter book and vol. of press cuttings. Bodleian MSS. Afr. s 116 and 117.

WILSENACH, H. O., Poems. MS. Submitted by Mrs. L. E. de Klerk, Stellenbosch.

B: PUBLISHED POETRY

ADAMS, Capt. W. A., *Rus Divinum*. London: Fisher Unwin, 1900.

— *Horae Fugaces*. London: Fisher Unwin, 1902.

ADCOCK, A. ST. JOHN, *Songs of the War*. London, 1900.

AIGNER, WALTER, *Gedenkblätter an den Krieg in Süd-Afrika*. Leipzig, 1903.

ALLAN, Sir WILLIAM, *Songs of Light and Shade*. Sunderland: Hills & Co., 1901.

— *Songs of Love and Labour*. London: Brown, Langham, 1903.

ALLHUSEN, BEATRICE M., and GERALDINE ROBERTSON-GLASGOW, *Verses*. Hampstead, 1905.

ANDERSON, 'THISTLE' M. C., *Verses at Random*. London: Alexander Gardner, 1901.

ANEMA, SEERP, *Poëzie*. Wageningen, 1903.

Antwerpen-Transvaal, Antwerp. 1902.

ARENDT-MORGENSTERN, OLGA, *Gedichte*. Berlin, 1903.

AUCHINLECK, SYDNEY E., *For the Honour of the Queen*. Dublin: Hodges, Figgis, 1900.

AUSTIN, ALFRED, *Songs of England*. Enlarged ed. London: Macmillan, 1900.

— *Sacred and Profane Love*. London: Macmillan, 1908.

BAKER, ADA B., *A Palace of Dreams*. Edinburgh: Blackwood, 1901.

BARLOW, GEORGE, *To the Women of England*. London: Henry Glaisher, 1901.

— *Poetical Works*. 11 vols. London, 1902–14.

BATE, HENRY, *The Transvaal War: First Canto*. London: Stoneman, 1900.

BATES, BENJAMIN FRANKLIN, *The Anglo-Saxon Union: or, Hands Across the Sea*. Cape Town, 1902.

BAUDOT, L., *Salut au Président Kruger*. Paris, n.d.

BEAUSSEIN, E., *Le Songe de Joë Chamberlain*. Aix, 1901.

BEAVAN, HARRIET A., *The 'Bobs' Reciter for Bands of Hope, Temperance Societies, and Sunday Schools*. London: John Heywood, n.d.

BEGBIE, HAROLD, *The Handy Man*. London: Grant Richards, 1900.

BELLOC, HILAIRE, *Verses*. London, 1910.

BENGOUGH, JOHN WILSON, *In Many Keys*. Toronto: William Briggs, 1902.

BENNET, NORMAN, *The Little Bugler*. London, 1900.

BESNARD, M. P., *et al.*, *Au Profit des Boërs*. Orléans, 1902.

BLANDIGNIÈRE, ADRIEN, *Les Minerviennes de la paix*. Monaco, 1900.

BONNAUD, DOMINIQUE, *Le Débarquement de Kruger à Marseille*. Paris, n.d.

BORTHWICK, J. D., ed., *Poems and Songs on the South African War*. Montreal: Gazette Pub. Co., 1901.

BOWLES, FRED. G., *Songs of Yesterday*. London: Unicorn, 1902.

BOYER, LUCIEN, *La Balle 'Dum-Dum'*. Paris, 1899.

BREITMANN (pseud.), *Der Junge Breitmann in South Africa*. London, 1900.

BRIDGES, ROBERT, *Poetical Works*. Oxford: Clarendon Press, 1912.

BRINK, MELT J., *Nationale en Afrikaanse Gedigte*. Cape Town, 1916.

BUCHANAN, ROBERT, *Pat Muldoon: or, Jack the Giant-Killer Up-to-date*. London: International Arbitration League, n.d.

— *Complete Poetical Works*. 2 vols. London: Chatto & Windus, 1901.

BUCKTON, ALICE M., *The Burden of Engela: A Ballad-Epic*. London: Methuen. 1904.

The Bulletin Reciter: A Collection of Verses for Recitation from ' The Bulletin' 1880–1901. Ed. A. G. Stephens. Sydney: *Bulletin*, 1902.

BUNGE, RUDOLF, *Burenlieder*. Dresden, 1901.

Buren-Lieder, aus der Bierzeitung der Scharfen Deutschen Ecke zu Kapstadt. Munich: J. F. Lehman, 1901.

BUTLER, A. G., *The Choice of Achilles*. Oxford: Clarendon Press, 1900.

BUTLER, GUY, ed., *A Book of South African Verse*. London: Oxford University Press, 1959.

BUTLER, HAROLD E., ed., *War Songs of Britain*. London: Constable, 1903.

CABUY, ARTHUR, *Cause divine de la guerre Anglo-Boër*. Brussels, 1900.

CAMPBELL-STRICKLAND, AMY, *A Call to Arms*. London, 1916.

CANTACUZÈNE, CHARLES-ADOLPHE, *Sonnets en petit deuil*. Paris, 1901.

CASSELTON, WALTER, *Verses*. London: Grant Richards, 1903.

CATRICES, LOUIS, *Les Boërs: ou, la guerre au Transvaal*. Paris, 1901.

CELLIERS, JAN F. E., *Die Vlakte en Ander Gedigte*. 4th, revised ed. Pretoria: *Volksstem*, 1917.

— *Die Lewenstuin en Ander Nuwe Gedigte*. Pretoria: Van Schaik, 1925.

CENTURION (pseud.), *Ante-Room Ballads*. London: Routledge, 1905.

Charivari-Album: Boërs et Anglais. Paris, n.d.

CHESTERTON, G. K., *Poems*. London: Burns & Oates, 1915.

CHEVALIER, ALBERT, *Mafekin' Night*. London, n.d.

CHILDE-PEMBERTON, HARRIET L., *Love Knows—and Waits*. London: John Long, 1906.

CHOLLET, LOUIS, *Chants de révolte*. Paris, 1904.

CLAY, P. S., *Ode to Lord Roberts*. London, 1900.

CLIFFORD, ETHEL, *Songs of Dreams*. London: John Lane, Bodley Head, 1903.

COCHRANE, ALFRED, *Collected Verses*. London: Longmans, Green, 1903.

COLDSTREAMER [Harry Graham], *Ballads of the Boer War*. London: Grant Richards, 1902.

COOPER, TONY, *Let 'Em All Come*. Revised version. N.p., n.d.

COPPÉE, FRANÇOIS, *Dans la prière et dans la lutte*. 8th ed. Paris, 1901.

COYLE, EDWARD, *The Empire*. London, 1905.

CRAIG, R. S., *In Borderland*. Hawick, 1899.

CROSBY, ERNEST, *Swords and Ploughshares*. London, 1903.

CROSLAND, T. W. H., *The Absent-Minded Mule*. London: Unicorn, 1899.

— *The Five Notions*. London: Grant Richards, 1903.

— *Collected Poems*. London: Martin Secker, 1917.

CUNNINGHAM-FAIRLIE, A., *Glimpses in Rhyme*. Lovedale, ?1900.

DAVAREND, R. P., *Un Brave: La Vengeance d'un Boër*. Valognes, 1900.

DAWSON, W. H., *War Songs 1899–1900*. Hobart, 1901.

The Death of Young Cronjé. Cape Town, n.d.

DESCHAMPS, PHILIPPE, ed., *Le Livre d'or du Transvaal*. Paris, 1901.

— *La Mort d'un héros: Hommage à la mémoire du colonel Georges de Villebois-Mareuil*. Paris, 1901.

— *La Reine Wilhelmine: Poésies dédiées à sa Majesté la Reine des Pays-bas*. Paris, 1901.

DES HAYES, EMMANUEL, *Mes rêves*. Paris, 1903.

DE SOUDAK, LOUIS, *Étapes sanglantes: Aux Boërs*. Paris, 1900.

DE VEYGE, HENRI, *La Justice des choses: Ode aux Boërs*. Paris, 1900.

DOBELL, BERTRAM, *Rosemary and Pansies*. London, 1904.

DOBSON, AUSTIN, *Carmina Votiva*. London, 1901.

— *Complete Poetical Works*. Oxford: Clarendon Press, 1923.

DOCKING, A. SHIPWAY, *The Great War 1899–1900*. London: Greening, 1902.

DRAKE, Corpl., *John, the Swell: A Poem Founded on an Incident at the Battle of Spion Kop*. Ladysmith, 1900.

DRAPER, W. H., *Poems of the Love of England*. London: Chatto & Windus, 1914.

DUM-DUM [John Kaye Kendall], *At Odd Moments*. Bombay: *Times of India*, 1900.

DUVAL, DENIS, *Back Numbers*. London: Henry J. Drane, 1904.

E., L. A., *Voyage du Pôle Nord à Capetown. Poème satirique*. Honfleur, 1901.

EARLE, WALTER, *Home Poems*. London, 1900.

EDWARDS, G. C., *The Relief of Ladysmith: A Reservist's Story*. Pietermaritzburg, n.d.

An Empire's Greeting: Coronation Odes. Supplement to *Good Words*. London, 1902.

EVANS, GEORGE ESSEX, *Collected Verses*. Ed. Firmin McKinnon. Sydney: Angus & Robertson, 1928.

EVERARD, GEORGE, *Good-Bye, Daddy*. Words by Laurence Barclay. London, 1900.

FACQ, LOUIS, *Dix contre un*. Paris, ?1900.
FAIRBRIDGE, KINGSLEY, *Veld Verse*. London: David Nutt, 1909.
FAŸS, VITO, *Pour les Boërs*. Paris, 1900.
FRÉMIN, GEORGES, *Le Colosse de Fachoda; Les Boërs; A l'Angleterre; Kruger fessant la Queen!; Abandon des Boërs par les chefs d'états du monde* (and others.) Paris, 1899–1901.
FRIEDRICH, ERNST, *John Bull und die Buren: Ein hochbegeistertes Heldengedicht*. Dresden, 1900.
FURSY, HENRI [Henri Dreyfus], *Chansons de la boîte*. Chansons Rosses, 3e série. Paris, 1902.
GARDNER, DRIVER W., *The Fate of the 14th Battery*. Privately printed, 1899.
GARNETT, RICHARD, *The Queen and Other Poems*. London, 1901.
GERARD, WILLIAM, *Una: A Song of England in the Year Nineteen-Hundred*. London: Paul, Trench, Trübner, 1900.
GERRARD, R. ELLIS, *Ballads of Battle and Poems of Peace*. Newcastle-upon-Tyne: North of England Printing Co., 1914.
GIBBON, PERCEVAL, *African Items*. London: Elliott Stock, 1903.
GRANDERYE, A., *John Bull en guerre*. Pintenville-les-Nancy, 1900.
GRANDMOUGIN, CHARLES, *Pour la patrie!* Paris, 1902.
GROVÉ, A. P., and C. J. D. HARVEY, eds., *Afrikaans Poems with English Translations*. Cape Town: Oxford University Press, 1962.
GUENIN, ALFRED, *La chanson des Boërs*. Langres, 1900.
GUIRAUDON, GABRIEL, *Gloria Victis: Episode de la guerre Anglo-Boër*. La Réole, 1900.
GWYNNE, JOHN, *Homer 2nd's Bulliad: A Satire of the South African Campaign*. Milwaukee, Wis., 1900.
HALES, A. G., *Poems and Ballads*. London: Erskine Macdonald, 1909.
HALLEY, FERNAND, ed., *Pour les Boërs*. Rouen, 1902.
HAMILTON, F. J., *Sunbeams through the War-Cloud*. London: Elliott Stock, 1900.
HARDY, THOMAS, *Poems of the Past and the Present*. London, 1901.
HARMAN, E. G., *Poems*. London: Arnold, 1920.
HARMAN, HENRY A., *Freedom's Footprints*. Springfield, Mass., 1899.
HASLAM, ANTHONY, ed., *Anthology of Empire*. London: Grayson & Grayson, 1932.
HENLEY, W. E., *For England's Sake: Verses and Songs in Time of War*. London: David Nutt, 1900.
— *Hawthorn and Lavender*. London: David Nutt, 1901.
HIGHTON, E. GILBERT, *The Siege of Mafeking: A Patriotic Poem*. London, 1900.
HILL, ROLAND, *Voices in Dreamland*. London: Paul, Trench, Trübner, 1900.

HOLE, W. G., *Poems Lyrical and Dramatic*. London: Elkin Matthews, 1902.

HORDIJK, A. PIJNACKER, *Tegan Haman met Esther en Mordechai*. Naaldwijk, 1901.

HORSFALL, EDITH, *Great Britain*. Harrogate: W. D. Dobson, 1911.

HOUSMAN, A. E., *Last Poems*. London: Richards Press, 1922.

— *Collected Poems*. London: Jonathan Cape, 1939.

HYSPA, VINCENT, *Chansons d'humour*. Paris, 1902.

INGRAM, PERCY T., *Songs of the Transvaal War*. Grantham, n.d.

IVES, GEORGE, *Eros' Throne*. London: Swan Sonnenschein, 1900.

IVES, HERBERT, *Britons and Boers*. London, n.d.

JACKSON, Mrs. C. N., *Gordon League Ballads*. 2nd series. London: Skeffington, 1903.

JOHNSON, LIONEL, *Complete Poems*. Ed. Iain Fletcher. London: Unicorn, 1953.

KAMMERER, J., ed., *Gedenkblätter aus dem Burenkrieg*. Elberfeld, 1903.

KENNEDY, ARTHUR CLARK, *Avenged*. London, 1899.

KETT, GEORGE, *Lyrics of Empire*. Privately printed, n.d.

KIPLING, RUDYARD, *The Absent-Minded Beggar*. London: *Daily Mail*, 1899.

— *The Five Nations*. London: Methuen, 1903.

KLOOS, WILLEM, *Verzen III*. Amsterdam, 1913.

KNIGHT, WILLIAM, ed., *Pro Patria et Regina*. Glasgow: James MacLehose, 1901.

KOSTER, EDWARD B., *Verzamelde Gedichten*. Rotterdam, 1903.

LANG, JOHN and JEAN, eds., *Poetry of Empire*. London: T. C. & E. C. Jack, n.d.

LANGBRIDGE, FREDERICK, *Ballads and Legends*. London: Routledge, 1903.

— ed. *Ballads of the Brave*. 4th, revised, ed. London: Methuen, 1911.

LAURILLARD, ELIZA, *Laatbloeiers*. Schoonhoven, 1904.

LAWSON, HENRY, *Collected Verse*. Ed. Colin Roderick. 3 vols. Sydney: Angus & Robertson, 1967.

LAWSON, Sir WILFRID, *Cartoons in Rhyme and Line*. London: Fisher Unwin, 1905.

LE BRETON, JOHN [M. Harte Potts and T. Murray Ford], *Come, Follow the Drum*. London: John Macqueen, 1900.

LE FEBURE, DENYS, *The Lone Trek*. London: Elkin Matthews, 1908.

LE GALLIENNE, RICHARD, *New Poems*. London: John Lane, 1910.

Leiden-Zuid-Afrika Album. Leiden, 1899.

LEIPOLDT, C. LOUIS, *Oom Gert Vertel en Ander Gedigte*. 2nd ed. Cape Town: H.A.U.M., 1917.

LELIÈVRE, LÉO, *Gloire aux Boërs! Chanson patriotique; Le Héros du Transvaal, ou Kruger en France; La Marche des Boërs;* etc. Paris, ?1900.

LEMAIRE, LÉON, *Recueil de récits et chansons Boërs.* Orléans, n.d.

— *Le Fou, ou le carême sanglant.* Orléans, 1902.

LIENHARD, FRITZ, *Burenlieder.* Leipzig: *Heimat,* 1900.

— *Boerenliederen.* Tr. J. F. Sikken. Amsterdam, 1900.

LINDSAY, Lady CAROLINE BLANCHE, *For England.* London, n.d.

LUCAS, ST. JOHN, *Poems.* London: Constable, 1904.

LYSAGHT, SIDNEY ROYSE, *Poems of the Unknown Way.* London: Macmillan, 1901.

LYSTER, LYNN [T. L. Millar] *Flag Lyrics.* Pietermaritzburg, n.d.

— *On Service: War Lyrics.* Pietermaritzburg, n.d.

— *Ballads of the Veld-Land.* London: Longmans, Green, 1913.

MACLEOD, Mrs. E. S., *For the Flag: Lays and Incidents of the South African War.* Charlottetown, 1901.

MALHERBE, D. F., *Karroo Blommetjies.* Cape Town, 1909.

MANN, ARTHUR M., *Songs for the Front.* 3 parts. Cape Town, n.d.

MAQUARIE, ARTHUR, *The Voice in the Cliff.* London: Simpkin Marshall, 1909.

MARAIS, EUGENE N., *Versamelde Gedigte.* Pretoria: Van Schaik, 1933.

MAYER, FRIEDRICH, *Cecil, der moderne Faust.* Berlin, 1905.

McLOUGHLIN, Lance-Corpl. J., *How the Lancashires Took Spion Kop.* N.p., n.d.

MENZIES, G. K., *Provincial Sketches.* Paisley: Alexander Gardner, 1902.

MEREDITH, GEORGE, *Last Poems.* London: Constable, 1909.

MILDMAY, AUBREY N., *In the Waiting Time of War.* London: Swan Sonnenschein, 1900.

MILLER, JOAQUIN, *Chants for the Boer.* San Francisco, 1900.

M'IVER, IVER, *Caught on the Wing.* London, 1911.

MOLENAAR, M., ed., *Nederland en Afrika: Gedichten.* Maassluis, n.d.

— *Transvaal Gedichten.* Sneek, 1902.

MOME [G. Murray Johnstone], *The Off-Wheeler Ballads.* London: John Ouseley, 1910.

MONTOYA, G., *La Moderne Épopée: Les Boërs.* Paris, 1902.

MORGAN, ROBERT, *Poems.* Liverpool, 1900.

MORRIS, Sir LEWIS, *Harvest Tide.* London: Paul, Trench, Trübner, 1901.

NEUMAN, B. PAUL, *Pro Patria.* London: Brown Langham, 1905.

NEWBOLT, HENRY, *The Sailing of the Long Ships.* London: John Murray, 1902.

— *Poems New and Old.* London: John Murray, 1912.

NIJGH and VAN DITMAR, *Huldeblad van Nederlandsche Letterkundigen.* Rotterdam, 1900.

NORTON, SMEDLEY, *Bramcote Ballads*. London, 1904.

OATEY, G. H., *Comrade Jim: A Story of the War*. Falmouth: Edwin T. Oliver, 1900.

OFFERMAN, HEINRICH, *Die Heldin von Transvaal*. Bonn, n.d.

OGILVIE (pseud.), *Cronjé's Siegen und Sinken: Ein Sang aus Burenlanden*. Dresden, 1901.

OMOND, T. S., *Scattered Verses*. Tunbridge Wells: R. Pelton, 1904.

Oranje-Vrijstaatsche Oorlogs Liederen-Bundel. N.p., 1901.

PARNELL, C. A., *Old Tales and New*. Dublin: Sealy, Bryers, Walker, 1905.

PATERSON, A. B., *Rio Grande's Last Race*. Sydney: Angus & Robertson, 1902.

Pfui Chamberlain! Berlin: *Lustige Blätter*, n.d.

PHILLIPS, STEPHEN, *New Poems*. London: John Lane, The Bodley Head, 1908.

PLOMER, WILLIAM, *The Fivefold Screen*. London: Hogarth Press, 1932.

PRÉSEAU, CHARLES, *Un Héros*. Brussels, n.d.

Der Protest der Deutschen gegen die englische Barbarei im Burenkriege. Munich, 1902.

PYKE, WILLIAM THOMAS, ed., *The Coo-Ee Reciter*. London: Ward, Lock, 1904.

RAWNSLEY, H. D., *Ballads of the War*. London: Dent, 1900. 2nd, enlarged, ed., 1901.

REDDING, J. SHELDON, *The Absent-Minded Beggar's Apology*. London: Geo. Vickers, 1900.

REHM, ALBERT, *Verzen*. Rotterdam, 1901.

REITZ, F. W., *Oorlogs en Andere Gedichten*. Potchefstroom: *Het Westen*, 1910.

RENK, ANTON, *Tiroler und Buren*. Innsbruck, 1901.

RÉTY, MARIUS, *Vive Kruger!;* and *Hommage au Président Kruger*. Paris, n.d.

RIFFARD, LÉON, *Une Douzaine de sonnets*. Evreux, 1900.

RILEY, Corpl. M., *Siege of Ladysmith*. N.p., n.d.

ROBEY, W. C., *The Pretoria Dinner Party: or, In Walked England*. London, n.d.

ROBISON, WILLIAM HERBERT, *Australia at the Front*. Rockhampton, 1903.

RODDY, J. W., *And Britain's Blest with Righteousness?* and *The Fate of Dullstroom*. New York: Grafton Press, 1901.

ROSTAND, EDMOND, *A Kruger*. Cambo, 1900.

ROUGHTON, WILL, *Onward*. Kirton Lindsey, 1900.

ROUTH, R. S., *Lines on the War*. Stockbridge, 1900.

ROWLEY, THOMAS, *The Maid of Malta*. London, 1913.

RUDLAND, MARSTON, *Poems of the Race*. London, 1901.

RUNCIE, JOHN, *Songs by the Stoep*. London: R. A. Thomson, 1905.

SCHUMANN, J. H. L., *Two Songs*. Cape Town: R. Müller, n.d.

SCOTT, R. P., and KATHARINE T. WALLAS, eds., *The Call of the Homeland*. London: Blackie & Son, 1907.

SELMER, LOUIS, *Boer War Lyrics*. New York: Abbey Press, 1903.

SERVICE, ROBERT, *Songs of a Sourdough*. London: Fisher Unwin, 1907.

SHADWELL, BERNARD, *America and Others Poems*. Chicago, 1899.

SHEPHERD, H., *Sad Memories: A Story of the Anglo-Boer War in Verse*. Klerksdorp, 1901.

SHIELL, ANTHONY GEORGE, *Pro-Boer Lyrics*. 4th, enlarged, ed. Brighton, n.d.

SIDNEY-WILLMOT, P. C., and OWEN HARRIS, *Irregular Lines and Moanings from the Veldt*. Ermelo, 1902.

SKRINE, JOHN HUNTLEY, *The Queen's Highway and Other War Lyrics 1899–1900*. London: Elkin Matthews, 1900.

SLATER, FRANCIS CAREY, ed., *The Centenary Book of South African Verse*. London: Longmans, Green, 1925.

SLEEPER, JOHN F., *The Marion of the Free State*. New Jersey: Sherwood Press, 1901.

Songs of the Veld. London: *New Age*, 1902.

The South African War: Some Poetry Published in England and the United States. N.p., n.d.

SPIERS, KAUFMANN C., *Guido and Veronica*. London: David Nutt, 1903.

STEINWEG, EMIL, *Burenlieder*. Marienburg. 1901.

STOREY, HEDLEY VICARS, *Britannia Poems*. Oxford: Clarendon Press, 1910.

SWINBURNE, ALGERNON, *A Channel Passage*. London: Chatto & Windus, 1904.

TER HAAR, B., *Het Volk van Nederland aan Zijne Broeders in Transvaal*. Nijmegen, 1896.

THOMA, LUDWIG, ed., *Der Burenkrieg*. Munich, 1900.

— *Grobleiten: Simplicissimus Gedichte von Peter Schlemihl*. Munich, 1901.

— *Neue Grobleiten*. Munich, 1903.

THOMPSON, FRANCIS, *Works*, vol. ii. London: Burns & Oates, 1913.

Tit-Bits Monster Book of Patriotic Poems. London: *Tit-Bits*, 1900.

TOMBLESON, Capt. JOHN, *Bothasberg and Other Verses*. London: Walter Scott, 1910.

TOTIUS [J. D. du Toit], *By die Monument*. 5th, revised, ed. Potchefstroom: Nasionale Pers, 1917.

— *Rachel*. Potchefstroom: A. H. Koomans, 1913.

— *Trekkerswee*. Potchefstroom: Nasionale Pers, 1915.

TRENCH, HERBERT, *New Poems*. London: Methuen, 1907.

TRETHEWAY, CHARLES, *Britain's Sons; or, We Will Bump Old Kruger*. Canning Town, 1900.

TRIMBLE, W. COPELAND, *Inniskilling Fusiliers at the Battle of Inniskilling Hill*. Enniskillen, n.d.

TURBERVILLE, WILLIAM, *The Saxon Saga*. London: Chapman & Hall 1902.

TYLEE, EDWARD SYDNEY, *Trumpet and Flag and Other Poems of War and Peace*. London: Putnam's Sons, 1906.

VAN DER MEULEN, E., and C. S. HULST, *An Epistle to Ahab . . . Dedicated to Joseph Chamberlain*. Grand Rapids, Mich., n.d.

VAN LOOY, JAC., *Gedichten*. Leiden, 1932.

VAN PONTEN, KEES, *Pillen voor Joe*. Amsterdam, n.d.

VERGOUWEN, J. P., *Gedenkklanken voor Zuid-Afrika*. Goes, 1900.

VERWEY, ALBERT, *Dagen en Daden*. Amsterdam, 1901.

— *Oorspronkelijk Dichtwerk*. 2 vols. Amsterdam, 1938.

VICTORY, LOUIS H., *Imaginations in the Dust*, vol. i. London: 1903.

VON BROCKDORFF-AHLEFELDT, Countess LOUISE, *Aus dem Burenkrieg: Gedichte*. Riga, 1901.

VON STERN, MAURICE REINHOLD, *Blumen und Blitze*. Linz, 1902.

— *Gesammelte Gedichte*. Linz, 1906.

VRIJMAN, C., *Burenlieder*. Dresden, 1902.

WALLACE, EDGAR, *The Mission that Failed*. Cape Town: *Cape Times*, 1898.

— *Poems for the Period: War! and Other Poems*. Cape Town, n.d.

— [as 'Dennison Joe'], *Poems for the Period*, No. 2: *Nicholson's Nek!* Cape Town, n.d.

— *Writ in Barracks*. London: Methuen, 1900.

War Songs. McGlennon's Standard Series, No. 16. Manchester, n.d.

WASON, RIGBY, ed., *Some Volunteer Verse*. London: Hazell, Watson & Viney, 1905.

WASZKLÉWICZ-VAN SCHILFGAARDE, Mme DOUAIRIÈRE B. DE, ed., *Carmen pro Invictis*. The Hague, 1901.

WATSON, WILLIAM, *For England*. London: John Lane, The Bodley Head, 1904.

WATT, LAUCHLAN MACLEAN, *The Grey Mother and Other Poems, being Songs of Empire*. London: Dent, 1903.

WHEELER, POST, *Poems*. London: Elkin Matthews, 1905.

WOUTERS, D., ed., *Na Veertig Jaar: Zuid-Afrika en het Lied van de Straat in Nederland in het Laatste Kwart der Negentiende Eeuw*. Nijmegen, 1940.

— *Krüger Klaagt aan*. ?Utrecht, 1942.

Y ALDWIN, W. B., *British and Boer: Satirical and Patriotic Verses.* Port Elizabeth, 1900.

Zuid-Afrika Album. Rotterdam: *Vaan van het Noorden,* 1902.

ZUIDEMA, WILLEM, *Voor Zuid-Afrika: Rijm en Onrijm.* Amsterdam, 1900.

C: PERIODICALS AND NEWSPAPERS (Place of issue, other than London, or some indication of the character of the publication is added where such information seems useful.)

Academy
Afrikaanse Patriot (Cape)
Ally Sloper's Halfholiday
Anglo-Saxon Review
Answers
L'Assiette au beurre (Paris)
Athenaeum
Atlantic Monthly
Black and White Budget
Blackwood's Edinburgh Magazine
Bookman
Bookman (New York)
Brandwacht (Boer campaign paper)
Brotherhood
Bulletin (Sydney)
Burenfreund (Berlin)
Cape Argus (Cape Town)
Cape Illustrated Magazine (Cape Town)
Cape Times (Cape Town)
Clarion
Coming Day
Commonwealth
Concord
Cossack Post (Campaign paper)
Cri du Transvaal (Paris)
Daily Chronicle
Daily Express
Daily Mail
Daily News
Daily Telegraph
Daylight (Norwich)
Deutsches Wochenblatt

Diamond Fields Advertiser (Kimberley)
Eastern Province Herald (Port Elizabeth)
Echo
Empire Review
Englishwoman's Review
Ethical World
Fortnightly Review
Forward!
Friend (Bloemfontein)
Friend (Quaker)
Gids (Amsterdam)
Globe (Toronto)
Globe and Laurel (Royal Marines)
Graaff-Reinet Advertiser (Cape)
Graaff-Reinetter (Cape)
Grahamstown Journal (Cape)
Gram (P.O.W., Pretoria)
Graphic
Great Thoughts
Green Howards' Gazette
Grocott's Daily Mail (Grahamstown, Cape)
Grouse (Campaign paper)
Guardian
Herald of Peace and International Arbitration
Household Brigade Magazine
Humanitarian
Idler
Imperial and Colonial Magazine and Review

M

Jong Transvaal (Boer campaign paper)
Jugend (Munich)
Justice
Kamp Kruimels (Boer P.O.W. paper)
King and Country
Kladderadatsch (Berlin)
Krijgsgevangene (Boer P.O.W. paper)
Labour Leader
Ladysmith Bombshell (Siege paper)
Ladysmith Lyre (Siege paper)
Literary World
Literature
Lustige Blätter (Berlin)
Mafeking Mail Special Siege Slips
Manchester Guardian
McClure's Magazine (New York)
Mercure de France
Methodist Weekly
Midland News (Cradock, Cape)
Morning Leader
Natal Mercury
National Review
Nederland (Amsterdam)
New Age
New Century Review
Nieuwe Gids (Amsterdam)
Nineteenth Century
Ons Klyntji (Cape)
Ons Tijdschrift (Amsterdam and Cape Town)
Op! Voor Transvaal (Amsterdam)
Orcana Oyster (Campaign—see Atthill, section *D*)
Outlook
Owl (Cape Town)
Oxford Magazine
Pall Mall Gazette
Pall Mall Magazine
Paris-Pretoria (Paris pro-Boer)
Pavonia Piffler (Campaign paper)
Pearson's Magazine

Pick-Me-Up
Poetische Flugblätter
Poets' Corner
Prikkeldraad (Boer P.O.W. paper)
Punch
Queen's Own Gazette (Royal West Kent Regt.)
Rambler
Rand Post (Johannesburg pro-Boer)
Regiment
Review of Reviews
Revue Franco-Allemande
Revue des poètes (Paris)
Revue socialiste (Paris)
Reynold's Newspaper
Rire (Paris)
Royal Magazine
Saint Andrew
Simonstown & District Chronicle (Cape)
Simplicissimus (Munich)
Skyview Parrot (Boer P.O.W. paper)
Slate
South African News (Cape Town)
Southern Cross (Cape Town)
Speaker
Spectator
Sphere
Standard and Diggers News (Johannesburg pro-Boer)
Star
Strever (Boer P.O.W. paper)
Success
Temple Magazine
Thin Red Line (Argyll & Sutherland Highlanders)
Thrush
Tick (Boer P.O.W. paper)
The Times
Times of Natal (Pietermartizburg)
Transvaal (Ghent pro-Boer)
Truth

Türmer (Stuttgart)
Tweemaandelijksch Tijdschrift (Amsterdam)
Uilenspiegel (Dutch satirical)
Uitenhage Chronicle (Cape)
Uitenhage Times (Cape)
Under the Union Jack
La Vie pour rire (Paris)
Volksstem (Pretoria)

Voor de Boeren (Amsterdam)
War Against War
Ware Jacob (Rotterdam)
Westminster Review
With the Flag to Pretoria
Woche (Berlin)
World
Zuid-Afrikaan (Cape pro-Boer)

D: OTHER SOURCES (Works quoting original Boer War poems or songs are marked by an asterisk.)

Anon., 'English Patriotic Poetry', *Quarterly Rev.* 192 (1900), 520–41.
— 'The True Poet of Imperialism', *Macmillan's Mag.* 80 (1899), 192–5.
*ABBOTT, J. H. M., *Tommy Cornstalk: Some Account of the South African War from the Point of View of the Australian Ranks*. London: Longmans, Green, 1902.

ADAMSON, JOHN WILLIAM, *English Education 1789–1902*. Cambridge: Cambridge University Press, 1930.

ADCOCK, A. ST. JOHN, ed., *For Remembrance*. London: Hodder & Stoughton, 1918.

ALTICK, RICHARD D., *The English Common Reader*. Chicago: University of Chicago Press, 1957.

AMERY, L. S., ed., *'The Times' History of the War in South Africa 1899–1902*. 7 vols. London: The Times, 1900–9.
— *My Political Life: England Before the Storm 1896–1914*. London: Hutchinson, 1953.

ANDERSON, OLIVE, 'The Reactions of Church and Dissent towards the Crimean War', *J. of Ecclesiastical History*, 16 (1965), 209–20.

ANTONISSEN, ROB., *Die Afrikaanse Letterkunde van die Aanvang tot Hede*. Pretoria: H.A.U.M., 1955.

*ARTHUR, Capt. Sir GEORGE, *The Story of the Household Cavalry*. 2 vols. London: Constable, 1909.

ASHTON, JOHN, ed., *Modern Street Ballads*. London, 1888.

ASSELBERGS, W. J. M. A., *Geschiedenis van de Letterkunde der Nederlanden*, vol. ix: *Het Tijdperk der Vernieuwing van de Noordnederlandse Letterkunde 1885–1950*. Brussels, 1951.

*ATHILL, Capt. A. W. M., *From Norwich to Lichtenburg via Pretoria*. Norwich, 1909. (Includes the *Chit* and the *Orcana Oyster*, two campaign papers, as appendices.)

AUBERON, REGINALD, *The Nineteen Hundreds*. London: Allen & Unwin, 1922.

BAILEY, J. O., *The Poetry of Thomas Hardy: A Handbook and Commentary.* Chapel Hill: University of North Carolina Press, 1970.

*BARBIER, PIERRE, and FRANCE VERNILLAT, eds., *Histoire de France par les chansons*, vols. vii and viii. Paris: Gallimard, 1956–61.

BARKER, DUDLEY, *Prominent Edwardians*. London, 1969.

BARNETT, CORRELLI, *Britain and Her Army 1509–1970*. London: Allen Lane, The Penguin Press, 1970.

BATHO, E. C., and BONAMY DOBRÉE, *The Victorians and After: 1830–1914*. 3rd, revised, ed. London: Cresset Press, 1962.

BAYLEN, JOSEPH O., 'W. T. Stead and the Boer War: The Irony of Idealism', *Canadian Hist. Rev.* 40 (1959), 304–14.

BELOFF, MAX, *Imperial Sunset*, vol. i: *Britain's Liberal Empire 1897–1921*. London: Methuen, 1969.

BENTLEY, NICOLAS, ed., *Russell's Despatches from the Crimea*. London: André Deutsch, 1966.

BERGERAT, ÉMILE, *Poèmes de la guerre 1870–1871*. Paris, 1871.

BERGONZI, BERNARD, *Heroes' Twilight: A Study of the Literature of the Great War*. London: Constable, 1965.

BERLAGE, HEINRICH, *Über das englische Soldatenlied in der zweiten Hälfte des neunzehnten Jahrhunderts*. Dissertation. Münster, 1933. Emsdetten, 1933.

BILLINGTON, R. C., *A Mule-Driver at the Front*. London: Chapman & Hall, 1901.

BILLY, ANDRÉ, *L'Époque 1900*. Paris, 1951.

BILSE, Lieut. OSWALD FRITZ, *Life in a Garrison Town*. Tr. Arnold White. London: John Lane, The Bodley Head, 1904.

BINYON, LAURENCE, *The Death of Adam*. London: Methuen, 1904.

BLACKIE, JOHN STUART, *War Songs of the Germans*. Edinburgh, 1870.

BLOCH, IVAN S., *Is War Now Impossible?* Tr. W. T. Stead. London: Grant Richards, 1899.

BLUNT, WILFRID SCAWEN, *My Diaries*. 2 vols. London: Martin Secker, 1919.

BOAS, F. S., *Wordsworth's Patriotic Poems and their Significance Today*. Eng. Assoc. Pamphlets, No. 30. London, 1914.

*BODELSEN, C. A., 'The Red White and Blue: A Footnote to English Literary History', *Eng. Studies*, 19 (1937), 158–64.

BOESCHENSTEIN, HERMANN, *German Literature of the Nineteenth Century*. London: Arnold, 1969.

BOND, BRIAN, 'Recruiting the Victorian Army 1870–92', *Victorian Studies*, 5 (1962), 331–8.

BOOTH, Gen. WILLIAM, *In Darkest England and the Way Out*. London: Salvation Army, 1890.

BRADBURY, MALCOLM, *The Social Context of Modern English Literature*. Oxford: Blackwell, 1971.

BRAILSFORD, HENRY NOEL, *The Broom of the War-God*. London: Heinemann, 1898.

BRANDT, JOHANNA, *Het Concentratiekamp van Irene*. Amsterdam, 1905.

*BRINK, J. N., *Recollections of a Boer Prisoner of War at Ceylon*. Cape Town: H.A.U.M., 1904.

A British Officer, *Social Life in the British Army*. London: John Long, 1900.

A British Officer, 'The Literature of the South African War 1899–1902', *American Hist. Rev.* 12 (1907), 299–321.

BROOKE-HUNT, VIOLET, *A Woman's Memories of the War*. London: James Nisbet, 1901.

BROPHY, JOHN, and ERIC PARTRIDGE, *The Long Trail: What the British Soldier Sang and Said in the Great War 1914–18*. Revised ed. London: André Deutsch, 1965.

BROWN, W. SORLEY, *The Life and Genius of T. W. H. Crosland*. London: Cecil Palmer, 1928.

BROWNING, ELIZABETH BARRETT, *Poetical Works*. Oxford: Clarendon Press, 1911.

BROWNLEE, JAMES H., ed., *War-Time Echoes: Patriotic Poems . . . of the Spanish-American War*. Akron, Ohio: Werner Co., 1898.

*BROWNLIE, Maj. W. STEEL, *The Proud Trooper: The History of the Ayrshire (Earl of Garrick's Own) Yeomanry*. London: 1964.

BRUNSCHWIG, HENRI, *French Colonialism 1871–1914: Myths and Realities*. London: Pall Mall Press, 1966.

BUCHAN, JOHN, *Memory Hold-the-Door*. London: Hodder & Stoughton, 1940.

BUCHANAN, ROBERT, 'The Voice of the Hooligan', *Contemp. Rev.* 76 (1899), 774–89.

BUCKLEY, JEROME H., *William Ernest Henley: A Study in the 'Counter-Decadence' of the 'Nineties*. Princeton: Princeton University Press, 1945.

BÜLOW, PAUL, *Friedrich Lienhard: Der Mensch und das Werk*. Leipzig, 1923.

BURTON, RICHARD, *Collected Poems*. Indianapolis: Bobbs-Merrill, 1931.

BUTLER, JEFFREY, *The Liberal Party and the Jameson Raid*. Oxford: Clarendon Press, 1968.

BYRON, Lord GEORGE GORDON, *Childe Harold's Pilgrimage*. London: John Murray, 1870.

CAPLAIN, JULES, *Villebois-Mareuil: Son Idée. Son Geste*. Paris, 1902.

CARLYLE, THOMAS, *Sartor Resartus, and On Heroes, Hero-Worship, and the Heroic in History*. London: Dent Everyman, 1908.

CARRINGTON, C. E., ('Charles Edmonds'), *A Subaltern's War*. London: Peter Davies, 1929.

— *The British Overseas: Exploits of a Nation of Shopkeepers*. Cambridge: Cambridge University Press, 1950.

— *Kipling: His Life and Work*. London: Macmillan, 1955.

CARTER, A. C. R., *The Work of War Artists in South Africa*. London: *Art Journal*, 1900

Cassell's History of the Boer War 1899–1902. 2 vols. London: Cassell, 1903.

CECIL, ROBERT, *Life in Edwardian England*. London, 1969.

CHAPPLE, J. A. V., *Documentary and Imaginative Literature 1880–1920*. London: Blandford Press, 1970.

CHIROL, Sir VALENTINE, *The Cambridge History of British Foreign Policy*, vol. iii: 1866–1919. Cambridge: Cambridge University Press, 1923.

CHURCHILL, WINSTON SPENCER, *From London to Ladysmith via Pretoria*. London: Longmans, Green, 1900.

CLARK, G. KITSON, *The Making of Victorian England*. London: Methuen, 1962.

CLARKE, I. F., *Voices Prophesying War 1763–1984*. London: Oxford University Press, 1966.

COMBES, PAUL, *Cent ans de lutte: Les héros Boers*. Paris, 1901.

CONRAD, JOSEPH, *The Nigger of the 'Narcissus'*. 1897; Harmondsworth: Penguin, 1963.

COOK, E. T., *The Rights and Wrongs of the Transvaal War*. Revised ed. London: Arnold, 1902.

CORBIÈRE, ÉDOUARD-JOACHIM (TRISTAN), *Les Amours jaunes*. 1873; ed. Yves-Gérard le Dantec. Paris: Gallimard, 1953.

CORELLI, MARIE, *A Social Note on the War: Patriotism or Self-Advertisement?* Birmingham, 1900.

*CORNER, WILLIAM, *The Story of the 34th Co. (Middlesex) Imperial Yeomanry from the Point of View of Private No. 6243*. London: Fisher Unwin, 1902.

COULTON, G. G., *Public Schools and Public Needs*. London, 1900.

COUSINS, GEOFFREY, *The Defenders: A History of the British Volunteer*. London: Frederick Muller, 1968.

CRANE, STEPHEN, *War is Kind*. New York: Fred. A. Stokes, 1899.

CRESWICKE, LOUIS, *South Africa and the Transvaal War*. 8 vols. London: Caxton Pub. Co., 1900–3.

CRISP, ROBERT, *The Outlanders: The Men Who Made Johannesburg*. London: Peter Davies, 1964.

CRONWRIGHT-SCHREINER, S. C., *The Life of Olive Schreiner.* London: Fisher Unwin, 1924.

CRUSE, AMY, *After the Victorians.* London: Allen & Unwin, 1938.

*CUTLACK, F. M., *Breaker Morant: A Horseman Who Made History. With a Selection of his Bush Ballads.* London, 1962.

CYRAL, HENRI, *France et Transvaal: l'Opinion française et la guerre sud-africaine.* Paris, 1902.

DAICHES, DAVID, *Some Late Victorian Attitudes.* London: André Deutsch, 1969.

DAVENPORT, T. R. H., *South Africa: A Modern History.* Johannesburg: Macmillan, 1977.

DAVIS, R. HARDING, *With Both Armies in South Africa.* New York, 1900.

DAVIS, WEBSTER, *John Bull's Crime; or, Assaults on Republics.* New York, 1901.

DAXOR, P., *Poésies martiales.* Paris, 1900.

DE BANVILLE, THÉODORE, *Idylles prussiennes.* Paris, 1872.

DE LA REY, Mrs. J. H., *A Woman's Wanderings during the Anglo-Boer War.* London: Fisher Unwin, 1903.

DENNISON, Maj. C. G., *A Fight to a Finish.* London: Longmans, Green, 1904.

DENOON, DONALD, *A Grand Illusion: The Failure of Imperial Policy in the Transvaal Colony during the Period of Reconstruction.* London: Longman, 1973.

DÉPASSE, FRANÇOIS, 'Un crime', *Courier du Nord Est,* 1 March 1900.

DE WATTEVILLE, Col. H., *The British Soldier: His Daily Life from Tudor to Modern Times.* London: Dent, 1954.

DE WET, Gen. C. R., *The Three Years War.* London: Constable, 1902.

DILKE, Sir CHARLES W., *Greater Britain.* London: John Murray, 1868.

*DISHER, M. WILSON, *Winkles and Champagne: Comedies and Tragedies of the Music Hall.* London: Batsford, 1938.

DOBELL, SYDNEY, *England in Time of War.* London, 1856.

DONALDSON, JOSEPH, *Recollections of the Eventful Life of a Soldier.* Glasgow, 1825.

DOUGLAS, Sir GEORGE, 'A New Note of Poetic Melancholy', *Bookman,* 21 (1901–2), 131–2.

DOWDEN, EDWARD, 'The Poetry of Mr. Kipling', *New Liberal Rev.* 1 (1901), 53–61.

DOYLE, ARTHUR CONAN, *Songs of Action.* London: Smith, Elder, 1898.

— *The Great Boer War.* Final ed. London: Nelson, 1903.

DU FRESNEL, Le Comte, *Rimes d'un soldat.* Paris, 1903.

EDWARDES, MICHAEL, 'Rudyard Kipling and the Imperial Imagination', *Twentieth Century*, 153 (1953), 443–54.

ELTZBACHER, O., 'The Disadvantages of Education', *Nineteenth Century*, 53 (1903), 314–29.

ENSOR, R. C. K., *England 1870–1914*. Oxford: Clarendon Press, 1936.

FABER, RICHARD, *The Vision and the Need: Late Victorian Imperialist Aims*. London: Faber, 1966.

FAULKNER, HAROLD U., *Politics, Reform, and Expansion 1890–1900*. New York: Harper, 1959.

FERGUSON, JOHN, ed., *War and the Creative Arts*. London: Macmillan, 1972.

FERGUSON, JOHN H., *American Diplomacy and the Boer War*. Philadelphia: University of Pennsylvania Press, 1939.

FERRY, HENRI, *L'École et le régiment*. Paris, 1904.

FISHER, JOHN, *That Miss Hobhouse*. London: Secke & Warburg, 1971.

FITCHETT, W. H., *Fights for the Flag*. London: Smith, Elder, 1898.

FRISWELL, J. H., ed., *Songs of the War*. London, 1855.

FROUDE, J. A., *Oceana; or, England and Her Colonies*. London: Longmans, Green, 1886.

FULLER, J. F. C., *The Last of the Gentlemen's Wars*. London: Faber, 1937.

*FUNKE, ELISABETH, *Die Diskussion über den Burenkrieg in Politik und Presse der deutschen Schweiz*. Zürich, 1964.

GALBRAITH, JOHN S., 'The Pamphlet Campaign of the Boer War', *J. of Mod. Hist.* 24 (1952), 111–26.

GANGHOFER, LUDWIG, *Die eiserne Zither*. Stuttgart, 1914.

GANN, L. H., and PETER DUIGNAN, *The Burden of Empire: An Appraisal of Western Colonialism in Africa South of the Sahara*. London, 1968.

GARDNER, BRIAN, *Mafeking: A Victorian Legend*. London: Cassell, 1966.

GAZEAU, JACQUES, *L'Impérialisme anglais: Son évolution*. Paris, 1903.

*GILBERT, SHARRAD H., *Rhodesia—and After, being the Story of the 17th and 18th Battalions of Imperial Yeomanry*. London: Simpkin Marshall, 1901.

GILDEA, Col. JAMES, *For King and Country, being a Record of Funds and Philanthropic Work in Connection with the South African War*. London: Eyre & Spottiswoode, 1902.

GODARD, JOHN GEORGE, *Racial Supremacy, being Studies in Imperialism*. London: Simpkin Marshall, 1905.

GOLLWITZER, HEINZ, *Europe in the Age of Imperialism 1880–1914*. London: Thames & Hudson, 1969.

GRAY, RONALD, *The German Tradition in Literature 1871–1945.* Cambridge: Cambridge University Press, 1965.

GREEN, H. M., *A History of Australian Literature*, vol. i: 1789–1923. Sydney: Angus & Robertson, 1961.

GREEN, ROGER LANCELYN, ed., *Kipling: The Critical Heritage.* London: Routledge & Kegan Paul, 1971.

*GREGORY, Lady ISABELLA, *Poets and Dreamers: Studies and Translations from the Irish.* Dublin: Hodges Figgis, 1903.

HAFERKORN, H. E., comp., *Bibliography of the South African War 1899–1902.* Washington, D.C., 1924.

*HALES, A. G., *Campaign Pictures of the War in South Africa.* London: Cassell, 1900.

HALÉVY, ÉLIE, *Imperialism and the Rise of Labour 1895–1905.* Tr. E. I. Watkin. 2nd, revised, ed. London: Ernest Benn, 1951.

HAMER, D. A., *Liberal Politics in the Age of Gladstone and Rosebery: A Study in Leadership and Policy.* Oxford: Clarendon Press, 1972.

HARDY, FLORENCE E., *The Life of Thomas Hardy 1840–1928.* London: Macmillan, 1962.

HARGREAVES, REGINALD, *This Happy Breed: Sidelights on Soldiers and Soldiering.* London: Skeffington, 1951.

HART, B. H. LIDDELL, ed., *The Letters of Private Wheeler 1809–28.* London, 1951.

HAYES, CARLTON J. H., *A Generation of Materialism 1871–1900.* 1941; New York: Harper & Row, 1963.

HEMANS, Mrs. FELICIA, *Poetical Works.* London: Ward, Lock, n.d.

HENLEY, WILLIAM ERNEST, ed., *Lyra Heroica: A Book of Verse for Boys.* London: David Nutt, 1892. 6th ed., 1900.

— *The Song of the Sword.* London: David Nutt, 1892.

— *Poems.* London: David Nutt, 1898.

HIBBERT, CHRISTOPHER, ed., *The Recollections of Rifleman Harris as Told to Henry Curling.* London: Leo Cooper, 1970.

HILL, ALSAGAR HAY, *Poor Law Rhymes.* London, 1871.

HILLEGAS, HOWARD C., *The Boers in War.* New York: Appleton, 1900.

HIMMELFARB, GERTRUDE, *Victorian Minds.* London: Weidenfeld & Nicolson, 1968.

HOBHOUSE, EMILY, *Report of a Visit to the Camps of Women and Children in the Cape and Orange River Colonies.* London:*Commonwealth*, 1901.

— *The Brunt of the War and Where It Fell.* London: Methuen, 1902.

HOBSON, J. A., *The War in South Africa.* London: James Nisbet, 1900.

— *The Psychology of Jingoism.* London: Grant Richards, 1901.

HOBSON, J. A., *Imperialism: A Study*. 1902; 3rd, revised, ed. London: Allen & Unwin, 1938.

HOFFMAN, DANIEL G., *The Poetry of Stephen Crane*. New York: Columbia University Press, 1957.

HOLLAND, B. H., 'War and Poetry', *Edinburgh Rev.* 196 (1902), 29–54.

HOLT, EDGAR, *The Boer War*. London: Putnam, 1958.

HOME, Lieut. WILLIAM, *With the Border Volunteers to Pretoria*. Hawick: W. & J. Kennedy, 1901.

HOOD, THOMAS, *Poetical Works*. Ed. W. M. Rossetti. 2 vols. London: Ward, Lock, n.d.

HOWARD, CHRISTOPHER, *Splendid Isolation: A Study of Ideas concerning Britain's International Position and Foreign Policy during the Later Years of the Third Marquis of Salisbury*. London: Macmillan, 1967.

HOWE, SUSANNE, *Novels of Empire*. New York: Columbia University Press, 1949.

HUTTENBACK, ROBERT A., 'G. A. Henty and the Imperial Stereotype', *Huntington Lib. Q.* 29 (1965), 63–75.

HYNES, SAMUEL, *The Edwardian Turn of Mind*. London: Oxford University Press, 1968.

The Intelligence Officer [Col. Lionel James], *On the Heels of De Wet*. Edinburgh: Blackwood, 1902.

JAMES, Col. LIONEL, *High Pressure*. London, 1929.

JANICKE, KARL, *Das deutsche Kriegslied*. Berlin, 1871.

JEAN-AUBRY, G., *Joseph Conrad: Life and Letters*. 2 vols. London: Heinemann, 1927.

JEBB, RICHARD, *Studies in Colonial Nationalism*. London: Arnold, 1905.

JERRAM, CHARLES S., *The Armies of the World*. London, 1899.

JOHNSTON, JOHN E., *English Poetry of the First World War*. Princeton: Princeton University Press, 1964.

JOHNSTONE, Capt. G. MURRAY, *The Avengers and Other Poems from South Africa*. London, 1918.

JONES, ERNEST, *Battle-Day and Other Poems*. London, 1855.

JONES, PETER D'A., *The Christian Socialist Revival 1877–1914*. Princeton: Princeton University Press, 1968.

JONES, WILLIAM, *Quaker Campaigns in Peace and War*. London: Headley Bros., 1899.

JULLIAN, PHILIPPE, *The Symbolists*. London: Phaidon, 1973.

*KEMP, Col. Sgt. R. E., ed., *Khaki Letters from my Colleagues in South Africa*. London, 1901.

KENNEDY, J. M., *English Literature 1880–1905*. London: Stephen Swift, 1912.

KINGSLEY, CHARLES, *Andromeda and Other Poems*. London: John W. Parker, 1858.

KIPLING, RUDYARD, *Departmental Ditties*. 1886; enlarged ed. London: George Newnes, 1899.

— *Barrack-Room Ballads*. London: Methuen, 1892.

— *The Second Jungle Book*. London: Macmillan, 1895.

— *The Seven Seas*. London: Methuen, 1896.

— *Stalky & Co.* London: Macmillan, 1899.

— *The Sin of Witchcraft*. London, 1901.

— *The Science of Rebellion*. London, 1902.

— *Traffics and Discoveries*. London: Macmillan, 1904.

— *Something of Myself*. London: Macmillan, 1937.

KOSS, STEPHEN, ed., *The Pro-Boers: The Anatomy of an Antiwar Movement*. Chicago: Chicago University Press, 1973.

KROMHOUT, J., *Leipoldt as Digter*. Pretoria: Van Schaik, 1954.

KRUGER, RAYNE, *Good-bye Dolly Gray: The Story of the Boer War*. London: Cassell, 1959.

Ladysmith Historical Society, *Siege Diaries*, No. 4. Ladysmith, 1973.

LAMPRECHT, HELMUT, ed., *Deutschland, Deutschland: Politische Gedichte vom Vormärz bis zur Gegenwart*. Bremen, 1969.

LANE, MARGARET, *Edgar Wallace: The Biography of a Phenomenon*. London: Heinemann, n.d.

LANGER, WILLIAM, *The Diplomacy of Imperialism 1890–1902*. 2nd ed. New York: Knopf, 1951.

LAWSON, HENRY, *Letters 1890–1922*. Ed. Colin Roderick. Sydney: Angus & Robertson, 1970.

LEAL, FERNANDO, *Dieu garde le Tsar!* Paris, 1899.

*LEATHER-CULLEY, Mrs. J. D., *On the War Path: A Lady's Letters from the Front*. London: John Long, 1901.

LECONTE DE LISLE, CHARLES, *Le Soir d'une bataille*. Paris, 1871.

— *Le Sacre de Paris*. Paris, 1871.

LE GALLIENNE, RICHARD, *The Romantic '90s*. London: Putnam, 1926.

LESLIE, SHANE, *Mark Sykes: His Life and Letters*. London, 1923.

LEVER, CHARLES, *Charles O'Malley, the Irish Dragoon*. 2 vols. Dublin: William Curry, 1841.

*LEWIS, CAROLINE [Harold Begbie *et al.*], *Clara in Blunderland*. London, 1902.

LINDENBERG, E., *Onsydige Toets*. Cape Town, 1965.

LING, PETER, ed., *Gentlemen at Arms: Portraits of Soldiers in Fact and Fiction, in Peace and at War*. London: Peter Owen, 1969.

LLOYD, A. L., *Folk Song in England*. 1967; London: Panther, 1969.

LLOYD, J. B., *1,000 Miles with the C.I.V.* London: Methuen, 1901.

LOCHHEAD, MARION, *Young Victorians*. London: John Murray, 1959.
LOGAN, W. H., ed., *A Pedlar's Pack of Ballads and Songs*. Edinburgh, 1869.
LONDON, JACK, *The People of the Abyss*. London: Isbister, 1903.
LONGFELLOW, HENRY WADSWORTH, *Poetical Works*. London: Routledge, 1894.
LUCAS, JOHN, ed., *Literature and Politics in the Nineteenth Century*. London: Methuen, 1971.
*LUSHINGTON, FRANKLIN and HENRY, *Wagers of Battle 1854–1899*. London: Macmillan, 1900.
MACDONAGH, MICHAEL, 'The Ballads of the People', *Nineteenth Century*, 54 (1903), 458–71.
MACDONALD, DONALD, *How We Kept the Flag Flying: The Story of the Siege of Ladysmith*. London: Ward, Lock, 1900.
MACINNES, COLIN, *Sweet Saturday Night*. London: MacGibbon & Kee, 1967.
MACK, EDWARD C., *Public Schools and British Opinion since 1860*. London: Methuen, 1941.
*MACKINNON, HEDLEY V., *War Sketches: Reminiscences of the Boer War in South Africa*. Charlottetown, 1900.
MACLEAN, A. H. H., *Public Schools and the War in South Africa*. London: Stanford, 1903.
MACLEAY, JOHN, ed., *War Songs and Songs and Ballads of Martial Life*. London: Walter Scott, 1900.
MALHERBE, V. C., *Eminent Victorians in South Africa*. Cape Town: Juta, 1972.
MARAIS, J. S., *The Fall of Kruger's Republic*. Oxford: Clarendon Press, 1961.
MARKS, ALFRED, *The Churches and the South African War*. London, 1905.
MARLOW, NORMAN, *A. E. Housman: Scholar and Poet*. London: Routledge & Kegan Paul, 1958.
MARRIOTT, J. A. R., 'The Imperial Note in Victorian Poetry', *Nineteenth Century*, 48 (1900), 236–48.
*MAURER, S. F., *England und Transvaal*. Stuttgart, n.d.
*MEINTJES, JOHANNES, *Stormberg: A Lost Opportunity*. Cape Town: Tafelberg, 1969.
— *Sword in the Sand: The Life and Death of Gideon Scheepers*. Cape Town: Tafelberg, 1969.
MELVILLE, HERMAN, *Battle-Pieces and Aspects of the War*. New York: Harper, 1866.
MENDELSSOHN, SIDNEY, *South African Bibliography*. 2 vols. London: Kegan Paul, 1910.

MONTGOMERY, JOHN, *1900: The End of an Era*. London: Allen & Unwin, 1968.

MORRIS, JAMES, *Pax Britannica: The Climax of an Empire*. London: Faber, 1968.

MORRIS, WILLIAM, *Chants for Socialists*. London, 1884.

MOUNTENEY-JEPHSON, R., *Sword and Song*. London: Simpkin Marshall, 1895.

MUDDIMAN, BERNARD, *The Men of the Nineties*. London: Henry Danielson, 1920.

*MUNRO, HECTOR H. ('Saki'), *The Westminster Alice*. London, n.d.

*NAUDÉ, J. F., *Vechten en Vluchten van Beyers en Kemp*. Rotterdam, 1903.

NIENABER, P. J., *Afrikaanse Skrywers aan die Woord*. Cape Town, 1947.

NOYES, ALFRED, *The Enchanted Island*. Edinburgh: Blackwood, 1909.

— *The Wine-Press: A Tale of War*. Edinburgh: Blackwood, 1913.

*OGDEN, H. J., *The War Against the Dutch Republics in South Africa*. Manchester: National Reform Union, 1901.

OMOND, G. W. T., *The Boers in Europe*. London: Black, 1903.

OWEN, WILFRED, *Poems: A Selection*. Ed. Dominic Hibberd. London: Chatto & Windus, 1973.

PARSONS, I. M., ed., *Men Who March Away: Poems of the First World War*. London: Chatto & Windus, 1965.

PEEL, Hon. SIDNEY, *Trooper 8008, I.Y.* London: Arnold, 1901.

**Pen Pictures of the War by Men at the Front*. London: Simpkin Marshall, 1900.

PENNER, C. D., 'Germany and the Transvaal before 1896', *J. of Mod. Hist.* 12 (1940), 31–58.

PERHAM, MARGERY, *Lugard: The Years of Adventure 1858–98*. London, 1956.

PIENAAR, PHILIP, *With Steyn and De Wet*. London: Methuen, 1902.

PIERSON, STANLEY, 'John Trevor and the Labour Church Movement in England', *Church History*, 29 (1960), 463–77.

PORTER, B., *Critics of Empire: British Radical Attitudes to Colonialism in Africa 1895–1914*. London: Macmillan, 1968.

PRESBER, RUDOLF, *Die Brücken zum Sieg: Kriegsgedichte*. Berlin, n.d.

PRICE, RICHARD, *An Imperial War and the British Working Class: Working-Class Attitudes and Reactions to the Boer War 1899–1902*. London: Routledge, Kegan Paul, 1972.

PRESTON, THOMAS, ed., *Patriots in Arms: Addresses and Sermons . . . in Praise of the Volunteer Movement*. London: Whittaker, 1881.

PRUDHOMME, RENÉ SULLY, *Poésies*. Paris, 1872.

PURCELL, Dr., 'Songs of the Veld and Other Poems', *Africana Notes and News*, 11 (1955), 220–1.

RALEIGH, Sir WALTER, *Letters 1879–1922*. Ed. Lady Raleigh. 2 vols. 2nd ed. London: Methuen, 1928.

*RALPH, JULIAN, *War's Brighter Side: The Story of 'The Friend' Newspaper Edited by the Correspondents with Lord Roberts's Forces, March–April 1900*. London: C. Arthur Pearson, 1901.

— *At Pretoria*. London: C. Arthur Pearson, 1901.

RAYNAUD, ERNEST, *La Mêlée symbolistes 1870–1910*. 3 vols. in 2. Paris, 1918–20.

*REITZ, DENEYS, *Commando: A Boer Journal of the Boer War*. London: Faber, 1929.

— *Trekking On*. London: Faber, 1933.

*REITZ, HJALMAR, *De Dochter van den Handsopper*. Amsterdam, 1903.

*RENAR, F., *Bushman and Buccaneer: Harry Morant, His Ventures and Verses*. Sydney: Dunn, 1902.

RIMBAUD, ARTHUR, *Œuvres complètes*. Ed. Roland de Renéville and Jules Monquet. Paris: Gallimard, 1946.

ROBERTSON, J. M., *Wrecking the Empire*. London: Grant Richards, 1901.

ROBINSON, A. M. LEWIN, 'Edgar Wallace at the Cape', *Q. Bull. of the South African Lib.* 28 (Sept. 1973), 2–10; (Dec. 1973), 53–4.

ROBINSON, R., and JOHN GALLAGHER, *Africa and the Victorians: The Official Mind of Imperialism*. London: Macmillan, 1961.

RODD, Sir JAMES RENNELL, *The Violet Crown*. London: Arnold, 1913.

ROPPEN, GEORG, *Evolution and Poetic Belief: A Study in Some Victorian and Modern Writers*. Oslo, 1956.

*ROSS, P. T., *A Yeoman's Letters*. London: Simpkin Marshall, 1901.

*ROSSLYN, Earl of, *Twice Captured: A Record of Adventure during the Boer War*. Edinburgh: Blackwood, 1900.

ROTH, H. LING, and J. T. JOLLEY, eds., *War Ballads and Broadsides of Previous Wars 1779–95*. Bankfield Museum Notes, 2nd series, No. 5. Halifax, 1915.

SAGARRA, EDA, *Tradition and Revolution: German Literature and Society 1830–90*. London: Weidenfeld & Nicolson, 1971.

SANDISON, ALAN, *The Wheel of Empire: A Study of the Imperial Idea in Some Late 19th and Early 20th Century Fiction*. London: Macmillan, 1967.

*SCHOLTZ, G. D., *Europa en die Tweede Vryheidsoorlog*. Johannesburg, 1939.

SCHREINER, OLIVE, 'The African Boer', *Ethical World*, 1 Sept.–20 Oct. 1900.

— *Trooper Peter Halket of Mashonaland*. London: Fisher Unwin, 1897.

— *Thoughts on South Africa*. London: Fisher Unwin, 1923.

SCHREINER, OLIVE, *Letters 1876–1920*. Ed. S. C. Cronwright-Schreiner. London: Fisher Unwin, 1924.

SCHUTTE, G. J., 'Koningin Wilhelmina en Zuid-Afrika', *Zuid-Afrika*, 49 (1972), 25.

SCOTT, JAMES, *Souvenir of the Siege of Ladysmith*. Pietermaritzburg, 1900.

SEELEY, Sir JOHN, *The Expansion of England*. London, 1883.

SEMMEL, BERNARD, *Imperialism and Social Reform 1895–1914*. Cambridge, Mass., 1960.

SHAW, GEORGE BERNARD, 'Civilization and the Soldier', *Humane Rev.* 1 (1900), 298–315.

— , ed., *Fabianism and the Empire*. London: Grant Richards, 1900.

SILKIN, JON, *Out of Battle: The Poetry of the Great War*. London: Oxford University Press, 1972.

SIMON, BRIAN, *Education and the Labour Movement 1870–1918*. London, 1965.

SIMS, GEORGE R., *Prepare to Shed Them Now: The Ballads of George R. Sims*. Ed. Arthur Calder-Marshall. London: Hutchinson, 1968.

SMITH, ALEXANDER, *Sonnets on the War*. London: David Bogue, 1855.

SMITH, GOLDWIN, *In the Court of History: An Apology for Canadians Who Were Opposed to the South African War*. Toronto, 1899.

SMITH, WARREN S., *The London Heretics 1870–1914*. London: Constable, 1967.

SOMERVILLE, G. G., *The Retreat from Moscow*. London: Ideal Pub. Co., 1899.

Songs and Sonnets for England in War Time. London: John Lane, The Bodley Head, 1914.

South Africa Conciliation Committee. Pamphlet collections in Library of Parliament, Cape Town, and State Archives, Pretoria.

SOUTHEY, ROBERT, *Poetical Works*. London: Routledge, 1894.

SPALIKOWSKI, E., *Strophes et chansons de la paix*. Paris, 1903.

SPENDER, HAROLD, 'War and Poetry', *Pilot*, 1 (1900), 477–8.

STEAD, W. T., *Shall I Slay My Brother Boer?* London: Stop the War Committee, 1899.

— *Joseph Chamberlain: Conspirator or Statesman?* London: S.W.C., 1900.

— *The Candidates of Cain*. London: S.W.C., 1900.

— *How Not to Make Peace*. London: S.W.C., 1900.

— *Methods of Barbarism*. London: S.W.C., 1901.

STEEVENS, G. W., *With Kitchener to Khartum*. Edinburgh: Blackwood, 1898.

— *From Capetown to Ladysmith*. Edinburgh: Blackwood, 1900.

— *Things Seen: Impressions of Men, Cities, and Books*. Edinburgh: Blackwood, 1900.

STEINMETZ, LEE, ed., *The Poetry of the American Civil War*. East Lansing: Michigan State University Press, 1960.

STEVENS, BERTRAM, ed., *The Golden Treasury of Australian Verse*. London: Macmillan, 1912.

STEWART, J. I. M., *Rudyard Kipling*. London: Victor Gollancz, 1966.

STIRLING, JOHN, *The Colonials in South Africa*. Edinburgh: Blackwood, 1907.

STOKES, ERIC, 'Milnerism', *Hist. J.* 5 (1962), 47–60.

Stop the War Committee, Pamphlet collections in Library of Parliament, Cape Town, and State Archives, Pretoria.

STUART, JOHN, *Pictures of War*. London: Constable, 1901.

STURT, GEORGE, *Journals 1890–1927*. Ed. E. D. Mackerness. 2 vols. Cambridge: Cambridge University Press, 1967.

SURTEES, Private HENRY, *The March to Khartum and Fall of Omdurman 1898*. N.p., 1899.

SWART, KOENRAAD W., *The Sense of Decadence in Nineteenth-Century France*. The Hague, 1964.

SYKES, JESSICA, *Side-Lights on the War in South Africa*. London, 1900.

SYMONS, JULIAN, ed., *An Anthology of War Poetry*. Harmondsworth: Penguin, 1942.

TAILLEFER, NUGENT, *Rondeaus of the British Volunteers*. London: Lamborn Cock, 1871.

TENNYSON, ALFRED Lord, *Poetical Works*. London: Oxford University Press, 1953.

THACKERAY, WILLIAM M., *Ballads and The Rose and the Ring. Works*, vol. xxi. London: Smith, Elder, 1879.

THOMPSON, BRUCE, 'Canon Rawnsley: "The Guardian of the Lakes" ', *National Trust News*, No. 14 (1972).

THOMPSON, FRANCIS, *Letters*. Ed. John E. Walsh, New York: Hawthorn, 1969.

THOMPSON, LEONARD M., *The Unification of South Africa 1902–10*. Oxford: Clarendon Press, 1960.

THOMSON, DAVID, *England in the Nineteenth Century 1815–1914*. Pelican History of England, 8. Harmondsworth: Penguin, 1950.

THORNTON, A. P., *The Imperial Idea and Its Enemies*. London: Macmillan, 1959.

TINT, HERBERT, *The Decline of French Patriotism 1870–1940*. London: Weidenfeld & Nicolson, 1964.

TUCHMAN, BARBARA W., *The Proud Tower: A Portrait of the World before the War 1890–1914*. London: Hamish Hamilton, 1966.

TUCKER, ALBERT V., 'Army and Society in England 1870–1900: A Re-assessment of the Cardwell Reforms', *J. of British Studies*, 2 (1963), 110–41.

TUPPER, MARTIN, *A Batch of War Ballads*. London, 1854.

TURNER, E. S., *Gallant Gentlemen: A Portrait of the British Officer 1600–1956*. London: Michael Joseph, 1956.

TWAIN, MARK [Samuel Clemens], *More Tramps Abroad*. London: Chatto & Windus, 1897.

UNGER, F. W., *With 'Bobs' and 'Kruger'*. Philadelphia: Coates, 1901.

UNTERMEYER, LOUIS, ed., *Modern American Poetry*. 4th ed. London: Jonathan Cape, 1932.

*VAN HELSDINGEN, JOHANNA, *Vrouwenleed: Persoonlijke Ondervindingen in den Boerenoorlog*. Cape Town: H.A.U.M., 1904.

*VAN ROOYEN, G. H., 'Kultuurskatte uit die Tweede Vryheidsoorlog', *Huisgenoot*, 7 June 1935.

VEALE, F. J., *Advance to Barbarism*. London: Mitre Press, 1968.

VEBER, JEAN, *Les Camps de reconcentration au Transvaal*. Paris: *l'Assiette au beurre*, 1901.

— *Das Blutbuch von Transvaal*. Berlin: *Lustige Blätter*, n.d.

— *De Boeren-Kampen*. Amsterdam, 1901.

VEBER, PIERRE, and LOUIS LACROIX, *L'Œuvre lithographié de Jean Veber*. Paris, 1931.

VILJOEN, Gen. BEN, *My Reminiscences of the Anglo-Boer War*. London: Hood, Douglas, Howard, 1902.

VILLARD, EMILE, *Guerre et poésie: La Poésie patriotique française de 1914–1918*. Neuchatel, 1949.

VIS, W. R., *Tien Maanden in een Vrouwenkamp*. Rotterdam, 1902.

*VISAGIE, L. A., *Terug na Kommando*. Cape Town, 1945.

VON PFLUGK-HARTTUNG, J., ed., *Krieg und Sieg 1870–71: Kulturgeschichte*. Berlin, 1896.

WALLACE, EDGAR, *Unofficial Despatches on the Boer War*. London: Hutchinson, 1901.

— *Edgar Wallace by Himself*. London: Hutchinson, 1932.

WALSH, WALTER, *The Moral Damage of War*. London: Brimley Johnson, 1902.

WATSON, WILLIAM, *The Purple East*. London: John Lane, The Bodley Head, 1896.

— *The Year of Shame*. London: John Lane, The Bodley Head, 1897.

WAUGH, A., 'The Poetry of the South African Campaign', *Anglo-Saxon Rev.* 8 (Dec. 1900), 42–58.

WHARTON, H. M., ed., *War Songs and Poems of the Southern Confederacy 1861–65*. Philadelphia, 1904.

WHITMAN, WALT, *Leaves of Grass, Complete Poetry and Prose*. Ed. Malcolm Cowley. New York, 1948.

WILKINSON, RUPERT, *The Prefects: British Leadership and the Public School Tradition*. London: Oxford University Press, 1964.

WILKINSON, SPENSER, *The Illustrated London News Record of the Transvaal War 1899–1900*. London: *Illustrated London News*, 1900.

WILSON, EDMUND, 'The Kipling that Nobody Read', *Atlantic Monthly*, 167 (1941), 201–14.

— *Patriotic Gore: Studies in the Literature of the American Civil War*. New York: Oxford University Press, Galaxy Books, 1966.

WILSON, MONICA, and L. M. THOMPSON, eds., *The Oxford History of South Africa*, vol. ii: 1870–1966. Oxford: Clarendon Press, 1971.

WILSON-MOORE, C. and A. P., *Diggers' Doggerel: Poems of the Veldt and Mine*. Cape Town: Argus Printing Co., 1890.

WINN, WILLIAM E., ' *Tom Brown's Schooldays* and the Development of "Muscular Christianity" ', *Church History*, 29 (1960), 64–73.

*WINSTOCK, LEWIS, *Songs and Music of the Redcoats: A History of the War Music of the British Army 1642–1902*. London: Leo Cooper, 1970.

WITHERBEE, SIDNEY A., ed., *Spanish-American War Songs: A Complete Collection of Newspaper Verse during the Recent War with Spain*. Detroit, 1898.

*WITTON, Lieut. GEORGE R., *Scapegoats of the Empire: The Story of the Bushveld Carbineers*. Melbourne, 1907.

WOODHOUSE, PETER, *Democritus his Dream; or, The Contention between the Elephant and the Flea*. London, 1605.

WORDSWORTH, WILLIAM, *The Prelude*. Ed. J. C. Maxwell. Harmondsworth: Penguin, 1971.

WRIGHT, Henry C., *Defensive War Proved to be a Denial of Christiantiy*. Dublin, 1864.

WRIGHT, PATRICIA, *Conflict on the Nile: The Fashoda Incident of 1898*. London: Heinemann, 1972.

WYNDHAM, GEORGE, *Letters*. Ed. Guy Wyndham. 2 vols. Edinburgh: Constable, 1915.

Y. Y. 'The Literary Harvest of the War', *Bookman*, 22 (1902), 131–3.

YEATS, WILLIAM BUTLER, *Autobiographies*. London: Macmillan, 1955.

YOUNG, G. M., *Victorian England: Portrait of an Age*. 2nd ed., 1953; rpt. London: Oxford Paperbacks, 1960.

ZOLA, ÉMILE, *The Downfall: A Story of the Horrors of War*. Tr. Ernest A. Vizetelly. London: Chatto & Windus, 1892.

Index